The Spanish Colonial Settlement Landscapes of New Mexico, 1598–1680

The Spanish Colonial Settlement Landscapes of New Mexico, 1598–1680

ELINORE M. BARRETT

University of New Mexico Press ✦ Albuquerque

© 2012 by the University of New Mexico Press
All rights reserved. Published 2012
Printed in the United States of America
First paperbound printing, 2015
Paperbound ISBN: 978-0-8263-5084-8

20 19 18 17 16 15   1 2 3 4 5 6

LIBRARY OF CONGRESS CATALOGING-IN-PUBLICATION DATA

Barrett, Elinore M.
The Spanish colonial settlement landscapes of New Mexico, 1598–1680 /
Elinore M. Barrett.
  p. cm.
Includes bibliographical references and index.
ISBN 978-0-8263-5083-1 (cloth : alk. paper) — ISBN 978-0-8263-5085-5 (electronic)
1. Land settlement—New Mexico—History—17th century. 2. Human geography—
New Mexico. 3. Spaniards—New Mexico—History—17th century.
4. New Mexico—History—To 1848. I. Title.
F799.B36 2012
978.9′01—dc23
                                                    2011027116

BOOK DESIGN
Composed in 10.25/13.5 Minion Pro Regular
Display type is Minion Pro

To James J. Parsons, geographer

Contents

Maps, Tables, Appendix Tables, and Abbreviations | ix

Preface | xiii

Acknowledgments | xv

PART ONE: The Context of Settlement

CHAPTER ONE
The Spanish Entrada | 3

CHAPTER TWO
The Natural Landscape | 7

CHAPTER THREE
The Pueblo Landscape | 14

CHAPTER FOUR
The Spanish Institutional Landscape | 19

CHAPTER FIVE
The Mission Landscape | 36

CHAPTER SIX
The Mining Landscape | 42

PART TWO: The Demographic Landscape

CHAPTER SEVEN
The Oñate Era | 51

CHAPTER EIGHT
The Post-Oñate Era | 59

PART THREE: The Settlement Landscapes

CHAPTER NINE
San Gabriel | 69

CHAPTER TEN
The Villa of Santa Fe | 75

CHAPTER ELEVEN
The Santa Fe River Valley | 100

CHAPTER TWELVE
The Española Basin | 108

CHAPTER THIRTEEN
The Far North | 122

CHAPTER FOURTEEN
The Galisteo Basin and Pecos Jurisdiction | 125

CHAPTER FIFTEEN
The Santo Domingo Basin | 129

CHAPTER SIXTEEN
The Middle Rio Grande Region | 135

CHAPTER SEVENTEEN
The Estancia Basin | 150

CHAPTER EIGHTEEN
The Southern Rio Grande Region | 155

Conclusion | 161

Appendix Tables | 165

Maps | 205

Notes | 213

Works Cited | 255

Index | 268

Maps, Tables, Appendix Tables, and Abbreviations

MAPS

1.	Seventeenth-Century New Mexico Pueblos	205
2.	Spanish Landholdings in New Mexico, 1610–80, an Approximation	206
3.	Zaldívar's Route to the Eastern Plains from San Gabriel, 1599	207
4.	Urrutia Map of Santa Fe, 1766	208
5.	Santa Fe Placenames and Seventeenth-Century Hydrologic Features	209
6.	Known Seventeenth-Century Spanish Landholdings: Santa Fe River Valley	210
7.	Known Spanish Landholdings: Española Basin, 1680	211
8.	Known Seventeenth-Century Spanish Landholdings: Middle Rio Grande Region	212

TABLES

1.	Average Annual Precipitation, Albuquerque, New Mexico, 1602–80 and 1950–95	9
2.	Average Seasonal Temperatures, Santa Fe, New Mexico, 1602–80 and 1950–95	10
3.	Number of Frost-Free Days, Selected Sites in New Mexico	11
4.	Number of New Mexico Pueblos: 1598, 1641, and 1680 by District and Language	15
5.	Seventeenth-Century New Mexico Missions	37

APPENDIX TABLES

A. Palmer Drought Severity Index Values for New Mexico, 1598–1680 — 165
B. Precipitation, Albuquerque, New Mexico, 1602–80 — 167
C. Precipitation, Southern Rio Grande Basin, New Mexico, 1600–1680 — 170
D. Temperature, Santa Fe, New Mexico, 1602–80 — 171
E. Known New Mexico Encomenderos, 1610–80 — 174
F. Known New Mexico Alcaldes Mayores, 1610–80 — 182
G. Spanish Men in New Mexico before 1601 — 186
H. Spanish Men Who Brought Families to New Mexico before 1601 — 190
I. Colonists Who Signed the October 2, 1601, Loyalty Petition — 192
J. Additional Colonists Who Remained in New Mexico after 1601 — 193
K. Known Spanish Families in New Mexico in the Early Post-1601 Years — 195
L. Known *Vecinos* of Santa Fe, 1610–32 — 197
M. Spanish Settlers Reported Killed in the 1680 Revolt — 199
N. Known Spanish Men Descended from Original New Mexico Colonists — 201

ABBREVIATIONS

AASF — Archives of the Archdiocese of Santa Fe
AGI — Archivo General de Indias, Seville
AGN — Archivo General de la Nación, Mexico City
AH — Archivo Histórico, Museo de Antropología e Historia, Mexico City
ARMS — Archaeological Records Management System, Laboratory of Anthropology (LA), Santa Fe, a division of the Museum of New Mexico
BN — Biblioteca Nacional, Madrid
BNM — Biblioteca Nacional, Mexico City

LA	Laboratory of Anthropology, Museum of New Mexico, Santa Fe
SANM	Spanish Archives of New Mexico in the New Mexico State Records Center and Archive, Santa Fe
ZL	Special Collections, Zimmerman Library, University of New Mexico, Albuquerque

Preface

☩ THE PATTERN OF SPANISH SETTLEMENT IN NEW MEXICO BETWEEN 1598 and 1680 has been known in a general way, but sparse documentation and limited archaeological work have hindered delineation of a more specific pattern. This study represents an attempt to utilize the documentary and archaeological information that is available with the hope of achieving a more concrete picture of the Spanish settlement landscape of New Mexico in the early colonial period. During that time there was only one officially designated urban center, the provincial capital, Santa Fe. Although many Spanish colonists or members of their extended families maintained a residence in Santa Fe, they mainly lived on their rural properties, which by midcentury were widely distributed throughout the colony and tended to be located particularly in the vicinity of Pueblo villages. Because the Spanish colonists did not migrate into an empty land but one that had been occupied by Pueblo farming people for many centuries, it is important to take up how Spanish settlement was shaped by this native occupation as well as by the number of people—natives and colonists—who were involved, the institutions and technology introduced by the Spaniards, and by the characteristics of the natural environment. It should be stated at the outset that this study does not include the Zuni and Moqui (Hopi) Pueblo areas, where Spanish occupation was mainly represented by religious and civil authorities.

Because settlement is the theme of this study, and acquisition of land is basic to settlement, the absence of land grant records, which were probably destroyed by rebelling Pueblo people who took over the government buildings (*casas reales*) in Santa Fe in 1680, has posed the greatest problem in carrying out this investigation.[1] Initially, land was acquired by means of these grants (*mercedes de tierra*), which were made by the governor in the name of the Spanish Crown, which held the right to all conquered lands. Information about the location of colonists' landholdings or place of residence, therefore, consists of references made in passing that have been gleaned from other documents, such as those of the Inquisition, surviving reviews of gubernatorial administrations (residencias), or post-reconquest petitions reclaiming land held by a family prior to the 1680 Pueblo revolt. The result is an incomplete picture of settlement and one that does not reflect a particular date but rather a composite of dates stretching over an eighty-year period, the preponderance of data coming from the 1660s, when many properties were in the hands of children or grandchildren of the original colonists. A 1695 post-reconquest survey of former Spanish properties in the area north of Santa Fe, ordered by Governor Diego de Vargas, is the only known systematic treatment of landholding. Family alliances worked out through the genealogical investigations of Fray Angélico Chávez and José Antonio Esquibel have helped establish the location of settler's properties, including land acquired by latecomers whose property was the dowry of a bride from a landowning family. Published collections of documents by George Hammond and Agapito Rey, George Winship, Richard Flint and Shirley Cushing Flint, Charles Hackett, Charles Hackett and Charmion Shelby, J. Manuel Espinosa, and John Kessell, Rick Hendricks, Meredith Dodge, and Larry Miller, as well as the work of France V. Scholes, are the source of most of the documentary material used in this study, and that material is supplemented by reports of Hispanic archaeological sites to be found at the Laboratory of Anthropology of the Museum of New Mexico in Santa Fe.

Acknowledgments

⁜ THIS STUDY OF SEVENTEENTH-CENTURY SPANISH SETTLEMENT IN NEW Mexico owes much to the help of many people, above all to José Antonio Esquibel, who not only critically reviewed the manuscript but generously provided material from his archival research related to the early history of New Mexico. Anyone perusing the endnotes and works cited sections of this book will become aware of my great debt to him for greatly enhancing the quality of this study. The chapter on Santa Fe has been greatly improved by the unpublished material provided by Cordelia T. Snow and James E. Ivey as well as by their comments and the review of this and other chapters by Ms. Snow, whose generosity and encouragement have meant much to me. The writings and personal communications of archaeologists Cordelia T. Snow, David H. Snow, Stephen S. Post, Stephen C. Lentz, and Michael P. Marshall have made it possible to incorporate archaeological findings into my study, as have data in the files of the Archaeological Records Management System at the Laboratory of Anthropology in Santa Fe, whose staff was most helpful. My understanding of the hydrologic features of seventeenth-century Santa Fe owes much to a map of the cienega published by urban planner and historian Linda Tigges and the dissertation research of geographer Tara Plewa. The draft article on the Comanche Springs site by archaeologists Ann F. Ramenofsky and David Charles Vaughn and their comments have shed new light on this settlement. Gerald Gonzalez and Francisco Sisneros have shared information about their family histories. James E. Ivey has provided me with a publishable copy of the 1766 Urrutia map. It is further a privilege to be able to include in this study a copy of a rare 1599 map showing the Spaniards' first settlement, San Gabriel. Permission to publish this map was granted by the Archivo General de Indias in Seville, Spain, and a copy has been made available through the courtesy of Joseph P. Sánchez, historian and director of the Spanish Colonial Research Center. Thanks, also to Nancy Brown-Martínez and other staff members of the Center for Southwest Research and Special Collections in Zimmerman Library at the University of New Mexico for help in finding needed materials. Natalie Heberling, a recent MA graduate of the Department of Geography has made maps 1, 2, 6, 7, and 8. Map 5 was created by Andrew Ruiz at the Map and Geographic Information Center of the University of New Mexico using shape files provided by the City of Santa Fe, GIS Division. I wish also to acknowledge the generous support of the Department of Geography at the University of New Mexico, my academic home for many years, whose administrator, Jasmin Knight, has provided much appreciated support and, along with Hays Barrett and Susan Pinter, has given me much-needed technical assistance. I am grateful to all I have mentioned as well to the many others unmentioned for the help they have given me, but I alone am responsible for any errors or omissions in this work.

PART ONE

The Context of Settlement

CHAPTER ONE

The Spanish Entrada

✢ THE EXPEDITION OF GOVERNOR JUAN DE OÑATE WAS NOT THE FIRST Spanish entry into New Mexico, but it was the first authorized to establish a permanent colony. From the reports of Álvar Núñez Cabeza de Vaca in 1536 and Fray Marcos de Niza in 1539, Spanish authorities had become interested in New Mexico as a field for the extension of empire and conversion to Christianity of the reported settled native population.[1] The large expedition led by Francisco Vázquez de Coronado explored much of New Mexico in 1540–42 without finding the fabulous riches previously reported, but the existence of a numerous village-dwelling agricultural people was not forgotten and inspired Fray Agustín Rodríguez to apply to the viceroy for permission to undertake missionary work in Pueblo country.[2] He and two other religious, along with a military contingent of nine led by Captain Francisco Sánchez Chamuscado, traveled widely, visiting pueblos as well as areas farther afield from June 1581 until April 1582, when they returned to Santa Barbara in the northern province of Nueva Vizcaya.[3] Fray Agustín and one other religious remained behind, and it was to discover their fate that another expedition was mounted later in that year.[4] A frontiersman, Antonio de Espejo, volunteered to underwrite the expedition, and he, along with fourteen soldiers and Fray Bernadino Beltrán, who obtained authorization for the undertaking, set off in November 1582, returning ten months later in September 1583.[5] They reported that Fray Agustín and his companion had been killed and provided additional information about the Pueblos. The chronicles of these three expeditions, as well as that of the unauthorized 1590–91 entrada by

Captain Gaspar Castaño de Sosa, provided Oñate with considerable advance knowledge of the land and people he set out to colonize.[6]

The cumulative information about New Mexico led the authorities in Spain and Mexico City to consider a colonizing expedition. Among the prominent citizens who applied to lead the enterprise was Juan de Oñate, scion of a wealthy and distinguished family that was associated with the discovery of the rich silver mines of Zacatecas.[7] After what was probably an extended period negotiating its terms, Viceroy Luis de Velasco II approved the contract that awarded leadership of the expedition to Oñate on September 21, 1595.[8] A new viceroy, Gaspar de Zuñiga y Acevedo, Count of Monterey, arrived soon thereafter and gave the contract provisional approval in October, pending further examination of its terms.[9] At the end of December Viceroy Monterey made known the modifications of the contract that he required—most notably rejection of Oñate's authority to deal directly with the Crown rather than with the viceroy.[10] Although opposed to the limitations placed on the powers granted him in the original contract, Oñate was forced to accept them. In the meantime, he had gone about recruiting financial support, personnel, and supplies for the expedition, which was a private enterprise underwritten by him, his family, and other supporters but that conformed with the royal ordinances of 1573 for new discoveries and settlements.[11] While Oñate was preparing for the expedition, mainly in his home province of Nueva Galicia, a contender for leadership, Pedro Ponce de León, submitted a petition to the Council of the Indies in Seville. Ponce de León's application offered more favorable terms in the eyes of the council members, who strongly recommended him to the king.[12] As a result, suspension of Oñate's contract was ordered on May 8, 1596.[13] Viceroy Monterey, who was now strongly supporting Oñate to the Crown and council, received the cedula in July 1596.[14] By the time it reached Oñate in September, he was dealing with an inspector, Lope de Ulloa y Lemos, a royal notary whom the viceroy had sent to the expedition headquarters in May to carry out an inspection and accounting of personnel, arms, provisions, livestock, and other items in order to ensure that Oñate was carrying out the terms of his contract.[15]

Oñate withheld news of the contract suspension from members of the expedition in the hope that it could be held together long enough to realize a reversal of fortunes. Problems with Ponce de León resulted in a decree issued February 18, 1597, that lifted the suspension of Oñate's contract, but the news did not reach him until the fall.[16] In the meantime, the long delays had led to many defections among the colonists and much dissatisfaction on the part of those who had sold their worldly goods to underwrite their share of the expedition. Although many colonists were still scattered in different parts of northern New Spain, Oñate was able hold onto most of the recruits and to prevail on Inspector Ulloa y Lemos to carry out the inspection, which took place during December 1596 and January 1597, mainly at the mines of Casco but also at Santa Barbara and La Puana, where a total of 205 soldier-colonists were mustered.[17] The viceroy, on receipt of the royal decree lifting the suspension, sent Juan de Frías Salazar to join Oñate in Santa Barbara and carry out a further inspection.[18] Since the Ulloa y Lemos inspection, the condition of the expedition had further deteriorated, and the Frías Salazar muster, carried out near the mines of Todos Santos from December 22, 1597, to January 8, 1598, had yielded only 129 soldier-colonists, making it necessary for Oñate to have a family member post bond for an additional eighty soldiers to be recruited later.[19] Finally on January 26, 1598, almost two and a half years after Viceroy Luis de Velasco had approved his contract, Juan de Oñate was able to lead his expedition northward into New Mexico.[20]

This caravan, consisting of an estimated five hundred people, some seven thousand head of livestock, and eighty-three carts and wagons, took a new, more direct, route from the Río Conchos via the San Pedro River and reached the Rio Grande (their Río del Norte) on April 20, 1598.[21] After the expedition traveled 6 leagues (15.6 miles) west along the Rio Grande, Oñate declared a day of celebration on April 30, when he took possession of "all the kingdoms and provinces of New Mexico."[22] On May 4 the expedition reached a place today called El Paso where they crossed to the east side of the river and headed north toward Pueblo country along what came to be called the Camino Real.[23] The first settlements were reached near Black Mesa on May 28 after the expedition had traversed 22 leagues (57.2 miles), including a waterless stretch of some 10 leagues (26 miles) called the Jornada del Muerto (see map 1, p. 205).[24] Oñate and a party of men had left six days earlier in order to prepare the way for the expedition and especially to secure food supplies, which they brought back to the caravan on June 12.[25] Leaving orders for the army to join him at the place he had chosen to settle, Oñate then moved quickly northward with his men. They found most of the pueblos along the way deserted by their fearful residents.[26] On June 30 they reached Kewa (Santo Domingo) Pueblo. There, on July 7, they held a council during which the heads of seven Pueblo provinces pledged obedience to the Crown.[27]

Traveling north from there, possibly up the canyon of the Santa Fe River to avoid the impassable canyon of the Rio Grande (present White Rock

Canyon), they passed through the Santa Fe River valley, where there were no occupied pueblos at that time, and entered the Española basin, home of the Tewa people. There, having returned to the Rio Grande, they passed through Bove (San Ildefonso Pueblo) and Caypa (Santa Clara Pueblo) before reaching their destination, Ohkay Owingeh (San Juan Pueblo), on July 11.[28] They stayed only two days before leaving to continue their reconnaissance—traveling north to Taos, east to Pecos, and west to the Jemez pueblos. They arrived back at Ohkay Owingeh on August 10, only a week before the remainder of the expedition arrived on August 18.[29]

From the beginning it seems that Oñate intended to settle his colonists in this area not only because it reportedly possessed substantial resources but because it had limited contact with the earlier Spanish expeditions that had explored New Mexico.[30] As a consequence, the Tewa people had little experience with the abuse visited on some of the pueblos to the south, especially by the Coronado expedition of 1540–42. One of Coronado's captains, Francisco de Barrionuevo, on a mission to round up provisions, visited a province he called Yuque-Yunque, where he found "two beautiful pueblos on opposite sides of the river" from which the people fled when he and his men arrived. The pueblos contained abundant provisions, beautiful glazed pottery, and jars filled with a shiny metal (lead) that they used to glaze their pottery—an indication that silver mines might also be found in the area.[31] Barrionuevo's men proceeded to plunder the two pueblos, but this negative experience was countered by better treatment fifty years later when the next Spanish expedition to reach this far north, that of Gaspar Castaño de Sosa, came through the area in 1591.[32] The fact that he took care not to antagonize the local people he encountered and was generously supplied with provisions at the Tewa pueblos was known to Oñate and probably played a crucial role in his decision to establish his headquarters in this area, particularly at the two beautiful pueblos described by Captain Barrionuevo (Ohkay Owingeh and Yunque Owingeh).

CHAPTER TWO

The Natural Landscape

✢ WHAT SEEMS TO HAVE STRUCK OÑATE'S COLONISTS MOST ABOUT THE landscape of New Mexico was its climate. Several of his captains who were in Mexico City reporting to the treasury official Francisco de Valverde in the summer of 1601 characterized the climate as one of extremes. According to one, the summers were as intensely hot as the winters were cold—"ocho meses de invierno y quatro de infierno."[1] The most common complaint was that the winters were prolonged and bitterly cold with heavy snow. The frost lasted from October through March, and there was snow on the ground until May. The winters were so cold that in places the Rio Grande froze over, permitting it to be crossed on horseback.[2] Smaller streams near the colonists' headquarters at San Gabriel also froze, and settlers had to melt the ice in order to obtain drinking water.[3] However, they noted that enhanced stream flow and increased soil moisture from melting snow in May were often more important for successful crop production than summer rainfall, so that the sparse rainfall during the summer was not necessarily detrimental, though they did emphasize the overall aridity of the province.[4] Fray Alonso de Benavides, custodian of New Mexico from 1626 to 1629, supported these general characterizations of the climate, although his statements are more exaggerated. According to him, "Snow remained on the ground most of the year," and from November through February, "all rivers, large and small, are frozen over so solid that iron-bound wagons, heavily laden, cross them, and vast herds of cattle go over them at full gallop," while on the other hand, during June, July, and August, "even in the shade of the houses tallow candles and salt pork melt."[5]

However, based on climate reconstructions, the New Mexico through which the expedition led by Juan de Oñate traveled in the summer of 1598 was not very different from the arid-semiarid landscape it had traversed after leaving the Parral district in northern New Spain, but it was different from what they were accustomed to in the central part of New Spain where temperatures were milder and rainfall was higher. The statements of sixteenth- and seventeenth-century explorers and settlers about long, bitterly cold winters and oppressively hot summers should be viewed from that perspective; it also should be kept in mind that they were probably commenting on climate extremes, while climate reconstructions reflect average conditions. This time period is well within the Little Ice Age (ca. 1450–1850), but temperature reconstructions for western North America indicate that this region did not share with eastern North America and Europe the greatly lower temperatures associated with the Little Ice Age.[6] Although climate in New Mexico can be characterized as dry, it is not everywhere the same; in the area north of La Bajada Mesa, where elevations are markedly higher (Santa Fe lies at 7,000 feet compared with Albuquerque at 5,000 feet), temperatures are somewhat lower and precipitation a little higher (see map 2, p. 206). But drought, mild or severe, is a frequent phenomenon everywhere in New Mexico. Of the eighty-three years of the early colonial period, 1598–1680, seventy-four, or 89 percent, would be considered dry based on values derived from the Palmer Drought Severity Index (PDSI) for Santa Fe (appendix table A). During this time several periods of extremely dry conditions prevailed, causing crops to fail. Unfortunately, such was the case when the first colonists arrived. The PDSI for Santa Fe indicates that the average value for the four years 1598–1601 was minus 1.074, where values below 1.00 indicate dryness. The average value for the preceding four years was 2.793 and for the succeeding four years 0.955. The following eight years (1602–9) saw only one year above 1.00 and an average of 0.446. Thus, early colonists had to contend with very difficult conditions, and the Pueblo people, on whose crop production the Spaniards largely depended, suffered a shortfall themselves. The Spaniards' consumption of the surpluses that the Puebloans had accumulated in previous, more favorable years and the prevailing famine conditions from 1598 to 1601 probably contributed to the large-scale desertion of the colony in 1601.[7]

This terrible period was followed by a series of relatively wetter years, particularly the three years 1610–12 when the villa of Santa Fe was officially established and the average PDSI value for Santa Fe was 2.013. During the following eleven years relatively good rainfall years alternated with bad years giving an average of 0.845 (incipient wet conditions) with a high value of 2.701 (unusually moist) and low of minus 1.703 (mild drought), which indicates a high degree of variability. Altogether the years 1610–23 constituted the longest period of "wet" years prior to the 1680 revolt, a situation not encouraging for agriculture but one that was better than that during the next fifty-seven years when twenty-six years had minus values and only sixteen measured above 1.00. The worst years were 1664–76, thirteen years that averaged minus 0.527 with only one year above 1.00. The resulting severe and prolonged drought was a major factor in the famine that led to abandonment of the native pueblos and Spanish estancias in the Estancia basin in the 1670s (appendix table A, Chupadera Mesa). Precipitation reconstructions based on tree-ring data for Albuquerque follow the pattern outlined here (appendix table B) and, in addition, show values similar to those of modern day as seen in table 1.

Table 1. Average Annual Precipitation,* Albuquerque, New Mexico, 1602–80 and 1950–95

YEARS	WINTER	SPRING	SUMMER	FALL	ANNUAL TOTAL
1602–80	0.82	2.33	3.08	2.39	8.37
1950–95	1.36	1.47	3.43	2.28	8.53

Sources: For 1602–80 data, see appendix table B. 1950–95 data are from the Midwestern Climate Center, a cooperative project of the National Climate Data Center and the Illinois State Water Survey, Champaign, Illinois.

*Inches.

These average annual values of 8.37 inches for 1602–80 and 8.53 inches for 1950–95 for the Albuquerque area, along with those for the Southern Rio Grande region (appendix table C), mean that crops would have had to have been irrigated in all but those years when precipitation was well above average. Reconstructed temperature values for Santa Fe derived from tree-ring analysis are also not very different from present average seasonal temperature values (appendix table D). The average summer temperature for 1602–80 was 68.48 degrees Fahrenheit compared with 68.50 degrees for 1950–95, and in winter, average temperatures were 49.60 and 50.50 degrees respectively (table 2).

Table 2. Average Seasonal Temperatures,* Santa Fe, New Mexico, 1602–80 and 1950–95

YEARS	WINTER	SPRING	SUMMER	FALL	ANNUAL TOTAL
1602–80	32.80	52.11	68.48	50.51	49.60
1950–95	31.80	48.20	68.50	51.10	50.50

Sources: For 1602–80 data, see appendix table D. 1950–55 data are from the Midwestern Climate Center, a cooperative project of the National Climate Data Center and the Illinois State Water Survey, Champaign, Illinois.

*Degrees Fahrenheit.

It should be emphasized that such average precipitation and temperature data mask the extreme values and high degree of variability that characterize the generally dry climate of the region that the colonists had to deal with and that they were at pains to report.

According to the Valverde informants, planting only began with the melting of snow in May and harvesting took place in August. They were probably referring to agricultural practices in the area around their settlement at that time, San Gabriel, in the Española basin. When Governor Vargas was in the nearby Santa Cruz River valley in 1695, he stated that the region was so cold that planting did not begin until early May after the sun had taken some of the chill from the land.[8] Growing conditions farther south were seen to be more favorable, and colonists began to move into areas south of Santa Fe early in the seventeenth century. The Spanish colonists who came to New Mexico in the 1690s had the same impression and sought to be relocated from Santa Fe and the Santa Cruz River valley to "a more temperate location" in the Middle Rio Grande region.[9] Modern growing-season data show an increase in the number of frost-free days southward and in areas with lower elevation (table 3).

Because plant growth generally does not take place when the soil is below 40–42 degrees Fahrenheit, the actual growing season is shorter than the number of frost-free days, making northern areas and the Estancia basin marginal for growing the staple crop, maize (corn), which can take between about 80 and 135 days to reach maturity, depending on the variety.[10] It is estimated that traditional native maize required about 120 days, and, although varieties were undoubtedly developed by Puebloans that were adapted to varying climatic conditions, in general, maize productivity is greater where the growing season is longer and summer temperatures higher.[11] Colonists were also attracted to more southerly regions along the Rio Grande where

Table 3. Number of Frost-Free Days, Selected Sites in New Mexico

STATION	NUMBER OF FROST-FREE DAYS*	ELEVATION IN FEET
Taos	130	7650
Española	164	5643
Santa Fe	155	7000
Albuquerque**	182	4955
Estancia	134	6107
Socorro	186	4585

Source: National Climatic Data Center (www.srh.noaa.gov).

*Number of days between the median date of the last occurrence of 32 degrees Fahrenheit in the spring and the median date of the first occurrence of 32 degrees Fahrenheit in the fall.
**Albuquerque South Valley station.

more land to grow wheat and water to irrigate it were available. The difficulties of cultivating crops in the northern regions were brought out in 1776 by Fray Francisco Atanasio Domínguez. Referring to Picurís Pueblo lands in the Far North, he stated that "frijol and chile do not yield a crop because of the cold" and "maize usually freezes, but not consistently."[12]

The Rio Grande owes its perennial flow to its source farther north in present southern Colorado where higher precipitation and a greater snowpack contribute significantly to its volume as it flows south through the structural basins (grabens) of the Rio Grande Rift valley of New Mexico. South to about its confluence with Galisteo Creek, the Rio Grande is bordered by the southern ranges of the Rocky Mountains (the Jemez Mountains on the west and the Sangre de Cristo Mountains on the east). Southward it enters basin and range topography characterized by lesser mountain ranges, the most prominent being the Sandia-Manzano chain bordering the east side of the Middle Rio Grande region (Albuquerque-Belen basin). Here tributaries are much diminished, most being nonperennial, and during years of extreme drought surface flow can even cease along some reaches of the Rio Grande in summer.[13] The Rio Grande is an aggrading stream that before modern times migrated freely across its floodplain, especially below Cochiti Pueblo. The river's shifting sandy substrate differed there from its gravel pavement northward, where the river is also more confined.[14] Flooding during spring runoff would not only moisten the soil but renew it with a fresh layer of silt.[15] Flooding also caused major and minor shifts of the river's channels. A major shift sometime in the distant past had established the Rio Grande's main channel east of where it is at present, most notably the stretch from below Algodones (just above the Rio Grande-Jemez River junction) to the southern outskirts of present Albuquerque (Rio Grande-Tijeras Arroyo junction), until sometime after 1710 when, having built up its channel bottom above its natural levees, it began to shift back to its present western channel.[16] The aggrading condition of the river contributed to elevation of the water table in the surrounding floodplain, creating marshy areas in low-lying places, especially those alongside the river (called yazoos) that could not drain properly because the adjacent riverbed was higher.[17] There are a number of yazoos along the Rio Grande sustained by a high water table and periodic flooding of the Rio Grande, but the one that was noted in the seventeenth century was called Esteros de Mexía, a wetland composed of marshes, swamps, and shallow ponds mainly used by the Spanish colonists for grazing livestock (see map 8, p. 212).[18] It was located in the Barelas district of present Albuquerque between about Central Avenue and the Barelas Bridge, the Rio Grande's main channel being located to the east roughly between Twelfth and Second streets.[19] These hydrologic conditions made farming precarious. In 1698, a reason given for refusing the request of colonists in Santa Cruz to move south to the Alameda area in the Middle Rio Grande region was that widespread flooding of the Rio Grande in that area caused the destruction of acequias and crops.[20]

Besides wetlands, Spaniards found discontinuous groves of native cottonwood (*Populus fremontii*) and willow (*Salix* sp.) along the Rio Grande.[21] In 1540 Hernando de Alvarado, one of Coronado's captains, mentioned "some cottonwood groves," referring to the area roughly between Isleta and Bernalillo (their Tiguex Province).[22] The explorer Antonio de Espejo, coming up the Rio Grande in 1583, noted many cottonwood groves once he reached the southernmost Pueblo settlements.[23] One of the most extensive of these gallery woodlands mentioned in the documents bordered the Rio Grande on the east from about present Alameda south to the Esteros de Mexía (see map 8, p. 212).[24] Originally known as the Bosque Grande de San Francisco Xavier, it came to be known as the Bosque Grande de doña Luisa, named for Luisa (Montoya) de Trujillo, whose estancia was located at the southern end of the bosque.[25] Spaniards mentioned other cottonwood groves south of present Albuquerque, such as one in the area of Valencia referred to in 1626 and others in the vicinity of Tome, noted in 1766 by the military engineer Nicolás de Lafora as he traveled along the eastern margin of the Rio Grande through "un llano cubierto de una alameda de bastante extension."[26] He also said that on the whole journey from the ruins of Senecú Pueblo in the south to

Santa Fe the group's animals never lacked pasture—which consisted mainly of gramma grass.[27] The riparian vegetation, which also included open grassy areas, or vegas, provided valuable resources to Spanish settlers as well as travelers even though it was subject to modification under the shifting conditions of erosion and deposition associated with seasonal flooding. Riparian resources were, of course, much less well developed elsewhere in New Mexico where smaller, nonperennial water courses were the norm. Away from rivers and streams, extensive grasslands predominated up to 6,000–7,000 feet, providing optimal conditions for the livestock Spaniards brought with them. These grasslands consisted of various types of bunch grass, particularly blue gramma and in the south, black gramma.[28] With increasing elevation, grasslands become interspersed with woody species, most commonly one-seed juniper (*Juniperus monosperma*), and in the 6,000–7,500 foot zone juniper and piñon pine (*Pinus edulis*) became dominant.[29] The seed of the piñon tree was prized not only by Puebloans but also by the Spaniards, for whom it became an important commodity that they exported to the population centers of northern New Spain. At higher elevations (7,200–8,500 feet) ponderosa pine (*Pinus ponderosa*) provided a more valuable wood for construction along with other coniferous species such as Englemann spruce (*Picea engelmannii*) and Douglas fir (*Pseudotsuga menziesii*), found above 8,500 feet.[30]

On the whole, the natural landscape of New Mexico presented Spaniards with difficult conditions for settlement. No substantial deposits of precious metals were found that could sustain the colony, and the aridity of the province limited productive crop agriculture in most years to those few areas with sufficient water for irrigation during the growing season. Limited water resources especially prevailed in the southern parts of the province and in the Estancia basin to the east, although dryness and the enclosed nature of the basin created extensive salt pans that provided a resource that the Spaniards exploited. Ranching, however, was greatly enhanced by the extensive grasslands that dominated much of the landscape. The groves of cottonwoods helped maintain stream embankments and provided a place for campsites, shelter for some game animals, and an inferior firewood. Juniper and piñon pine made for excellent firewood, and piñon nuts provided an edible item for local consumption and export. Timber for construction was not readily accessible to most settlers, especially in the southern part of the province, and it took special effort to obtain posts for corrals and vigas for buildings. As a result, structures, even churches and government buildings, were made mainly of adobe bricks.

CHAPTER THREE

The Pueblo Landscape

☥ AS THE MEMBERS OF THE OÑATE EXPEDITION MADE THEIR WAY UP the river they called the Río del Norte (Rio Grande), traveling some 175 miles from Senecú, the southernmost pueblo, to their destination at San Juan (see map 1, p. 205), they passed loose groupings of villages or pueblos. These pueblos were mainly located on tributary streams, although some were built on benchlands along the margins of the Río del Norte itself. Subsequently, the expedition encountered two pueblos farther north and others to the east in the Estancia basin and to the northeast in the Pecos River drainage as well as to the west in the Jemez Mountains and on the peñol of Ácoma.[1] In all, there were about eighty pueblos inhabited by some fifty to sixty thousand people.[2] These pueblo groupings, which occupied specific drainage areas, were distinguished by different languages, all of which are related to the Tanoan family, except one group whose language was Keres, a distinct linguistic stock (table 4).[3]

Traveling through the southernmost Pueblo district, which stretched some sixty miles from Black Mesa near present San Marcial to about the Rio Grande-Abó Arroyo junction and including the Socorro basin, they passed nine pueblos inhabited by Piro-speaking people.[4] To one of these pueblos (Teypama [LA 282]), they gave the name "Socorro" because its people generously furnished them with maize, whereas they found other pueblos deserted, their inhabitants having fled at the approach of the Spaniards.[5] Traveling north some eighteen miles from Teypama, they camped at deserted Sevilleta Pueblo for a week, waiting for supplies of maize to be brought in. While

Table 4. Number of New Mexico Pueblos: 1598, 1641, and 1680 by District and Language

DISTRICT	NUMBER OF PUEBLOS			LANGUAGE*
	1598	1641	1680	
Far North	2	2	2	Northern Tiwa
Chama River	1	0	0	Tewa
Española Basin	8	8	8	Tewa
Pajarito Plateau	1	0	0	Tewa
Galisteo Basin	3	4	4	Tano
Pecos	1	1	1	Towa
Ácoma	1	1	1	Keres
Santa Fe River Valley	0	1	1	Keres?
Santo Domingo Basin	5	3	3	Keres
Lower Jemez River	5	2	2	Keres
Jemez Mountains	11	1**	1**	Towa
Middle Rio Grande	21	5	4	Southern Tiwa
Estancia Basin				
Northern	5	3	0	Southern Tiwa
Southern	6	3	0	Tompiro
Southern Rio Grande	11	3	4	Piro
Total	81	37	31	

Source: Barrett, Conquest.

*All languages except Keres belong to the Tanoan family.
**Incomplete.

they waited, a small party explored the Abó Pass area, which gave entry to the Estancia basin.[6] There they would later find five Southern Tiwa pueblos along the eastern margin of the Manzano Mountains and six Tompiro pueblos farther south. The expedition then moved some seventy miles north through the Middle Rio Grande region (Albuquerque-Belen basin) where they encountered an additional twenty-one pueblos belonging to Southern Tiwa people and where they noted many planted fields on both sides of the river.[7] To the north and west of the Rio Grande-Jemez River junction were five Keresan pueblos located along the lower Jemez that were not visited at this time, nor were the eleven or so Towa-speaking Jemez pueblos located farther north up the river into the Jemez Mountains or the western frontier pueblo of Ácoma, whose members spoke Keresan. The expedition continued north along the Rio Grande through the Santo Domingo basin where there were five pueblos, all of whose inhabitants spoke Keresan. They were blocked from following the river farther north because it entered an impassible canyon, and so they moved east, following Galisteo Creek before turning north toward San Marcos Pueblo, a pueblo that might have been inhabited by Keres and/or Tano people (see map 1, p. 205). Eastward in the Galisteo drainage were three pueblos inhabited by people who spoke Tano, a dialect of Tewa. Farther east still was the frontier pueblo of Pecos, whose inhabitants spoke the same language as the Jemez people—Towa. From San Marcos Pueblo the expedition moved north, crossing the Santa Fe River valley where there were no occupied pueblos at that time, into the Española basin where they found eight Tewa-speaking pueblos, one of which, Ohkay Owingeh (San Juan), was their destination. Beyond, the two northernmost pueblos, Taos and Picurís, were occupied by speakers of Northern Tiwa.

Members of the Oñate expedition found what had been reported by earlier Spanish explorers: a people living in permanent homes and practicing agriculture.[8] Their settlements consisted of roomblocks arranged around one or more plazas where their subterranean ceremonial chambers, called "kivas," were located. The multistoried roomblocks, which each contained a number of houses, were made of puddled adobe (although in some areas stone was used). Each level was set back from the one beneath, creating rooftop terraces where much of the activity of daily living took place. Because the roomblocks lacked ground-floor doors, access to the interior was gained by means of ladders and openings in the ceilings of rooms. In the smaller pueblos, the roomblocks were usually two stories high and typically the pueblo consisted of thirty to forty houses; larger pueblos had roomblocks four to five or more stories high and contained up to four hundred houses with numerous plazas and kivas.[9] The smaller pueblos had about two hundred inhabitants and the largest ones eight hundred to a thousand residents.[10] The chroniclers of previous Spanish expeditions reported that the pueblos were larger, better constructed, and more numerous as they traveled north.[11] But the Piro pueblos (as well as those pueblos in the districts farther north) were noted as having whitewashed interiors with walls "well decorated with monsters, other animals, and human figures."[12]

The Puebloans also took pains to decorate their clothing, which was made of various materials—cotton or yucca fibers, turkey feathers, rabbit skins, and deer or buffalo hides.[13] The tasks of spinning and weaving were mainly the work of men using upright looms.¹⁴ According to the early explorers, the men, to cover their privy parts, wore a small colored cotton cloth, which they tied at their hips. Over that they wore a cotton blanket or manta, also hand painted or embroidered, that reached to the knees and was fastened at the shoulders. It was also mentioned that many men wore shirts and, on occasion, long robes made of turkey feathers or the skins of hares. The women wore colored and embroidered skirts that were tied at the waist with an embroidered, tasseled cotton sash. They covered their upper bodies with a cotton manta, also decorated, that was fastened over the left shoulder. Both men and women had footwear with buffalo hide soles and dressed deerskin uppers.¹⁵ Clothing made of animal skins was more commonly worn by people in the northern pueblos than by those in the south, although all wore them during cold weather.¹⁶ The availability of cotton cloth was a boon to the Spanish colonists, who were in much need of it after their long journey, and it became a major item of tribute. Throughout the prerevolt period (1598–1680), the Spaniards also made use of Puebloan ceramic ware, both decorated and utilitarian, that the women produced using the coiling method in the absence of knowledge of the potter's wheel.¹⁷ Early explorers noted the high quality of the ceramics. The chronicler of the Coronado expedition stated that "throughout all of these provincias there is pottery glazed with lead and jars of consummate workmanship and very many shapes. That was something to see."¹⁸

However, the products of which the Spanish colonists were most in need were the foodstuffs Puebloans produced. They principally grew maize, beans, and squashes. Maize was their most important crop, and it also became the chief item of tribute collected by the Spaniards. Crops were raised in irrigated fields where streams could be diverted by means of ditches and dams; otherwise they depended on snowmelt and rainfall to moisten soils directly, though these sources were not reliable given the semiarid climate.¹⁹ Despite the harsh agricultural conditions, Puebloans were able to produce surpluses to store against the inevitable droughts, and it was these stores that were much needed by Oñate's colonists, who had run low on provisions even before they reached Pueblo country—marking the beginning of the Spaniards' ongoing need for Puebloan crops.²⁰ The digging stick (*coa*) and hoe were the agricultural implements used by the Puebloans. Only with the arrival of the Spaniards were the plow and draft animals introduced, but they were not taken up by Pueblo farmers.²¹ Their animal husbandry was focused on raising turkeys, of which they had large flocks that they kept in corrals.²² It was reported that they were not raised for food but to provide feathers for making cloaks that were worn in cold weather.[23] Cotton was mainly grown in the southern part of the region—the Piro, Southern Tiwa, and Keres districts. People in other pueblos obtained it as raw cotton or finished cloth through trade, particularly with the Moqui (Hopi) far to the west, where cotton cultivation was an important activity.[24] Unfortunately, over time, less cotton was produced, as Spanish labor demands, diminished cultivable lands, droughts, and increased Apachean raids took their toll. At the same time, the Spanish mission and civil authorities, as well as some encomenderos, supplied the Puebloans with wool to weave on the treadle looms they introduced; by the end of the prerevolt period in 1680, the Spaniards had converted Pueblo textile production mainly to woolen products.[25]

Trade networks among the Puebloans were a source of food, cotton, and other items, such as salt from the salt pans in the Estancia basin. And they exchanged their maize and cotton cloth for meat, hides, tallow, and fat, which they obtained from the surrounding nomadic Apachean tribes, especially those who exploited the vast herds of bison that inhabited the plains to the east. These items of exchange also benefited the Spaniards as they took over Puebloan trade networks.[26] But more than anything, it was the labor of a sedentary agricultural people that was of the greatest value to the Spanish colonists.

CHAPTER FOUR

The Spanish Institutional Landscape

Encomienda

✢ ONE OF THE MOST DISTINCTIVE SPANISH COLONIAL INSTITUTIONS brought to New Mexico was the encomienda, a means by which the Spanish Crown could reward men who played a leading role in the conquest of new territories, the reward being the right to collect a designated amount of tribute from specified villages of native peoples.[1] This institution was meant to help colonists sustain themselves in the new land and at the same time ensure for the Crown continued settlement of the colony. Juan de Oñate, who with his family underwrote the costs of colonizing New Mexico, was given the right to grant encomiendas to those of his men he considered deserving—a decision made largely based on the roles they played and the arms, horses, and other materiel they provided.[2] In New Mexico, the encomienda could be granted after five years' residence in the colony, and the grantees, or encomenderos, could hold this privilege for their lifetimes and those of two successive generations; in addition, they became eligible for the much sought-after title of hidalgo.[3] The encomenderos were obliged to defend the colony when called on to do so and to protect the missionaries as they sought to convert the Puebloan people to Christianity.[4] They were also required to maintain a residence in Santa Fe, once the villa was established.[5] By the time New Mexico was colonized in 1598, the tribute to which encomenderos were entitled did not include personal service. Rather, every Pueblo house was assessed each year one fanega of maize (2.6 bushels) and one manta (piece of cotton cloth measuring about 5.5 square feet) for which a buffalo hide or deer skin could be substituted, for example, by those in northern pueblos where cotton could not be grown.[6] Tribute was collected in May and October, the latter date being when Puebloans most likely paid their maize tribute from their newly harvested grain.[7] In the late 1620s, the missionary custodian Fray Alonso de Benavides noted the conflict between the encomenderos and Puebloans over the collection of tribute. When several families moved into a single house in order to lessen their payment, the encomenderos insisted that the tribute be collected on the basis of households.[8]

Only a partial picture of the encomienda establishment in New Mexico is available because records of such grants were destroyed in the 1680 revolt (or otherwise lost), and no copies have been discovered. What is known comes from passing references in other documents in which a colonist is mentioned as an encomendero, sometimes along with the name of his tribute pueblo or pueblos. No encomiendas were granted before 1601 according to two of Oñate's captains who were in Mexico City in that year. When questioned by the treasury official Francisco Valverde, they replied that no such grants had been made but that is not surprising given the five-year residence requirement.[9] The first known grant was made in 1606 to Juan Martínez de Montoya, who came to New Mexico with reinforcements that were sent in 1600 to make up the shortfall in the number of soldiers called for in Oñate's contract. On October 6, 1606, Governor Juan de Oñate certified the services of Martínez de Montoya in New Mexico, granting him the encomienda of the Jemez pueblos for three lives.[10] After the Santa Fe cabildo rejected the viceroy's appointment of Martínez de Montoya as interim governor, he left the colony in 1608 with the permission of acting governor Cristóbal de Oñate.[11] It is unknown if his father, Juan de Oñate, made any other encomienda grants before he resigned as governor in 1607.[12] Martínez de Montoya's brief tenure as an encomendero in New Mexico probably did not afford him an opportunity to collect tribute from the remote and hostile Jemez people and, in the probable absence of other encomenderos, the settlers continued to obtain food and cloth from the Puebloans during the governorship of Oñate in the manner described by the Valverde witnesses in 1601: groups of armed men, at times accompanied by the governor, went from pueblo to pueblo, even from house to house, collecting the one cotton blanket, or a substitute deer skin or buffalo hide, that was due each year. Once a month, or whenever needed as one witness stated, soldiers went out at the governor's order to collect maize, but whether a fixed amount was assessed each house is unknown.[13] Tribute items were distributed by the governor according to need.[14] Personal service was also exacted, although it was not legal. Services mentioned by the Valverde witnesses included bringing wood and water to the Spaniards at San Gabriel, helping with the planting, weeding, and harvesting of Spaniards fields, tending their livestock, and repairing their dwellings.[15]

Undoubtedly, the new governor, Pedro de Peralta, made encomienda grants but how many or to whom is not known, and it is likely that during his administration the aforementioned amounts of tribute were set in place. The earlier manner of tribute collection continued for some time for those pueblos not yet granted in encomienda, with Governor Peralta dividing the items among the settlers who were not encomenderos.[16] In the 1640s, in the aftermath of the murder of Governor Luis de Rosas, the viceroy set the number of encomiendas in New Mexico at thirty-five, which included the Zuni and Hopi pueblos that numbered about ten.[17] There were about thirty-seven Rio Grande pueblos at that time, making it possible for some encomenderos to have more than one tribute pueblo. The governor who was sent to investigate the Rosas affair, Alonso Pacheco de Heredia, was accused of revoking and regranting encomiendas of those found guilty, diverting to himself the tribute collected while the ensuing litigation took place.[18] When an encomendero was arrested by the civil authorities or the Inquisition or when he had to be absent from the colony or when an encomienda was inherited by a woman or minor, the governor had the opportunity to intervene by appointing one of his partisans as *escudero*.[19] This person's duties included overseeing collection of the tribute and taking on the military obligation of the encomendero until the matter was settled and a permanent replacement named, who could also be a person in the governor's favor.[20] The escudero, however, received only part of the tribute for his services, while the governor impounded the remainder, giving him the opportunity to appropriate (illegally) some of the tribute for his own ends.[21] In the late 1650s, when Governor Bernardo López de Mendizábal required all encomenderos to present their papers for review and verification and returned some encomiendas to their original holders who had been dispossessed by his predecessor, he created further dissension among the members of the encomendero class.[22]

These examples suggest that the encomienda system in New Mexico was not fixed or secure but subject to the vicissitudes of politics. Nevertheless, the right to collect tribute gave encomenderos an edge in accumulating what little wealth there was in this largely subsistence economy and a means of supporting less fortunate family members and other dependents. After about 1640 this source of income was reduced as the Puebloan population had come to be greatly diminished as the result of epidemics, Spanish exploitation, and Apachean raids. It is, therefore, not surprising that Governor Pacheco de Heredia proposed exacting tribute from individuals (heads of households) rather than houses.[23] In the early years of colonization, there were about eighty pueblos, by 1630 about seventy, by 1641 about thirty-seven, and in 1680 about thirty-one (table 4).[24] Nevertheless, in the 1640s the total number of Spaniards remained small—less than two thousand—compared with the tributary population which numbered about 15,600 in 1641, and maize tribute continued to be a significant part of the Spaniards' economy.[25]

The known encomenderos of the prerevolt period are listed in appendix table E. It provides only a partial picture of the encomiendas granted in New Mexico. The data are not sufficient to construct the encomienda establishment for any given year or even a period such as a decade, and the years included in the table are merely those of the document in which the encomendero happens to be mentioned. A number of pueblos do not appear in appendix table E, but undoubtedly they belonged either to an unknown encomendero or one listed in this table; the Crown did not claim any Puebloan villages for itself.[26] It can be noted from appendix table E that some encomendero families held many tribute pueblos, while others had only one or part of one. About seventeen of the encomendero families listed were founded by men who came to New Mexico in 1598 or 1600 or in the first decade of the seventeenth century. Of these families, twelve had members who were in New Mexico in 1680: Archuleta, Carvajal, Durán y Chávez, Gómez Robledo, Griego, Herrera, Hinojos, López de Ocanto, Madrid, Martín Serrano, Montoya, and Tapia. Genealogical research has revealed that over time, alliances among encomendero families gave rise to "clans" that constituted an elite among the New Mexico settlers.[27]

Land

It was apparent from the earliest days of colonization that land would be the principal basis of survival in New Mexico. By virtue of conquest, all land became property of the Spanish Crown, and Governor Oñate by virtue of his contract with the Crown to "discover, pacify, and conquer New Mexico" was given the authority to grant land to his colonists contingent on their "remaining in the conquest" for five years.[28] The absence of land grant records for New Mexico greatly limits knowledge about when they were initiated as well as their number, size, and location. The further lack of information about landholding during the governorship of Juan de Oñate in surviving records might indicate that he did not make any land grants (mercedes de tierra), but he must have been under pressure to make such grants to reward his men for their contribution to establishing the colony and for their loyalty in remaining in the face of the desertion of 1601. Evidence that at least some of the colonists were moving to the Santa Fe River valley and the fact that as early as 1601 Juan Luján claimed he was settled in La Cañada (Santa Cruz River valley)—both areas where there were no occupied pueblos—suggest that colonists were wanting to move out of the confined and illegal situation of their headquarters at San Gabriel and that they were receiving permission from Governor Oñate to do so (see map 1, p. 205).[29]

Certainly land grants were made once Oñate's successor Governor Pedro de Peralta arrived in early 1610 and New Mexico became a Crown colony, although, again, there are no records of such grants. His instructions from the viceroy spelled out the components of the grants he should make to the colonists, all of whom were expected to maintain a residence in the capital he was charged with establishing.[30] These grants, which required ten years' residence to confirm, presumably took into account those held by the colonists who had moved to Santa Fe earlier. They provided for house lots (*solares*), garden and orchard land (*suertes*), and cropland (*caballerías*) as well as the water needed to irrigate these lands. Land grants for grazing livestock, which the Spaniards introduced to New Mexico, were not mentioned in Governor Peralta's instructions, but they were likely the subject of separate grants—for large livestock, *sitios de ganado mayor* and for small livestock, *sitios de ganado menor*. These livestock grants allowed the Spaniards to take advantage of New Mexico's extensive grasslands, lands that had never before been grazed by domestic animals. Such grants, located throughout the province, probably were supplemented by mercedes for house lots and lands where crops introduced by the colonists, especially wheat, could be grown.

There were, however, regulations about where lands granted to Spaniards could be located in relation to settlements of local people—an expression of the Crown's concern for the protection of native peoples and their lands.[31] In general the Crown held that native people were to have whatever lands and waters they occupied and required: "Tengan comodidad de aguas, tierras y montes, entradas y salidas, y labranzas y un exido de una legua de largo."[32] In New Mexico, the recognized amount of land that Pueblos could claim was a league (2.6 miles) measured in each cardinal direction.[33] Spaniards were forbidden to reside on or near Puebloan land, and, to afford them protection, buffer zones were specified. Traditionally, Spanish grazing operations involving ganado mayor (cattle and horses) had to be at least 1.5 leagues (3.9 miles) from the cultivated fields of native people and a half league (1.3 miles) distant from pueblo boundaries in the case of ganado menor (sheep and goats).[34] However, complaints of noncompliance, mainly voiced by the friars, were so numerous that the viceroy in 1621 issued a decree that doubled the width of the buffer zones, specifying that they also applied to the soldiers' horse herd.[35] But abuses continued, especially the destruction of Pueblo crops by Spanish cattle. In 1633, the missionary at the pueblo of Cuarac (Quarai) charged that the governor gave settlers permission to establish an estancia for raising cattle and sheep on the Pueblo's cultivated fields.[36] It was not uncommon for encomenderos to establish properties on or near lands of their tribute pueblos. In one particularly abusive case, Governor López de Mendizábal ordered the encomendero of Pojoaque Pueblo, Antonio de Salas, to tear down his house and leave the pueblo. But Salas claimed that the people of the pueblo asked him to take up residence there and that it had been approved by the previous governor. He added that in New Mexico the presence of an encomendero provided pueblos with protection from Apache and Navajo raids and, because previous governors recognized this, it had become common practice not only in the Tewa area where he lived but also in the Rio Abajo and the Salinas districts.[37]

Grants of land from the governor were not the only means by which a settler could acquire land. A settler who sided with the clergy in the ongoing competition for power between religious and civil authorities in New Mexico might find it difficult to obtain a land grant from the governor, but there were other methods of land acquisition. Purchase from an owner, some type of barter arrangement, marriage to a Puebloan woman, or marriage into a landholding Spanish family were all possibilities, in addition to illegal means such as encroachment on Pueblo lands. How prevalent any of these methods was is unknown because land dealings are rarely mentioned in the surviving documents. Receipt of land as a dowry is the method of land acquisition best documented, either as it is mentioned directly or can be inferred from records of family relationships. In the 1650s, Cristóbal de Anaya Almazán purchased the Estancia de San Antonio from Tomé Domínguez, and when he married Domínguez's daughter, her family augmented the estancia with land that was her dowry.[38] Francisco Xavier was first known in New Mexico in 1658 when he came as a wagon train escort. He stayed and married Graciana Griego, daughter of Juan Griego II, from whom he likely received a dowry of land.[39] The post-reconquest lists of former Spanish landholdings indicate that Xavier's estancia was located near that of his father-in-law.[40] The Pajarito estancia was carved out of lands of Isleta Pueblo, possibly in the 1620s by the pueblo's missionary for his family.[41] In 1638, the estancia appeared to be in the hands of Andrés López de Gracia, possibly the friar's son, and in the 1660s the Pajarito property belonged to Andrés's daughter, probably her dowry when she married Francisco Ramírez de Salazar.[42] In 1663, the inhabitants of Isleta Pueblo lodged a complaint against Francisco for taking some of their land, possibly part of a long-standing complaint stemming from the estancia's origin.[43]

As the Puebloan population declined, some villages were abandoned and survivors were congregated in the larger, remaining pueblos. They retained their right to their old lands unless they were relocated too far away to conveniently work them, in which case they were to be given other equivalent land.[44] Only after the governor had declared vacant lands (*tierras baldías*) abandoned were they eligible to be granted to others.[45] This stricture also applied to encomenderos, who were forbidden to take over lands of their tribute pueblos when members died.[46] The severe decline in the Puebloan population in the late 1630s meant that large areas of land became available to be granted to Spaniards, and it was likely then that they dispersed in greater numbers, particularly to the Rio Abajo (area south of La Bajada Mesa, see map 2, p. 206), where the greatest number of pueblos had been abandoned.[47] Part of this dispersal could also have been prompted by the political turmoil in Santa Fe following the murder of Governor Luis de Rosas in 1642, when many residents fled to the missionary headquarters at Kewa (Santo Domingo) Pueblo and then sought to acquire some of the former Pueblo agricultural land to the south.[48]

An idea of the expansion of Spanish landholdings can be gained from ecclesiastic censuses made in 1641 and from 1663 to 1666 that show that the total number of properties increased from some twenty-five to more than fifty-five.[49] In 1641, about 64 percent of these estancias were located in the Middle Rio Grande region (Albuquerque-Belen basin) and by the mid-1660s this figure was 80 percent. The number of estancias noted in the censuses could refer not just to those that belonged to the missions but to all Spanish landholdings in the jurisdiction of the church-convent where the religious needs of the local settlers as well as those of the Puebloans were administered by the clergy.[50] In the 1641 census, eight estancias are listed for Santa Clara Pueblo, fourteen for Isleta Pueblo, and an indeterminate number for Sandia Pueblo, while the 1663–66 census mentioned several estancias each at Santa Fe and Nambé Pueblo, six at San Ildefonso Pueblo, three at San Marcos Pueblo, thirty at Sandia Pueblo, fourteen at Isleta Pueblo, and two at Socorro Pueblo.[51] However, Spanish landholdings in general were widely scattered rather than clustered around villages, a pattern that emerged early in the seventeenth century, as the viceroy's 1609 instructions to Governor Peralta suggest.[52] In 1639, former governor Francisco Martínez de Baeza mentioned that below Santa Fe to the southernmost pueblo of Senecú, a distance of 50 leagues (130 miles), Spaniards had ten or twelve estancias along the Rio Grande.[53] In 1680, Governor Antonio Otermín complained that it was easy for the rebels "to carry out their evil designs" because Spanish settlement was composed entirely of estancias quite distant from one another.[54]

However, concentrations did develop in certain areas where there were favorable lands, water, and labor resources or where family alliances grew up through godparentage or intermarriage. In part 3 of this volume, which is concerned with the distribution of landholders, it can be seen that certain families or alliances of families had numerous properties, often in several geographic districts, which in many cases they had secured not only by being on favorable terms with the governor but through marriages in which land constituted the bride's dowry.[55] The Middle Rio Grande region continued to be a major area of Spanish landholdings. In 1681, during an attempt to retake the province, Governor Otermín reported seventeen estancias on both sides of the Rio Grande along a 3-league (7.8 miles) stretch south of Alameda Pueblo known as the Atrisco valley.[56] Other areas of concentration were in the Angostura-Bernalillo section of the Santo Domingo basin, the Santa Fe River valley below the villa, the Santa Cruz River valley, and the stretch of the Rio Grande south of Ohkay Owingeh (San Juan) Pueblo to the Rio Grande–Santa Cruz River junction (see map 2, p. 206). It is clear from map 2 that Spanish landholdings as well as pueblos were especially few and far between south of Isleta Pueblo, the result, most likely, of the loss of Pueblo population and villages caused in large part by the epidemics of the late 1630s.

The settlement pattern that emerges from the records that are available would probably not be greatly altered even if more information about

Spanish landholders before 1680 was discovered. This pattern basically conforms in large part to that of the preexisting pueblos whose inhabitants had long before identified the areas most favorable for agriculture, particularly areas where crops could be irrigated. Although Spanish innovations such as livestock grazing and a more developed irrigation technology made it possible to utilize more extensive land areas, access to labor was a compelling factor that led Spaniards to locate close to pueblos, particularly the larger pueblos where the Franciscan missionaries built their convent-churches that served both the Puebloan and Spanish populations. Major exceptions to this pueblo-related pattern were the Santa Cruz and Santa Fe river valleys where there were no occupied pueblos when Spanish colonists arrived in New Mexico. With the demise of many pueblos after about 1640, especially in the Middle and Southern Rio Grande regions, many Spanish properties were left at great distances from the few remaining pueblos, but a pattern had already begun to take shape. Access to the Camino Real was an important factor in the location of many estancias, its route following the east side of the Rio Grande where many pueblos were located.

Although the scattered information about where the colonists lived reveals what is probably a fair approximation of the overall pattern of settlement, it is harder to determine how they utilized their land. If land grant records were available, there would be data on the number of sitios, caballerías, or suertes each petitioner was granted, and thus not only the size of the property would be known but also how much land was intended for grazing, field crops, and horticulture. Lacking this information about the size of the grant and the nature of its operations, it can only be inferred from the descriptive terms in use: hacienda, estancia, and rancho. In New Mexico, the distinctions among these terms are not clear, and they were frequently used interchangeably.[57] Generally speaking, a hacienda is thought to have been a large landed estate on which various crops and livestock were raised.[58] The estancia is considered to have been a more modest establishment, often mainly devoted to raising livestock (estancia de ganado) but also used in part for growing crops, whereas a rancho (a term rarely encountered in prerevolt documents but probably not an uncommon type of landholding) would have been a small, mainly subsistence operation. A difference of opinion has arisen over whether the hacienda or the estancia was the prevalent type of landholding in prerevolt New Mexico. One view holds that the hacienda was the predominant form, especially among the more prominent citizens of the province.[59] The other opinion states that the limited economy of New

Mexico, dominated as it was by the governors and clergy, did not provide opportunity for settlers to develop the hacienda of the agro-industrial type that evolved in Mexico and therefore that the estancia was the typical type of landholding, especially the estancia de ganado.[60] It has been shown that the word "estancia" is mentioned in the documents much more frequently, but it should be recognized that this term covered a range of size and type of operation, and in the case of the few settlers who held numerous encomiendas and extensive landholdings, the character of the estancia was closer to that of the hacienda.[61] Use of the term "hacienda" was at times a means of conferring prestige on a landowner as a hacendado. In the 1695 survey of prerevolt properties in La Cañada, most were referred to by that designation even though some had previously been called estancias.[62] Because in New Mexico the terms "hacienda" and "estancia" did not have distinct definitions, the nature of agricultural activities can only be known in a very general way. For example, when Governor Martínez de Baeza mentioned the estancias scattered along the Rio Grande, he said they were planted with wheat and maize, irrigated with water from the river, but it can be assumed that away from the river the land was mostly used for stock raising.[63]

It would seem that New Mexico offered land without limit to the Spanish colonists, but the prior claims of the Puebloans and access to water, to labor, to mission churches, to the capital, and to routes of travel—particularly to the Camino Real—put desirable land at a premium such that acquisition was subject to considerable competition, particularly in the context of the church-state rivalry.

Labor

Use of Puebloan labor was vital to the survival of the Spanish people in New Mexico whether they were encomenderos, settlers without encomiendas, Crown officials, or members of the clergy. However, access to native labor was subject to Crown regulation. Tribute labor, as well as slavery, was outlawed.[64] The tribute to which encomenderos were entitled consisted of goods, not labor, and they as well as other settlers could legally utilize native labor only by paying for it.[65] Although it was Crown policy that native peoples should not be forced to work against their will and should be well treated, it was also recognized that they would not willingly work for Spaniards, and therefore a system of forced, paid, rotational labor was devised, that is, a labor draft, referred to as repartimiento.[66] Labor drafts could be initiated to provide labor for specific projects, such as various kinds of public works, or for ongoing or seasonal work such as in mines or in agriculture. The conditions of labor—such as type of work, frequency and length of time, and pay—were specified in order to protect workers from abuse, but violations were such that the Crown attempted to do away with the system.[67] The repartimiento system was thus on the wane in New Spain by the time New Mexico was colonized, but it continued to be utilized there up to the time of the 1680 revolt. A report of the Junta General de Hacienda in Mexico City dated March 12, 1697, noted that the uprising in New Mexico in 1680 was largely the result of misuse of the Indians in repartimiento.[68] Governor Otermín, on the other hand, claimed in 1680 that the revolt was not the result of "repartimiento or other drudgery," but his statement, nevertheless, indicates that this labor recruitment practice was in use up to the end of the early colonial period.[69]

In New Mexico, the earliest labor draft was raised by Governor Oñate shortly after he arrived at Ohkay Owingeh (San Juan) Pueblo in August 1598, when he recruited some fifteen hundred Puebloans to construct an irrigation ditch for his colonists; the San Juan people also built the Spaniards' first church and then remodeled Yunque Owingeh Pueblo to accommodate them.[70] Although it is not likely that the San Juan people were paid for their work, Governor Oñate had been instructed by the viceroy that not only should the Indians not be forced to work against their will but that they should be enticed to work by good treatment and pay.[71] During Oñate's governorship "peoples came from all the pueblos to help in planting, weeding, cultivating the land, to work in the harvest, to serve in the houses, and to tend the livestock," according to two of the governor's men who were questioned by the treasury official Francisco de Valverde in Mexico City in 1601.[72] Again, there is no mention of compensation for the work. When Oñate's successor, Governor Pedro de Peralta, undertook construction of the newly founded villa of Santa Fe in 1610, he ordered relays of workers called up from several pueblos, some of which were a considerable distance away.[73] No pay is mentioned, but the governor did provide the workers with food. A further indication that the labor draft was used in the prerevolt period is found in the 1696 petition of residents of the newly formed Villa Nueva de Santa Cruz in the Santa Cruz River valley asking Governor Vargas "to grant us Indian laborers from the pueblos during the planting season, as was formerly done; . . . it is understood that we will be obliged to pay these Indian laborers as they were customarily paid before."[74]

Beyond Santa Fe, the administration of repartimiento was the responsibility of the district *alcaldes mayores*, appointed by the governor.[75] Those needing laborers would make their needs known to these officials, and they would arrange with pueblo officials to have the work done. But the repartimiento system in New Mexico was no more free of abuse than it was in New Spain, and this is evident in the viceroy's instructions to Governor Juan de Eulate and missionary custodian Fray Estéban de Perea in 1621 ordering them, among other things, to see to the good treatment of the Indians and not permit illegal use of their labor.[76] In the case of levies or repartimientos of Indian laborers, work could be permitted for no other purpose than tilling and herding, and wages must be duly paid. At the time, the rate of pay per day was a half *real* and food or one real without food, with the monetary value paid in food. This amount was raised to one real plus food in 1659 by Governor López de Mendizábal, much to the settlers' chagrin.[77] Furthermore, according to the viceroy's letter, the number of workers recruited for a given levy should be limited to 2 percent of the total number of laborers in each pueblo, although they were allowed to recruit up to 8 percent in periods of heavy demand such as planting and harvesting. But they were not supposed to hire groups as large as forty or a hundred, as had been reported, which left pueblos short of labor for their own needs.[78] The prohibition of other illegal uses of native labor reiterated by the viceroy included the allotment of women as servants in the houses of Spaniards, unless they went voluntarily and with their husbands, and the practice of using Pueblo men as burden bearers, particularly for hauling piñon, hides, salt, and other items of trade long distances, a practice that was of concern because it was so widespread.[79] Diego de Guadalajara, encomendero of Sevilleta and Alamillo pueblos, was mentioned in 1663 as holding people from Sevilleta as "slaves" at his hacienda, where he used them to carry salt from Las Salinas in the Estancia basin for the governor.[80] Even when after three years the governor ordered the Sevilletans returned to their pueblo, it is likely they continued to carry salt from the salt pans some fifty miles away. The missionary custodian was instructed that the native residents of the mission pueblos should be used only "for things necessary for the church and the convenience of the living quarters" and then only "with the greatest moderation."[81]

Reforming labor practices, especially enforcing the obligation to pay for labor, lay with the governors but they, too, needed workers for their various enterprises—which in themselves were illegal—and thus were opposed to any reform.[82] Nor did the alcaldes mayores, who if not encomenderos were at least landowners, wish to pay for the labor they needed, and they were in a position to manipulate labor recruitment in their jurisdictions.[83] Among the encomenderos it was likely common practice to exchange their tribute goods for labor, which may be one reason why they located their rural properties near their tribute pueblos. Francisco Gómez, the most powerful encomendero, and his son and heir, Francisco Gómez Robledo, did not collect tribute goods from Tesuque Pueblo for forty years because its people rendered service in lieu of goods.[84] And it is likely that the same practice prevailed at the family's six other encomienda pueblos. Access to labor to haul salt and other goods for the governor from the Estancia basin to the family's Las Barrancas estancia in the Southern Rio Grande region was probably the reason Francisco II exchanged his right to half of Sandia Pueblo for half of more conveniently located Abó Pueblo.[85] Although nonencomenderos were probably less successful in avoiding payment for the labor they needed, nonpayment or partial payment was not uncommon despite the possibility of being cut off from repartimiento labor for noncompliance. That Spaniards were successful in exploiting Puebloan labor is seen in the Puebloans' complaint at the time of the revolt that they were so burdened with work that they had little time left to care for their own fields.[86]

Governors, in particular, required a lot of native labor for their commercial activities. Even though such activities were illegal, they were widely engaged in, the production of cotton cloth and woolen stockings for export being one of the more important.[87] A governor who was especially notorious for his commercial activities was Bernardo López de Mendizábal.[88] In 1661, thirteen pueblos had claims against him for nonpayment of their labor in producing some fourteen hundred pairs of stockings.[89] The scale of the work commanded by this governor can be seen in the three hundred fleeces he provided to the inhabitants of Socorro Pueblo with the demand that they make six hundred pairs of stockings.[90] Some governors set up workshops (*obrajes*) in Santa Fe to produce these goods, where long hours and conditions of virtual servitude prevailed.[91] Many Puebloans were requisitioned by governors such as López de Mendizábal to carry salt and piñon nuts long distances to points on the Rio Grande for transshipment south to destinations in northern New Spain.[92] He made further claims on labor in calling on Puebloans to process hides for export, to prepare leather and fabricate it, and to cut and haul timber to make carts in which to ship his goods.[93] Although enslavement of Puebloans was not common, Spaniards did make use of indigenous slaves, especially as household servants, even though it was illegal. From time to time governors would give written permission to soldiers to capture orphaned Pueblo children for this purpose, justifying it as a means of securing guardianship for them.[94] Apacheans captured in warfare, often provoked for this purpose, were also made slaves and were either used in the colony or sent to the mining areas of northern New Spain. Governors especially made large-scale use of such slaves in their enterprises.[95] The drain on the labor supply by governors not only deprived Puebloan workers of time to meet their own needs but diminished the number of workers available to the settlers, especially after about 1640 when the Puebloan population was greatly diminished.

Although the ratio of Spaniards to Puebloans was favorable to the former in the early decades of the prerevolt period, after about 1640 this situation changed somewhat, especially in the Rio Abajo, where population decline and abandonment of pueblos were greatest.[96] The Puebloan population located along the Rio Grande and some of its tributaries in 1600 numbered about 50,000 people living in some eighty-one pueblos.[97] The Spanish population in 1601 after the desertion was about 190, which included 72 men—34 with families. By 1641 the Puebloan population numbered 15,575 living in thirty-seven pueblos, while the Spanish population in 1639 consisted of some 200 Spanish men capable of bearing arms and an estimated total of about 1,000 persons.[98] Unfortunately, there are no data that would indicate what proportion of the total Puebloan population was working-age men, but a rough calculation of 5 to 1 would give 10,000 workers in 1600 and 3,115 in 1641. However, with regard to access to labor, it is not total numbers of workers but their geographic distribution that is important. While Spanish exploitation and Apachean raids had been responsible for a declining Puebloan population, a severe smallpox epidemic in the late 1630s and 1640 contributed to large-scale population loss and abandonment of pueblos. But not all areas were equally impacted. The Española basin, where the majority of Spaniards had their rural properties at the time, lost about three quarters of its Puebloan population between the 1620s, when there were about 6,000 Puebloans, and 1641, at which point there were only 1,500 left, although none of the eight pueblos had been abandoned.[99] The Middle and Southern Rio Grande regions, to which more Spaniards were beginning to move, were hardest hit, losing 86 and 93 percent of their Puebloan populations, declining to about 1,000 and 400 respectively, with the number of pueblos decreasing from eighteen to five and from fourteen to three.[100] This population loss and abandonment of pueblos meant more land that could be claimed by Spaniards but at the same time that a smaller number of Pueblo men would be subject to the labor draft. In the Estancia basin, none of the six pueblos was abandoned in the 1620s to 1641 period, and with almost 3,000 people, it had a larger population than any other region, but it attracted few Spanish settlers because of its remoteness, restricted water resources, and exposure to Apachean raids. These raids, in conjunction with drought and epidemic disease, caused the Estancia basin pueblos to be abandoned in the 1670s and with them the estancias of the seven Spanish families known to have been living near the Salinas pueblos. By 1680 the Puebloan population of New Mexico numbered about 15,000 persons living in thirty-one pueblos.[101] There were about 1,350 to 1,500 Spanish persons (excluding servants) of which some 200 were men able to bear arms.[102]

Governance

The governor of the New Mexico colony as representative of the viceroy in Mexico and the Spanish Crown held broad powers, especially to maintain the security and integrity of the colony and to make land and encomienda grants.[103] The colonists were represented by the cabildo, or council, whose members were drawn from the prominent landowning/encomendero class and who were elected by them—men who had the status of *vecino* (a landowning and tax-paying citizen) and who were required to maintain a residence in the capital.[104] The cabildo had the authority to make ordinances for the governance of the villa and also acted as an advisory council for the province as a whole; however, its decisions were subject to approval by the governor.[105] The governor's authority also extended to the appointment of regional administrators (alcaldes mayores) whom he selected from members of the vecino class and who were required to live in their districts during their term of office. These officials carried out the orders of the governors not only in overseeing the orderly functioning of the pueblos in their districts but also in mediating differences among settlers and between settlers and Puebloans.[106] One of their most important functions was supervising the distribution (repartimiento) of Puebloan workers among the settlers. Carrying this out could give rise to many disputes and also gave these officials the opportunity to illegally divert such labor to their own properties, although they were forbidden to own land in their districts while they held office, a stricture that was seldom observed.[107] For nonencomendero settlers who did not have access to (illegal) tribute labor, the alcalde mayor was a very important person. He was also important to the governor in organizing production and transport of commodities to be exported to northern New Spain.[108]

In his contract, Governor Oñate was given the authority to divide the territory of New Mexico into "districts of alcaldías mayores," but it is uncertain when such districts were created.[109] They are first mentioned in 1643 in the wake of the murder of Governor Rosas, when his successor Governor Alonso Pacheco de Heredia appointed six men to the office: Fernándo Chávez y Durán (Durán y Chávez), Diego de la Serna, Juan Luján, Diego Pérez Granillo, Juan Ramírez de Salazar, and Andrés López de Gracia (appendix table F).[110] He did not specify the districts over which they presided, and it was only later in the 1660s when in various documents alcaldes mayores are mentioned that the districts, or *jurisdicciones* as they were then called, became apparent; however, it is generally assumed that they were first designated in the 1640s.[111] The 1640s seems a late date for establishing a system of local officials, and it is possible the men named by Governor Pacheco were not the first to hold this office, but by that time there was a definite need for them. In response to the "mini–civil war" caused by the Rosas affair, many Santa Fe residents had reason to move elsewhere; at the same time agricultural land was becoming available in the wake of pueblo abandonments caused by epidemics at that time as well as by the accumulated effects of Spanish exploitation and Apachean raiding. As more Spanish landholdings were established in areas farther from the capital, such as in the Middle and Southern Rio Grande regions, and surviving Pueblo people were congregated into a much-reduced number of villages (see map 1, p. 205) the need for a system of local administrators became great. By 1660 the growing number of Spanish settlers in the area south of the Rio Grande-Jemez River confluence and the increasing Apachean attacks in that area occasioned the division of New Mexico into the Rio Abajo and Rio Arriba for administrative purposes. At the same time, the governor created the office of lieutenant governor, who was given command over the Rio Abajo region.[112] This innovation by the governor also emphasizes the continued importance of the alcaldes mayores. A 1661 document names six jurisdictions, possibly the same ones established in the 1640s. In this document they are referred to as: Los Piros, Isleta y Sandia, Cochiti, Los Tanos, Los Tewas, and Las Salinas.[113] Possibly the Jemez pueblos constituted a separate jurisdiction or were included within the jurisdiction of Cochiti. The names of jurisdictions differed somewhat in various documents as seen in appendix table F, but whether, for instance, Isleta y Sandia was officially divided into two districts or the use of two separate names was merely a function of local usage is not known, as is the case with the jurisdiction of "Los Tewas" which was more commonly known as "La Cañada" and included the Northern Tiwa–speaking pueblos of Picurís and Taos.

CHAPTER FIVE

The Mission Landscape

✝ ALTHOUGH TWENTY FRANCISCAN MISSIONARIES ACCOMPANIED Governor Oñate to New Mexico in 1598, and he assigned them to the various pueblos as one of his firsts acts upon arrival, little missionary work was accomplished during the first few years of the colony. In the fall of 1601, all but three of the religious personnel then in New Mexico accompanied the majority of the settlers who deserted the colony at that time.[1] Additional friars were sent to New Mexico, but only three remained by the time the new governor arrived in early 1610.[2] Needless to say, expansion of the mission establishment during the Oñate era was limited. Only two intermittently served missions besides the one at the capital, San Gabriel, were established (table 5): San Ildefonso, located some twelve miles south along the Rio Grande, and Santo Domingo, another thirty miles farther south (see map 1, p. 205).[3]

Additional missionaries came with Governor Pedro de Peralta in 1610, and at this time permanent church-convents were built at San Ildefonso and Kewa (Santo Domingo). During the following decade, eight other missions and three *visitas* (visiting parishes) were established besides the Hermita de San Miguel in Santa Fe. One mission was at Nambé Pueblo among the Tewa of the Española basin, or La Cañada as it was then known. Two were at the Tano pueblos of Galisteo and San Lázaro in the Galisteo basin. Among the Keres in the Santo Domingo basin, where the mission at Kewa (Santo Domingo) Pueblo was made headquarters of the Franciscan missions in New Mexico, the pueblos of Cochiti and San Felipe were made visitas. In the adjacent lower Jemez River valley, Zia Pueblo was made a mission and

Table 5. Seventeenth-Century New Mexico Missions*

MISSION PUEBLOS	DATE ESTABLISHED	COMMENT
San Gabriel	1598–99	Church-convent; was abandoned ca. 1610.
Santa Fe	ca. 1610	Called Hermita de San Miguel.
San Ildefonso	1610	Church-convent.
Santo Domingo	1610	Became mission headquarters beginning in 1610.
Galisteo	1610–12	First permanent Tano mission.
Sandia	1610	Established in 1610 or soon thereafter.
Isleta	1612 (late)	Possibly established in early 1613.
Zía	1613, possibly 1610	First mentioned in 1613 but was possibly founded in 1610.
Nambé	1613	Convent.
San Lázaro	1613	Established as a visita of Galisteo by 1621.
Chilili	1613–14	Convent.
Cochiti	1614	Visita of Santo Domingo.
Santa Ana	1614	Visita of Zía.
San Felipe	1615	Visita of Santo Domingo.
Pecos	1619	Permanent mission.
San Felipe	1621	Convent.
Picurís	1621	Abandoned in 1625 and reestablished in 1628.
Taos	1621 or early 1622	Reestablished ca. 1627.
Jemez (San Jose)	1621 (late)	Abandoned in 1630s.
Jemez (San Diego)	1621–22	Abandoned in 1623 and refounded between 1626 and 1629.
Abó	ca. 1622	Convent.
Socorro	1626	Convent.
Quarac	ca. 1626–28	Convent.
Santa Clara	ca. 1628	Convent.
Ácoma	1629	Convent.
Senecú	1629	Convent.
Tajique	ca. 1629	Convent.

Table 5. continued

MISSION PUEBLOS	DATE ESTABLISHED	COMMENT
Las Humanas	ca. 1629	Soon abandoned, becoming a visita of Abó until reestablished between 1659 and 1660.
Tabirá	ca. 1629	Visita of Las Humanas by the 1660s.
Tenabó	ca. 1629	Church.
Sevilleta	ca. 1630–34	Convent.
Alamillo	ca. 1638	Replaced Sevilleta.
San Marcos	ca. 1638	Convent.
San Juan	by 1641	Visita of Santa Clara.
Pojoaque	by 1641	May have been a visita of San Ildefonso.
Jacona	by 1641	May have been a visita of San Ildefonso.
Cuyamungue	by 1641	Visita of Nambé.
Tesuque	by 1641	Visita of Santa Fe.
La Ciénega	by 1641	Visita of San Marcos.
San Cristóbal	by 1641	Visita of Galisteo.
Puaray	by 1641	Visita of Sandia.
Alameda	by 1641	Church-convent.

Sources: Scholes and Bloom, "Friar Personnel"; Scholes, "Documents."

*The term "convent" in the usage of the time denoted a mission church-convent complex; visitas by contrast, had only a small chapel and were visited by the clergy periodically.

a visita was established at Santa Ana Pueblo. Farther south in the Middle Rio Grande region, missions were established at Sandia and Isleta Pueblos in 1610 and 1612 respectively, and in between 1613 and 1614 a mission was established at Chilili Pueblo on the east side of the Manzano Mountains, a remarkably remote location at that time.[4] At another remote location was the mission established in 1619 at Pecos Pueblo on the eastern frontier.[5]

The foundation of missions was even more intense during the 1620s. Some of this activity involved infilling within the areas where missions had already been established.[6] With the building of a convent at the Keres pueblo of San Felipe in 1621, it was upgraded from its status as a visita, while the Tano pueblo of San Lázaro was downgraded to a visita of the Galisteo mission that same year. On the east side of the Manzano Mountains convents were built at Quarac (Quarai) between 1626 and 1628 and at Tajique in 1629. Among the Tewa in the Española basin, a mission was established at Santa Clara in 1629. New geographic expansions included Taos and Picurís in the Far North in 1621, which were abandoned and then reestablished in 1627 and 1628.[7] Missions were first founded among the Jemez Pueblos in 1621 and then reestablished later at the end of the decade.[8] To the far west, Ácoma mission was founded in 1629.[9] An early extension to the south was the convent built at Abó Pueblo in 1622 at the major pass between the Estancia basin and the Rio Grande, and at nearby Tenabó Pueblo, a church was built in 1629.[10] Farther south along the Rio Grande convents were built at Socorro Pueblo in 1626 and at Senecú, the southernmost pueblo, in 1629.[11] In the extreme southeast, a convent and church were built at Las Humanas Pueblo in 1629 and a church at Tabirá Pueblo the same year.[12] The work of custodian Fray Alonso de Benavides in the second half of the 1620s was especially notable for the founding of missions and the expansion of their geographical range.[13] By 1630 mission church-convents had been established at the principal pueblos from Taos in the north to Senecú in the south, east to Pecos and Las Humanas, and west to Ácoma. In the following decade, between 1630 and 1634, a convent was built in at Sevilleta on the Southern Rio Grande region, and in 1638 it was replaced by the convent built at Alamillo.[14] Ecclesiastic censuses of 1641 and 1663–66 indicate that, with minor changes in status, this was the pattern of mission location.[15]

A principal Crown objective in maintaining the New Mexico colony after the desertion of 1601 was support of the Christianizing mission of the Catholic Church, and the civil authorities were charged with aiding this enterprise. It was customary to have the residents of each pueblo supply their missionary with basic needs such as water, firewood, and food from fields set aside for that purpose. In addition, they were expected to help with chores related to his religious duties.[16] Other items needed by the clergy were brought by the triennial supply train. However, in order to obtain the credit needed to purchase these goods for their missions, and presumably also to enhance their influence in the colony, they engaged in agriculture and ranching, producing commodities that they exported to the mining centers in northern New Spain. These activities, which went beyond meeting mere subsistence needs, brought them into conflict with Spanish settlers and the civil administration over the use of land and Puebloan labor.[17] Some of these problems are brought out in a complaint to the viceroy made in

1639 by the Santa Fe cabildo.[18] They claimed that the missionaries kept many more Puebloans working for them than were needed to perform the personal services they were supposed to provide and for which the missionaries were not obliged to pay. According to the cabildo, the friars utilized many Puebloans to tend their large herds of cattle and horses and work their very large fields of wheat and maize. Each missionary had from one to two thousand sheep, while only a few settlers had as many as five hundred, and most had no more than a hundred, and although each missionary had twenty to forty horses, many poor soldier-settlers had none and were thus unable to carry out their obligation to defend the colony. Furthermore, the civil government was, they stated, hampered, because the clergy claimed control of the supply trains and, despite an order from the viceroy that his Majesty's carts should be under the orders of the governor, they withheld the lion's share of the arms and the iron that was needed to shoe the horses as well as make ploughshares.[19]

Expansion of the clergy's farming and ranching activities took place largely on Pueblo land, but it has been suggested that the clergy also acquired other land beyond those boundaries.[20] In addition, they attempted to prevent settlers from obtaining land in the vicinity of pueblos by claiming that the settlers' livestock would destroy the fields of the Puebloans. Using various methods of intimidation, such as denial of holy sacraments, threats of excommunication, taxation through use of the bull of the Santa Cruzada, and even vigilantism, the clergy was often successful in suppressing the establishment of settler landholdings, especially in the most attractive areas.[21] Their apparent success is seen in the Santo Domingo basin in the vicinity of Kewa Pueblo, where the Franciscan headquarters was located. In the admittedly patchy records available, no settler landholdings between Cochiti and San Felipe pueblos, a distance of some fourteen miles along the Rio Grande, are mentioned.[22] And, it has been suggested that many of the settler properties in New Mexico belonged to those who supported the clergy.[23] Whether the estancias mentioned in the 1641 and 1663–66 censuses belonged to the clergy or to the settlers (and this is a matter of interpretation, as discussed in chapter 4), the clergy through its position in the pueblos was a powerful force in the administration of agricultural land, producing surpluses for export to New Spain as well as providing relief locally in times of famine. Its control of a substantial part of the agricultural land added to its power as a force in the colony.

The clergy and settlers had disputes over labor in addition to conflicts over land. The labor demands of the clergy's mission economy competed with the settlers' need for labor, particularly after about 1640 when the Puebloan population was substantially diminished. The Franciscans defended their extensive farming and ranching activities by claiming that they needed to maintain large stores of food to supply the population during the frequent droughts and famines.[24] The clergy also earned money to support their missions by using Puebloan labor, both male and female, to produce woven cloth and knitted stockings for export.[25] In 1663, they were accused of putting Puebloans to work weaving in mission workshops (obrajes) and not paying them for their labor.[26] One product of these obrajes was frieze and sackcloth, the rough woolen cloth friars used for their garments.[27]

CHAPTER SIX

The Mining Landscape

✣ THE INTEREST OF SPANIARDS IN MINERAL WEALTH IN THEIR NEW World possessions is well known and was no less true of the explorers and colonists who came to New Mexico. Its first explorer, Francisco Vázquez de Coronado, made this clear when he stated in 1540 that "if there is any [gold or silver], we shall get our share of it, and it shall not escape us through any lack of diligence in the search."[1] But neither he nor the explorers who followed him made any significant finds, although they made inquiries, did some exploring, and took note of the Puebloans' turquoise and lead mining in the Cerrillos Hills near San Marcos Pueblo, the lead being used by Puebloans to glaze their pottery (see map 2, p. 206 and map 6, p. 210).[2] Nevertheless, Juan de Oñate, leader of the first colonizing expedition and scion of a successful Zacatecas mining family, brought along equipment for mining and ore processing, intending to pursue further the search for precious metals.[3] In his initial reconnaissance in July 1598, Oñate had ore extracted from mines that he called Escalante that were located near San Marcos Pueblo, and during the first few years of the colony he made numerous claims about the many silver mines of high grade ore in the province.[4]

Oñate's nephew, Vicente de Zaldívar, was particularly active in early mining efforts. Zaldívar claimed that he explored the mines of San Marcos (also called San Mateo) and Anunciación as well as many others, which, he said, were rich in silver. He also claimed that he was the first to extract silver using both smelting and amalgamation methods, for which greta and quicksilver had been brought from New Spain.[5] According to Zaldívar, the mines of Anunciación were located near some salinas (salt lakes) that he had discovered, presumably those of the Estancia basin.[6] The mines of Anunciación might thus have been located north of the San Pedro Mountains near Arroyo Tuerto in the headwaters of Tunque Arroyo (see map 2, p. 206). In 1601, one of Oñate's men testified that he had heard there were rich mines at the pueblo of El Tuerto.[7] This general location east of the Sandia Mountains on the west side of San Pedro Mountain in the vicinity of the present village of Golden is some forty miles from the Estancia basin salt lakes and, therefore, not exactly "near" them but is the most likely location, given that it was the mining area nearest these deposits.[8] According to some of the same men who testified in 1601 before treasury official Francisco de Valverde in Mexico City, Zaldívar was not only involved in assaying the silver content of the ore obtained at mines near San Marcos Pueblo but was building a device to crush ore and extract metals.[9] However, this testimony is divided as to whether this enterprise was located near San Marcos Pueblo or at El Tuerto. It was reported by two defecting officers in 1602 that there were no mines and the silver thus far encountered was of poor quality.[10] During the first stressful years of the colony, before the desertion, diggings were probably small scale and superficial, yielding only ores of low grade. Despite the claims of Governor Oñate and his nephew, the failure early on to find rich ore deposits or evidence of precious metals among the Puebloan people was one of the main reasons for the massive defection of colonists in 1601, but those who remained persisted in their efforts to discover mines.

Spanish mining activities in the ensuing years seem to have been mainly centered on the Cerrillos Hills and the San Pedro Mountains, where Puebloans had previously been engaged in mining and where they continued to extract lead for glazing their pottery. In 1608, Juan Martínez de Montoya, listing his services to the Crown, stated that he had participated in the discovery of mines at a place he called the "Real de San Buenaventura, Real de Minas" where he lived for a while before returning to the capital, San Gabriel, to build the house which he occupied until 1608, when he left the colony.[11] Where the "real" was located has been something of a mystery, but recently an intriguing suggestion has placed it at Las Humanas Pueblo and the mines at the saline lakes of the Estancia basin (see map 2, p. 206).[12] The Real de San Buenaventura is not mentioned again in available documents, but it is not unlikely that the salt deposits were exploited by the Spaniards from the earliest years of the colony. However, the idea of New Mexico as a place where rich metallic mines were to be found persisted. Even the viceroy, circa 1602, expressed the belief that the province, with its mountainous terrain that was a continuation of that of the rich mining province of Nueva Vizcaya to the south, should contain rich ore deposits.[13] This idea was given further support in the 1626–27 report of missionary Fray Gerónimo Zárate Salmerón, who extolled the widespread occurrence and richness of New Mexico's mines.[14] He wrote that in 1617 three Flemish miners, Juan Fresco, Juan Descalso, and Rodrigo Lorenzo, came to New Mexico from Mexico City to look for mines; they must have been successful, as they went back to New Spain to purchase more equipment, returning in 1625.[15] On arriving in Santa Fe, they were attacked and their workshop and equipment destroyed. This hostility probably stemmed from several factors: their being foreign, their intention to carry on the work of former governor Pedro de Peralta, whose interest in mining was the cause of much controversy, and jealousy of any success they might have.[16] Although Juan Descalso is not heard of again in the records available, Rodrigo Lorenzo is noted in 1639 as a silversmith who lived on San Francisco Street in Santa Fe.[17] Juan Fresco or Fresqui also remained in New Mexico, but where he lived is unknown. He most probably pursued his calling as a miner, possibly in the Cerrillos Hills and the San Pedro Mountains, while maintaining a residence in Santa Fe where his family lived. His son Juan II was noted as a vecino of the Rio Abajo in 1661, an indication that sometime earlier Juan I might have moved to that area and engaged in mining there.

It is likely that Spaniards in New Mexico continued to pursue mining in the Cerrillos Hills and San Pedro Mountains in the years leading up to the 1680 revolt, although the much sought-after silver bonanza eluded them. It is at four smelter sites in the New Placers district near Golden, where archaeologists have found sherds of ceramics produced during the middle to late 1600s, that ores from the nearby San Pedro Mountains were most probably processed. Ceramic evidence as well as the absence of stone tools at mine and smelter sites in the Cerrillos Hills indicates that they, too, were Spanish workings.[18] These ores may have been valued as much for their lead and copper content as for any silver they might have contained. Copper for making implements and lead for bullets were much needed by the colonists. One lead mine, located in the "Cerro de San Marcos" was owned by Francisco de Madrid, who came to New Mexico about 1603. Knowledge of this mine comes from the time of the reconquest, when Governor Vargas sent Francisco's son Roque to find his father's lead mine in order to relieve the shortage of shot.[19] The Madrid family's property, located in the Santa Fe River valley about five miles below the villa on the south side of the Santa Fe River, was about fifteen miles from the mines (see map 6, p. 210). Closer yet was Los Cerrillos, the estancia of the Márquez family, who might also have been involved in mining as well as raising livestock. Evidence of iron mining is also very scant. What is known comes from an investigation conducted by archaeologists at the Comanche Springs site (in the vicinity of Comanche Canyon), where a small-scale bloomery processed ore from the Manzano Mountains in the latter part of the seventeenth century (see map 8, p. 212).[20] The crucial need for iron for shoeing horses, among other things, meant that the colony was mainly dependent on imports from New Spain that came on the triennial supply train, as discussed in chapter 5.[21]

Not only is information about the location and nature of mining operations in early colonial New Mexico scarce but so too is knowledge about how the industry was officially administered and how labor was procured. As owner of all mineral resources, the Crown had the right to require mines to be registered and their production taxed. Possibly there were treasury offices (*cajas reales*) in mining districts such as the Cerrillos Hills and San Pedro Mountains where mines were registered, ores assayed, and the silver taxed.[22] The term "*real de minas*" does not appear in the available seventeenth-century records except for in Juan Martínez de Montoya's reference to the Real de Minas de San Buenaventura, but that may be the result of the scarcity of such documentation. The manual labor involved in the mining and processing of ore was probably not carried out by Spaniards, but how labor was acquired is only rarely mentioned in the available documents. Because mine-related operations in New Mexico were small in scale and to some degree sporadic, a formal system for supplying labor probably did not exist. Where mines were owned by encomenderos, these men might well have followed the common, but illegal, practice of requiring tribute to be paid in labor rather than goods, or the work might also have been carried out by detribalized native men (*genizaros*) or landless men of mixed race, who were paid in food or other goods. Those who committed a crime also might find themselves sentenced to work in the mines, as was the case for a native from Galisteo Pueblo who stole some goods from the *palacio* in 1662 and was given to Toribio de la Guerta (Huerta) "para las minas."[23] The small scale of metals mining might not have required the use of repartimiento.

A nonmetallic mineral resource of value to the Spaniards and available in abundance was salt. Reports from the expeditions of Chamuscado

(1581–82) and Espejo (1583) mentioned the saline lakes east of the Sierra Morena (Manzano Mountains) that extended for 5 leagues (13 miles), which contained salt of high quality—comparable to that produced from sea water (see map 2, p. 206).[24] These saline lakes, of which there are some seventy of various sizes, occupy shallow depressions in the floor of the Estancia basin, which once contained an old Pleistocene lake with no exterior drainage. Salts remained in the lake sediments as the lake dried up, particularly in the depressions created by wind scour, where, over time, successive filling during the rainy season followed by drying concentrated the salts through a combination of capillary action and solar evaporation. These salt deposits together cover some 13,500 acres in the lowest part of the basin, occupying an area some sixteen miles long and six miles wide.[25] They are about eighteen miles east of the Spanish and Puebloan settlements along the east side of the Manzano Mountains and some fifty miles from the Rio Grande via Abó Pass.

Who had right of access to these salt lakes in the early years of the colony is unclear. Because of the poverty and remoteness of the colony, the Crown apparently did not choose to exercise its monopoly right (*estanco*) or to establish a concession (*asiento*) for the exploitation of the salt deposits of the Estancia basin.[26] They might have been open to all, as in prehistoric times.[27] Juan Martínez de Montoya might have attempted to exploit these deposits before he left the colony in 1608. The Spaniards needed salt not only for themselves but also for their livestock and their mining operations. Because the mines were small in scale, the demand for salt, where the amalgamation process was used, was limited. However, there was eventually greater demand for Estancia basin salt from the much larger silver mining operations to the south. Even before then, New Mexico's governors, who engaged in whatever enterprises they could find that would make them a profit, began to exploit the salt deposits by arranging with encomenderos in the area to have their tributaries harvest the salt annually and transport it to convenient collection places, where it was sold.[28] As early as 1630 the clergy complained about the hardship imposed on natives in transporting salt for the governor.[29] It was reported that men from Tabirá Pueblo in the Estancia basin loaded salt at the "salt marsh" and carried it to the house of Sargento Mayor Francisco Gómez, whose estancia, Las Barrancas, was located on the Rio Grande, some fifty miles away via Abó Pass.

Prior to 1655, mining interests from the Parral district in present Chihuahua were sending annual caravans seven hundred miles to the Estancia basin to obtain salt, large quantities of which were needed in the amalgamation or "patio" process that prevailed in the mining districts of northern New Spain.[30] Presumably local sources of supply were no longer abundant, and the long journey to the Estancia basin to obtain this vital ingredient was justified, greatly expanding the demand for New Mexico salt and the profits to be made by governors who regularly sent Puebloan workers to gather salt to be sold to Parral miners.[31] Governor López de Mendizábal was particularly active in promoting the export of salt. On several occasions during his term, he sent accumulated goods, including salt, to Parral to be sold by his agent.[32]

Governor López de Mendizábal called on his alcalde mayor for the Salinas district, Nicolás de Aguilar, to administer the harvesting and transport of salt with the help of mine superintendent Antonio de Ávalos.[33] Ávalos supervised teams of workers from the Estancia basin pueblos, who camped at the salt pans at the end of the dry season (April–July) after the lakes had dried out during the fall and winter and before the summer monsoon rains began.[34] By then a crust of salt crystals (mainly sodium chloride) had formed that could be scraped off the underlying sediments. The quality of the harvested salt was graded on the basis of the amount of sediment mixed in with the salt crystals. The highest grade of crystalline salt was used for human consumption, whereas lower grades (saltierra) were used for processing ore in the "patio" process, for livestock, for saltpeter in making gunpowder, for making soap, and for other operations depending on the degree of silt contamination.[35] As Governor López de Mendizábal and his successors came to monopolize the production of salt in the Estancia basin, friction with the Apachean tribes, whose access to the deposits was thus curtailed, contributed to their increased raiding of settlements, which eventually led to abandonment of both Puebloan and Spanish settlements in the Estancia basin in the early 1670s.[36] This situation not only put an end to exports of salt to Parral but made it necessary to mount armed convoys to obtain salt in the Estancia basin during the years leading up to the 1680 revolt when the Spaniards were forced to retreat to the El Paso area.

The "mining" of salt in the Estancia basin might have been one of the more conspicuous features of the mining landscape of New Mexico in the seventeenth century, whereas the mining of metals was confined to smaller areas, but it is unlikely that either gave rise to permanent settlements. However, because documentation is sparse and archaeological evidence limited, it would appear that knowledge of the seventeenth-century mining landscape of New Mexico is far from complete.

PART TWO

The Demographic Landscape

CHAPTER SEVEN

The Oñate Era

✣ IN 1598 GOVERNOR OÑATE BROUGHT 129 SOLDIER-SETTLERS TO NEW Mexico, according to the final muster conducted by Juan de Frías Salazar on January 8, 1598, at the mines of Todos Santos in the Parral district of Nueva Vizcaya in northern New Spain.[1] When Frías Salazar reported the total to the viceroy, he mentioned that there were other men near the muster site who did not present themselves, possibly because they had committed offenses, but he was sure some of them intended to join the expedition.[2] Many other men and families had assembled in Nueva Vizcaya earlier but had returned to their homes because of the prolonged delays in obtaining royal authorization for the expedition. Even after musters were carried out in February 1597 in the area of the Santa Barbara mines, continued delays occasioned further defections. Some 133 men who answered early roll calls were absent from the final muster, although three turned up on the 1600 muster of reinforcements.[3] Despite the lack of the full complement of two hundred men that Oñate's contract required, the expedition was permitted to leave for New Mexico on condition that the deficiency would be made up.[4] A muster for that purpose, conducted by Juan de Gordejuela Ybarguen and Juan de Sotelo Cisneros, was held August 28–29, 1600, at San Bartolomé in Nueva Vizcaya. The expedition left for New Mexico on September 5, and the reinforcements, numbering eighty-one men, arrived on December 23 at San Gabriel.[5] In all, some 248 Spanish men (including Oñate and his son) came to New Mexico during the three years from August 1598 to August 1601. In addition to those on the muster rolls of 1598 and 1600, thirty-four were mentioned in other documents of this period, including the history written by Captain Gaspar Pérez de Villagrá, who was a prominent member of the original expedition. During this period there was a loss of 31 men, who died under various circumstances, deserted, or returned to New Spain on missions, leaving a total of 217 Spanish men (excluding missionaries). Details of these data are summarized in appendix table G. A letter written by one of the colonists to the viceroy on March 22, 1601, stated that the colony consisted of more than five hundred persons—men, women, and children—a figure that presumably included missionaries, family members, and servants.[6]

Further support for a figure of some two hundred Spanish men in New Mexico in the spring of 1601 comes from testimony ordered by the viceroy and given in July 1601 to the treasury official Francisco de Valverde y Mercado by two of Oñate's captains. In response to a question asking how many Spaniards were in New Mexico at the time they had departed, the two captains said there were about two hundred soldiers.[7] Another member of that party said there were about 150, and the fourth estimated between 150 and 160.[8] The latter two had come to New Mexico only three months earlier with the reinforcements and were probably less familiar with the size of the colony. However, when the viceroy wrote to the king a year later on March 8, 1602, he alluded to a total of 160 when he mentioned that ninety men had left on an exploring expedition to Quivira, leaving seventy persons (men?) at San Gabriel, their headquarters (see map 1, p. 205 and map 3, p. 207).[9] The viceroy might also have obtained this total from another Valverde witness who testified on April 23, 1602, that when he arrived in New Mexico with the reinforcements of eighty men, they joined the eighty men who were there with Governor Oñate.[10] Despite this testimony, which seemed to have influenced the viceroy, the documentation listing the names of more than two hundred Spanish men gives greater weight to this figure, even after taking losses into account. Therefore, it is probably fair to say that about two hundred Spanish soldier-colonists were in New Mexico in the summer of 1601 when Governor Oñate undertook an expedition to Quivira in what is today central Kansas.[11] He had already visited all parts of the Rio Grande Pueblo region, and Vicente de Zaldívar, his nephew, had explored the buffalo plains to the east and made a failed attempt to reach the South Sea (Gulf of California) to the west. The trip to Quivira was a further attempt to locate sources of wealth that would quell the dissatisfaction of his colonists with what they perceived to be the meager resources of New Mexico. Dissatisfaction was evident as early as March 1599 when Governor Oñate reported to the viceroy that more than forty-five soldiers and officers attempted to desert the colony upon "not finding bars of silver on the ground right away."[12]

Because Governor Oñate undertook to colonize New Mexico, it is important to know how many of his soldier-colonists brought families. He himself brought only his teenage son. There was no systematic listing of the families who came in 1598, but twenty-two men who came in that year mentioned that they had families with them (appendix table H). The muster of reinforcements includes a list of eight married women, and Villagrá mentioned an additional eight wives, making a total of thirty-eight families.[13] The Valverde witnesses who testified in July 1601 gave the number of married men as forty-one to forty-two or, according to one of them, as many as fifty.[14] It is possible that the number of families was greater, but it is also likely that the long delays involved in obtaining authorization for the expedition discouraged many families from undertaking the journey. There was, however, potential for the formation of additional families in the marriages that probably took place between the single men and the adult daughters and sisters who came with their families. Bernabé de las Casas, who came with Governor Oñate in 1598 and returned to Nueva Vizcaya to lead the reinforcements to New Mexico in 1600, mentioned that he had settled down and married.[15] Others may well have followed his example. Among the many single soldiers who came to New Mexico in 1598 and 1600, there were probably others who married during those first three years. Hence, there might well have been as many as fifty families in New Mexico in the summer of 1601 when Oñate left on his expedition to Quivira. By all accounts though, unless the number of colonizing families (that is, families that included a wife, not just an elder man and his adult sons) was greatly underdocumented, this number was very small in proportion to the number of single men, and it was also a very small number for the purpose of founding a sustainable colony in an area so remote from the center of the Spanish population and Spanish authority in New Spain.

The colony became even less viable after a massive desertion took place while Governor Oñate was away in Quivira from June 23 to November 24, 1601.[16] Sometime between early September and early October a large number of the colonists he left behind and all of the missionaries except their custodian departed for the mining settlement of Santa Barbara in Nueva Vizcaya, reaching the royal authorities before Oñate's men could overtake and arrest them.[17] The number of men who were still part of the colony after the defection consisted of those who had remained in San Gabriel, the colony's headquarters at that time, and those who returned from Quivira with Governor Oñate. In San Gabriel on October 2, 1601, twenty-five men signed a petition—accompanied by the testimony of ten of them—to be presented to the viceroy claiming loyalty to Governor Oñate (appendix table I).[18] It is not certain if these were all of the Spanish men who did not desert to Santa Barbara while Governor Oñate was still in Quivira, nor is it known precisely how many men Oñate took with him because there is considerable variation in the numbers reported for the expedition. These estimates range from a high of 113–14 given by one of the Valverde witnesses who said he saw a list of expedition enrollees that contained that many names. He also said that the total number of men capable of bearing arms was between 150 and 160, 40–45 of which remained at San Gabriel.[19] The ten loyal colonists testified affirmatively to item five on their questionnaire, which stated that ninety-four men went to Quivira.[20] In the official report of the expedition, Oñate stated that he took more than seventy men.[21] The viceroy wrote to the king on March 8, 1602, that there were ninety mounted soldiers, and on March 13, 1602, he wrote that the number was eighty to ninety soldiers.[22]

From the data available it would seem that some ninety men went to Quivira with Oñate. If he took 90 men out of a total of some 200, about 110 remained in San Gabriel, and if the 25 who signed the loyalty petition constitute the true number of men who did not defect, presumably 85 soldier-colonists, or about 43 percent of the total, fled to the Santa Barbara mines. If Oñate took fewer men to Quivira, the number who deserted would, or course, be even greater. Upon his return he therefore had only about 115 men under his command—the twenty-five who had remained loyal and the ninety men who had gone to Quivira. This number was further diminished when many of those returning from Quivira left to pursue the deserters under the leadership of Oñate's nephew and *maese de campo*, Vicente de Zaldívar.[23] They also went on with him to Mexico City, where some gave testimony in April 1602 to Valverde.[24] Zaldívar did not return to New Mexico at that time, and it is probable that most of those who accompanied him did not return either, but it is known that three—Diego de Ayardi, Isidro Suárez de Figueroa, and Rodrigo Zapata—did return as part of the 1603 supply train escort bringing new missionaries to New Mexico.[25] Three loyal colonists, Gerónimo Márquez, Cristóbal Baca, and Asencio de Archuleta, were also part of that escort (appendix table I).[26] Presumably they had joined Zaldívar's pursuit of the defectors and followed him to Mexico City but then returned to New Mexico. Seven other loyal colonists were possibly also among those who accompanied Zaldívar but, because they are not heard of again, they might not have returned to New Mexico.

The claim by one of the Valverde witnesses that Governor Oñate left 40–45 men behind in San Gabriel when he left for Quivira does not seem credible because, given that at least 25 men remained loyal to Oñate, that would mean only 15–20 colonists would have defected—hardly a significant number, even if the overall total was 150 to 160, as he stated. The viceroy, who also seemed to think the total number of men was 160, said 70 (men?) stayed in San Gabriel and that of those, one-third (23) to one-fourth (18) remained after the others defected. But other documents indicate that his estimates are too low.[27] Analysis of the genealogical work of Fray Angélico Chávez and José Antonio Esquibel reveals an additional thirty-eight men who were still in New Mexico early in the seventeenth century after the desertion, and another twelve men are mentioned in various Oñate-era documents dated not long after (appendix table J). These men could have been among the probable ninety who had gone to Quivira with Oñate but did not join Zaldívar in pursuit of the fleeing defectors, leaving about forty who did follow him. These forty were possibly joined by ten of the loyal colonists, only three of whom are known to have returned to New Mexico with the 1603 supply train. Altogether Oñate might have suffered an attrition of some 47 men in addition to the 85 defectors, a total of 132 men, or about two-thirds of the original 200 soldier-colonists. If the fifty men who did not follow Zaldívar are added to the remaining eighteen loyal colonists, the result is that only sixty-eight men, or about one-third of the original soldier-colonists, stayed in New Mexico after the 1601 desertion. These figures can only be conjectural because the records are so incomplete, but they are compatible with information provided later in connection with Oñate's 1604–5 expedition to the Gulf of California and with a 1609 viceregal order concerning the number of armed men in New Mexico.[28]

The number of families in New Mexico also diminished after the desertion. Of the fifty families estimated to have come from New Spain, only seventeen remained—a loss of some two-thirds (appendix table K). While this number was augmented by some seventeen new families that appear to have been formed in New Mexico by the time of the defection or shortly thereafter, this early post-1601 colony still consisted of only some thirty-four families, half of which were formed in New Mexico. The total Spanish population probably amounted to less than 200 persons: 34 single men; 17 pre-1601 families of 6 persons each, for a total of 102; and 17 newly formed families of approximately 3 each for a total of about 187. Among the post-1601 colonists, there was a much higher proportion of men with families than there had been among the earlier population. Of the possible sixty-eight men who were in New Mexico in the early post-1601 years, thirty-four, or half, had families, compared to the four-to-one pre-1601 ratio. Given the dire condition of the colony and its ongoing dependence on the Pueblo people for food, it is not surprising that about 43 percent of the men and 66 percent of the families who had come from New Spain deserted. Their loss was partly compensated for by newly formed families, but the number was still exceedingly small—enough so as to question the viability of the colony. What likely sustained it, however, was that it contained a much higher proportion of families and was made up of people who knew what conditions in New Mexico were like and who had presumably decided that it offered them a better future than they might be able to find elsewhere. In the meantime, the purpose of the colony had changed. Rather than serve to expand the territory and sources of wealth under Spanish control, the colony primarily served to protect the Pueblo people who had been converted to Christianity, and its approximately seventy soldier-colonists were considered adequate for that purpose.[29] This purpose was reaffirmed by the king in 1608 when he appointed a replacement for Governor Oñate, who had tendered his resignation the previous year.[30]

The colony was not only depleted in numbers of people; it also lost a number of its most prominent members. Even before the defection, Oñate had lost eleven men who held the rank of captain and/or were office holders. Among the latter were the maese de campo, the *procurador general*, and the *secretario* and *notario real* of the expedition—Juan de Zaldívar, Gaspar Pérez de Villagrá, and Juan Pérez de Donís, respectively (appendix table G). Among the deserters, the colony lost its *tesorero, contador, proveedor general*, and *sargento mayor* in addition to some five men who held the rank of captain. The officeholders were respectively: Luis Gasco de Velasco, Alonso Sánchez, Diego de Zubía, and Antonio Conde de Herrera.[31] The five captains were: Bernabé de las Casas, Gregorio César, Alonso de Quesada, Francisco Donís, and Alonso Vayo (Valle).[32] It is probable that Lieutenant Governor Francisco de Sosa Peñalosa, who was the *alférez real* and the wealthiest colonist, also left New Mexico with his extensive family not long after 1601; he is not mentioned again. Although his office obliged him to remain at San Gabriel while Governor Oñate was away in the land of Quivira, his sympathies were with the defectors.[33]

In the years following 1601 until sometime in late 1609 or early 1610 when a new governor arrived, the size of the colony does not seem to have grown and may have even decreased somewhat. Governor Oñate took thirty soldiers with him on the 1604–5 expedition to discover the Gulf of California, and fifty to fifty-three "persons of all ages" were left in San Gabriel, according to Fray Francisco de Escobar and three other members of the expedition.[34] Unless they greatly underestimated the number of people who remained in San Gabriel, these figures indicate a decline from the probable 68 men and 34 families, possibly totaling some 187 people, who remained in New Mexico in 1601 after the desertion. The colony's population may have reached its nadir in this early post-defection period. There is no further information about eighteen of the sixty-eight men after mid-decade nor about another nine after 1610, a total of twenty-seven, including five men who had signed the October 2, 1601, loyalty petition—men who probably left the colony with Governor Oñate in 1610. Despite the lack of information about the changing population of New Mexico, which may at least partially be ascribed to the scarcity of documents, a general picture does emerge from the surviving records, which suggests the 1601–10 decade was one of considerable population flux. Besides losses, there were some additions, including two men who came at this time and founded families that became prominent in New Mexico: Francisco Madrid in 1603 and Francisco Gómez in 1604.[35] By 1609 there might have been some fifty soldier-settlers, but only thirty possessed arms according to a decree issued in January of that year in which the viceroy ordered that ten to twelve soldiers be recruited for New Mexico and that arms be sent to equip an additional ten of the men who were already in the colony, thus achieving an armed force of about fifty.[36] Fray Francisco de Velasco, writing to the viceroy in April of that year in support of maintaining the colony, recommended an even larger number of soldiers and requested "that the contingent of seventy to eighty soldiers from New Mexico be completed," but there is no evidence that the colony received any of these proposed reinforcements.[37]

It can be seen from these data that the number of soldier-colonists in New Mexico numbered only about fifty almost a decade after the 1601 desertion. They were probably not all the same fifty people because during these eight years there must have been among the colonist families a number of boys who came of age, married, and started families. In addition, men coming to New Mexico with the triennial supply trains were a source of new people. Francisco Madrid was one such person; he came in 1603 as wagon driver (*chirrionero de los carros*) for the caravan that brought new missionaries to New Mexico.[38] During ensuing decades it was government policy to encourage escort soldiers to remain in New Mexico in order to increase the population.[39] These gains were probably balanced by losses incurred when colonists died or returned to New Spain. One prominent example is Captain Juan Martínez de Montoya, who came to New Mexico in 1600 with reinforcements and served Oñate in many campaigns but whose appointment as interim governor by the viceroy in 1608 was rejected by the cabildo in San Gabriel.[40] Governor Oñate had resigned in 1607 and was replaced by his son Cristóbal after the cabildo rejected the viceroy's choice.[41] Martínez de Montoya was then granted permission to leave New Mexico along with two friars who were taking reports to the viceroy. With the arrival of Governor Peralta in late 1609 or early 1610, the colony suffered the loss of Oñate and his supporters but at the same time gained the soldiers and officials that the new governor brought with him—Peralta was instructed to take twelve soldiers for protection.[42] Sixteen officers accompanied him to New Mexico, but nine were from New Mexico.[43] Juan de Oñate left with his son and possibly those of his officers still in the colony, who were tried with him in Mexico City in 1614 and banished from New Mexico for varying periods of years.[44] Only Captain Gerónimo Márquez, who was tried in absentia, seems to have remained in New Mexico in defiance of his sentence of perpetual banishment. Later documents show that he and his sons were active in the colony—according to one source, they were a law unto themselves and inveterate troublemakers.[45] At least two grandsons, Pedro and Bernabé, were still in the colony at the time of the 1680 revolt according to the Otermín muster, and others on this list with the Márquez name were also probably relatives.[46]

CHAPTER EIGHT

The Post-Oñate Era

✢ AS LATE AS 1620, THE VICEROY WROTE TO THE KING THAT SANTA FE, the new capital officially established in 1610, was the only Spanish town in New Mexico and that it contained fifty residents (vecinos).[1] The king had been informed a few years earlier in a letter from the Santa Fe cabildo dated 1617 that there were forty-eight soldier-residents.[2] The question arises as to whether these figures represent only those who were full-time residents of Santa Fe or whether, because the villa was the only official Spanish settlement, all Spanish men in New Mexico who were tax-paying citizens (vecinos) were considered residents of the capital. By this time colonists had begun to settle elsewhere in the province, but as vecinos they also would have maintained a house in Santa Fe where some members of the family would have lived, as was customary in Spain and its colonies. This was especially true of those favored with encomienda grants, who were required to maintain a residence in the capital even though they spent most of their time at their rural properties.[3] The requirement that encomenderos live in Santa Fe is seen in the case of Andrés Hurtado, who in 1661 was ordered by the then-governor Bernardo López de Mendizábal to maintain a house in Santa Fe, although Hurtado complained that he could not afford it.[4] It seems likely that in addition to the fifty vecino-residents of Santa Fe, there were an unknown number of additional colonists of lesser means and status living on rural properties elsewhere who did not have a house in the capital. Although this scenario is speculative, it would help account for the natural increase in the number of men in the colony after 1601 as well as for the immigrants that are known to have arrived in New Mexico. Even so, it would seem that almost twenty years after the desertion, the number of Spanish soldier-settlers in New Mexico had not increased greatly. In the late 1620s the Spanish population of Santa Fe reported by the missionary custodian Fray Alonso de Benavides numbered as many as 250, of which there were 50 men who possessed arms—apparently the official figure that continued to be repeated.[5] He further noted that most of the Spanish men were married. The remainder of Santa Fe's total population of one thousand was, according to Benavides, composed of mestizos and Indians, most of whom were servants. Some forty-two vecinos known to have resided in Santa Fe between 1610 and 1632 have been identified (appendix table L).

By 1638 the villa of Santa Fe was still the only official Spanish settlement, and it remained so for the rest of the pre-1680 period. In his report of that year, Fray Juan de Prada, custodian of the New Mexico missionaries, stated that Santa Fe had a (Spanish) population of about two hundred persons, of whom about fifty could bear arms.[6] The following year former New Mexico governor Francisco Martínez de Baeza stated that Santa Fe had a few more than fifty inhabitants (that is, male residents or vecinos) with established homes and families, who formed a moderate-sized settlement.[7] However, that same year, 1639, the cabildo, in a letter to the viceroy, reported that there were thirty families in the villa.[8] Martínez de Baeza's claim notwithstanding, it is possible that Santa Fe was experiencing a reduction in its population related to the turmoil surrounding the 1637–41 administration of Governor Luis de Rosas and his murder in 1642. Eight men, the majority of whom were citizens of Santa Fe, were executed for the killing, and many others implicated in the plot fled the villa.[9] Still others may have left to take up lands newly available for settlement as the result of a major epidemic in the late 1630s and early 1640s that seriously decimated the Puebloan population, especially in desirable districts to the south such as the Middle and Southern Rio Grande districts.[10] This epidemic might have also affected the Spanish population in New Mexico, including those living in Santa Fe, where population decline seemingly persisted as late as 1661, when Governor López de Mendizábal mentioned that Santa Fe consisted of only thirty-eight small adobe houses (*casillas*), nine of which were occupied by widows, while other settlers lived in outlying districts on estancias and ranchos.[11] Whereas Martínez de Baeza stated in 1639 that "there are perhaps in the entire [province?] and its settlements two hundred persons, Spaniards and mestizos, who are able to bear arms," missionary custodian Fray Alonso de Posada claimed in 1661 that "this land does not have more than a hundred [male] citizens, more or less, and among this number are mulattoes, mestizos."[12] Although neither of these statements is probably entirely accurate, it would seem that the Spanish population of both the villa of Santa Fe and the province of New Mexico as a whole experienced a period of decline beginning in the late 1630s and persisting at least into the early 1660s.

By 1679, a year before the Pueblo revolt, there were almost 170 Spaniards and *castas* in the colony who could bear arms, but most lived outside of the capital on the frontiers and on their rural properties, according to the missionary custodian Fray Francisco de Ayeta.[13] This number included a contingent of forty-three men—forty convicts and three volunteers—of the fifty he had requested in 1677, who arrived in Santa Fe from Mexico City on February 12, 1678.[14] They were sent to the convents at Galisteo and Senecú to guard the frontiers against Apache attacks, thus leaving the number of settler-citizens in the province at about 127, a number somewhat higher than the 100 estimated by Fray Alonso de Posada in 1661. But examination of the 1680 and 1681 musters of refugees indicates that there were probably even more citizens, perhaps as many as two hundred. By this time Santa Fe had about seventy vecinos.[15] Part of the increase in the number of Spanish men in New Mexico resulted from the inclusion of some men of mixed race in the population figures. In his 1661 report, Fray Alonso mentioned that among the citizens (vecinos) of New Mexico were counted "mulattoes, mestizos, and all who have any Spanish blood, even though it is slight."[16] Increasingly during the eighty years after the first colonists came to New Mexico, it became less and less accurate to refer to a "Spanish" population. Following the 1601 mutiny, few Spanish women remained in the colony, and few came to stay in the ensuing years, thus resulting in an increase in the number of progeny with less and less Spanish biological heritage. As they became the majority, they claimed the status formerly accorded only to the Spanish colonists from New Spain. In this study, use of the term "Spanish" takes into account this change from a biological to a social designation.

The scarcity of information about the overall size of the Spanish population in New Mexico during the 1602–80 period is partly compensated for by estimates Governor Antonio Otermín made of the number of refugees who fled during the 1680 Pueblo revolt and by the muster he conducted on September 29 and October 2, 1680, at La Salineta, a post about three hundred miles south of Santa Fe and some ten miles north of the Spanish settlements in the El Paso area.[17] Governor Otermín reported that the refugees were composed of two groups—one from the Rio Arriba led by him and consisting of some one thousand people and another of about fifteen hundred from the Rio Abajo led by the lieutenant governor Alonso García.[18] The total of 2,500 included 325 Puebloans—mainly Piro and Tiwa from the Rio Abajo and 8 Tewa.[19] Adding to the 2,175 that are left after excluding the Puebloans the more than 400 people (including 21 religious) who were reported killed in the revolt gives an estimated non-Puebloan prerevolt population of some 2,575, including women, children, servants, clergy, the recently arrived convict contingent, and families of mixed race.[20] In order to determine how many of the 2,175 non-Pueblo refugees estimated by Otermín were considered Spanish settlers, it is necessary to examine the muster that Otermín held at La Salineta. Governor Otermín stated that 1,946 persons of all classes were present at the muster, mentioning that many other refugees did not stay but went on to El Paso without his permission.[21] The muster yields a total of 1,668 non-Pueblo persons, resulting in a discrepancy of 507 persons compared with the 2,175 of his earlier estimate.[22] Although such a large gap might be partly explained by the inexact nature of Otermín's estimates, he did say that many did not stay for the muster, and it is not unreasonable to suppose that as many as five hundred bypassed the roll call, keeping in mind that the exhausted and ill-fed refugees knew that the supply train from Mexico City had arrived in El Paso, only ten miles away. Although some provisions were brought to them at La Salineta, many refugees were anxious to reach the source of succor as quickly as possible.[23] Adding these 500 people to the 1,668 non-Pueblo refugees at La Salineta gives a total of 2,168.

To arrive at the number of people among the refugees who made up the Spanish settler population, the 2,168 figure must be further refined. Starting with the 1,668 non-Puebloans who stayed for the muster and subtracting the 14 men of mixed race who reported 103 family members, 1 non-Spanish woman with 8 family members, 30 clergy and their servants, and 14 members of the convict contingent with their 18 dependents—188 persons—yields a total of 1,480 Spanish settlers and their servants reported by the 127 non-convict men and 7 women heads of household.[24] Deducting their servants would give the Spanish population, but only sixty-four of these 134 Spanish heads of household on the muster reported their servants separately (a total of 408). Undoubtedly, however, there were many more servants—possibly some 500 in all.[25] Subtracting this latter number of servants from the 1,480 total leaves some 980 refugees who might be considered Spanish.[26] But those who bypassed the muster must be considered. Of the approximately five hundred people who did not attend the roll call, the twenty-six members of the convict contingent who were not either killed (three) or on the muster (fourteen) were likely part of this group, and most probably they were single men. If they are excluded, the great majority of the remaining 474, possibly 400 of them, might be assumed to belong to Spanish settler families. These families might have numbered about thirty-six, using the average number of eleven persons per household of the refugees who did answer the muster. Applying the factor of 3.7 servants per family derived from the refugees who answered the muster to the thirty-six families who did not stay for the muster and deducting their 133 servants from 400 leaves a total of 267 Spaniards, which when added to the 980 who answered the roll call gives an estimated total population of 1,247 refugees who could be considered Spanish.

In order to obtain an estimate of the Spanish settler population in New Mexico on the eve of the revolt, the number killed in 1680 must be added (appendix table M). Eight men were reported killed along with their families, a total of 58, using a family size of 7.3, not counting servants. An additional 10 nonconvict men were killed but not their families. Taking into account the 12 women who were killed with their families but whose husbands survived yields a total of 76, using a reduced family size of 6.3. Altogether some 144 Spanish settlers and family members might have been killed, and when added to the 1,247 refugees, the prerevolt Spanish population would have been 1,391, or approximately 1,400. Given that in the early years after the 1601 desertion, 68 men, 34 with families, or a total of 187, remained in New Mexico, the Spanish population appears to have grown more than sevenfold over the course of eighty years, a growth that can be mainly attributed to natural increase and the changing racial definition of the term "Spanish" rather than to immigration, which was limited. However, the Spanish population was still very small and was greatly outnumbered by the Pueblo people, who numbered about thirteen thousand on the eve of the revolt, having declined from some fifty thousand in 1598.[27] In light of the manipulation of the data, these figures must, however, be considered speculative.

Ascertaining how many Spanish men were in New Mexico prior to the revolt also presents problems. Governor Otermín claimed that fewer than 100 men capable of bearing arms accompanied him on the retreat from Santa Fe and that some 120 were in the division led by the lieutenant governor.[28] When the 40 surviving convicts are subtracted from Otermín's estimated 220 and the 18 nonconvict Spanish men who were killed (appendix table M) are added, the result is a prerevolt total of 198.[29] But using the 127 nonconvict men listed on the 1680 muster, the estimated 36 who bypassed the muster, and adding the 18 nonconvict Spanish men who were killed yields a prerevolt total of 181 Spanish men. There is also the number reported by the commissary Fray Francisco de Ayeta in 1679, that is, 170 men capable of bearing arms.[30] However, this figure includes some low-ranking men of mixed race (castas) and the recently arrived forty-three-man convict contingent, leaving possibly some 120 nonconvict Spanish men. The difference can perhaps be accounted for by different definitions of "men capable of bearing arms" used by Otermín and Ayeta and/or the estimated nature of their figures. In view of the congruence of the data from Otermín's estimates and the 1680 muster, Ayeta's figure seems low, and a prerevolt total of close to two hundred nonconvict Spanish men capable of bearing arms is not an unreasonable estimate. The gap between these figures shows how inexact they are, but they give a general idea of the number of Spanish men, most heads of households, living in New Mexico in 1680 before the revolt, a figure that is about triple the sixty-eight that remained after the 1601 desertion.

Many descendants of original colonists who continued to live in New Mexico during the years up to 1680 when they were forced to leave can be identified from the Otermín musters. His 1680 muster contains the names of nineteen and possibly four other families whose members were descended from those on the Oñate-era musters, the family connections having been worked out mainly by Fray Angélico Chávez (appendix table N). The adult male members of these twenty-three families number fifty-four on the 1680 muster, and an additional thirty-five men belonging to these and an additional four families can be identified on roll calls taken in the El Paso settlements in 1681. When the three men from these families who were reported killed in the revolt are also added, that suggests there would have been at the time of the revolt a total of at least ninety-two Spanish men, members of twenty-seven families, who were descended from some of the original sixty-eight colonists who remained after the 1601 desertion. The men listed on the 1680 and 1681 musters constituted 45 percent of the approximately two hundred nonconvict Spanish men in New Mexico on the eve of the revolt. When considering just the 54 men on the 1680 muster, their proportion is similar—slightly over 40 percent of the 127 non-convict total. Other descendants might have bypassed the 1680 and 1681 musters, but they cannot be identified. In addition, others might have been absorbed into other settler families or taken different family names, or, in other cases, the family might have died out or its members may have left the colony. But at least 40–45 percent of the nonconvict Spanish men in 1680 are known to have belonged to families that remained in New Mexico throughout the period from 1601 to 1680.

The remaining approximately 60 percent of the Spanish population was made up of post-1601 immigrants and their progeny. They came not as part of officially organized colonization but consisted mainly of individuals who came to New Mexico for various reasons—government service, business, or work on the supply trains—found wives among the eligible women and stayed. Otermín's 1680 muster lists seventy-eight Spanish men (excluding convicts), representing some fifty-seven families who were not descended from the original settlers. An additional fifty-five post-1601 settlers who were not on Otermín's musters have been identified by Chávez and others.[31] Together they constituted about 67 percent of the estimated two hundred prerevolt Spanish men in New Mexico. The 78 nonconvict men who answered Otermín's 1680 muster made up about 60 percent of the 127 nonconvict respondents. Because the data are scarce and fragmentary, it is not possible to know in most cases when the post-1601 newcomers arrived and began contributing to the growth of the population. There might have been other post-1601 immigrants, but they or their descendants are not identifiable as living in the colony at the time of the revolt. The musters held in El Paso from September 22 to October 16, 1681, show that, with few exceptions, the Spanish population of New Mexico was native born.[32]

PART THREE

The Settlement Landscapes

CHAPTER NINE

San Gabriel

✝ THE TEWA PUEBLOS OF OHKAY OWINGEH AND YUNQUE OWINGEH, where Juan de Oñate established the first Spanish settlement in New Mexico, are located at the confluence of the Chama River and the Rio Grande (see map 1, p. 205). They were two of the most northern pueblos of a region that extended along the Rio Grande Rift valley 175 miles to the south of the confluence and 40 miles to the north. Yunque Owingeh was situated in the floodplain west of the Rio Grande and above the Chama, and Ohkay Owingeh was built opposite Yunque Owingeh about a quarter mile away on a low terrace east of the Rio Grande. The more extensive arable lands lay west of the Rio Grande, where they could be more easily irrigated than others because of their location near the smaller Chama River. Yunque Owingeh was established sometime in the later 1200s and Ohkay Owingeh a little later, perhaps around 1300.[1] Their proximity led to frequent contact, including intermarriage, between the two peoples, so that they came to consider themselves a single people inhabiting two pueblos, with Ohkay Owingeh eventually becoming the larger of the two.[2] Other Tewa-speaking people inhabited seven pueblos to the south, mainly in the Tesuque-Pojoaque drainage.

During the week between August 10, 1598, when Oñate and his advance party returned to San Juan (their name for Ohkay and Yunque) and August 18, when the remainder of the expedition arrived, Oñate was able to recruit a large body of San Juan people to assist in working on an irrigation ditch (acequia) for his planned "city of our father, Saint Francis," and within less than a week after the main part of the expedition arrived work was begun on a church.³ This church, dedicated to San Juan Bautista, was completed two weeks later on September 7. At this point, questions arise as to where the ditch and church were located and where the approximately five hundred people of the expedition were accommodated during those early days after their arrival. It is possible that during the week between Oñate's return to San Juan and the arrival of the main body of the expedition the governor was able to negotiate with the leaders of the San Juan people not only the construction of the irrigation ditch but also a place for the colonists to stay, namely Yunque Owingeh Pueblo. Until it was made ready, they might have camped in their tents just outside Ohkay Owingeh or Yunque Owingeh, or some might have temporarily moved in with local families or into some of the empty houses, which all pueblos have.⁴ Eyewitnesses stated that the church was large enough to accommodate all members of the "camp"—an indication that their situation at that point was temporary.⁵ If it had been decided that the Spaniards would take over Yunque Owingeh, it seems likely that the church and ditch would have been constructed near that pueblo.⁶ According to San Juan traditional knowledge, all Spanish ditches were west of the Rio Grande.⁷ It is also likely that renovation of Yunque Owingeh was soon undertaken—anxious as the Spaniards must have been to have a place of their own and anxious as their hosts would have been not to have strangers living among them. It is probable that the principal alteration of Yunque Owingeh took place after its inhabitants moved out to join their relatives in Ohkay Owingeh, although some probably stayed behind to finish modifying the pueblo and to attend to the needs of the Spaniards.⁸ And it is likely that by the time Oñate returned from his aborted trip to the South Sea (Gulf of California) in late December 1598, the colonists had found shelter from the very cold New Mexico winter in a remodeled Yunque Owingeh.⁹

Although the place Oñate returned to was called San Juan, the name appears to have referred to the two-pueblo complex, not just to the pueblo of Ohkay Owingeh. This interpretation is speculative, however, because the known documents do not indicate where the ditch and church were built or just when the Spaniards took over Yunque Owingeh. Some scholars believe that the Spaniards initially established their capital at Ohkay Owingeh, which they called San Juan, and then at a later date, perhaps by mid-1599 or as late as mid-winter 1600–1601, moved to Yunque Owingeh, which they named San Gabriel.¹⁰ The continued use in the Oñate documents into early 1599 of the name San Juan or San Juan Bautista to refer to the Spaniards' headquarters could support this interpretation, but no such move is ever referred to in these documents, and it does not take into account that Ohkay Owingeh and Yunque Owingeh were regarded by their inhabitants as a single settlement and that the name San Juan initially applied to both.[11] According to Tewa tradition, Oñate established the first capital of New Mexico at Yunque, or old San Juan.[12] In this view, San Juan refers to the combined pueblo complex of which Yunque Owingeh was the older part and would thus explain the continued use of San Juan as the name of the capital in the correspondence of this early period of settlement, which was the same time that the Spaniards were living in Yunque Owingeh. The name San Juan de los Caballeros, first used by Oñate's captain Gaspar Pérez de Villagrá, probably referred to the magnanimity of the San Juan people as a whole in accommodating the Spaniards; the name San Juan de los Caballeros is not found in the Oñate documents.[13]

As late as February 1599 the colony's headquarters were still referred to as San Juan or San Juan Bautista, as seen in the report dated February 23, 1599, that Vicente de Zaldívar presented to Governor Oñate on the expedition he had led east to the buffalo plains from September 15 to November 8, 1598.[14] In 1599 a map indicating where he and his party had traveled was made in Mexico City for the viceroy based on information supplied by Miguel, a native that Zaldívar brought back with him. This map shows San Gabriel as the starting place of the trip (see the lower right corner of map 3, p. 207).[15] The presence of San Gabriel on the map and San Juan in Zaldívar's report shows that the two names were in use at the same time and the map could provide evidence that the Spaniards were living in Yunque Owingeh, which they named San Gabriel, at the time of Zaldívar's expedition. Although there is no direct evidence to indicate when the Spaniards named Yunque Owingeh "San Gabriel," it is likely they did so at the time they took it over. The name, however, probably only gradually took precedence over San Juan as the official name of the Spanish settlement.

Documents from New Mexico during the remainder of 1599 and 1600 do not cite the name of the Spaniards' capital, but by the time the reinforcements arrived in late December 1600, it was called San Gabriel.[16] From this time forward the capital continued to be referred to as San Gabriel, and it is this name that is used in later documents when referring back to the founding of the colony.[17] In a letter written on March 22, 1601, from San Gabriel, Captain Luis de Velasco stated that "we came to a pueblo where the governor ordered a halt. It is the one from which I am writing to your lordship. We have been here three years."[18] Further evidence that Yunque Owingeh/San Gabriel was the Spaniards' capital from the earliest days of the colony is seen in the July 1601 testimony of another of Oñate's captains, who, when queried about how the governor had established his camp, stated that it was established in a pueblo named San Gabriel.[19] Another witness, who had come to New Mexico with the reinforcements in December 1600, claimed that the original 1598 expedition proceeded until it reached the pueblo of San Gabriel, which was the place where don Juan de Oñate established his headquarters.[20] No mention is made in any of these statements about a move of the colony's headquarters from San Juan to San Gabriel, that is, from Ohkay Owingeh to Yunque Owingeh. Eventually the Spaniards abandoned San Gabriel, but the San Juan people have continued to the present to live in Ohkay Owingeh.

Evidence of Spanish occupation of Yunque Owingeh was found in the east and west mounds (houseblocks) when the site was excavated from 1959 to 1962.[21] Work at the site indicated that the Spaniards lived in the second story of the houseblocks and used the ground floor for storage (this conclusion was arrived at based on the absence of ground-floor fire pits) as did the San Juan people and Puebloans in general; the houseblocks, constructed of coursed adobe, were subdivided into houses or apartments. The distinctive non-Puebloan features included doorways cut down to floor level, doorways to connect rooms, cobblestone hearths or "tables," Spanish-type fire pits, and domed ovens. Windows cut into the walls were not found in the reduced walls of the site but were reported by Spaniards testifying in July 1601.[22] The west mound, which showed little architectural modification, was probably used as a barracks for the single men, while the east mound was fashioned into apartments for officers and their families.[23] This work included shoring up some walls, plastering the interior of the two main roomblocks, and providing openings for ventilation to meet the Spaniards' complaints that the pueblo buildings were smoky and vermin infested.[24] The excavation provided evidence that the roomblocks had at least two to three terraced stories but did not reveal how many rooms it contained overall.[25] However, two Spaniards testifying in July 1601 said they took over a pueblo that had approximately four hundred houses.[26] Excavation also revealed part of the San Miguel church built of small blocks of volcanic tuff that possibly by the time of the arrival of the reinforcements in December 1600 had replaced the original, San Juan Bautista, that most likely had been made of temporary jacal construction, given the rapidity with which it was built.[27] No fortifications were found nor were any built according to the July 1601 witnesses, who claimed that its strong location (between two rivers) and the gentle, peaceful nature of the local people made it unnecessary.[28]

From the beginning, Governor Oñate wanted his colonists to build their own capital, his "city of Saint Francis." That this did not happen can be attributed to reluctance to commit the necessary time and labor when so many were dissatisfied with what they saw in New Mexico and wished to abandon the colony.[29] This dissatisfaction was evident soon after the colonists arrived in New Mexico, as seen in Oñate's report to the viceroy that same month, August 1598, that forty-five men planned to desert the colony.[30] Although they were prevented from doing so, resentment continued and found expression in the 1601 desertion. Oñate also wanted his colonists to produce their own food. But they were not farmers, and initially they made little effort to grow crops, despite the irrigation ditch that he ordered constructed for them. The Spaniards, having exhausted their stores of grain even before they reached New Mexico, mainly lived off the dwindling number of livestock they brought with them and food supplies requisitioned from the pueblos, often by force. Armed soldiers were sent out every month, or as needed, to all of the pueblos to bring in maize to San Gabriel, where it was then distributed to the more than five hundred persons of the expedition.[31]

The scarcity of food was cited as one of the reasons for abandoning New Mexico. The spokesmen for this faction, which included the clergy, stated that they had exhausted the reserve stores of maize in the pueblos, that they as well as the Pueblo people were starving, and the drought that year meant further privation.[32] Members of the faction who favored remaining in New Mexico painted a very different picture of the situation, stating that there was an abundance of food, that they had planted wheat every year in increasing amounts, that they had established a flour mill, and that many were no longer dependent on Pueblo food supplies.[33] Further evidence of this divide comes from testimony given in July 1601 to treasury official Francisco de Valverde by four captains Oñate had sent to Mexico City. Two who had come with Governor Oñate in 1598 gave favorable reports about the number of livestock, pastures, and wheat harvested, but the two who had come with the reinforcements in 1600 reported that the supply of livestock was dwindling and that wheat was grown only near the Spanish camp where there was water for irrigation.[34] Although both factions were undoubtedly exaggerating, it is very likely that after three years there was something of a food crisis, which was only partly relieved by the departure of a substantial part of the colony in the fall of 1601.

It is probable that the remaining colonists, dedicated as they were to staying in New Mexico, were more willing to engage in farming activities themselves. Although certain colonists stated that the natives sowed and harvested wheat for the Spaniards, others reported that it was the Spaniards who plowed the fields, which seems likely because it was they who introduced the plow and oxen to pull it, a technology previously unknown to the Puebloans.[35] It was further noted that although they employed the local people to cultivate vegetables, they raised their own type of beans as well as the chile they brought with them from New Spain.[36] They probably initially planted their crops near San Gabriel, where some Spaniards had acquired individual lands.[37] But because the delta between the Chama River and the Rio Grande constituted the main cropland of the San Juan people and because Spanish colonial law forbade the takeover of land worked by native people, the Spanish settlers might have begun to move farther afield— possibly to the nearby Santa Cruz River valley or to the larger, more centrally located Santa Fe River valley twenty-eight miles to the south, neither of which were permanently occupied by Pueblo people at that time (see map 1, p. 205).[38] The attack on San Gabriel by "Navajo Apaches" in 1606 or 1607 gave the Spaniards another reason to want to leave.[39] They might also have been eager to move out of their converted pueblo and into housing of a type more familiar to them. However, San Gabriel was probably not completely abandoned when the new capital was transferred to Santa Fe in 1610. Instead, it likely withered away gradually.[40] Of the colony that consisted of about sixty settlers in 1608–9, some families that had already been farming near San Gabriel probably continued to do so, at least for a few years—particularly families in which the men were married to San Juan women.[41] Evidence is scarce, but the 1665 statement by Isleta settler Francisco García Holgado that he was born in San Gabriel de Iunque in 1615 suggests that some Spaniards were still living there after 1610.[42]

Although San Gabriel was sometimes referred to as a villa, it did not have that status officially. Under the terms of his contract Governor Oñate had the authority to designate the status of his headquarters, but he seemingly never did so.[43] Fray Francisco de Velasco in his memorial of April 9, 1609, in which he urged maintaining the New Mexico colony, also suggested conferring on San Gabriel the status of a villa; however, that advice was obviated by the transfer of the capital to Santa Fe.[44] In 1620 the viceroy informed the king that "there are no other Spanish towns [in New Mexico] except the villa of Santa Fe which contains fifty residents."[45] And Santa Fe remained the sole officially designated Spanish settlement until the reconquest period of the 1690s.

CHAPTER TEN

The Villa of Santa Fe

✝ RELOCATION OF THE SPANISH COLONISTS' CAPITAL FROM SAN GABRIEL to Santa Fe brought a number of advantages. From an administrative point of view, its relocation farther south and also east of the Rio Grande on the main north-south route gave the Spanish authorities better access to a larger number of pueblos (see map 1, p. 205). But of prime importance was the absence of permanently occupied pueblos in the Santa Fe River valley, not only making it possible to establish a Spanish settlement that was in conformance with colonial law that proscribed Spaniards from living near places inhabited by native people, as was the case at San Gabriel, but also giving them access to abundant land, water, pasture, and woodland resources—resources that Puebloan people in the surrounding areas probably utilized only intermittently.[1] Although the Santa Fe area had a long history of occupation by native people, the high mark of Pueblo settlement occurred "between the fourteenth and early fifteenth centuries when 3,000 to 5,000 people possibly lived along the Santa Fe River and its major tributaries."[2] A number of large pueblos were built in the area during the 1200–1325 Coalition Period but all had been abandoned by 1425, possibly owing to a conjunction of unfavorable environmental conditions and strife related to population influxes.[3]

The Santa Fe River valley might be better described as a piedmont plain that extends from the foothills of the Sangre de Cristo Mountains westward some twelve miles to the Caja del Rio Plateau, thus having the protection of the mountains to the east and extended visibility to the west (see map 6,

p. 210).⁴ The capital, located near where the Santa Fe River emerges from a narrow band of foothills, had at hand good crop and pasture land on the plain as well as piñon and juniper that extended into the foothills and pine and fir higher in the mountains where summer grazing was also available. The river, partly fed by snowmelt from the mountains, which reach elevations of 10,000–12,000 feet, and partly by summer-dominant rains, provides a usually reliable supply of water. But in this region of semiarid climate, average annual rainfall of about fourteen inches in Santa Fe cannot always sustain a permanent stream flow, especially given the high degree of precipitation variability, which ranges between five and twenty-five inches.⁵ At 7,000 feet, mild summer temperatures, which average near 70 degrees Fahrenheit, with an average maximum of 84 degrees, minimize evaporation, but both rainfall and temperatures and a variable frost-free growing season constitute conditions for growing such basic crops as maize or wheat that are marginal for dry farming and make successful farming dependent on irrigation in all but a series of above-average rainfall years (tables 2 and 3).⁶ Climate reconstructions based on tree-ring analysis indicate that the Spaniards were favored with such conditions in the early years after Santa Fe was officially established as their capital in 1610 (appendix table A).⁷ But by 1693 a returning settler, Juan Lucero de Godoy, who had lived in Santa Fe for fifty years, noted the scarcity of water there, claiming that it hardly sufficed to irrigate the sown fields of the seventy settlers who had lived there in his time.⁸ That the scarcity of water was a persistent problem can be seen in the 1760 statement made by visiting bishop Pedro Tamarón y Romeral in which he noted that the Santa Fe River "dries up entirely in the months just before the harvest when only an inadequate small spring remains for drinking water in addition to the wells."⁹

The advantages offered by the Santa Fe River valley had probably already brought some of Oñate's colonists to this area before the villa was officially founded by the new governor, Pedro de Peralta, most likely early in 1610.¹⁰ His instructions from the viceroy hinted as much when they stated that Peralta's first responsibility was the foundation and settlement of "la villa que se pretende," an indication that it was the colonists, or some of them, who had been petitioning for a new capital.¹¹ Claims that Santa Fe was first settled in 1605 were at one time based on an abbreviated quotation from Fray Alonso de Posada (who was in New Mexico circa 1650–64), but his statement referred to the discovery of the Gulf of California, not to Santa Fe.¹² At the time when this mistake became apparent, there was no further evidence to support a 1605 founding date.[13] Later, in 1929, when the 1609 instructions to Governor Peralta to establish a capital city in New Mexico were published, the date when he most probably arrived in New Mexico, 1610, became the accepted date for the founding of Santa Fe.[14] Although 1610 was the official date, other documents dated 1607–8 related to Juan Martínez de Montoya, prominent colonist and encomendero, refer to a place called Santa Fe, indicating that it was some sort of post or settlement before its official founding as a villa and the capital of New Mexico.[15] The full text of these documents (which recently became available) contain a 1608 statement that Martínez de Montoya had established a plaza called Santa Fe ("el haber hecho Plasa en Santa Fe"), presumably making him founder of the initial settlement.[16] Martínez de Montoya, who, as secretary of war and government, was left in charge of the colony while Governor Oñate was away on his 1604–5 expedition to the Gulf of California, might have, along with some of the other colonists, undertaken a search for a better place to settle.[17] Recognizing the advantages of the Santa Fe site, they could well have requested permission to establish a plaza there when Oñate returned in April 1605. Additional evidence to support settlement at the Santa Fe site prior to 1610 is the birth there circa 1605 of a son to Juan Griego, an original settler who came to New Mexico in 1598.[18] A less certain case is that of original settler Hernán Martín Serrano, whose son, named for him, was born in 1608 or earlier (dates vary) and was described as a "natural de Santa Fe"; however, on another occasion, he gave his birthplace as El Yunque (that is, San Gabriel).[19] Limited as this evidence is, it is sufficient to establish that some Spaniards were living at the Santa Fe site before 1610, possibly as early as 1605.

In 1608 the king decreed that the colony of New Mexico should be maintained in order to protect the Christianized native population and preserve "nuestra sancta fee catholica," which is possibly where the name "Santa Fe" came from.[20] The number of settlers who moved to Santa Fe before its official founding in 1610 is not known with any certainty, but available records of a somewhat later date contain the names of nine persons described as founding settlers (e.g., *primero fundador, antiguo poblador, vecino antiguo,* or *vecino fundador*), who might well have been already living at the site at the time its status as villa and provincial capital was made official. These men were Pedro Durán y Chávez, Francisco Gómez, Juan Griego, Juan López Holguín, Francisco Madrid, Hernán Martín Serrano, Juan Rodríguez Bellido, Juan Pérez de Bustillo, and Alonso Varela Jaramillo, all of whom were in New Mexico by 1605.[21] In addition, there was Juan Martínez de Montoya, who led the move to the Santa Fe site, although he left the colony in 1608, and Blas de Valencia, whose son Francisco was born in Santa Fe in 1607 or 1611. There were probably others whose names are not mentioned in the scant records available.[22]

The presence of a group of Spanish colonists already living in the Santa Fe River valley could have been the factor that determined the location of the new capital when Governor Peralta arrived with his mandate to establish a villa.[23] After Governor Oñate resigned in 1607, the viceroy named Martínez de Montoya to replace him, but he was rejected by the cabildo in San Gabriel.[24] It has been suggested that the reason for his rejection by a body that had been appointed by Oñate was a rivalry between the two men and that when Martínez de Montoya returned to Mexico in 1608, he lobbied the viceroy to move the capital to Santa Fe, a settlement that he had played a leading role in establishing.[25] Hence when Peralta did arrive in late 1609 or early 1610 with orders to establish a new capital, its location had probably already been decided, including its specific site at the head of the valley where access to water for irrigation and other uses was perceived to be optimal, particularly on the north side of the Santa Fe River where the plaza was established (see map 4, p. 208). Beginning in 1610 most colonists probably made the move from San Gabriel to Santa Fe to take up land being granted by the new governor. Some, particularly those who were married to San Juan women, might have continued to reside in San Gabriel at least for a time, and others who had already moved elsewhere, such as to the Santa Cruz River valley, also called La Cañada, continued to live there although they also acquired land in the villa, as was required of all vecinos. By 1617 the cabildo reported forty-eight soldiers and residents in the villa.[26] Unfortunately, because all government records in the villa were destroyed by the Pueblo people who took over Santa Fe in 1680, records of land grants, including any that might have been made in 1610 or before, have been lost.[27] Spaniards were not the only people moving from San Gabriel to Santa Fe. When Santa Fe was established, the considerable number of Mexican warriors, attendants, and their families who had accompanied the Spaniards to New Mexico formed a satellite community on the south side of the river called the Barrio de Analco ("analco" being a Nahuatl term meaning "the other side of the river"), where they were subsequently joined by local natives who became servants of the Spaniards (see map 4, p. 208).[28]

What Santa Fe was like during the 1610–80 period is largely a matter of conjecture, not only because the records were destroyed, but also because four centuries of building and rebuilding has obliterated or obscured nearly all evidence of pre-1680 structures. As a result, it can only be inferred from a few surviving sources such as "La ynstrucción a Peralta," the 1573 royal ordinances for the laying out of new towns, and statements about Santa Fe in documents from the 1680–96 revolt and reconquest period as well as from the eighteenth century, in addition to reports on archaeological work that is still being carried out. This scarce information, which is not always clear or consistent, has been interpreted in different ways with the result that only an approximation of what Santa Fe might have been like before 1680 can be achieved. Governor Peralta had instructions from the viceroy about how the villa was to be organized. The lands of the villa (*propios*) were to consist of six *vecindades* with a square reserved for royal offices (*casas reales*) and other public buildings. A vecindad was the amount of land to be apportioned to each resident or vecino. The six belonging to the villa totaled some 3,822 acres, which could be rented to bring in income for the villa or used for further expansion.[29] Each resident was to receive 2 lots, or solares (1.72 acres), for a house and garden. In addition each was granted 2 suertes (105.76 acres) for planting fruits and vegetables, 2 suertes for a vineyard and an olive grove, and 4 caballerías (423.28 acres) of cropland—presumably for planting grain. They were also given the right to the water needed to irrigate these lands, which would have totaled some 637 acres for each settler.[30] The amount of land actually parceled out to each resident is unknown, but because the governor's instructions indicate that they were expected to produce food, they probably received, in addition to lots for a house and house garden, an allotment of land in the villa for raising some crops and a few livestock at least sufficient to sustain themselves. As a result, it is likely that Santa Fe from its inception was a dispersed settlement in which residents lived on semiurban properties rather than closely clustered near the central plaza of the villa. The residence pattern probably resembled a smaller, but otherwise not very different, version of the villa shown on the 1766 Urrutia map (see map 4, p. 208).[31] In 1760 visiting bishop Dr. Pedro Tamerón y Romeral described Santa Fe as an open place with houses far apart, and in 1776 visiting father commissary Fray Francisco Atanasio Domínguez said it was a place that did not conform to the status of a villa and that it consisted "of many small ranchos at various distances from one another, with no plan as to their location."[32] This dispersed pattern might have had its beginning in the years before Santa Fe's founding as a villa, and the location of its plaza might have also been determined then.[33]

The 1573 royal ordinances instructed settlers to set up a tent or other temporary shelter as soon as their lots had been assigned.[34] Those settlers who moved from San Gabriel early in 1610 undoubtedly were pressed for time to prepare fields and plant crops and, even with conscripted Pueblo labor, had little time to devote to building houses. It has been suggested that these initial buildings were constructed of wattle and daub or jacal, methods that produce structures that are not very durable but that require much less time to build than those made of adobe bricks.[35] It is possible that these methods were also used to construct the initial government buildings (casas reales) and church in order to have places in which to carry out civil and religious functions until more permanent adobe brick structures could be constructed.[36] Settlers continued to rely on Pueblo labor as they had at San Gabriel even though the supply of labor was farther away. The closest pueblos were Tesuque, located about nine miles to the north, Cuyamungue, which was six miles beyond Tesuque, and La Bajada, which was some twenty miles to the southwest (see map 6, p. 210). Tribute labor was outlawed, but royal officials such as alcaldes mayores could require pueblos to supply workers for public and private needs under the repartimiento system of rotational forced paid labor, a practice subject to much abuse.[37] The demise of La Bajada Pueblo (LA 7) early in the seventeenth century might have been related to the Spaniards' removing its residents to a pueblo in the La Cienega area of the Santa Fe River valley in order to have a closer supply of labor for the villa. The site of this pueblo, called La Cienega, has not been discovered, but it was probably located about twelve miles below the villa in the area that today carries that name (see map 6, p. 210).

What might be called the urban component of Santa Fe was centered on the plaza, government buildings, and the church. Archaeological work, difficult as it is to conduct in a built-up area, has contributed the only concrete information about the physical arrangement of this core area in the prerevolt era, in addition to revealing the existence of pre-1425 Pueblo ruins in the vicinity of the Museum of Fine Arts, the city hall, La Garita Hill, and the San Miguel chapel (see map 5, p. 209).[38] A major attraction this site had for earlier Pueblo people as well as Spanish colonists was undoubtedly the availability of a good water supply.[39] In addition to the Santa Fe River and some half-dozen arroyos emerging from the foothills immediately to the north and east, there was an extensive wetland (cienega) that was fed from springs and runoff from the arroyos as well as from the westward flow of groundwater. A recent study of the Santa Fe River has established that the cienega lay in an abandoned channel or oxbow of the river created when the river changed course.[40] Its extent varied according to changing climatic and hydrologic conditions, but soil sample analyses indicate that in the early seventeenth century it stretched from its western edge in the vicinity of present Grant and Marcy streets eastward, passing north of the Palace of the Governors, east of the cathedral, and south to the Santa Fe River (see map 5, p. 209).[41] Its springs provided water for irrigation and domestic use and supported vegetation that was used for livestock fodder. The cienega could also act as a defensive barrier. All of these advantages must have been especially attractive to the Spaniards as they looked for a new site for their capital. Another source of water was a small stream that flowed from a large spring in the cienega located southeast of the present cathedral and that followed a course westward along what later became Water Street, joining the Santa Fe River just north of Guadalupe Church (see map 5, p. 209).[42] This stream, which was called El Rio Chiquito, is mentioned in late seventeenth- and early eighteenth-century documents and probably existed at the beginning of the seventeenth century. Interestingly, the 1766 Urrutia map shows neither the cienega nor the Rio Chiquito, but it is most likely they existed then as well as in the seventeenth century. Although there was the potential for flooding from these sources of water, in an otherwise dry land they would have been attractive in 1610, if not earlier.[43] Spaniards used the Rio Chiquito to irrigate fields and gardens located between it and the Santa Fe River. Water from the cienega was channeled to the casas reales on the north side of the plaza as well as to the church-convent complex to the east, and it also provided for the needs of those settlers whose lots were located nearby. The ditch (acequia) that brought water to the casas reales is mentioned by Governor Otermín in 1680 and Governor Vargas in 1692.[44] There have been differing views about the source of this water, but it most likely originated in the large spring located northeast of the plaza between present Otero and Cienega streets south of East Marcy Avenue, from which its waters were directed along what is now Palace Avenue to the Palace of the Governors, which was then located somewhat south of its present location.[45] Archaeological evidence for such an acequia has been revealed by recent excavation on the plaza in front of the entrance to the Palace of the Governors.[46]

Laying out the plaza was probably the first step taken to establish the villa. It can be argued that a plaza had already been created by Martínez de Montoya and others in 1607 or 1608 as a *plaza de armas*, but it is likely that a formal town plaza was established by Governor Peralta. His instructions from the viceroy do not include guidelines for establishing the plaza aside from stating that a square should be set aside for the purpose of erecting royal and other public buildings, but he was probably familiar with and attempted to follow the specifications in the royal ordinances of 1573, which called for a plaza with a length at least equal to one and one half times its width.[47] Excavations at the northwest corner of the current Palace of the Governors and at the parking structure at the corner of San Francisco Street and Cathedral Place help establish the original east-west dimension of the plaza—from approximately Lincoln Avenue on the west eastward to present Saint Francis Cathedral (see map 5, p. 209).[48] This east-west axis of the rectangular plaza can be seen on the 1766 Urrutia map, the earliest known map of Santa Fe. The position of the present palace helps establish the plaza's northwest corner, but there is disagreement about the southern border— whether it reached nearly to the Rio Chiquito or some distance above it.[49] If the plaza extended south to just above the Rio Chiquito, it would approximate the maximum measurements set out in ordinance 112, which, converted to English feet was 731 by 486, or 6.1 acres.[50] But if the topography of the area is taken into account, a relatively flat space for the plaza would be bounded on the south by a river terrace somewhat more than a hundred feet north of the north bank of the Rio Chiquito, on the west by an increased down-slope gradient, and on the north and east by the cienega. Within this space a plaza of average size according to the royal ordinances (548 by 365 English feet, or 4.6 acres) could be accommodated.[51] Most likely it was a plaza of medium size that was laid out by Governor Peralta in 1610. An attempt to correlate a plaza of this size with the 1766 Urrutia map shows that the southern boundary falls about half way between the street that enters from the west—presumably present San Francisco Street—and where the Rio Chiquito would be located.[52] Evidence that the southern boundary of the plaza did not extend to the Rio Chiquito comes not only from the topography of the area but also from land transfer records between 1696 and 1707 that indicate that some residents had house and garden lots between the plaza and the Rio Chiquito at least in the late prerevolt years and one possibly as early as 1628.[53] Although this plaza seems large for a population of less than fifty vecino families, it served the community for many space-requiring needs, including the foraging and grazing of domestic animals attached to the casas reales, grain threshing and milling, reception of supply caravans from Mexico City, fiestas, religious processions, and military reviews. Ordinance 122 called for a separate site for such "filth producing" activities as slaughtering and tanning, and they might well have been carried out elsewhere.[54] In addition, there was probably the anticipation that, as the capital city, Santa Fe would grow to need a large main plaza.

The government buildings located on the plaza included a residence for the governor. The Palace of the Governors from the beginning was most likely located on the north side of the plaza in the general area of where it is today and where it is shown on the 1766 Urrutia map. Besides the argument for continuity, the main evidence for this location is excavation work that uncovered seventeenth-century foundations and floors in an area now occupied by the west end of the current palace building.[55] These structures date from the mid-seventeenth century, but they lie over trash dated to 1610–40, making it likely that the original 1610 palace was built somewhere on this site on the north side of the plaza at its west end. A more recent excavation unearthed a 1640–80 foundation adjacent to the north wall of the present palace offices, giving further support to the supposition that this is where the seventeenth-century palace was located.[56] It can be assumed that the Palace of the Governors initially contained quarters for the governor and his family, kitchens, storerooms, and a place to conduct official business, but the casas reales also consisted of other buildings including housing for the families that served Governor Peralta and his successors, stables and corrals for horses and other livestock, and various workshops, as well as an arsenal and a meeting place for the town council. The lack of any evidence as to where these other structures were originally located has led to differing theories. A long-held view states that they were arranged around a large compound stretching north and west of the palace—west to Grant Avenue and north to Federal Place.[57] But excavation in this area has not yielded evidence of seventeenth-century structures.[58] Although the exact dimensions of the cienega in the seventeenth century cannot be known precisely, recent work identifying its extent suggests that the construction of buildings in a large part of this area would have been limited.[59] A current view holds that the casas reales were located around the plaza.[60] Peralta's instructions make clear that it was to have a space on which to erect buildings for royal and other public purposes that a square or plaza should be set aside, a directive based on ordinance 126, which also forbade the assignment of lots on the plaza to individuals.[61] Given the location of the Palace of the Governors on the north side of the plaza, it is likely that the other structures that made up the casas reales would also be located nearby on the plaza, but precisely where on the plaza is so far unknown. However, recent test excavations in back of buildings on the west side of the plaza indicate the presence of seventeenth-century structures that might possibly include the *casa de cabildo*, the meeting place of the town council.[62]

What defenses Santa Fe had in the early years after its founding are not known but it is possible there were none of a formal nature. Although the viceroy in 1608 mentioned a presidio in New Mexico, and it has been suggested that the plaza established by Martínez de Montoya was a military camp, Santa Fe lacked an official presidio until 1693 or 1694.[63] It is possible that the viceroy was simply referring to a corps of soldier-colonists rather than to an officially constituted body that manned a fortified site. Even later, in 1639, the cabildo was begging the viceroy to establish an "army base" in the villa to deal with the "hostile heathen."[64] But in the earlier years the Spaniards probably did not feel threatened. They had not fortified their previous capital, San Gabriel, because they did not perceive the Pueblo people to be a menace, and the Navajo-Apache were not yet a significant threat, although they did attack San Gabriel in 1606 or 1607.[65] Furthermore, as noted, the topographical situation of the Santa Fe River valley afforded some protection, as did the Barrio de Analco located south of the river.[66] For these reasons the Spaniards felt free to build their houses in a scattered pattern away from the urban core rather than heed the 1573 ordinances that required that the houses of a town be arranged so as to serve as a "defense and barrier."[67] Whatever defensive arrangements there were probably centered on the casas reales and not on the villa as a whole. The 1573 ordinances stipulate that a palisade or ditch be constructed around the plaza as soon as possible, but it is not known if either was actually constructed.[68] To some extent the core area was protected by its location between the cienega and the Santa Fe River. In the absence of an official presidio, the casas reales might have served that function, the buildings placed in a defensive arrangement around the plaza, but there is insufficient evidence to know just what form they took initially.[69]

There is better evidence to support the location of the main church. According to the royal ordinances the church should not be located on the plaza, nor should it be surrounded by other buildings but rather should be so sited that it could be seen "from all sides."[70] Statements made by Governor Otermín during the 1680 siege of Santa Fe suggest that the church and convent were located below the hills on the east side of the villa where fighting took place.[71] The location of the church on the 1766 Urrutia map fits this description, and subsequent churches, including the present cathedral, have been built in this area; therefore, it is not unlikely that the earliest church set the precedent for locating the main church near but not on the east side of the plaza.[72] This original church with its convent is first mentioned in 1613 in connection with a conflict between Governor Pedro de Peralta and custodian Fray Isidro Ordóñez. On July 7, the governor was excommunicated and his chair in the church thrown into the street; however, he ordered it retrieved and placed inside the church door near the baptismal font, "and there among the Indians he sat down," an indication that the latter did not yet have a church of their own in their Barrio de Analco.[73] The *parroquia* was probably a simple structure consisting of only a single nave and likely not substantially built.[74] The viceroy's letter of 1621 mentioned an existing church in need of repairs.[75] There is some indication that this early church or the one built in the 1620s was fronted by a courtyard or plaza of its own facing the principal plaza, which would have thus enhanced the church's visibility and provided space for religious activities.[76]

Santa Fe in its earliest years was a rudimentary place that came to be considered unsatisfactory by its governor and possibly by many of its residents. This dissatisfaction is reflected in a letter Governor Juan de Eulate received in 1621 from the viceroy in Mexico City which, in part, refers to a previous request by the governor and cabildo to move the villa to a better defensive site "on a squared location with four Towers" and to erect a church and government buildings.[77] The viceroy denied the request to move the villa but specified substantial amounts of tools and materials that he was sending to make the needed building repairs.[78] Although the preferred site for the move is not mentioned, it could have been to higher ground south of the Santa Fe River. Governor Vargas, after wresting control of the casas reales from the occupying Puebloans, wrote to the viceroy in January 1693 suggesting such a move, citing the heavy frosts, fogs, and noxious vapors related to the swamp on the eastern margin of the urban core as reasons to relocate away from this "miserable" place.[79] Seemingly, the cienega was no longer the attractive feature that it appeared to be when Santa Fe was initially settled. In 1620, the viceroy, in a letter to the king, mentioned that Santa Fe had fifty residents, showing no apparent growth from the forty-eight soldiers and residents reported by the cabildo in 1617.[80] By the late 1620s the population of Santa Fe was reported by the custodian and commissary Fray Alonso de Benavides to be about 1,000, of which 250 were Spaniards, including 50 men who could muster arms, most of whom were married, while the remainder of the population was made up of native people and mestizos.[81] The population of the villa continued to be reported as about fifty vecinos, apparently, as noted in chapter 8, a standard figure that came to be repeated. Encomenderos, who numbered thirty-five, were required to maintain a residence in the villa, and other settlers may have found it convenient to do so as well—some family members would have maintained the residence while they mainly lived on their rural properties located elsewhere in the colony. Of the Spanish settlers who lived in Santa Fe in the period 1610–32, forty-two have been identified (appendix table L).

With the governor and leading residents concerned about the deteriorated state of the capital's buildings and the promise of help from the viceroy, Santa Fe apparently underwent a certain amount of urban renewal beginning in the 1620s. It was probably at this time that buildings of adobe brick construction replaced whatever earlier jacal or wattle and daub structures remained. The church was one structure in need of reconstruction. According to Fray Alonso de Peinado, who likely directed construction of the villa's first church in 1610, foundations were laid as early as 1622 for a new church and convent "that will be the best in this land."[82] This construction might have been set in motion by his interest in building churches and by the pending election of Fray Alonso de Benavides to the custodianship of the New Mexico missions, which took place the following year, although he did not arrive in Santa Fe until January 1626.[83] It appears that by then the church had been completed or nearly so. Upon his arrival he was accommodated in one of the cells of its convent and the following day was installed in the church with considerable pomp, attended by all the local dignitaries including the governor, who was described as seated at the transept of the church.[84] That this church was built with a transept would distinguish it from the parroquia built in 1610.[85] Fray Alonso claimed that during his tenure he built a church and convent for Santa Fe that "would shine in whatsoever place."[86] Was Fray Alonso claiming credit for building the new parroquia or was he referring to the San Miguel chapel that is first mentioned in 1628?[87] The lack of clarity on this point in the statements he makes in his memorials of 1630 and 1634 has given rise to differing opinions among scholars about which church he built. But the church with a transept in which Fray Alonso was installed does not accord with his complaint about a church that was a "poor hut" and in a state of collapse.[88] That he brought with him large quantities of building materials and tools as well as church furnishings, including an altar screen (retablo) and an image of the Virgin (La Conquistadora), indicates that he intended to build a church.[89] And that he did so is seen in his statement that "they, their wives and children personally aided me considerably by carrying the materials and helping to build the walls with their own hands."[90] It would seem that it was the church of the inhabitants of the Barrio de Analco that Fray Alonso referred to as a "poor hut" and that they helped him build a new one. When the new governor arrived in 1631, his reception was held in the "Iglesia de San Miguel," not only an indication that at the time the parroquia might not have been available but also that the San Miguel chapel had been rebuilt.[91] This church or chapel of San Miguel was commonly referred to as a hermitage, indicating its status as under the administration of the parroquia as well as its location some distance away from the plaza of the villa.[92] In 1693, Governor Vargas remarked that the small church or hermitage named for archangel St. Michael had served as parish church for Indians from Mexico City who lived in the villa of Santa Fe.[93] San Miguel was located south of the Santa Fe River in the Barrio de Analco, where it still stands at the present intersection of Old Santa Fe Trail and East De Vargas Street (see maps 4, p. 208 and map 5, p. 209).[94] The location of the new parroquia is not mentioned, but its foundations were still visible after it had been destroyed during the 1680 revolt and its successor was built nearby, that is, east of the plaza.[95]

The 1573 ordinances called for a hospital that would serve the poor and those sick with noncontagious diseases to be located near the church and its cloister and another for those with contagious diseases to be located in a place "where no harmful wind passing through it may cause harm to the rest of the town."[96] In Santa Fe, it was the San Miguel hermitage that served the poor and sick. In addition to its chapel, it had attached friars' cells, part of which served as an infirmary that was referred to as *el hospital* or *la enfermería*, where a friar dispensed care to the population of the villa.[97] When the hospital was established is unknown, but possibly it was at the time Fray Alonso had San Miguel rebuilt. It was definitely in existence in the late 1630s when, as a result of Governor de Rosas's dispute with the church, San Miguel, including the infirmary, was partly destroyed and was not rebuilt for another decade.[98] In addition to the infirmary in the San Miguel convent, perhaps there was a hut somewhere on the outskirts of the villa that housed those with contagious diseases.

In his letter, the viceroy also mentioned that the casas reales were in disrepair, and they were most likely enlarged and/or rebuilt more substantially as part of the urban renewal initiated in the 1620s. Archaeological investigations indicate that the palace has been rebuilt or remodeled many times, making it difficult to discern what it was like at that time, as is the case with the casas reales in general. Perhaps it was in the 1620s that separate structures, called for by the 1573 ordinances, were built to serve as the arsenal and the casa de cabildo, which in this instance also included a jail.[99] It is possible that the casas reales extended east from the palace beyond present Washington Avenue, perhaps as far as Sena Plaza (see map 5, p. 209), but the lack of archaeological evidence of their location (except for the palace) makes it nearly impossible to know the location and layout of the casas reales of prerevolt Santa Fe.[100] A document from the mid-1660s mentioned that running along the *plaza principal* were the *casas reales de palacio*, casa de cabildo, convento, parroquia, and at least one house owned by encomendero Francisco Gómez Robledo located at one of the corners of the plaza.[101] Just where on the plaza the casa de cabildo was sited or on which corner the house was located are not mentioned, but this statement does indicate that they were on the plaza. Knowledge of the location of the palace is more secure but information about its configuration in the 1620s is lacking. Fortunately, major restoration of the palace initiated by Governor Bernardo López de Mendizábal between July 1659 and October 1661 gives an idea of how it evolved.[102]

Although the population of Santa Fe might have reached its nadir during the administration of Governor López de Mendizábal (as discussed in chapter 8), he saw fit to enlarge and refurbish the palace. By the mid-1660s it consisted of some eighteen rooms built around an interior patio that was apparently reached through a wide corridor (*el corridor grande del patio*), its doors facing the main plaza.[103] It was probably a two-story structure, its roof crowned with parapets (*pretilez*).[104] During 1661 the collapsed tower (*torreon*) was rebuilt, indicating that it was part of the palace compound and possibly one of at least two that were positioned at the southeast and southwest corners of the compound. Perhaps the adobe brick floor laid in a diagonal pattern that was excavated in an area at the west end of the current Palace of the Governors dates from this period. Rooms in the palace included one for reception (*sala de recibimiento*), next to which on its east side was an apartment (*aposento*) for the governor and his wife that consisted of a sleeping room and, on the street side, a drawing room (*sala de estrado*).[105] On the interior side was a bedroom (*recamara*) for the women servants. There was also possibly a separate room for bathing. The governor had an office (*cuarto al escritorio*), and there was another for his secretary. The closet (*alacena*) for the archive might have been part of these offices. The governor's wife had her own drawing room as well as a dressing room. The governor had a room built to serve as a chapel ("un aposento que havia echo para capilla"). There was a dining room ("sala donde estava la Mesa") and a kitchen (*cuarto de cocina*) as well as a kitchen garden (*huerta*). A series of four small rooms ("cuarto . . . que tiene Cuatro piesas de biviendo") that ran alongside this garden was also added by the governor. A room in the palace was set aside as a jail, in addition to the one in the casa de cabildo. A storehouse (*almacén*) is mentioned and also a store maintained by the governor for the sale of chocolate and other luxury items. There was a harness room, and nearby was likely a place for the coach of the governor's wife.[106] Neither stables nor corrals are mentioned, but perhaps they were located north of the palace buildings along with the vegetable gardens and orchard that supplied the occupants of the palace.[107] Barracks, various workshops, such as forges, and storage structures as well as the casa de cabildo were probably located on the plaza. Because previous governors might have made additions or repairs to the palace, it is difficult to know how the *palacio* of the 1620s would have compared to the palace after it was refurbished by López de Mendizábal. Possibly it was not quite as large, but the main unknown is when the components of the palace came to be built around an interior patio. Perhaps Governor Eulate and the cabildo had such a plan in mind when, in 1620, they requested of the viceroy a squared defensive site with four towers.[108]

The viceroy's 1621 letter indicates that there was by then increased concern to provide for the defense of the villa, especially defense of the casas reales or, more particularly, the palace. Although the viceroy refused the request to move the villa to a better defensive site, there is documentary evidence that fortifications were built, including at least two of the four towers requested. The existence of two towers is supported by the statement of two Spanish refugees from Taos who, escaping past Santa Fe during the 1680 siege, observed that "the dwelling of the governor was on fire in two places and that only two small towers were left on it"—a statement that might indicate the towers were part of the palace compound.[109] Governor Otermín in a letter to the viceroy dated April 5, 1682, stated, referring back to the era of Governor Phelipe Sotelo (1625–29), that Sotelo built only two towers in which to store gunpowder to ensure the defense of the villa ("solo hico dos torreones o Cubos para segurar la polvera para la defensa de la Villa").[110] At the time, the complaint of the clergy that Governor Sotelo's fortifications endangered the church and convent indicates that at least one of the towers was being built on the east side of the casas reales/palace, suggesting that the palace extended eastward to the vicinity of church property.[111] This statement could also imply that the towers were part of a palace compound, which would be in accord with the rebuilding of a tower undertaken by Governor López de Mendizábal early in the 1660s as part of his restoration of the palace. But Governor Otermín's 1680 report that he had to "sally forth into the plaza of the casas reales" in order to prevent the rebels from setting fire to the doors of the fortified tower that housed "nuestra Señora de las casas reales" could indicate either that the towers were part of the palace compound or that they were built at the corners of the plaza where the other government buildings were possibly linked by walls to form a defensive barrier around the plaza.[112] Not knowing whether "casas reales" referred to the palace only, to the other government buildings, or to both makes it difficult to determine the configuration of the villa's urban core.

According to Governor Otermín, the "casas reales had been in ruins and falling down, with many gates open and without even doors at the principal entrance." Prior to the outbreak of the revolt, he had them repaired so that "within said casas reales something more than a thousand persons, five thousand head of sheep and goats, four hundred horses and mules, and three hundred head of beef cattle" could be gathered without crowding.[113] The question remains whether the governor meant by "casas reales" the principal plaza surrounded by linked government buildings or the palace compound. Was the principal entrance the one to the plaza or to the palace compound? Otermín's description of the principal entrance whose doors had to be replaced and where he placed his two small cannon could fit either the plaza or the palace compound. He further stated that with the siege of Santa Fe underway, "I endeavored to fortify myself in the casas reales and to make a defense without leaving their walls."[114] He could have been referring to walls that linked the buildings that made up the casas reales surrounding the plaza or he could have been referring to the walls of the palace compound. Unfortunately, no evidence of walls surrounding either has been found by archaeologists. The plaza would certainly have been large enough to enclose the people and livestock that Governor Otermín mentioned, but it is questionable if the patio of the palace compound would have been unless it had, by this time, been enlarged or a second, larger, patio had been created—in which case the governor might have been referring to the more secure space in the palace compound.

Much of this speculation about whether the defenses of the villa centered on the palace compound or included the plaza shows that the matter cannot be resolved on the basis of a few statements made by the governor at the time of the revolt or the meager archaeological evidence presently available. That the term "casas reales" at times seems to refer to the palace and at other times to the plaza with its government buildings adds to the difficulty of determining the layout of the urban core and its defenses. One interpretation would place the palace compound, with a single entrance and towers at least at two of its corners, on the north side of the plaza with the other buildings of the casas reales facing inward around the remaining perimeter of the plaza and linked by walls with gates where necessary, thus forming another line of defense. When Governor Vargas arrived at Santa Fe in 1692 on his initial reconnaissance of the colony and again the following year to reclaim it, he found at the site of the villa a fortified pueblo with four towers in place of the palace compound and fields (milpas) of the occupying Puebloans planted up to within a harquebus shot of their fortress. Other buildings of the Spaniards, including the parroquia, had been razed to their foundations.[115] Although the Spaniards' plaza area and palace compound had been greatly modified, the fortified pueblo had some characteristics that might suggest parallels with the Spaniards' palace. The fortress's massive walls or ramparts that were topped by parapets were likely more impressive than those of the palace compound, but they both had a single gate, and on the inside there was a patio—two in the case of the pueblo and possibly two as well in the case of the palace. The Puebloans used the same water supply for their fortress as the Spaniards had used for their palace, each in turn cutting off this supply to defeat the other in 1680 and in 1692.[116] More importantly, the towers of the Puebloan fortress, two on the north face and two on the south, would suggest that the towers mentioned in 1680 were part of the palace compound rather than located at the corners of the plaza. Needless to say, the above reconstruction of the villa's defenses rests on fragmentary information that could be interpreted in different ways.

It is probable that Governor Peralta attempted to carry out the requirements of the 1573 royal ordinances with regard to a street pattern for Santa Fe when he formally laid out the plaza, and a further attempt at conformity was probably made during the urban renewal of the 1620s. Ordinance 114 stipulates that two streets should extend from each corner of the plaza and that four main streets should enter it at the middle of each side.[117] A street plan that followed the first part of the ordinance undoubtedly took shape, and its persistence can be seen in the 1766 Urrutia map (see map 4, p. 208). It shows one street (present Palace Avenue) on the north side of the plaza and a second street, Camino Real (present San Francisco Street), on the south side. The original street plan around the plaza was largely obliterated when Puebloans took over Santa Fe between 1680 and 1693 and planted their milpas on part of the plaza and the surrounding area. Post-reconquest landowners extended their plantings into the former streets and also blocked them with their houses. To make the streets passable and restore them to their original dimensions, the governor in 1715 ordered a survey and appointed a group of elderly men who had lived in the villa all of their lives to carry it out.[118] From their report it can be discerned that there was a street on the east side of the plaza that extended north of the northeast corner of the plaza, through the cienega and probably on to the road to Tesuque Pueblo. Southward the street ran past the parroquia that was being rebuilt at the time, through the intersection with San Francisco Street at the southeast corner of the plaza and across the Santa Fe River to the San Miguel church. The survey crew then went west along San Francisco Street, where they found "an alley which was there in former times going out to the river on the south side of the curve," very probably present Shelby Street.[119] They continued along San Francisco Street to the southwest corner of the plaza to a former street that had been very wide and "capable of going north to the hills," possibly present Lincoln Avenue that borders the west side of the present plaza and possibly did so in the prerevolt period.[120] The team then noted that beyond the plaza and the gunpowder tower, there had been only a footpath along the (western) wall of the palace and its garden.[121] It would seem that in prerevolt times the wide street on the west side of the plaza dwindled to a footpath beyond its northwest corner, where the house of Pedro Luján was located.

Ordinance 114 also calls for streets that enter the plaza at its midpoints, but evidence for such streets, aside from present Shelby Street, is lacking. An attempt to show that this requirement was carried out proposes that San Francisco Street entered the plaza at the midpoint of its west side rather than at its southwest corner and, accordingly, that the plaza must have extended south to just above present Water Street (then the Rio Chiquito).[122] Such a plaza would approximate the dimensions of a plaza of maximum size as set forth in ordinance 112, but it would be at odds with the topographic features of the plaza. It is doubtful that a precursor of present Washington Avenue entered the midpoint of the plaza's north side because of the likelihood that the casas reales/palacio extended eastward beyond it and because the northern exit from the plaza was more likely in the area of the present Sena Plaza (see map 5, p. 209).[123] On the east side of the plaza, church lands and the cienega could have precluded a midpoint street. Thus, it is likely that there were at least streets on the four sides of the plaza, as was common in Spanish colonial towns, but in the absence of supporting documentary or archaeological data, any reconstruction of the prerevolt street pattern beyond the plaza must remain speculative. Whether streets located away from the plaza conformed to the grid pattern typical of Spanish colonial towns seems unlikely.[124] Given the scattered location of residents' properties, the street pattern might have consisted of pathways along these property lines, as suggested by the Urrutia map and the 1715 survey. As late as 1776 Fray Francisco Atanasio Domínguez stated that Santa Fe had only one quasi street, the one that ran north-south in front of the church plaza.[125]

The main roads leading in and out of Santa Fe shown on the Urrutia map were most likely the same ones in use during the prerevolt period. The road north, the Camino de la Cañada, took a northwesterly direction, probably approximating the route of present Old Taos Highway (see map 4, p. 208 and map 5, p. 209). The Camino de Tesuque (not shown on the maps) was mentioned in a 1693 land claim as leading from a road that ran between two prerevolt properties located north and west of the palace compound; the one closest to the palace was located near a "pueblo quemado" (possibly LA 1051, which is known by that name), the site being located beneath the present Civic Center.[126] This road is likely the extension of the prerevolt footpath that ran along the west side of the palace compound that was noted by the 1715 survey team.[127] It would appear that the Camino de Tesuque followed two routes to reach Tesuque Pueblo from the villa.[128] From the northwest side of the plaza (as described above), it followed the route of Old Taos Highway, and from its northeast side it continued north along the route of present Bishop's Lodge Road (see map 5, p. 209). The Urrutia map also shows a number of routes leading south from the villa. One of these, Camino del Alamo, led southwest to the estancia of El Alamo by way of the canyon of the Santa Fe River or via the Camino de los Carros (a cutoff from Agua Fria to Alamo) and on to the missionary headquarters at Kewa (Santo Domingo) Pueblo and beyond. The Camino del Alamo and the Camino de los Carros were also known as the Camino Real (see map 6, p. 210).[129] The Camino Real, following the route of present Agua Fria Street, entered the plaza at present San Francisco Street, which in 1704 was known as La Calle Real (see map 5, p. 209).[130] Although no entrance is shown on the south side of the plaza, one has been proposed at present Shelby Street/Old Santa Fe Trail, where the wagon trains coming north could enter the plaza after detouring east from

Kewa Pueblo along Galisteo Creek to avoid La Bajada escarpment.[131] Besides this road, known as Camino de Galisteo, another road, Camino de Pecos, led from the southeast corner of the plaza through the Barrio de Analco to Pecos Pueblo farther east.

Although the residential layout of Santa Fe was generally dispersed, the prestige associated with location near the plaza influenced prominent citizens to establish their houses and gardens there. A number of such properties have become known mainly through research in the land records of the early eighteenth century that refer to prerevolt landholdings. One of the two Santa Fe residences owned in 1659 by New Mexico's most prominent vecino-encomendero, Francisco Gómez Robledo, was located on a corner of the plaza—"que cae en la esquina de la plasa Rl desta villa."[132] The house of Francisco, whose father was a founder of the villa, appears to have been located on the northeast corner of the plaza according to information cited in a 1703 land claim made by Antonia González Bas, a member of the neighboring González Bernal/Bas family (see map 4, p. 208).[133] The house consisted of three rooms (aposentos) in addition to a living room (sala) and a patio and garden (huerta).[134] The González Bernal lands, which had belonged to family founders Sebastián González and his wife Isabel Bernal, were bounded on the north by the cienega, on the south by the acequia, which ran in front of the "villa" (that is, Palace of the Governors on present Palace Avenue), the house of Francisco Gómez on the west, and that of Juan de Moraga on the east.[135] According to this claim, the land had belonged to Isabel, whose father, Juan Griego I, was a founder of the villa and owner of other land nearby "to the rear of the casas reales," between the cienega and the villa (palace) (see map 5, p. 209).[136]

By the 1660s a parcel of Griego land belonged to Diego López del Castillo, who possibly acquired it when he married María Griego, granddaughter of Juan Griego I and one of the 1703 Griego claimants. Her sister Juana Bernal married Diego de Moraga, and this might have been the basis of the landholding of their son Juan de Moraga that was located to the east of the land claimed by Antonia González Bas.[137] Another sister, Catalina, whose husband was Diego de Trujillo, was also a claimant. Alonso del Río was mentioned in the 1703 land claim as a resident of this neighborhood, possibly having inherited property originally acquired by Alonso del Río, who came to New Mexico with Oñate in 1598. A 1713 land claim mentioned the house and orchard that had belonged to Juan del Río, a probable relative of Alonso, who was married to Ana de Moraga.[138] His land was bounded by the cienega, the intake of the *acequia madre* (that which ran in front of the palace), the lands of the convento, and the hills and land of Diego Durán. The latter's lands were formerly part of the property of Juan de Moraga that was described as near the church and "from the dam as far as the cienega."[139] Diego returned to New Mexico in 1693 as an adult, and there is a question whether his father, Salvador, owned land in this part of the villa prior to the revolt. They were likely members of the Durán family founded by Juan Durán (a.k.a. de la Cruz), who came to New Mexico in 1598.[140]

Family connections suggest that most of the properties mentioned in the land claims of 1703 and 1713 had their origins in the grants made by Governor Peralta in 1610 or, in the cases of Francisco Gómez and Juan Griego I, possibly in grants made a few years earlier. The ready availability of water from springs in the cienega and attendant fodder for livestock probably made this part of the villa highly desirable to the vecinos of Santa Fe at that time it was founded. Francisco Xavier, a high-ranking vecino of the villa during the latter decades of the prerevolt era, also seems to have been a resident of the northeast part of the villa. At the time of the revolt, his house, as well as that of Francisco Gómez Robledo, were mentioned as being in the area where the Spaniards were battling the Puebloans who were ensconced in the heights above the villa (i.e., Fort Marcy Hill; see map 5, p. 209).[141] Xavier came to New Mexico in 1658 with Governor López de Mendizábal and at the time of the revolt was maese de campo and secretary of government and war.[142]

There were undoubtedly other residents of the villa who also lived in the area north and east of the plaza before the 1680 revolt, but even less is known about who lived elsewhere in the plaza area. Documentation is available, however, that suggests there were residents living south of the plaza in the prerevolt years. Post-reconquest land claims records give the names of residents who lived between the plaza and the Rio Chiquito and south to the Santa Fe River. The availability of water also made this area attractive. Land claims dated 1696 give evidence that a number of important early families lived in this area.[143] In that year, Isabel Jorge de Vera requested title to land with a house and garden that formerly belonged to her grandfather, Antonio Baca, who was the son of original colonist Cristóbal Baca, making it possible that the landholding dated back to the grants Governor Peralta made in 1610.[144] The land Isabel was requesting apparently stretched from the plaza south across the Rio Chiquito to the Santa Fe River (see map 5, p. 209), bordering the property of Lorenzo Madrid to the east and that of

Juana Domínguez to the west. It was noted in a 1707 document that Isabel split this property into two parts north and south of the Rio Chiquito.[145] Bordering lands of Lorenzo Madrid and the Baca family and close to the Rio Chiquito was the holding of Antonio de Albizu, who most likely acquired it when he married Gregoria Baca, daughter of Antonio Baca, or when Antonio was executed in 1643 for his part in the murder of Governor Luis de Rosas.[146] Antonio Baca's neighbor to the east, Lorenzo Madrid, could have acquired his land through marriage to Antonia Ortiz (Baca), who was possibly related to Ana Ortiz, wife of Cristóbal Baca. Lorenzo, who was the younger son of Francisco de Madrid I (who came to New Mexico in 1603), inherited the family encomienda and returned to New Mexico with Governor Vargas in 1693 to reoccupy family land.[147]

In 1696, Ana de Archuleta was requesting land that was bounded by that of Lorenzo Madrid, probably on the north, and by "the road north of the [Santa Fe] river between some plum trees."[148] She was the granddaughter of Asencio de Archuleta, who came to New Mexico in 1598 and probably was granted land in the villa by Governor Peralta in 1610. His son and heir, Juan, was beheaded in 1643 for his part in the murder of Governor Rosas, and the family's land in Santa Fe as well as its encomienda "de los tributes de Jémes" were inherited by Asencio's daughter Gregoria.[149] It is this land that belonged to her aunt Gregoria that Ana was requesting. Gregoria's relationships with the Pérez de Bustillo family suggest that this family also owned land in the area, although it is not so stated in the document. Gregoria's mother was Ana Pérez de Bustillo, who was the wife of Asencio de Archuleta and daughter of original colonist Juan Pérez de Bustillo; Gregoria's husband was Diego de Santa Cruz, possibly the adopted son of Juan Pérez.[150] It should also be noted that Juan Pérez's son Simón married Juana Baca, daughter of Cristóbal Baca, and Cristóbal's son Antonio was married to Yumar, daughter of Juan Pérez.[151] When Ana de Archuleta made her request in 1696, she was the widow of Luis Durán, member of the Juan Durán (a.k.a. Juan de la Cruz, a 1598 colonist) family, and it is likely that he was a landowner in this area south of the plaza as a result of this marriage.[152] To the west of the Baca property and south of the plaza was the property of Juana Domínguez, daughter of Tomé Domínguez de Mendoza and wife of Domingo Luján whose forbearer, Juan Luján, came to New Mexico in 1600.[153] Her family had extensive prerevolt landholdings in the Rio Abajo, and perhaps it was Juana who maintained their Santa Fe residence. In 1680 she and her children were captured and held in the pueblos until rescued by her brother José

Domínguez in 1692.[154] Her husband, Domingo, returned in 1693 but was killed that year in an accident.

"Looking toward the plaza and the [gunpowder] tower of the palace" was the house of Pedro Luján at the northwest corner of the plaza, according to the 1715 survey team who said there was only a footpath along the west wall of the palace and its garden, never a street.[155] Pedro, who was a minor in 1680, returned to New Mexico with his wife in 1693. He was the son of Juan Luis Luján, who was a native of Santa Fe and related to the Ruiz Cáceres family whose founder, Juan, came to New Mexico in 1600.[156] Perhaps Pedro reclaimed land that had belonged to his family before 1680. A vecino who owned land north and west of the plaza was Juan González Lobón. His house was described as near a "pueblo quemado" that could have been the ruin of a prehistoric pueblo known by that name that is located beneath Santa Fe's present Civic Center (see map 5, p. 209).[157] The property of Juan's neighbor to the west, Juan Lucero de Godoy, was described as being on the outskirts of Santa Fe—only two harquebus shots away. Juan González Lobón's father, Domingo González, who was in New Mexico as early as 1608 and who married the daughter of pioneer colonist Juan de Vitoria Carvajal, undoubtedly received one of the land grants awarded by Governor Peralta in 1610.[158] Domingo's adult children were all living in Santa Fe in 1660, but it is not known if any family members were still living there in 1680.[159]

In 1693 Sargento Mayor Juan Lucero de Godoy told Governor Vargas that Santa Fe had seventy vecinos before the revolt, making it obvious that those mentioned here are only a small sample of the total, but they are the only ones for whom there is information about where in the villa they lived.[160] One prominent vecino-encomendero not mentioned is Hernán Martín Serrano II, whose father came to New Mexico in 1598.[161] Hernán operated an obraje in the villa in 1659 which most probably produced textiles for export.[162] This workshop, which used native labor, was probably located on his property, but where that was is unknown. Other vecinos very likely engaged in commercial enterprises from their places of residence that required warehouses (bodegas), such as the one owned in 1662 by Ana Robledo, wife of powerful encomendero Francisco Gómez.[163]

The villa had an official armorer, and the holders of this position might have also maintained a forge on their premises. Gaspar Pérez, who came to New Mexico in 1619 and died in 1646, was official armorer during that period.[164] Manuel Jorge was appointed official armorer in 1655 to succeed

Gaspar Pérez, and he might have been followed by Joseph Jurado, who was mentioned in 1662 as "armerero real de las provincias del Nuevo México" and who probably resided in Santa Fe.[165] Another blacksmith (*herrero*) who also lived in Santa Fe in the 1660s was Juan de Moraga, a property owner in the northeast part of the villa, whose father, Diego, was also a blacksmith who had a house near a spring in the cienega as early as 1628.[166] Matías Morán was a *carretero* and *carpintero* in Santa Fe who was involved in making ten carretas and three *carros* for Governor López de Mendizábal in the late 1650s and early 1660s.[167] Whether Matías was related to Juan Morán, who came with Oñate in 1598, or to Miguel Morán, who returned to New Mexico and was a member of the 1715 survey team, is unknown.[168]

Other businesses were undoubtedly conducted in the villa, such as that of silversmith Rodrigo Lorenzo, who lived on San Francisco Street in 1639.[169] Many craftsmen were Mexican Indians who lived in the Barrio de Analco across the river. One of the most prominent in midcentury was Juan Chamiso, a master mason (*albañil maestro*) who played a major role in the restoration of the palace ordered by Governor López Mendizábal.[170] In 1680 he, along with seven other Mexican Indians, was listed on Governor Otermín's muster of refugees in which he declared twenty dependents, including servants.[171] Another Mexican Indian, Francisco "Pancho" Balón, was noted as a blacksmith and deceased in 1626.[172] No one with his surname was among the refugees.[173] This very limited information gives only a partial view of the range of economic activities in which the residents of Santa Fe engaged and their location. Undoubtedly they were more numerous and varied despite the fact that the community remained small and depended on goods brought in on the triennial supply train.

Although the Santa Fe site possibly had a few settlers as early as 1605, there is now evidence that there was some settlement there at least by 1608, prior to its official founding as a villa and capital of New Mexico in 1610. During the seven decades between 1610 and 1680 it remained a small remote outpost of Spanish authority on New Spain's northern frontier—an administrative center for the colony of New Mexico that was chiefly maintained for geopolitical reasons and to support the missionary effort to Christianize the Puebloan peoples—a population that declined by some 75 percent during that period.[174] Because New Mexico lacked a viable mining economy and exported only small amounts of commodities such as hides, salt, piñon, cotton and wool textiles, and slaves to the mining districts farther south in New Spain (much of this trade monopolized by its governors and by the clergy), the villa did not have a significant commercial function that could serve as a basis for growth. The number of Spanish families increased only slightly from about fifty families after the 1601 desertion to some seventy when they were forced to leave in 1680.[175] Although the villa undoubtedly evolved from its rudimentary beginnings, only a sketchy and conjectural picture of what Santa Fe looked like in the prerevolt period can be gleaned from the limited documentary and archaeological data available.

CHAPTER ELEVEN

The Santa Fe River Valley

✣ MANY OF SANTA FE'S ORIGINAL SETTLERS AS WELL AS THOSE WHO CAME later sought land grants in the valley downstream from the villa (see map 6, p. 210). This area was attractive not only for its proximity to the capital but for the presence of many springs such as those in the Agua Fria and La Cienega sections of the valley. These springs were especially important because they contributed to the flow of the Santa Fe River, which, however, was not always adequate for irrigating fields, as noted by a colonist returning in 1693 who had lived in Santa Fe for fifty years before the revolt of 1680.[1] Ecclesiastic officials visiting in the eighteenth century also observed that the river could not provide water sufficient for irrigation except in very rainy years and that "often the river dried up entirely in the months before the harvest."[2] It was generally in a stretch between the Agua Fria and La Cienega areas, as well as below La Bajada, that the river seasonally ceased to flow above ground, except during years of heavy rainfall.[3] Thus, there were limits to the carrying capacity of the valley, and despite its location within easy reach of the capital, many colonists located their farming and ranching operations elsewhere in the province.

Documentary and archaeological records provide information about a number of seventeenth-century Spanish habitation sites in a zone along the Santa Fe River and its tributaries, stretching some fifteen miles below the villa to its confluence with Cienega Creek. At the time Santa Fe was officially declared the capital, all colonists were officially granted house and garden lots in the villa, but larger land grants were most probably located elsewhere, including some in the valley downriver from the villa. The owners of nineteen properties are specifically mentioned in the scattered documentary records, and archaeologists have identified twelve possible prerevolt Spanish habitation sites, but information about the owners is insufficiently precise to match any of them to the sites, with the possible exception of Roque de Madrid. Although this zone has been the subject of more historical and archaeological work than any other comparable area in New Mexico, only a partial picture of Spanish settlement has emerged because both historic documents and archaeological surveys are incomplete and because many sites have been destroyed as the area has become increasingly urbanized over recent decades. Particularly unfortunate was the destruction of land grant records following the 1680 Pueblo revolt.

On the outskirts of Santa Fe, "two harquebus shots away," was the "tract of residence and farm lands" of Juan Lucero de Godoy that he was reclaiming in 1693.[4] According to Juan, his lands and house were located opposite the thicket (monte) called Cuma, which was also described as two musket shots away from the villa when Governor Vargas's force was camped there prior to entering Santa Fe in December 1693.[5] Juan's farm lands stretched from the old road to Tesuque Pueblo on the east in the vicinity of a "pueblo quemado" to the property of his neighbor Juan González Lobón, along a dry arroyo on the north. On the west, they bordered the property of Luis Maese, where there was another "pueblo quemado."[6] To the south, his land reached to the Rio Grande. Juan's father, Pedro Lucero, who was in New Mexico by 1616, might have been the original grantee of this tract of land, and Juan, who was alcalde mayor of Santa Fe in 1680, continued to hold this property until he was forced to flee the revolt with his family.[7] His neighbor Luis Maese, who was possibly related to Juan Maese, who was in New Mexico in 1632, was also petitioning in 1693 for revalidation of his claim to land he held before the revolt, having passed muster with his family in 1681.[8] His neighbor to the west was Gerónimo Morán, who was mentioned as living in Santa Fe in 1642 and 1662 and who might have been related to Juan Morán, who came with Oñate in 1598; however, there is no further information about Gerónimo.[9] Nor is there any information about whether he was related to Matías Morán, a craftsman who lived in the villa.

Nicolás Durán ("el Mozo") and his wife, who lived in Santa Fe in 1659, had a property called Rancho Ribado that was located on the banks of the Santa Fe River.[10] He was the son of Ayudante Nicolás Durán and grandson of Juan de la Cruz I, who changed his surname to Durán after he arrived in

New Mexico in 1598 and who possibly originally acquired the land.[11] Nicolás the younger was apparently not alive in 1680, but Juan Durán II, possibly his son and great-grandson of Juan I, passed muster with an extended family that year.[12]

Miguel de Hinojos owned land on the Santa Fe River about 1 league (2.6 miles) below Santa Fe in 1661, property that he might well have inherited from his father, Hernando de Hinojos, who came to New Mexico in 1598.[13] Miguel was alcalde mayor of Cochiti Pueblo in 1661 and was reported residing in that jurisdiction, where he might also have owned land.[14] In that year he held one-third of the encomienda of Las Humanas Pueblo in the Estancia basin as escudero for Alonso Rodríguez Cisneros.[15] His name is not on the 1680 or 1681 musters, but he might have been dead by that time. Two men with the Hinojos (Ynojos) surname, Hernando II and Diego, who did pass muster, might well have been related to him.[16]

Farther downriver from Santa Fe, about four to five miles, in the vicinity of Agua Fria, was a cluster of Spanish properties. The attraction of this location was the presence of springs, as the name Agua Fria indicates. One of these properties was the abandoned "hacienda" of Roque de Madrid, 2 leagues (5.2 miles) from Santa Fe, which was identified during the reconquest by Roque, who was accompanying Governor Vargas.[17] It might have occupied the seventeenth-century component of the prehistoric pueblo site LA 2, which was located on the south side of the Santa Fe River in the Agua Fria area.[18] Roque was the grandson of Francisco de Madrid, who arrived in New Mexico in 1603, and son of Francisco II, who acquired the land when he married the daughter of Juan Ruiz de Cáceres I, thus establishing Juan, who had come to New Mexico in 1600, as an early landholder in this area.[19] Numerous members of the Madrid family were on the 1680–81 muster rolls, including Roque, who played a leading role in the reconquest.[20] The Pacheco family also lived in the Agua Fria area and was related to the Madrid family. At some point Francisco de Madrid II sold land to Gerónimo Pacheco, whose granddaughter, Juana de Arvide, later married Francisco's son Roque de Madrid.[21] Gerónimo was first mentioned in New Mexico in 1628, and his son Juan passed muster with his family in 1680.[22]

Another property on the south side of the Santa Fe River near the holdings of the Madrid and Pacheco families was that of Cristóbal Nieto.[23] Cristóbal's father José, who resided in the Salinas settlements in the 1660s, was a native of Santa Fe, and it might have been José who acquired the land originally, or Cristóbal might have received it as a dowry when he married Petrona

Pacheco, the daughter of Juan Pacheco and granddaughter of Gerónimo Pacheco.[24] The likelihood of this connection is reinforced by Roque Madrid's rescue of Petrona and her children when he returned to New Mexico in 1692 and found them at San Juan Pueblo, where they had been held after having been captured during the revolt.[25] The probability that the property of Cristóbal Nieto and his wife, Petrona Pacheco, was located near that of Gerónimo Pacheco would mean that land belonging to José Telles Jirón was located there as well because it was bounded on one side by the property of Cristóbal Nieto.[26] José Telles Jirón, who came to New Mexico in 1649 with Governor Ugarte y la Concha, had, in addition to this property, landholdings in the vicinity of Senecú in the extreme southern part of the colony.[27] In 1661 he was encomendero of San Felipe and Cochiti pueblos.[28] His Agua Fria property passed to Antonio Gutiérrez de Figueroa, a youth of nineteen when the latter married José's daughter Jacinta Telles Jirón, apparently not long before the revolt, at which time José escaped with members of his family to El Paso.[29]

According to a 1704 document, the granddaughters of Andrés López Sambrano were claiming a house and farm land he owned on the south side of the Santa Fe River "on the Cienega Road," although just where along this road was not stated.[30] The father of these women was Francisco Lucero de Godoy, who received this property as a dowry and added it to land that he already owned that bordered his father-in-law Andrés's property.[31] Like his brother Juan, Francisco also escaped the revolt with his family.

A property described as on the "other," or south, bank of the river was claimed after the reconquest by María Gutiérrez, who said she inherited it from her mother, María de Tapia, whose husband was Roque Gutiérrez.[32] Unfortunately, there is not enough information about the parents of María Gutiérrez or their antecedents to know how this property was acquired or where along the Santa Fe River it was located.[33]

Along the Santa Fe River, downriver from Agua Fria, a number of possible seventeenth-century Spanish habitation sites have been identified by archaeologists. On the north side of the river, about three quarters of a mile from Agua Fria, is a site (LA 69996) with several single rooms, or a roomblock, where seventeenth-century ceramics were found.[34] Almost 2 miles from Agua Fria (and 7.3 miles from the Santa Fe plaza) on the south side of the river is a nonstructural site (LA 146) whose ceramics indicate a possible prerevolt seventeenth-century occupation.[35] About two and a quarter miles below Agua Fria on the north side of the river is LA 16773, a Spanish rancho of one or two rooms that was first occupied in the seventeenth century.[36] And approximately three and a half miles farther downriver are the remains of a small linear house with at least two rooms, an exterior work area with cobbled surface and ramada, as well as several outbuildings (LA 16768).[37] Another habitation site, this one with the ruins of a tower (LA 16767), is a little over a mile farther down the river.[38] Another mile downstream on the south side of the river and some thirteen miles from Santa Fe is a large prehistoric pueblo site called La Cieneguilla (LA 16), which is located near springs at the head of the canyon of the Santa Fe River. Glaze F ceramics found on part of this site indicate a small Spanish occupation sometime during the seventeenth century.[39] About 1.5 miles southeast of LA 16 and 11.5 miles from Santa Fe is another prehistoric site (LA 44) that was occupied by Spaniards prior to 1680.[40] It is located on the north side of Arroyo Hondo about a half mile above its junction with Cienega Creek. This site, known as La Cienega, consists of what was a small L-shaped building characteristic of a Spanish habitation, not a pueblo, and therefore it is not likely the pueblo of La Cienega mentioned in prerevolt documents.[41] A Spanish rancho named La Cienega was mentioned by Governor Vargas in 1696, and this reference might well have been to the LA 44 site.[42] Less than a half mile south of LA 44 on Arroyo Hondo is another site, LA 163, whose ceramics indicate a possible Hispanic occupation in the prerevolt period.[43] Unfortunately, there are no descriptions of Spanish properties in this area that can be identified with these sites.

A known Spanish landholding in the La Cienega area was that of Simón Pérez de Bustillo. It was reported in 1613 that he went out from Santa Fe with several other vecinos to brand cattle in the La Cienega area 4 leagues (10.4 miles) away, indicating that Simón, and most likely his father Juan, both of whom had come to New Mexico with Governor Oñate in 1598, had acquired land here by this early date.[44] At least some of the men who accompanied Simón might have been his brothers-in-law, who possibly obtained land or extended their holdings by marrying into the Pérez de Bustillo family. Simón's sisters Catalina, Beatriz, and Yumar were married to Alonso Varela I, Hernando de Hinojos, and Antonio Baca respectively.[45] The estancia of Alonso Varela I, who came to New Mexico in 1598, was described in 1628 as "en la Sienega" and "at La Cienega" in 1632, but the 1613 document could put his landholding there at a much earlier date.[46] This estancia might have remained in the family, as his grandson Pedro Varela Jaramillo, who survived the 1680 revolt, appears to have owned it.[47] The 1613 document suggests that Hernando de Hinojos, also an original colonist, might have held land in this area, land that was inherited by his son Miguel, who, as noted, in 1661, also owned lands on the Santa Fe River 1 league (2.6 miles) downstream from the villa. Hernando extended his relationship to the nearby Anaya Almazán family when his daughter, Gerónima Pérez de Bustillo, married Francisco de Anaya Almazán II.[48] Miguel had likely died by the time of the revolt, but two men with the Hinojos (Ynojos) surname who survived the revolt, one in particular, Hernando, might well have been related to the original Hernando de Hinojos.[49]

The Baca family owned the estancia El Alamo, which was described as being 4 leagues (10.4 miles) from Santa Fe, in, as has been suggested, the area of present Rancho de las Golondrinas, a distance of some 12.5 miles.[50] If this property, known for its many springs, was acquired by Cristóbal Baca I, who came to New Mexico in 1600, it might have been inherited by his son Antonio. Antonio was executed in 1643 for his role in the murder of Governor Luis de Rosas, and by 1661 the property was in the hands of Antonio's daughter Ana Baca, who claimed that "tengo una estancia de labor quarto leguas desta villa que llaman El Alamo el año pasado de sesenta."[51] She was then the widow of Francisco López de Aragón, but it seems likely that the estancia belonged to her family. Ana's sister Gertrudis, who was married to Antonio Jorge de Vera, had a son Antonio who was born at El Alamo in 1654.[52] Four men with the Baca surname survived the revolt, but there is no information about whether any of them were owners of the El Alamo property. During the reconquest, Governor Vargas refers to the "abandoned hacienda of El Alamo."[53]

Francisco de Anaya Almazán II, who was related to the Pérez de Bustillo family through his marriage to Juan Pérez de Bustillo's granddaughter Gerónima, held a property located about thirteen miles from Santa Fe that was mentioned in a 1714 document as "La Cieneguilla of the Almazán family."[54] This large grant might have been made to Francisco's father, Francisco I, who was in New Mexico by 1626, but by 1661 it was in the hands of Francisco II, and his claim was reconfirmed by Governor Vargas in 1693.[55] The name of the grant suggests that the abandoned prehistoric pueblo La Cieneguilla (LA 16) was on or near Francisco's property, which was also only 1 league (2.6 miles) from La Cienega Pueblo, the only occupied pueblo in the Santa Fe River valley during the prerevolt period, a pueblo of which Francisco was encomendero.[56] Although the site of this pueblo has not been discovered, its name indicates that it was located in the La Cienega area, and it is likely that the Anaya Almazán landholding was somewhere between the present settlement of that name and the site of LA 16, which according to Governor Vargas was 5 leagues (13 miles) from Santa Fe.[57] Francisco's family was killed in the revolt, but he was able to escape and returned with Governor Vargas in 1693.[58]

An early seventeenth-century habitation site (LA 20000) about fifteen miles from Santa Fe is located on a stream that is tributary to Cienega Creek less than a mile above the latter's confluence with the Santa Fe River.[59] The site consists of a large house of some ten to fifteen rooms, adjacent corral, associated outbuildings, and the remains of what might have been a tower across the stream on a small rise.[60] Unfortunately, there is no evidence that would link this important site to its Spanish owner, although it has been suggested that one of the brothers-in-law of Simón Pérez de Bustillo, perhaps Alonso Varela Jaramillo, might have been its owner.[61] Below LA 20000 are two sites that could well have been occupied by Spaniards in the prerevolt period. Located at the junction of Cienega Creek and Mocho Arroyo is LA 165, and about two-thirds of a mile downstream at the junction of Cienega Creek, Alamo Creek, and the Santa Fe River is LA 164.[62] Among the many sites discovered in the Santa Fe River valley, there are undoubtedly other prerevolt Spanish habitation sites, but their identification has been obscured because some sites have been mistakenly interpreted as pueblos or because at others the ceramics could be interpreted as dating to the eighteenth century.[63]

During the prerevolt seventeenth century, there was only one occupied pueblo in the Santa Fe River valley, the one that was called La Cienega.[64] It might have been created by the Spanish authorities as a *reducción*, that is, a congregation of people from various pueblos that the Spaniards formed in order to have a nearby source of labor for the villa and the estancias in its hinterland. La Bajada Pueblo (LA 7), located on a hillock below the mouth of the canyon of the Santa Fe River (Las Bocas; see map 6, p. 210) and abandoned from early in the seventeenth century, might have provided the majority of the residents for this new pueblo. References to La Cienega Pueblo are found in documents that state that Francisco de Anaya Almazán was its encomendero; that it was located 1 league from Anaya Almazán family land; that it was a visita of San Marcos Pueblo in the 1640s and 1660s; and, according to Fray Gabriel de Torija, that it was located about half way on the route between Kewa (Santo Domingo) Pueblo and the villa of Santa Fe (map 6, p. 210).[65] In the early days of the revolt, Governor Otermín referred to a pueblo called La Cienega whose members had joined the uprising.[66] Unfortunately, the site of this pueblo has not been found, but its name suggests that it was located in the part of the valley known as La Cienega and its proximity to the property of the Anaya Almazán family provides another clue.

It is likely that there were other colonists who acquired land for grazing and raising crops in the Santa Fe River valley, given its proximity to the capital where they had grants of house lots and horticultural land, but because of the incomplete nature of the documentary and archaeological records, only a partial picture of the Spanish settlement pattern in the valley can be drawn.

CHAPTER TWELVE

The Española Basin

✣ ALTHOUGH THERE IS SOME EVIDENCE THAT COLONISTS WERE MOVING into the Santa Fe River valley before the official founding of the villa there in 1610, it is less certain when other early settlements away from the original capital of San Gabriel took place, but it probably happened at much the same time. Given the proximity of the Santa Cruz River valley to San Gabriel (see map 1, p. 205), it would not be surprising that, early on, some colonists were also attracted to this valley. Although smaller in area and volume of stream flow than the Santa Fe River valley, it was likewise bereft of occupied pueblos at that time. A substantial number of original colonists or their descendants are known to have owned land in La Cañada, the name then used to designate not just the Santa Cruz River valley specifically but also areas along the Rio Grande north to Ohkay Owingeh (San Juan Pueblo) and south to its junction with Pojoaque Creek, including the drainage area of the creek, an area roughly coterminous with the Española basin (see map 7, p. 211). Spaniards moving out from San Gabriel were initially attracted to the nearby Santa Cruz River valley, where there were no occupied pueblos, whereas most of the cultivable and irrigable land elsewhere in the basin was claimed by the Tewa people's eight pueblos.

The earliest known Spanish colonist to move away from San Gabriel was Juan Luján I, who testified on October 5, 1601, that he was settled in La Cañada.[1] He most probably meant that he was located in the Santa Cruz River valley, and it is interesting to note that a possible descendant, Miguel Luján, was a property owner in this area in 1680 (see map 7,

p. 211).² Many of the known settlers in the Española basin, as elsewhere in the colony, belonged to families whose founders were among the 1598 and 1600 colonists, and it is very possible that it was they who initially acquired the lands, even though the earliest documentation refers to the properties as belonging to their sons, grandsons, or other relatives. Although it cannot be proven that these original colonists settled in La Cañada in the very early years of the seventeenth century, the fact that Juan Luján made the move makes it likely that he was not alone in doing so. Very possibly he was accompanied by his fellow Canary Islander, Juan Ruiz de Cáceres. The absence of land grant records makes it difficult to know not only when and where Spaniards settled in the Española basin but also how many of them did so. As a result, the forty-nine names that scholars have gleaned from different sources, including residencias of governors and Inquisition records, cannot be presumed to be complete. Nor are all these settlers contemporaneous. Although there is almost no information about when known Spanish landowners acquired their properties in the Española basin, there is better information about those residing in the area in 1680. In March 1695 Governor Diego de Vargas, who was in the process of reconquering New Mexico, ordered Lieutenant Governor Luis (Pérez) Granillo to survey the prerevolt landholdings of Spaniards in the La Cañada district in order to ascertain where he could grant lands to newly arrived colonists and to where he could move the Tano people, who had moved onto former Spanish lands in the Santa Cruz River valley after the Spaniards were forced out in 1680. The lieutenant governor was accompanied by Matías Luján and Sargeant Juan Ruiz de Cáceres, both of whom were born and raised in the area and were interpreters of the Tewa language. The published versions of this survey do not cover all parts of the basin, either because the survey team did not visit them or because parts of the report were lost; however, other documents have been discovered that fill in the missing parts of the report, and altogether they identify the location of thirty-seven landowners in the Española basin in 1680 (see map 7, p. 211).³

Because Governor Vargas wanted to know how many colonist families could be accommodated, the Granillo survey also provides information about the relative size of the landholdings. Nearly all of the properties mentioned in the survey were described as having sufficient land for only a single family. Exceptions were the "haciendas" of Juan Griego II and Francisco Xavier that encompassed enough agricultural land and pastures for two families; the Sebastián González property, where three families had lived; and the lands of the Martín Serrano family, "los Martínezes," which were extensive enough for five families.⁴ In the survey, most properties are referred to as "haciendas," but, as discussed elsewhere, it is difficult to know what this term means with regard to size and type of operation or if it was being used to confer status. In other sources, some of these properties are referred to as estancias, for example, those of Melchor de Archuleta, Juan de la Cruz I, Juan Griego II, and Catalina Pérez de Bustillo, and even the largest property mentioned in the survey, that of the Martín Serrano family, was called an estancia. In New Mexico, the terms "hacienda" and "estancia" did not necessarily carry distinct connotations, as discussed in chapter 4.

Apparently the Granillo survey team did not visit the part of the Española basin north of the Rio Grande–Santa Cruz River junction, or, again, that part of their report has been lost; however, other documents yield the names of eleven Spanish settlers with landholdings along that five-to-six-mile segment of the Rio Grande, all but two of which were located on the east side of the river.

Francisco Gómez Robledo held two properties in this area. One was located 1 league (2.6 miles) to the north of Ohkay Owingeh, and the other was called "la estancia de Yunque," probably located on the west side of the Rio Grande in the vicinity of the old Yunque/San Gabriel settlement.⁵ His father, Francisco Gómez, who came to New Mexico about 1604, was encomendero of Tesuque and founded probably the most prominent landholding family in the province; his wife was Ana Robledo, and their children added her surname. By the time he died in 1656 or 1657, Francisco, his eldest son, seems to have become the principal manager of the family's many properties. At the time of the revolt he was maese de campo and was forced to flee with his extended family.⁶

Also on the west side of the Rio Grande were the lands of Alonso Martín Barba I. In post-reconquest documents, the boundaries of his property were described as the Río del Norte (Rio Grande) on the east, the Río del Norte–Río Chama junction on the north, Santa Clara Pueblo to the south, and the hills to the west, a huge property, probably comparable to that of Juan de Herrera east of the Rio Grande.⁷ Alonso I was on Oñate's 1597 muster and a signatory of the 1601 loyalty petition. In 1661 he was mentioned as a resident of La Cañada; his second wife, Francisca de Herrera Abrego, was related to families that held land on the east side of the Rio Grande north of that river's junction with the Santa Cruz River.⁸ At that time his son Alonso II was living in the Estancia basin, and by 1669 he was dead. A second son, Diego, had been executed earlier in connection with the Rosas affair, and a possible grandson, Esteban Barba, was killed at Santo Domingo Pueblo in 1680; however, other family members were on the 1680 and 1681 musters, indicating that Alonso I's line had not died out, but whether any of them still lived in La Cañada jurisdiction is unknown.[9]

The property of Juan de Herrera, located 2 leagues (5.2 miles) south of Ohkay Owingeh and 1 league below the border of the pueblo's lands, was a vast area encompassing much of the land in this area north of the Rio Grande-Santa Cruz River junction on the east side of the Rio Grande.[10] Juan came to New Mexico as a twenty-year-old in 1600 and possibly acquired this land early in the century. At some point he was granted the encomiendas of Santa Clara and Jemez pueblos. His two sons, Juan II and Antonio, who were on the 1681 muster, most likely held the family property until they were forced to leave in 1680.[11] Juan's neighbor to the north was Lucas de la Vega about whom nothing else is known.[12] On his west was the property of Ambrosio Sáez, who was also mentioned in the Granillo survey as a landholder in the area along the Rio Grande between Santa Clara and San Ildefonso pueblos. In the 1660s Ambrosio's property was in the Angostura area of the Santo Domingo basin, but having moved to the Española basin sometime before the revolt, he avoided the massacre of Spanish residents in the former area in 1680 and was able to escape to El Paso with his family.[13] South of Juan de Herrera's land was that of Domingo Martín Serrano. He was the grandson of original colonist Hernán Martín Serrano I, who established extensive landholdings in the Chimayó area of the upper Santa Cruz River valley, which were held by Domingo's brother Luis II at the time of the revolt, when all family members fortunately escaped.[14]

Adjoining other land that belonged to Juan de Herrera was the property that belonged to Juan de Archuleta II, but how Juan II acquired it from Juan de Herrera I is unknown.[15] His father, Juan I, was beheaded in 1643 for his part in the murder of Governor Luis de Rosas, and his brother Melchor inherited the family property on the south side of the Santa Cruz River, which might have been established by their grandfather Asencio who came to New Mexico in 1598.[16] Juan II died before the revolt, but one of the two men named Juan de Archuleta that were on the Otermín musters might have been his son.[17] Also adjoining land of Juan de Herrera was the rancho of 1598 colonist Juan Griego I, the southern boundary of which was the road that went eastward up the Santa Cruz River valley.[18] A ruined house on this land belonged to Juan's son Francisco Bernal, who used his mother's surname.[19] Sometime before 1631 Juan and Francisco had settled in the Bernalillo district of the Middle Rio Grande region, while Francisco's brother Juan Griego II inherited the La Cañada property, probably including a holding in the Santa Cruz River valley.[20] To the west of the Griego property were the lands of Juan de Abrego, but nothing more is known about him.[21] The land of Alonso del Río, with its house, maize fields, and orchard, was located near swamp land (cienega) at the junction of the Rio Grande and Santa Cruz River.[22] Alonso was the son of Diego del Río and possibly related to Alonso del Río, who came to New Mexico in 1598.[23] He also held land along the Santa Cruz River between where the Tanos of San Lázaro and San Cristóbal established their pueblos after the revolt, land that he possibly acquired as his wife's dowry when he married María González, a member of the Sebastián González family whose land was located in that area.[24] Alonso was with the Leyva party in the El Paso area at the outbreak of the 1680 revolt.

The heaviest concentration of known settlers in the Española basin before 1680 was in the Santa Cruz River valley. At the far end of the valley, some twelve miles from the Rio Grande on the Rio Quemado east of the Pueblo Quemado ruin (present Córdoba) along the road to Picurís Pueblo was the property of Alonso de Moraga.[25] Alonso's father, Diego, a blacksmith, was first mentioned in the surviving documents in 1628, when he was living in Santa Fe in a house that stood near a spring in the cienega that occupied part of the villa.[26] It seems that Diego acquired land in the Cañada de Chimayó in the early 1640s from Governor Alonso de Pacheco.[27] Although his son Alonso is cited as the owner in the Granillo survey, a brother Juan apparently shared it or preceded him as owner according to a petition filed by his daughter Antonia in 1697 claiming that land there belonged to her father, who had inherited it from his father Diego.[28]

Although not mentioned in the Granillo survey, it appears likely that Sebastián Montaño's property was located nearby. His sister María was married to Juan de Moraga. It is possible that Sebastián moved to this area sometime after 1669, when he left the Estancia basin because it was under heavy attack by Apachean bands and soon abandoned by other settlers.[29] Although there were people with the Montaño surname in New Mexico earlier, including Isidro Xuáres Montaño who came to New Mexico in 1598, there is no information available to connect them to Sebastián Montaño, who was among the 1680 refugees.[30]

Near the junction of the Rio Quemado with the Santa Cruz River were the lands of "los Martínezes" that stretched northwestward along the latter river to the Paraje de Chimayó.[31] In 1661 these lands were described as being eight leagues (twenty-one miles) from Picurís Pueblo.[32] According to the Granillo survey, this land was the property of Luis Martín (a.k.a. Luis Martín Serrano II), who was the grandson of Hernán I, who came to New Mexico in 1598, and son of Luis I, who was said to live on paternal lands at La Cañada where he was alcalde mayor of the Tewa jurisdiction in 1661 and dead by 1663.[33] Luis II, who claimed that he was raised in the outpost of Chimayó, presumably took over the family land when his father died and held it until 1680, when he was forced to flee with his large family.[34] Perhaps Pedro Martín Serrano, another son of Luis I who was not mentioned in the survey, occupied part of this land.[35] Hernán Martín Serrano II, elder brother of Luis I, was born in San Gabriel ("El Yunque") about 1607 and in 1632 gave his residence as La Cañada, probably on the family land in the Chimayó area, but he spent much time elsewhere, mainly in Santa Fe, where, as heir to the family encomienda, he looked after affairs, including properties in the Santa Fe River valley and in the Estancia basin.[36]

In the Chimayó area about 0.5 leagues (1.3 miles) west of the lands of the Martín Serrano family was the property of Juan Luis.[37] He was most probably Captain Juan Luis Luján, who was married to Isabel López del Castillo and who seems to have been related to the Ruiz de Cáceres and Luján families of this area, the name "Luis" possibly a corruption of Ruiz.[38] The founders of these two families, both named Juan, were fellow countrymen from La Palma in the Canary Islands and came to New Mexico in 1600.[39] Juan Ruiz de Cáceres might well have moved to the Santa Cruz valley in 1601 with his compañero Juan Luján. He also owned land in the Santa Fe River valley at an early date and later he acquired land in the Isleta jurisdiction of the Middle Rio Grande region, where he died about 1636.[40] Although it appears likely that Juan Ruiz de Cáceres established a property in the Santa Cruz valley and that Juan Luis was a descendant who at some point inherited the property, for lack of evidence it can only be surmised. An elderly Juan Luis and his son Juan Luis "el Mozo" were both recorded on the 1680 Otermín muster.[41] It is interesting to note that a member of the Granillo survey team, Juan Ruiz de Cáceres, was not mentioned as owner of this or any other property in La Cañada prior to the revolt, but he grew up in the area and was an interpreter of the Tewa language; thus it is very probable that he lived on ancestral land there.[42] By 1698 he had acquired the property formerly held by Alonso del Río located farther west along the Santa Cruz River.[43]

From the Juan Luis property the Granillo survey team continued west and crossed to the south side of the Santa Cruz River, where it encountered the property of Miguel Luján.[44] Although Miguel's relationship to Juan Luján I, who settled in La Cañada in 1601, is not known, it is likely that he was a descendant, and this land might well have been where Juan I established his estancia. A clue as to where in the district Juan I settled is found in the birthplace of a possible great-grandson, Matías Luján, who was born circa 1656 "at a place called San Cristóbal after the Reconquest, and there he had his residence before the Rebellion."[45] San Cristóbal refers to an area along the Santa Cruz River in the vicinity of present La Puebla to which Tano people from the San Cristóbal Pueblo in the Galisteo basin transferred their pueblo after the revolt.[46] This property was probably inherited by Juan Luján II, who at some point moved to the Taos valley, where he had an estancia in 1661 and in that year was mentioned as alcalde mayor of the Taos-Picurís jurisdiction.[47] The property might then have been taken over by Juan Luis Luján, possible son of Juan II, by the time his son Matías was born. These relationships, however, are a matter of speculation.[48] As noted, Juan Luis Luján, or Juan Luis, owner of the neighboring property, was related to the Ruiz de Cáceres family, and the wife of Miguel Luján was Elena Ruiz de Cáceres, sister of Juan Ruiz de Cáceres, who was, therefore, brother-in-law of Miguel.[49] Perhaps it can be surmised that Miguel as well as Matías was a son of Juan Luis and that it was the former who inherited the family land. Matías was also a member of the Granillo survey team and possibly brother-in-law by marriage of his fellow interpreter Juan Ruiz de Cáceres, neither of whom were mentioned as landowners in the Granillo report.

Bordering the Luján land on the west was the property of Marcos de Herrera, which consisted of a lot (suerte) and some agricultural fields.[50] His other property in the Española basin, the one where his family lived, was, according to the Granillo survey, in the area between the Rio Grande-Santa Cruz River junction and Santa Clara Pueblo.[51] Whether he was related to the Juan de Herrera who came to New Mexico in 1600, who owned an extensive property located along the Rio Grande above the Santa Cruz River junction, and who was encomendero of Santa Clara Pueblo has not been established.[52] Marcos's son Domingo was in the El Paso area with the Leyva expedition at the time of the revolt when his family was killed, but the whereabouts of Marcos at that time is unknown, although he might have been dead by then.[53]

Nicolás de la Cruz was also noted in the Granillo survey as a landowner in this area and was likely a descendant of encomendero Juan de la Cruz I ("el Catalán"), who came to New Mexico in 1598, as well as a relative of Pedro de la Cruz, who owned land farther downstream.[54]

Continuing west along the south side of the Santa Cruz River where the valley widens into a plain (*llano*) with meadows (vegas), the survey team encountered the estancia of Melchor de Archuleta, which was probably inherited from his grandfather Asencio, who came to New Mexico in 1598 with Governor Oñate, was granted an encomienda, and was dead by 1626.[55] Asencio's son Juan I, who was involved in the Rosas affair, was beheaded in 1643, and thus the property was inherited by Juan's son Melchor. His brother Juan II also resided in the Española basin on land located between Ohkay Owingeh and the Rio Grande–Santa Cruz River junction. The two Archuleta men on the Otermín musters are thought to be the sons of these brothers.[56]

Next came the property of Juan Griego II.[57] Juan II was born about 1605 in Santa Fe, providing evidence of settlement in that area before the official founding of the villa in 1610. His father Juan I, an encomendero, came to New Mexico with Governor Oñate.[58] It is likely that Juan I acquired the land in La Cañada, which he left to his son, who was mentioned in 1628, 1631, and 1662 as owning an estancia there, his father having moved to the Bernalillo area of the Middle Rio Grande region by 1631.[59] Juan II also inherited the family encomienda.[60] He was related to his de la Cruz neighbors through his marriage to Juana, daughter of encomendero Juan de la Cruz I.[61] Their son Blas escaped the revolt with an extended family.[62]

The Granillo survey team described the next property, that of Sebastián González, as extensive lands of better quality that had previously been held by Alonso del Río and two other families.[63] Another description of this property indicates that it occupied land on both sides of the river.[64] Two men named Sebastián González who passed muster in 1680 had mentioned that their home was in the Cañada district.[65] One was an adjutant who had owned lands near Santa Cruz (i.e., near where the villa of Santa Cruz de la Cañada was established in 1695), which others were asking for after the reconquest because he did not return to claim them.[66] He might possibly have been related to the González Lobón family founded by Domingo González, who came to New Mexico in 1600, in which case this landholding might have been established very early in the seventeenth century. The second man, who did return to New Mexico, might have been related to the González Bernal family founded by Domingo's brother Sebastián, who was first noted in New

Mexico in 1626 and whose children added their mother Isabel's surname, Bernal. From the Granillo survey it appears that by the time of the revolt this property belonged to Sebastián the adjutant.[67] Apparently, Sebastián purchased this land not long before the 1680 revolt from Alonso del Río, whose wife, María González, was likely related to Sebastián.[68] As mentioned, Alonso also owned land near the confluence of the Santa Cruz River and the Rio Grande. When Alonso passed muster in 1681, he claimed that his residence had been located at La Cañada.[69] This property was, by 1698, in the hands of Juan Ruiz de Cáceres, member of the Granillo survey team.[70]

The neighboring property was owned by Francisco Xavier, and according to the Granillo survey, a small tower was standing among the house ruins.[71] In 1697 a grant of land called San Cristóbal, located in La Cañada, was made by Governor Rodríguez Cubero to Pedro de Ávila.[72] Francisco Xavier was mentioned as its former owner. As in the case of the Luján family, the location described probably does not refer specifically to where the San Cristóbal Tanos had their pueblo but to the general area along the river occupied by Tano people after the revolt. Francisco was first known in New Mexico in 1658, when he came as a wagon train escort.[73] He married Graciana Griego, daughter of Juan Griego II, and her dowry might have been the source of his land.[74] By the time of the revolt, when he escaped with his family, he held the office of secretary for government and war and the rank of maese de campo.[75]

The last property before reaching the Rio Grande was that of Pedro de la Cruz, son of original colonist and encomendero Juan de la Cruz I ("el Catalán"); the latter was noted as having an estancia in this area in 1628 and the former in 1660 when he was fifty years old.[76] By 1680 Pedro was dead and no adult males with this surname appear on the 1680–81 Otermín musters.[77]

After inspecting the prerevolt Spanish properties along the Santa Cruz River, the Granillo team turned south and went along the east side of the Rio Grande reviewing the properties in the area between the mouth of the Santa Cruz River and Santa Clara Pueblo (1.5 miles). The landowners named in the Granillo survey were Bartolomé de Montoya II, Diego López Sambrano, and Marcos de Herrera.[78] Bartolomé II was the grandson of original colonist Bartolomé I, who moved his family from San Gabriel to Cuyamungue Pueblo in 1607. On March 5, 1607, testimony was given that his wife, María de Zamora, went to live at the pueblo of Cuyamungue, where heirs of the family continued to own land up to the time of the 1680 revolt, possibly owning more than one property in the Española basin.[79] Bartolomé II inherited the family encomienda of San Pedro (Paako) at the time his father Diego died in about 1660, and he apparently held it along with the land until he fled the revolt in 1680 with his family and other members of the Montoya clan.[80]

On the property of Diego López Sambrano, the Granillo team found a tower next to the ruined house.[81] Diego was born in Santa Fe about 1639, which means that his father Andrés was in the colony by at least that date and that although he was in Parral in 1642 giving testimony, he could have acquired land in the Española basin before then. Diego was living with his wife in Santa Fe in 1669, but according to the Granillo survey, he continued to own the property in the Española basin, which he held until he escaped with his family in 1680.[82] As mentioned, Marcos de Herrera's second property in the Española basin, the one where his family lived, was located in this area between the Rio Grande-Santa Cruz River junction and Santa Clara Pueblo. According to the Granillo survey, the house was located next to an arroyo and was carried away by a great flood.[83]

The last segment of the Española basin covered in the Granillo survey is a six-mile stretch of the Rio Grande between Santa Clara and San Ildefonso pueblos, an area where the properties were also located on the east side of the river.[84] It is here that Francisco Gómez Robledo had another property in the basin. Following on downriver, the survey team came upon the other property in this jurisdiction owned by Ambrosio Sáez, one that they estimated to be large enough for two or three families.[85] Ambrosio came to New Mexico in 1659 with Governor López de Mendizábal, and in the 1660s he held property in the Angostura area of the Santo Domingo basin as noted, but he apparently moved to the Española basin, where he was living at the time of the revolt.[86] The third landowner in this area mentioned in the Granillo survey was Agustín Romero II, whose property was near Black Mesa in the vicinity of San Ildefonso Pueblo.[87] His father, Agustín I, was the son of Bartolomé Romero, an original colonist and holder of many encomiendas; thus this property was possibly in the Romero family from very early in the seventeenth century, but how long it remained in the family unknown—his son Agustín II is not listed on any of the Otermín musters.[88]

It appears that there were other Spanish properties in the southern part of the Española basin, but they were not mentioned in the Granillo survey. They included the lands of two cousins of Agustín Romero II, Bartolomé and Pedro Romero de Pedraza.[89] They were sons of sons of Matías Romero and grandsons of Bartolomé Romero, who came to New Mexico in 1598 and possibly established family landholdings in this area early in the seventeenth century.[90] It was noted in 1696 that Bartolomé had a house at La Cañada, and it might have been located in the southern Española basin, given the location of his cousin Agustín's property and his brother Pedro's marriage to the stepdaughter of Antonio de Salas, who lived at Pojoaque Pueblo and was its encomendero.[91] These are slender clues, but they might indicate where in La Cañada the brothers' properties were located. Bartolomé also had property in the Taos area.[92] He escaped with Governor Otermín in 1680, indicating that he might have been one of the La Cañada refugees who joined the governor in Santa Fe and that the Romero family probably still had land at La Cañada at that time—although his brother Felipe Romero de Pedraza was a landowner in the Southern Rio Grande region.[93] At the time of the revolt, his brother Pedro apparently was away from home when his wife, Petronila de Salas, and their numerous children were killed in the Pojoaque massacre, but he is not listed on the Otermín musters of 1680 or 1681.[94]

Francisco Jiménez and his family were killed at Pojoaque Pueblo when the revolt broke out, indicating that they, too, might have lived in the southern Española basin.[95] Francisco's house in the La Cañada jurisdiction was still remembered after the reconquest.[96] He might have been related to Juan Jiménez, who was on the 1598 Oñate muster and to Juan Jiménez "el Mozo," possibly el Mozo's son; if so, landowning in the Española basin by the Jiménez family might date from early in the seventeenth century.[97]

By 1639 Antonio de Salas was encomendero of Pojoaque Pueblo, where he lived with his wife and where he had a rancho (in contravention of Crown law).[98] He was the stepson of Pedro Lucero de Godoy; hence he was probably not related to the Juan de Salas who was on the 1597 Oñate muster and who signed the 1601 loyalty petition.[99] Antonio's neighbors were Pedro Romero, whose wife Petronila de Salas was his stepdaughter, and Francisco Jiménez. However, with the exception of Petronila and her children, the Salas family seems not to have been part of the massacre at Pojoaque Pueblo; Antonio participated in the retreat and was on the 1680 muster.[100]

Francisco de Anaya Almazán II, a prominent landholder in the Santa Fe River valley, also owned an estancia near Pojoaque Pueblo according to the 1692 testimony of Francisco Naranjo, a Spanish-speaking member of San Felipe Pueblo.[101]

Pedro Márquez II lived with his Tewa wife, Lucía, at Nambé Pueblo, of which she was a member. He was the grandson of Gerónimo Márquez, an original colonist, and son of Diego, who maintained the family estancia Los Cerrillos near San Marcos Pueblo until he was executed in 1643 for involvement in the murder of Governor Luis de Rosas. Pedro and a son escaped the revolt, but his wife and daughter were captured and only rescued in 1692.[102]

During his reconnaissance of September 1694, Governor Vargas encountered the abandoned property of Sebastián de Herrera Corrales near the maize fields (milpas) of the Tesuque people.[103] Sebastián was most likely Sebastián de Herrera Corrales, who was first noted in New Mexico in 1661.[104] When the rebellion broke out in August 1680, he was in Taos, visiting there with his wife and her relatives, and because he was absent the day of the massacre, he escaped with his life, whereas the others did not.[105]

The only other property mentioned by the Granillo survey team was another belonging to Francisco Gómez Robledo, which was located 2 leagues (5.2 miles) north of Santa Fe and a league south of Tesuque Pueblo and which contained land for agriculture and livestock but only enough land for one family because of the difficulty of irrigating the hilly terrain.[106] This property might have been the first one established beyond Santa Fe by his father, Francisco Gómez, who came to New Mexico in 1604 and at some point was awarded the encomienda of Tesuque Pueblo.[107]

Additional settlers, not on the Granillo survey list, were mentioned as residents of La Cañada but without any indication of where in the district they were located.

Catalina Pérez de Bustillo was the daughter of Simón Pérez de Bustillo and niece of Catalina Pérez de Bustillo who married Alonso Varela Jaramillo.[108] Catalina and her husband, Pedro Márquez I (whose nephew was the Pedro Márquez living at Nambé Pueblo), the son of Gerónimo Márquez, were living in Santa Fe in 1626, but by 1631, after Pedro died, she was living as a young widow at her estancia in La Cañada, perhaps on land that had been her marriage dowry, indicating that her father or grandfather who owned land in the Santa Fe valley might have also been landholders in the Española basin; her husband's family owned lands in the Rio Abajo.[109]

The home of Sebastián González (Bernal/Bas) was in the La Cañada district before the revolt, but it was probably not the property in the Santa Cruz valley mentioned in the Granillo survey that belonged to the other person with the same name and that previously belonged to Alonso del Río. The aforementioned Sebastián González might have been related to the González Bernal family, founded by Sebastián González and his wife Isabel Bernal and, if so, indicates that this family, founded about 1626, owned property in the Española basin as well as in the Bernalillo area of the Middle Rio Grande region, as did the allied family founded by Juan Griego I.[110] Sebastián passed muster with his family in 1680.

Francisco Gómez de Torres, who led wagon trains to New Mexico in 1619 and 1621, might have been related to Juan de Torres, who was a member of the wagon train escort of 1608 and on Oñate's 1597 muster.[111] Francisco had a house in Santa Fe and an estancia at La Cañada. He died in 1636, and whether people with the Torres name living in the El Paso area after the revolt were descended from him is unknown.[112]

Luis de Quintana was a resident of La Cañada and its alcalde mayor at the time of the revolt when he escaped with his family, according to the 1680 muster.[113] Unfortunately, there is no record of when he came to New Mexico or when he acquired his La Cañada property.

Matías de Herrera was mentioned as a "vecino de La Cañada" in March 1662, but there is no information to link him to Juan de Herrera, who held extensive lands along the east side of the Rio Grande north of its junction with the Santa Cruz River, or to Sebastián de Herrera, whose land was near Tesuque Pueblo, nor to Marcos de Herrera, who held properties in the Santa Cruz River valley and on the east side of the Rio Grande above Santa Clara Pueblo.[114]

Juan López del Ocanto, who came to New Mexico in 1598, is not mentioned in any available records as a landowner, but he was encomendero of Nambé Pueblo, indicating that he probably owned land in the district and from an early date. His son Domingo, who passed muster in 1680, inherited his father's encomienda and probably any land his father owned.[115] Diego Pérez Romero, whose father, Gaspar Pérez, came to New Mexico in 1608, held the encomienda of Cuyamungue in 1662 (succeeded by Pedro de Montoya as escudero and then by Cristóbal Durán y Chávez) and may well have also owned land in the Española basin, as did a number of his mother's Romero relatives.[116] The encomenderos of San Juan, San Ildefonso, and Jacona pueblos are unknown but they, too, could have been landowners in this district with its considerable concentration of pueblos and hence sizable labor force. Asencio de Archuleta, Juan de la Cruz I, Juan Griego I, and Hernán Martín Serrano I were all encomenderos of unidentified pueblos whose families owned land in the Española basin and might have held any of these pueblos in encomienda.

Although no systematic archaeological survey of Spanish colonial sites in the Española basin has been made, there are two sites that possibly were established during the prerevolt period. Ceramic evidence at one site, located about five miles north of Ohkay Owingeh on the east side of the Rio Grande (Los Luceros Hacienda [LA 37549]), indicates Spanish occupation going back to the early seventeenth century.[117] In 1703 a large land grant stretching north from Ohkay Owingeh was made to Sebastián Martín Serrano, who built on this site a four-room house with two towers that he named La Soledad.[118] He was the son of Pedro Martín Serrano de Salazar and great-grandson of Hernán I, founder of this prominent landowning family in the Española basin.[119] But it is not known if their holdings included land north of Ohkay Owingeh prior to the revolt and thus whether Sebastián was reclaiming land previously held by the family on which the LA 37549 site was located.

The second site is located a short distance east of present La Puebla in the Santa Cruz River valley. It is the Montez site (LA 4994), a small adobe habitation with a tower also known as San Cristóbal de la Puebla.[120] The property of Francisco Xavier that was located in the part of the valley called San Cristóbal contained a tower among the house ruins, but according to the route of the Granillo survey team, it would have been located farther downriver.[121] The description of the location of Francisco's property could well refer to a more general area rather than a discrete location such as LA 4994, and the coincidence of towers may be just that—towers were not uncommon at that time. Hence, while it cannot be said that Francisco Xavier once occupied the Montez site, he did live in the area, probably farther downriver, and perhaps it was the home of another of the settlers in the area.

The geographic distribution of Spanish landholdings in the Española basin revealed by the Granillo survey and other documents can be seen as a fair approximation of the overall settlement pattern in the prerevolt era even though there may well have been other landholdings. It should also be noted that family properties were not static and could, over time, change in size, character, and ownership. What is impressive is the number of families who held land in the Española basin from the early years of the seventeenth century until the circumstances of the Pueblo revolt forced them to leave in 1680.

CHAPTER THIRTEEN

The Far North

✣ EARLY SPANISH LANDHOLDING IN THE FAR NORTH, A REGION THAT mainly encompasses land in the vicinity of Picurís and Taos pueblos, was probably related to expansion northward by families already living in the Española basin (see map 2, p. 206). Altogether, seven settler families are known to have resided in the Far North region in the seventeenth century. The information about property boundaries available for some of them indicates that their holdings were very extensive.

Juan Luján II, whose father was established in La Cañada (Santa Cruz River valley in the Española basin) in 1601, had an estancia in Taos valley by 1661 and was alcalde mayor of the Taos-Picurís district about that time.[1] He died in 1663, and possibly his heir was among the many Luján men who passed muster in 1680.[2]

Francisco Gómez Robledo also held the grant of an estancia "en los Taos" in the 1660s.[3] His father, Francisco Gómez, who was encomendero of half of Taos Pueblo, also had extensive properties in the Española basin and elsewhere, which his son inherited and held until he was forced to leave the colony with his family in 1680.[4] Both the Luján and Gómez Robledo families were among the earliest colonists in New Mexico.

A member of the Lucero de Godoy family, Diego, was living in the Taos valley in 1680, whereas most members of this family, founded by Pedro Lucero de Godoy I about 1616, lived in Santa Fe or on properties in the Santa Fe River valley downriver from the villa. It is not clear if Diego was the son or grandson of Pedro I—possibly the latter.[5] The connection with the Taos area was established with Pedro's marriage to Francisca Gómez Robledo, sister of Francisco Gómez Robledo, who could well have received some of her family's land as a dowry. Pedro I and Francisco each held half of the Taos encomienda.[6] Diego survived the revolt because he was in El Paso with the Leyva party at the time it began, but his family was massacred.[7] Diego did not return to New Mexico, but the vast extent of the Lucero de Godoy lands in the Taos valley is indicated in Antonio Martínez's 1716 petition to acquire this property. The boundaries were recorded as the mountains that are the source of the Río de Lucero on the north, an arroyo on the east, "being the nearest one to the pueblo of Taos," the Río del Norte (Rio Grande) on the west, and the junction of the Río de Taos and the Río del Norte on the south. The Río de Lucero separated the lands of Taos Pueblo to the east from those of Lucero de Godoy to the west.[8] While conducting his visitation of New Mexico in 1776, Fray Francisco Domínguez noted that the Taos valley was watered by four fair-sized rivers—the Taos River, the Río Lucero, Río de las Trampas de Taos, and the Río del Norte—and that an extensive cienega with lush pasture grasses was located a short distance west of Taos Pueblo.[9]

Domingo de Herrera, son of Marcos de Herrera, was born about 1650 in La Cañada, where his father was a landowner. In 1680 Domingo was described as a resident of Taos and undoubtedly lived there much earlier, possibly on land acquired by his father.[10] Like Diego Lucero de Godoy, Domingo survived the revolt because he was in El Paso with the Leyva escort party, while members of his extended family were all killed.[11]

Another Taos settler, Sargento Mayor Fernando Durán y Chávez, was also away when his family was killed by the rebelling Taoseños. He was likely a grandson of family founder Pedro Durán y Chávez, an original colonist, and in 1680 was reported to be residing in the Taos valley on lands located at present Ranchos de Taos, whereas the lands of most members of this family were located in the Middle Rio Grande region.[12] The boundaries of Fernando's lands recorded in 1710 and 1715 documents of the grant of his land to Cristóbal de la Serna are poorly described, but it appears that the property extended from north of Ranchos de Taos south to the crest of the mountains that divide the lands of Taos Pueblo from those of Picurís Pueblo.[13]

To the west of the Fernando Durán y Chávez landholding was that of Bartolomé Romero (possibly Bartolomé III). Information about this property comes from its sale in 1725 by Francisco Antonio de Guijosa to Baltasar Trujillo.[14] The land, previously granted to Guijosa and specifically mentioned as formerly belonging to Romero, extended from the southwest boundary of Taos Pueblo lands along the Río de Taos west of the property granted to Cristótal de la Serna and extending to Arroyo Hondo on the Rio Grande farther west.[15] Romero was mentioned as encomendero of Picurís Pueblo from 1659 to 1661 and was presumably the grandson of Bartolomé I, who came to New Mexico with Governor Oñate in 1598 and who might have originally acquired these lands.[16] Bartolomé III was forty-two years old in 1669 and could well have been alive at the time of the revolt, but he is not listed on any of the 1680–81 musters.[17]

Blas de Miranda owned land in the Taos valley sometime during the seventeenth century; he was in New Mexico as early as 1631.[18] His land might have been located halfway between Picurís and Taos pueblos if, by the time of the reconquest, it had become the outpost called Miranda mentioned by Governor Vargas in 1692.[19] In the course of archaeological work done in the Taos-Picurís area, no reported sites have so far been found that contain any evidence of seventeenth-century Spanish occupation.[20]

Two families who held encomiendas in the region might also have been landowners. Juan de Tapia (Fernández de Tapia), who came to New Mexico in 1600, was reported in 1625 to have held one quarter of Taos Pueblo.[21] He married Francisca Robledo, daughter of Pedro Robledo I, and thus was related to the Gómez Robledo clan.[22] One half of Picurís Pueblo was held by Francisco de Anaya Almazán I, which upon his death in 1662 passed to his son Francisco II as escudero for his elder brother Cristóbal, who had been imprisoned by the Inquisition.[23] Many encomenderos found it advantageous to locate in the vicinity of their subject pueblos in order to ensure collection of tribute and to have access to labor despite Crown laws meant to protect native land and labor. Marcos de las Heras, who came to New Mexico in 1677 as a volunteer with a contingent of convicts, was alcalde mayor of Taos at the time of the revolt; whether he was also a landowner in this jurisdiction is open to question.[24]

CHAPTER FOURTEEN

The Galisteo Basin and Pecos Jurisdiction

Galisteo Basin

✝ NINE SPANISH MEN ARE RECORDED AS LANDOWNERS IN THE Galisteo basin in the seventeenth century. This basin, in the northern part of the Rio Abajo, is defined here as the area tributary to Galisteo Creek that lies east of the Ortiz Mountains and southeast of the Cerrillos Hills (see map 2, p. 206). The four Tano pueblos are located in this area (see map 1, p. 205): San Cristóbal (LA 80), Galisteo (LA 26), San Lázaro (LA 91–92), and San Marcos (LA 98).[1]

In this region the Márquez family established an estancia named Los Cerrillos that was located near the western edge of the basin 2 leagues (5.2 miles) from the San Marcos Pueblo convent and some twenty miles southwest of the villa of Santa Fe.[2] It was the property of Diego Márquez, who was beheaded in 1643 for his role in the murder of Governor Luis de Rosas; however, his widow was still living there in 1660, and in 1680 it was in the hands of their son Bernabé when it was referred to as a rancho.[3] How early the Márquez family acquired this property is unknown. Diego's father, Gerónimo, an original colonist, was living in 1631 on his estancia at Acomilla in the Southern Rio Grande region, but earlier he might have been granted land to establish Los Cerrillos estancia, which he later left to Diego.[4]

In 1661 Gerónimo de Carvajal, an encomendero, was mentioned as owner of a "hacienda" (reported elsewhere as a rancho) named Nuestra

125

Señora de los Remedios de los Cerrillos in the jurisdiction of San Marcos Pueblo and as alcalde mayor of the Tano jurisdiction.[5] Gerónimo's wife was the daughter of Diego Márquez, and it was perhaps through this marriage that he acquired part of the Márquez's Los Cerrillos property.[6] His father Juan de Vitoria Carvajal, who came to New Mexico with Oñate, had an estancia in nearby Sandia jurisdiction, where his children were born in the 1630s, indicating that the Carvajal family was in the Rio Abajo by that time.[7] Gerónimo was dead by the time of the revolt, but his two adult sons, Antonio and Ambrosio, survived and one or both might have continued to hold the family property after their father's death.[8]

Another settler in the northern part of the Galisteo basin was possibly Cristóbal Enríquez, likely the son of Juan Rangel, who came to New Mexico in 1600.[9] Cristóbal's wife was a member of the Márquez family, and he was executed in 1643 along with Diego Márquez and others for involvement in the murder of Governor Rosas. In 1660 his daughter Estefanía was described as a vecina of Galisteo.[10] His son Cristóbal II might have held the family property until 1680, when he was forced to flee the province.[11] When, at the outbreak of the revolt, Governor Otermín ordered the families of Los Cerrillos to come to the villa, he was referring not only to those living at the estancia Los Cerrillos but to all the Spanish settlers in the Galisteo basin, nearly all of whom were located in the vicinity of the pueblos, which were their source of labor.[12]

Francisco García, born in San Gabriel del Yunque in 1608, the likely son of Álvaro García Holgado, who came to New Mexico in 1600, was living in Santa Fe as a soldier in 1632.[13] In 1636 Francisco mentioned that he was living in the Galisteo jurisdiction when testifying in support of the petition of Mateo Manzanares, who was a landowner in the Santo Domingo basin to the west.[14] Later he established residence near Isleta Pueblo, where his brother Juan was living, and in 1667 he was *justicia mayor* of Socorro Pueblo in the Southern Rio Grande region.[15] The García Holgado family was connected to the Leyva and Nieto families, who lived near Galisteo Pueblo, the largest of the Tano pueblos, and it is possible that Francisco's property was also in that area. In 1662 Francisco García, Pedro de Leyva, and José Nieto were mentioned as "todos cuñados" (brothers-in-law).[16] Francisco was fifty-seven years old in 1665 and might well have died before the 1680 revolt.

Pedro de Leyva, who had been in New Mexico since 1637, was married to Catalina García Holgado and was residing in the jurisdiction of Tajique in the Estancia basin in 1660s, where he held the position of alcalde mayor for the Salinas district.[17] But he might have been granted land in the Galisteo basin earlier, which his sons managed while he resided in the Salinas jurisdiction carrying out his official duties. It is likely he returned to the Galisteo basin in the 1670s, when the Salinas pueblos were abandoned. His sons, Nicolás and Juan, were killed in 1680 with members of their families, including their sister and mother, at their "hacienda" in the vicinity of Galisteo Pueblo, while their father and another brother were on a mission to El Paso to meet the supply train from Mexico.[18]

José Nieto's property in the Galisteo basin was 1 league (2.6 miles) from Galisteo Pueblo.[19] He was a native of Santa Fe, born about 1616 and somehow connected to the García Holgado family. In the 1660s he was living in the Salinas jurisdiction, where he was mentioned as alcalde mayor in 1668 as well as at the time of revolt.[20] It was possibly in the 1670s when Apache attacks forced abandonment of the Salinas pueblos that he acquired or returned to land in the Galisteo basin, and it was there that he and members of his family were killed, along with the Nicolás and Juan Leyva families, when the revolt broke out.[21]

The encomenderos of two of the four Galisteo basin pueblos have been identified, and they might also have been landowners in the area. San Cristóbal Pueblo was held by Antonio de Albizu from 1659 to 1661.[22] Antonio, also encomendero of Ácoma and Alameda pueblos, was mentioned only as living in the Rio Abajo—possibly in the 1660s—and that might have referred to land in the Galisteo basin. Juan Gómez was encomendero of San Lázaro Pueblo in the late 1610s and early 1620s, at the time of the Juan de Eulate administration.[23] This man was most likely Captain Juan Gómez de Luna, who journeyed to Mexico City to accompany Fray Gerónimo de Zárate Salmerón to New Mexico in 1621.[24] Given the lack of information about any property he might have owned elsewhere, there is the possibility that he was a landowner in the Galisteo basin. His wife's sister was married to Álvaro García Holgado.[25] He was still in the colony in 1664, aged seventy-three, but nothing more is known about him, including whether he was related to Diego de Luna, who owned land in the Middle Rio Grande region and passed muster in 1680.[26] There were two alcaldes mayores in the Galisteo basin (Tano district) who might also have been possible landowners. Diego González Bernal, son of early colonist Sebastián González, was alcalde mayor from 1659 to 1661 and again in 1663.[27] Francisco de Anaya Almazán II, son of an early colonist of the same name, was alcalde mayor of the jurisdiction in 1664.[28]

The vast Galisteo basin with its limited water resources and openness to Apache attacks did not seem to attract many Spanish settlers; however, the scattered and incomplete nature of the available information leaves open the possibility that there were other settlers besides the nine discussed, possibly the encomenderos or alcaldes mayores just mentioned. So far, no Spanish habitation sites have been discovered, but little archaeological work focused on such historic sites has been carried out in the Galisteo basin.

Pecos Jurisdiction

East of the Galisteo basin was the important frontier pueblo of Pecos (see map 2, p. 206), near which were lands held by Diego Pérez Romero about 1662.[29] His landholding, established to engage in trade with the Apaches, is the only one in this area mentioned in the available documents, but there might have been others eager to participate in this trade. Francisco Gómez Robledo, encomendero of Pecos and a cousin of Diego, might well have been one of them.[30] In 1662 Pecos Pueblo paid the following hides in tribute, which Francisco most probably exported for profit: sixty-six pronghorn skins, twenty-one white buckskins, sixteen large buckskins, and eighteen buffalo hides.[31] The Gómez family also had a strategically located property, Las Barrancas, in the Sevilleta jurisdiction of the Southern Rio Grande region, where goods were collected for transshipment south on the Camino Real.

CHAPTER FIFTEEN

The Santo Domingo Basin

☦ THE SANTO DOMINGO BASIN COMPRISES THE DRAINAGE AREA OF Galisteo Creek from the Ortiz Mountains/Cerrillos Hills on the east westward to the Rio Grande and from La Bajada escarpment on the north, south to the junction of the Rio Grande with the Jemez River and the north end of the Sandia Mountains (see map 2, p. 206). In this region, seventeen seventeenth-century Spanish settlers are mentioned in the available documents, and there are six known Spanish archaeological sites. Most of these holdings were clustered near the Rio Grande in the vicinity of Cochiti Pueblo and the Angostura area south of San Felipe Pueblo (see map 2, p. 206 and map 8, p. 212). East of the river was another cluster in the Las Huertas Creek/Placitas area at the north end of the Sandia Mountains. These last two areas fell within the Sandia jurisdiction.

Perhaps the earliest landholding to be established in the basin was that of Francisco Luján, son of Juan Luján I, who was living in La Cañada district by 1601. Whereas his father and older brother remained in the Española Basin and Far North, Francisco's sphere of action was in the jurisdiction of Cochiti Pueblo, where he was deputy alcalde mayor in 1643, his house reported to be near the pueblo 0.5 leagues (1.3 miles) east of the Rio Grande.[1] Unfortunately, information is not available about who, if anyone, took over the property after Francisco's death in 1663 or who of the many men with the Luján name listed on the 1680 and 1681 musters were his heirs.

The other seventeenth-century Spanish settler in this area was Cristóbal Fonte(s) or possibly Fuente(s).[2] He was alcalde mayor of Cochiti jurisdiction in 1663 and owner of the La Majada grant located east of the Rio Grande opposite Cochiti Pueblo.[3] Although Fontes's early family connections are unknown, his wife was possibly the daughter of Juan Varela de Losada, who was alcalde mayor of Cochiti from 1661 to 1662 and member of a family whose founder, Pedro I, came to New Mexico in 1598.[4] Fontes might have acquired his land as a dowry from his wife's family.

The Fontes and Luján properties were in the vicinity of the only known seventeenth-century Spanish archaeological sites in the area, LA 34 and LA 591, both of which are located within the one-league boundary of Cochiti Pueblo and were discovered during salvage excavations connected with construction of Cochiti Dam.[5] LA 34, also known as the Cochiti Springs site, is situated on the west bank of the Santa Fe River on a knoll overlooking the springs 2.7 miles southeast of Cochiti Pueblo.[6] LA 591, Las Majadas site, is located some 2.9 miles northeast of the pueblo on the east side of the Rio Grande near the mouth of White Rock Canyon above present Cochiti Dam.[7] A property with remarkably similar boundaries was described in a post-revolt application for a grant of land that had been "deserted since 1680," about a league (2.6 miles) from Cochiti Pueblo and bounded on the north by a small house, the lands of Cochiti Pueblo on the south, the Rio Grande to the west, and the La Majada mesa to the east.[8] Unfortunately, the former owner of this land is not given. The LA 34 site at Cochiti Springs consisted of an adobe structure containing about twenty rooms arranged around a central plaza with corrals constructed of basalt boulders located below on the floodplain.[9] It is reported to be the largest seventeenth-century rural site in New Mexico for which room counts can be estimated.[10] At LA 591, the L-shaped main structure, built of adobe bricks, consisted of five rooms.[11] In addition, there was an L-shaped three-room adobe outbuilding attached to a large corral made of cobbles. It has been suggested that LA 34 might have been the Luján property and that the Fontes property might have been at either LA 34 or LA 591, but information about where their properties were located is not sufficiently precise to make a definite connection.[12] Apparently both sites were abandoned before the revolt.[13]

South of Cochiti Pueblo along the Rio Grande, there are no known pre-revolt Spanish landholdings until San Felipe Pueblo is reached, some fourteen miles downriver. Kewa Pueblo is located about halfway between these pueblos and, although Spanish settlers may have owned properties in this vicinity, it is most likely that the Franciscans, who made this pueblo their headquarters, dominated landholdings in this area.

Some ten miles east of Kewa (Santo Domingo) Pueblo on Galisteo Creek, a small three-room Spanish dwelling (Signal site [LA 9142]) was discovered during excavations connected with construction of Galisteo Dam, indicating that there was some settlement away from the Rio Grande in this central part of the Santo Domingo basin.[14] The site yielded a considerable amount of majolica ware and was likely occupied for about a generation in the late prerevolt period.[15]

Perhaps the earliest settler property in the vicinity of San Felipe Pueblo was a "hacienda" that belonged in 1626 to Isabel de Bohórquez, wife of Pedro Durán y Chávez I and daughter of Cristóbal Baca.[16] It was located in Tunque Arroyo near San Felipe Pueblo, possibly near where the arroyo reached the Rio Grande.[17] Pedro held the encomienda of San Felipe, which their son Fernando I inherited about 1638.[18] The lands he inherited were described in the 1660s as in the jurisdiction of Sandia Pueblo—stretching from the boundary of San Felipe Pueblo south through Bernalillo to Atrisco (thus including land in the Middle Rio Grande region)—and were probably, in turn, inherited by his son Fernando II, who fled the revolt with his family in 1680.[19]

A property described as more than 3 leagues (more than 7.8 miles) from San Felipe Pueblo belonged in 1636 to Mateo Manzanares about whom nothing is known of his antecedents.[20] Nor is there any information about which direction from the pueblo his estancia was located. The Manzanares property could have been located up Tunque Arroyo in the vicinity of Tunque Pueblo, where there were springs, the pueblo having been abandoned by that time—but that is only speculation.[21] At some time Mateo acquired another property farther south in the Middle Rio Grande region, which was claimed by his daughter Ana de Sandoval y Manzanares after the reconquest.[22]

At the time the Spaniards were retreating from Santa Fe in late August 1680, Governor Otermín mentioned passing by a number of Spanish properties along the Rio Grande in the Angostura area between San Felipe Pueblo and the Rio Grande-Jemez River junction, where the present village of Algodones is located (see map 2, p. 206 and map 8, p. 212). The first property they encountered in this area was that of Cristóbal de Anaya Almazán located some 2 leagues (5.2 miles) south of San Felipe Pueblo.[23]

A quarter of a league (0.65 miles) downriver from Anaya's property was the estancia of Pedro de Cuéllar, who came to New Mexico in 1677 as part of a contingent of convicts who were meant to settle in the province.[24] He might have acquired this property as a result of marriage to a daughter of one of the landowning families in the area such as the Domínguez de Mendozas or the

Duran y Chávezes, the latter said to have had landholdings from the boundaries of San Felipe Pueblo down through Bernalillo to Atrisco.[25] Pedro's family was killed at the time of the revolt while he was away in the El Paso area with the Leyva party.[26]

Just below Pedro de Cuéllar lived Agustín de Carvajal and his wife, Damiana Domínguez de Mendoza, on land that she received as a dowry when she married her first husband, Álvaro de Paredes, in 1660—another indication that her family's lands at one time included properties in the Angostura as well as in the Bernalillo and Atrisco areas to the south.[27] Her father, Tomé Domínguez, was dead by 1656 and it was her elder brother, Francisco Domínguez de Mendoza, who inherited his father's lands and who probably gave the dowry to Damiana.[28] Damiana and Agustín were both found dead in the parlor of their house by the retreating Otermín refugees.[29]

A short distance away was another property belonging to Cristóbal de Anaya, the Estancia de San Antonio, which included land for raising livestock and three springs that fed irrigated farm land ("tierras de labor y asequia"). It also included a house with a parlor (sala), two other rooms (aposentos), and a kitchen (cocina), as well as a one-room outbuilding where meetings were held and that possibly served as a stopping place for travelers on the Camino Real, one of many along this arterial that linked the colony to New Spain.[30] Cristóbal, who was married to Leonor Domínguez de Mendoza, purchased the Estancia de San Antonio from his father-in-law, Tomé Domínguez, and it was augmented after Tomé's death about 1656 by a donation of land located west of the Rio Grande in the mountains that was made by his wife's brothers Francisco and Juan Domínguez de Mendoza.[31] As early as 1669 it was noted that Cristóbal and Leonor had a property located near that of Leonor's sister Damiana.[32] It was in this house that the refugees retreating from Santa Fe discovered the couple and their six children massacred.[33]

Ambrosio Sáez, who came to New Mexico in 1659 in the company of Governor López de Mendizábal, was also located in the Angostura area in the 1660s. He married Ana Rodríguez de Anaya, whose father was a son-in-law of the Anaya Almazán patriarch Francisco, and it was probably through this connection that he acquired land.[34] In 1693 Governor Vargas encountered his ruined "hacienda" 0.5 leagues (1.3 miles) off the road between San Felipe and Santa Ana pueblos in a wooded area along the banks of the Rio Grande.[35] However, he had moved to the Española basin by the time of the 1680 revolt, and he and his family thus escaped the killing that befell his former neighbors in the Angostura area.

To the west of the Angostura area at or near Santa Ana Pueblo, which is located some eight miles up the Jemez River from its junction with the Rio Grande, was the house of Andrés Hurtado I, encomendero of this and neighboring pueblos, who arrived in New Mexico in 1649.[36] He apparently had an estancia somewhere between Santa Ana Pueblo and Zia Pueblo, eight miles farther west, where he raised wheat and livestock (see map 8, p. 212). In 1661 Governor López de Mendizábal forced him to leave Santa Ana Pueblo and establish a house in Santa Fe as required of encomenderos (even though Andrés claimed he could not afford to do so) because it was forbidden for Spaniards to live in pueblos.[37] Andrés's sons Diego and Andrés II were on the 1681 muster.[38] Few, if any, other colonists were likely to have been attracted to the valley of the lower Jemez River because of its alkaline soils, the source of which was the Rio Salado that joined the Jemez River just west of Zia Pueblo (whose inhabitants mainly depended on upland dry farming).[39] Even before the Oñate colonists arrived, the people of Santa Ana Pueblo farmed land along the west side of the Rio Grande, mainly north of present Bernalillo, in order to ensure successful crop production.[40] Governor Vargas in 1693 mentioned the alkaline soil and bad water of Zia Pueblo.[41]

In addition to properties along the Rio Grande, there was seventeenth-century Spanish settlement in the southeastern part of the Santo Domingo basin on the northern edge of the Sandia Mountains centered on Placitas and lower Las Huertas Creek, where several major springs were located (see map 2, p. 206 and map 8, p. 212).[42] In 1631 a mulatto named Juan Antón was living at an estancia or rancho called El Paraje de las Huertas, noted in 1632 and 1661–62 as belonging to Diego de Trujillo.[43] The property was located in the Sandia jurisdiction 4 leagues (10.4 miles) from Sandia Pueblo, most likely along lower Las Huertas Creek.[44] It has been suggested that Trujillo's estancia was at or near the site called San José de las Huertas (LA 25674), located about 5.5 miles upstream from the Rio Grande, on the basis of ceramics dating from this time found at the site, although its principal Spanish occupation was in the eighteenth century.[45] Trujillo, encomendero of part of Picurís Pueblo, was sargeant major by 1662 and held many high positions such as lieutenant general for the Rio Abajo, alcalde mayor of the Zuni and Hopi jurisdiction, and maestro de campo. He survived the revolt and died in Casas Grandes in 1682.[46]

A ranch, described as near San Felipe Pueblo and also probably in the Las Huertas/Placitas area, belonged sometime before 1680 to the mestizo Naranjo brothers, Bartolomé, Francisco, and Juan.[47] They might have been descendants of Alonso Naranjo, who came with Oñate in 1598, and/or Diego Martín Naranjo, who was killed by Jemez people in the latter 1640s.[48] Bartolomé was killed in San Felipe Pueblo in 1680 by rebels when he refused to join them.[49] It has been suggested that the Naranjo rancho might have been located in present Placitas village next to a spring on upper Suela Arroyo at the Ojo Cuchilla site (LA 50329).[50] The uncertainty about whether this site was occupied by Spanish or Puebloan people might be related to occupation by acculturated native or mestizo people such as the Naranjos. The main structure was a large ten-room house of masonry-based adobe brick construction. High incidence of majolica sherds, including spindle whorls, and large room size would suggest Spanish occupation, but a substantial depression at the east end of the roomblock could be interpreted as a kiva. Whether or not Ojo Cuchilla was the location of the Naranjo property, this site was occupied in the seventeenth century as was San José de las Huertas.

Another property in the Las Huertas Creek area, Casa Acequia (LA 44534), was located 4.3 miles upstream from the Rio Grande and a little over 1 mile below San José de las Huertas. The house, a large single-story, eight-room masonry structure adjacent to an extensive irrigation ditch and field area, was occupied during the late prerevolt period, based on ceramic evidence.[51] The presence of majolica ceramics, including spindle whorls, large room size, and absence of a kiva depression indicate that Casa Acequia, unlike Ojo Cuchilla, was clearly a Spanish site.[52]

There were other officials associated with the Santo Domingo basin in the seventeenth century, mainly in the 1660s, who might also have owned land there even though they were not mentioned as such in surviving records. Two settlers, who each held half of the encomienda of Cochiti in the 1660s, were Diego Pérez Romero and José Telles Jirón.[53] Romero's father was Gaspar Pérez, an armorer who arrived in New Mexico in 1608 and who might have been the original grantee.[54] Telles Jirón, who came to New Mexico possibly about 1650, held the encomienda of San Felipe in 1661 but was living in the jurisdiction of Senecú in the far south where he owned an estancia in 1667.[55] Juan Varela de Losada, the alcalde mayor of Cochiti from 1661 to 1662, was one of five alcaldes mayores in the Santo Domingo basin in the 1660s who might also have been landowners there.[56] Other known alcaldes mayores of the Cochiti jurisdiction in the 1660s were Andrés López Sambrano, Miguel de Hinojos, and Francisco Romero de Pedraza.[57] Andrés de Peralta, who was killed at Kewa Pueblo during the 1680 revolt, was alcalde mayor of the jurisdiction at that time.[58]

CHAPTER SIXTEEN

The Middle Rio Grande Region

☩ THE MIDDLE RIO GRANDE REGION, FOR PURPOSES OF THIS STUDY, stretches along the Rio Grande from its confluence with the Jemez River some fifty miles to the south, approximately the Albuquerque-Belen basin (see map 2, p. 206). In early colonial times, the region encompassed part of the Sandia jurisdiction in the north, where there were three occupied pueblos throughout the prerevolt period—Sandia, Puaray, and Alameda—and the Isleta jurisdiction south from about Tijeras Arroyo, where Isleta was the only pueblo. The number of known settlers identified as landowners or residents in this region in the seventeenth century is fifty. Sandia jurisdiction contained the largest number: thirty-five, of which ten lived in the vicinity of Bernalillo and the others in the area occupied by greater Albuquerque today. The remaining fifteen settlers were located in the less densely occupied Isleta jurisdiction. In 1661 Governor López de Mendizábal stated that the jurisdictions of Isleta and Sandia had the most Spaniards—"donde ay mas Españoles en el Govierno."[1] The properties of twenty-eight settlers, for which location information is sufficient for mapping, are shown on map 8 (see p. 212).

Sandia Jurisdiction

Bernalillo in the seventeenth century was not a settlement but a scattering of ranches on both sides of the river to which this collective name applied.[2] The Rio Grande at that time followed a course east of present Bernalillo.[3] The earliest known property in this area was mentioned in 1614 in connection with the imprisonment of Governor Peralta in the convent at Sandia Pueblo and his escape to an estancia 2 leagues (5.2 miles) away (Hackett, *Historical Documents*, 3:64). Although in which direction from Sandia the estancia was located is not given, it is likely that it was to the north, which would put it in the area of Bernalillo. Unfortunately, the owner of the estancia is not mentioned.

Three other families seem to have had properties in the upper Bernalillo area sometime in the seventeenth century. Cristóbal Baca II, grandson of Cristóbal I, who came to New Mexico in 1600, had land "at the Angostura de Bernalillo" according to his son Manuel, who was requesting these lands in 1695.[4] Cristóbal II and his family, including Manuel, answered the 1680 muster.[5] Earlier in the century the Baca family owned the estancia El Alamo in the Santa Fe River valley, and possibly this Bernalillo property represented an extension of the family's holdings into the Rio Abajo.

The property of Juan Ramírez de Salazar was "situated on the banks of the Rio del Norte [Rio Grande] between the pueblos of San Felipe and Sandia in the most important and populous part of the kingdoms and provinces of New Mexico."[6] Juan was active in New Mexico in the 1640s. He played a role in the murder of Governor Rosas, and even though he was pardoned, he nevertheless fled the colony.[7] His property was confiscated and converted to a military post where one officer and fifteen soldiers were stationed, but it was no longer maintained by 1680.[8]

In 1701 Diego de Montoya II, a possible great-grandson of original colonist Bartolomé de Montoya I, owned a house and land in Bernalillo on the west bank of the Rio Grande "opposite weaver's bend," which his son Salvador later claimed to have inherited, and it is probable that Diego owned this land prior to the 1680 revolt.[9] Diego's father, Bartolomé II, had a property in the Española basin at the time of the revolt, and he also held the encomienda of San Pedro (Paako), which he inherited about 1660 from his father Diego I, both of which might have been originally granted to Bartolomé I.[10] When the property in the Bernalillo area claimed by Diego II was acquired is unknown. It could have been any one of three known seventeenth-century Spanish habitation sites, all on the west bank of the Rio Grande (in its present course) and north of present Bernalillo. One (LA 50230) is less than a quarter mile above the ruin of Kuaua Pueblo (LA 187), also known as Coronado State Monument (see map 1, p. 205), which was abandoned in the 1630s; the second is located on part of the Kuaua site; and the third (LA 4955), known as Casa Quemada (having been burned during the Pueblo revolt), a spacious four-room, L-shaped structure, is less than a half mile below Kuaua.[11] Another site (LA 50247), also located north of Bernalillo but east of the Rio Grande (near the intersection of Interstate 40 and Highway 550), consisted of a single room that was probably occupied in the late seventeenth century.[12]

Farther south was the property of Tomé Domínguez, who was in New Mexico by 1636. He had a house near Bernalillo 2 leagues (5.2 miles) above Sandia Pueblo in 1637, which he might have held until he died in 1656, when it was inherited by his elder son Francisco Domínguez de Mendoza, who passed muster with his family in 1680.[13]

Juan Griego I, who in 1631 was settled in the Bernalillo area, was one of the early landholders in the area.[14] Juan came to New Mexico in 1598 and was one of the founders of Santa Fe, as well as holder of an encomienda grant. Before moving to the Bernalillo area, he seems to have had an estancia in the La Cañada district, where his son and heir Juan II was living in 1628.[15] The wife of Juan I, Pascuala Bernal, is probably the source of the Bernalillo placename.[16] His second son, Francisco Bernal (who used his mother's surname), might have continued holding the Bernalillo property after his father's death, and his son, Francisco Bernal II, who passed muster in 1680 with an extended family, likely inherited it after his father's death.[17]

It is possible that there was also a property in this area belonging to the related González Bernal family. Sebastián González married Isabel Bernal, daughter of Juan Griego and Pascuala Bernal, and their children added Bernal to their surname. In 1731 Juan González Bas was in litigation over lands "above Albuquerque," lands that were probably in Bernalillo where he was residing in 1710, having claimed that he returned after the reconquest to reoccupy the house where he had been born.[18] He was likely the grandson of Sebastían González and Isabel Bernal and son of Juan González Bernal/Bas.[19] Sebastián González, who lived in La Cañada before the revolt, was his uncle.[20]

Across the Rio Grande from present Bernalillo was Santiago Pueblo (LA 326), which was abandoned in the 1630s, possibly as a result of the epidemic that devastated the Pueblo population at that time.[21] Sometime during the following decade, Juan Estevan de Fagoaga established an estancia named Santiago in the Sandia jurisdiction, and it is thought that the ruins of seventeenth-century Spanish structures discovered on part of the pueblo site might have belonged to him; however, conflicting information about whether his estancia was twelve leagues from Santa Fe or twelve leagues from Kewa (Santo Domingo) Pueblo make it difficult to identify his residence with a particular archaeological site.[22]

The larger grouping of known Spanish settlers in the Sandia jurisdiction was located south of that pueblo in the present Albuquerque area. Here, too, during the seventeenth century the Rio Grande followed a course on the east side of the valley, its channel running roughly between present Second and Twelfth streets, leaving a greater area for settlement on the west side of the river—then known as the Atrisco valley, which is where Alameda Pueblo was located—some six miles south of Sandia Pueblo.[23] One of the greatest concentrations of Spanish agricultural settlements in seventeenth-century New Mexico was in the Atrisco valley between Alameda Pueblo and the hacienda of Juan Domínguez de Mendoza 3 leagues (7.8 miles) to the south, where, in the aftermath of the revolt, Governor Otermín noted seventeen ruined properties located along both sides of the river.[24] Scattered seventeenth-century references to settlers in a similar area yield thirteen landowners who were mentioned or whose presence can be inferred (see map 8, p. 212), another five who were noted as residents of Sandia jurisdiction and most probably were also landowners, three who were living in the Rio Abajo and whose family connections would indicate residence and perhaps landholding in this area, and two who were requesting land in the 1690s reconquest period that was likely held by them or their families before the 1680 revolt. This reconstructed population of twenty-three settlers is based on references from various sources and dates during the prerevolt period, and it is not certain if the ten described as residents or "other" did live in the Atrisco valley. However, the total of at least thirteen to eighteen definite or likely landholders in the valley is close to Governor Otermín's count of seventeen, and a statement in another document that there were "before the outbreak of 1680, nineteen ranchos, haciendas, etc. of Spaniards in the vicinity of where Albuquerque now is" indicates that for this limited area, the number of known settlers is fairly complete—the only area for which estimated figures are available with which to compare the reconstructed number of settlers.[25] It should be noted that in this area substantial amounts of land became available for Spanish settlement. Even before the 1620s, pueblos Piedras Marcadas (LA 290) and Calabacillas (LA 289) had been abandoned, and beginning in the late 1630s, a major epidemic forced the abandonment of Maigua (LA 716), Chamisal (LA 22765), and Corrales (LA 288) pueblos and the congregation of surviving populations in the three remaining—Sandia (LA 294), Puaray (LA 717), and Alameda (LA 421).[26]

Antonio de Albizu was the encomendero of Alameda Pueblo, among others, possibly in the 1660s.[27] His father, Tomás de Albizu, was in New

Mexico by 1623 and an encomendero by 1632—probably also of Alameda—and another relative, Juana de Albizu, was the wife of Felis de Carvajal, landowner in the central Atrisco valley; thus, although Antonio was described only as resident of the Rio Abajo, it is likely that he, and possibly his father before him, was a landowner in Sandia jurisdiction in the vicinity of Alameda Pueblo.[28] In 1680 he fled the revolt with his family.

Some nine miles south of Sandia Pueblo and just below present Alameda village in what might be considered the northern part of the Atrisco valley, there was a cluster of settlers. On the west side was the large Estancia de San Antonio, owned in 1660 and up to 1680 by Alonso García, who was in New Mexico by 1636 and who was alcalde mayor of Sandia jurisdiction in 1660 and again in 1670 and lieutenant governor of the Rio Abajo region at the time of the revolt.[29] García might have acquired this estancia through his marriage to Teresa Varela of the Varela Losada family, important landowners in this area, whose founder came to New Mexico in 1598.[30]

A short league above García's property was Francisco de Ortega's Estancia de San Nicolás, which he owned in the 1660s and which was described as ten to twelve leagues (twenty-six to thirty-one miles) from Kewa Pueblo, from which "some thirty Indians transported piñon to his estancia for Governor López de Mendízabal."[31] He must have died before the revolt, but Tiburcio and Pablo de Ortega, who passed the 1680 muster with their families, might have been his heirs.[32]

Antonio Jorge de Vera, grandson of original colonist Juan Jorge, was a resident of the Rio Abajo in 1661 and might have acquired land in the Atrisco valley, where his daughter Ana's husband, Alonso García de Noriega, possibly helped manage his father's large Estancia de San Antonio. Antonio died before 1680, but his son Antonio—who was born at El Alamo, the property of his mother's Baca family in the Santa Fe River valley—might have inherited any land his father had and held it until he fled the revolt with his family.[33]

Although there is no record of prerevolt landholding in the Atrisco valley by the Griego family, whose known property was in the Bernalillo area, a number of descendants of Juan I answered the 1680 muster, and it is possible that some of them had settled in the present Albuquerque area where the family name persists as Los Griegos, a barrio of Albuquerque located north of Old Town plaza.[34]

Across the river from Alonso García's estancia was the "hacienda" that Luisa (Lucía) de Montoya and her husband, Francisco de Trujillo, owned in 1663.[35] She was possibly the daughter of encomendero Diego de Montoya I, and Francisco was the son of encomendero Diego de Trujillo, whose property, El Paraje de las Huertas, was located in the northern part of Sandia jurisdiction. Their landholding was more than 3 leagues (7.8 miles) south of Sandia Pueblo and about 6 miles south of Puaray Pueblo.[36] It was near the southern end of what came to be called the Bosque Grande de doña Luisa, a gallery forest of cottonwood trees that stretched from Alameda Pueblo south toward the "hacienda" of Mexía, which was located just above the northern end of the Esteros de Mexía, an extensive area of open wetlands (see map 8, p. 212). Five men with the Trujillo surname passed the 1680 or 1681 musters, at least some of whom might have been the heirs of Luisa and Francisco.[37]

Below the Trujillo-Montoya estancia and five leagues (thirteen miles) north of Isleta Pueblo was the "hacienda" of Mexía.[38] Who Mexía was is something of a mystery but there is a possibility that he was a descendant of Antonio Mejía, who came to New Mexico with the reinforcements in 1600; however, he is not mentioned in any other known documents.[39] On his first incursion into New Mexico in 1692, Governor Vargas reported that the property was destroyed and abandoned but had good open land with water and pastures and bordered on the Camino Real.[40] The Mexía property was probably another stopover place (*paraje*) on the Camino Real, which followed a route on higher ground to the east of the Rio Grande. The Esteros de Mexía consisted of ponds (charcos), swamps (esteros), and marshes (cienegas) that extended to the southern limits of Albuquerque near the mouth of Tijeras Arroyo.[41] These wetlands were sustained by a high water table, and although they were subject to seasonal flooding, they provided valuable grazing for the settlers' livestock.

Below the Mexía property on the east side of the Rio Grande was the Estancia de San Nicolás, where Felis de Carvajal and his wife were living in 1664 when he was encomendero of part of Senecú Pueblo.[42] Felis was born in 1635 at the estancia established by his father Juan de Vitoria Carvajal, an original colonist, which would make the estancia one of the earliest Spanish properties in the area. At one time, this estancia might have been much more extensive and might have included the estancia owned by Francisco de Ortega in the 1660s, which was also called San Nicolás. Felis's estancia was located opposite Atrisco 2.5 to 3 leagues (6.5 to 7.8 miles) south of Alameda Pueblo and 5 leagues (13 miles) north of Isleta Pueblo.[43] Juan's widow, Isabel Holguín, was noted in 1662 as living on her land in Sandia jurisdiction.[44] Other Carvajal properties that belonged to Felis's brothers Agustín and Gerónimo were located in the Santo Domingo basin and Galisteo basin respectively. Nicolás de Carvajal, who passed muster in 1681, might have been the son and heir of Felis, but there is no information about whether he returned to claim the estancia San Nicolás.⁴⁵

In 1695 Governor Vargas made a grant to Pedro López (del Castillo), who had returned after the exile in El Paso: "Pedro López. Grant of a tract of land on the Rio del Norte called San Nicolás opposite the agricultural lands of Atrisco and on the edge of the Esteros de Mexía."⁴⁶ Was Governor Vargas granting to Pedro the estancia that had belonged to Felis de Carvajal before the revolt or other land that also fits this description or had formerly been part of the Carvajal estancia but acquired by Pedro prior to the revolt? Possibly it was the latter, but unfortunately in existing records there is no mention of landowning or residence in the Middle Rio Grande region by members of the López del Castillo family to which Pedro apparently belonged—the earliest members of which, Matías and Diego, were in New Mexico in the 1620s and 1630s and resided in Santa Fe.⁴⁷

Across the Rio Grande in the midsection of the Atrisco valley were a number of estancias that had access to the Camino Real by means of the Barelas ford.⁴⁸ One of these west-side estancias was owned by Pedro Varela de Losada II, son of original colonist Pedro I.⁴⁹ It is likely that the part of central Albuquerque that came to be known as the district or barrio of Barelas is located on land that belonged to Pedro in the 1660s. In 1664 a meeting took place in Pedro II's house that was concerned with the founding of a villa in this area, "the villa de Cerralvo."⁵⁰ However, this proposed villa was not established. Pedro's brother Juan, who was alcalde mayor of Cochiti in 1662, was only mentioned as living in Sandia jurisdiction, but if he did not have an estancia of his own, he might have shared Pedro's, which their father might have acquired earlier in the century.⁵¹ Although neither Pedro II nor Juan answered Governor Otermín's musters in 1680 and 1681, a number of their descendants did, and perhaps some of them maintained the family landholdings up to the time of the revolt. One such person was Alférez Alonso Varela de Losada, who passed muster in 1680 with a numerous family.⁵² In 1668 when he was twenty-four years old, he testified that he was a resident of Sandia jurisdiction, possibly living on one of the Varela de Losada properties, if not his own.⁵³

The Hacienda de Atrisco, located near the Varela de Losada estancia on the west side of the valley, was the property of Juan Domínguez de Mendoza, son of Tomé I, who was in New Mexico by 1636.⁵⁴ It was located 3 leagues (7.8 miles) south of Alameda Pueblo and 4.5 leagues (11.7 miles) north of

Isleta Pueblo and probably was adjacent to the estancia of Pedro Durán y Chávez II.[55] Juan might well have acquired his land, or part of it, when he married Isabel Durán y Chávez, daughter of Pedro II and granddaughter of Pedro I, who came to New Mexico in 1600 and was probably one of the earliest settlers in this area.[56] Juan was appointed alcalde mayor of Isleta and Sandia jurisdiction and lieutenant captain general of the Rio Abajo and Salinas by Governor Bernardo López de Mendizábal and was also escudero of the Humanas encomienda in the 1660s.[57] He was still in possession of his property, whose gardens contained fruit trees, at the time of the revolt when he fled with his family.

The estancia of Juan's neighbor and father-in-law, Pedro Durán y Chávez II, was part of the holdings of Pedro's father, Pedro Durán y Chávez, and in the 1660s it was described as south of Sandia Pueblo and 4 leagues (10.4 miles) north of Isleta Pueblo on the Rio Grande.[58] Pedro's older brother Fernando I, lieutenant governor of the Sandia jurisdiction in 1638, was his father's principal heir (Pedro I was dead by 1637), becoming encomendero of San Felipe Pueblo and a major landholder in the area until he died shortly before 1669.[59] These lands were described as extending from the boundaries of San Felipe Pueblo down through Bernalillo to Atrisco. The son of Fernando I, Cristóbal, was reported living in Sandia jurisdiction in 1663, presumably on family lands.[60] At that time he was escudero of the half of the encomiendas of Zia and Cochiti, but later he either died or left the colony because his name does not appear on the Otermín musters.[61] In 1692 Cristóbal's cousin, Fernando II, who did answer the 1680 muster, was requesting a tract of agricultural land with an acequia madre located on the Rio Grande, commonly called Atrisco, that he inherited from his father Pedro II.[62]

In his request, Fernando II mentioned an old house located nearby that belonged to Juan de Perea, presumably another estancia owner in this area, possibly in the latter part of the century.[63] Three men with this name were on the El Paso musters of the early 1680s, but there is insufficient information to link any one of them to the Juan de Perea living in the Atrisco area.[64]

On the east side of the river 7 leagues (18 miles) south of Sandia Pueblo, 4 leagues (10.4 miles) below the Trujillo estancia, and north of Isleta was the hacienda of "Los Gómez," the most prominent landholding family in New Mexico, members of whom had properties in the Española basin, Taos jurisdiction, and the Southern Río Grande region as well as in the Sandia district.[65] This family was founded by Francisco Gómez, who came to New

Mexico in 1604, where he subsequently held all of the important posts in the colony short of the governorship, and by the 1620s he had been granted seven encomiendas (appendix table E).[66] How early the family acquired this particular property is unknown. Francisco I died in 1656, but his sons, particularly his heir Francisco Gómez Robledo, were active in the colony and continued to maintain the family properties up to the time of the revolt. They added their mother's name, Robledo, to their surname.[67]

Another early landholding was that of Diego Bellido, son of Juan Rodríguez Bellido, who came to New Mexico in 1600. Juan was one of the founders of Santa Fe and a supply train escort in 1606 and 1609.[68] Diego, who died early, had an estancia in the jurisdiction of "Los Tiguas" in 1631.[69] This description puts his property somewhere in either the Sandia or Isleta districts at a very early date, but nothing more can be said about this property or its founding family.

There is also little to say about Diego de Luna, who was in New Mexico in 1654. In 1662 he was a vecino of the Sandia jurisdiction and presumably a landholder somewhere in the district.[70] His tenure presumably extended to 1680, when he fled the revolt with his family.[71]

La Villa de Cerralvo

The villa of Santa Fe, from its founding in 1610, remained the only officially established Spanish settlement in New Mexico prior to 1680. However, there was an attempt to found a second villa as early as 1631. Documents from this time mentioned the proposed founding of "la Villa de Nuestra Señora de la Piedad de Cerralvo" (named for the viceroy Rodrigo Pacheco de Osorio, marqués de Cerralvo). One of these documents records payments made to *pobladores* who were being sent out to found this villa "que se comiensa a poblar."[72] One such prospective settler was Roque de Casaus, who came to New Mexico with the wagon-train escorts of 1625 and 1629 and who in 1639 was alcalde ordinario of Santa Fe, while another was Diego de Santa Cruz, who was listed as *alcalde ordinario* of this planned new villa. Both of these men were residents of Santa Fe at the time.[73] The location of this proposed villa is not stated, but it is possible that it was in what later came to be called the Rio Abajo (lands lying south of La Bajada Mesa). Here a growing number of settlers were acquiring land, especially in the district between Sandia and Isleta pueblos, where the concentration of Spanish landholdings was greatest and where seemingly there was need for another center of civil administration. The location could have been specifically in the vicinity of where Albuquerque was later founded in 1706. Despite what appears to have been concrete planning, the villa was not established, but this failed attempt does show how early in the colony's history substantial numbers of colonists were moving south from Santa Fe and more northern areas. However, the idea of founding a villa in this area did not die, and another attempt was made thirty years later when Governor Diego de Peñalosa was charged with settling the "villa de Cerralvo."[74] The location of this proposed villa was "the valley called Atrisco, this being the best site in all New Mexico." According to this document, the governor and twelve or fifteen persons who offered to make the settlement signed the order at the estancia of Pedro Varela de Losada II in 1664 (see map 8, p. 212). Again, however, the proposed "villa de Cerralvo" was not founded, perhaps because, as one scholar claims, the signatures on the agreement were forgeries and it was a ploy by the governor to cover a land grab.[75]

Isleta Jurisdiction

This district extended south along the Rio Grande from about Tijeras Arroyo to the vicinity of the present village of Tome. Over this distance of some nineteen miles, fifteen known Spanish families were described as either landowners or residents. Only eight properties can be located with any specificity, and they are widely distributed along the Rio Grande (see map 8, p. 212). In 1682 Governor Otermín mentioned that he passed six burned estancias in the ten miles between the hacienda of Juan Domínguez and Isleta Pueblo.[76] Unfortunately, the only property in this area mentioned in the existing historical records is the estancia Pajarito.[77] The only pueblo in this area was Isleta (LA 724), located seven miles south of the Rio Grande-Tijeras Arroyo junction. It should be noted that in this jurisdiction, too, epidemics in the late 1630s led to the abandonment of five pueblos: Pur-e Tu-ay (LA 489), Bei-jui Tu-ay (LA 81), Valencia (LA 953), Ladera del Sur (50257), and Casa Colorado (LA 50261).[78]

The earliest estancia, Pajarito, located in the northern part of Isleta Pueblo lands, was likely established in the 1620s by a friar of the pueblo for his family.[79] In 1638 the estancia appeared to be in the hands of Alférez Andrés López de Gracia, possibly a son of the friar, who moved south to Guadalupe del Paso in 1661 as its alcalde mayor, but some of his heirs seem to have stayed in the area.[80] The Pajarito property, or part of it, belonged in the 1660s to

Andrés's daughter María and her husband, Francisco Ramírez de Salazar.[81] In 1663 the inhabitants of Isleta Pueblo lodged a complaint against Francisco for taking some of their land, possibly part of a long-standing complaint stemming from the estancia's origin.[82] Francisco might have been related to Alonso Ramírez de Salazar, who was living with his wife at Isleta Pueblo in 1626, or even to Francisco Ramírez, who came to New Mexico in 1598.[83] Another daughter of Andrés, Isabel, was married to Pedro de Sedillo, who came to New Mexico in the second half of the seventeenth century and was described as living in the Rio Abajo, very possibly having settled on the part of the Pajarito lands to which his wife had a claim.[84] In 1666 he was described as a "soldado que viva junto al pueblo de Isleta."[85] Possibly the estancia was located on or near the site of the present village named Pajarito, five miles north of Isleta Pueblo. In 1680 Pedro and his family fled the revolt.[86] How long María and Francisco held their estancia is uncertain; by 1680 Francisco was alcalde mayor of Casas Grandes.[87]

As early as 1626 Juan López Mederos and his wife were residing at Isleta.[88] He might have been the Juan López Medel who came to New Mexico in 1600.[89] Although the extent of Mederos's landholdings is unknown, he might have given some of his land to his daughter Catalina as a dowry when she married Tomé Domínguez de Mendoza II. Or, if Juan was no longer living at that time, his land was probably inherited by his son Pedro who lived at the estancia in 1664, and he might have donated land to his sister Catalina as a dowry. Pedro and his family, along with his sister, her husband, and her extended family, fled the revolt in 1680.[90]

Cristóbal Holguín, a native of Santa Fe, was also living in Isleta jurisdiction in the 1660s. In 1661 he was described as a resident of the jurisdiction of Isleta living 2 leagues (5.2 miles) from the Isleta convent.[91] He was the son of Juan López Holguín, a colonist who came to New Mexico in 1600 and who was one of the founders of Santa Fe.[92] Although there is no direct record of land acquisition by this family, it might have been obtained as a grant by the father Juan or by Cristóbal through marriage to Melchora de Carvajal. His sister Isabel Holguín was the wife of Juan de Vitoria Carvajal, original colonist and landowner in the Sandia jurisdiction by the 1630s.[93] Cristóbal's son and heir Salvador escaped the revolt with his family in 1680.[94]

Cristóbal de Tapia owned land 2 leagues (5.2 miles) south of Isleta Pueblo on the west side of the Rio Grande and above the ruined pueblo of San Clemente (LA 81).[95] He was possibly related to Juan Fernández de Tapia, who probably came to New Mexico in 1598 and who by 1625 was encomendero of one-quarter of Taos.⁹⁶ Juan married Francisca Robledo and thus came to be related to the Francisco Gómez Robledo clan, whose founder, Francisco Gómez, established an estancia called Las Barrancas located farther south, possibly early in the century.⁹⁷ Francisco's contemporary, Juan Fernández, might also have been attracted to the Rio Abajo at that time and acquired by marriage the land that was eventually inherited by Cristóbal, who survived to answer the 1681 musters.⁹⁸

West of Cristóbal's land was a property that apparently was established by Mateo Manzanares, who also held land in the vicinity of San Felipe Pueblo in 1636. His property in the Middle Rio Grande region is known through the post-reconquest claim made by his daughter Ana de Sandoval y Manzanares.⁹⁹ The property, called San Clemente, was located in the vicinity of the pueblo ruin of that name (LA 81), also known as Bei-jui Tu-ay, which is about eight miles south of Isleta Pueblo. In 1716 it was described as "bounded on the east by the Rio del Norte [Rio Grande], on the west by the Rio Puerco, on the south by the house of Tomé Domínguez, and on the north by a ruin that is a little above the pueblo of San Clemente."¹⁰⁰ Ana's husband, Blas de la Candelaria, who died before 1680, is not mentioned in any of the seventeenth-century documents and was known to have been a New Mexico settler only through his wife and children. Ana returned to claim her paternal lands, which she and her husband possibly occupied before the revolt.¹⁰¹

The estancia of Francisco de Valencia was also located south of Isleta, but just how far is uncertain. Some sources say just 1 league (2.6 miles) from the pueblo, but others say 2 leagues north of the estancia of Tomé Domínguez de Mendoza II, even though Tomé's property is cited as being 4 leagues (10.4 miles) south of Isleta by one source and 11 leagues (28.6 miles) south by another.¹⁰² Because another source indicates that the two estancias were fairly close, the eleven-league distance is probably not correct; most likely these properties were located not far from the present villages of Valencia and Tome, which were probably established on the lands originally held by these two families, that is, on land eight and twelve miles south of Isleta Pueblo respectively.¹⁰³ The Valencia property could possibly have been established quite early (Francisco was probably the son of Blas de Valencia, who came to New Mexico in 1600) and on or near lands of Valencia Pueblo that was likely abandoned in the late 1630s.¹⁰⁴ Francisco's wife, María López Millán, was the sister of Andrés López de Gracia, and so Francisco was thus related to the family whose property, Estancia de Pajarito established in the 1620s, was located at the northern end of Isleta jurisdiction.¹⁰⁵ Francisco held important positions in the 1660s: encomendero of Isleta Pueblo, lieutenant general for the Rio Abajo, and alcalde mayor of Isleta in 1668 just before he died.[106] The estancia was seemingly maintained by his widow and son Juan until 1680, when the extended family fled to El Paso.[107]

Tomé Domínguez de Mendoza II was the son of Tomé I, who was in New Mexico at least by 1636 and was likely a landowner in the Middle Rio Grande region well before his death in 1656.[108] Tomé II, like his brother Juan, who held the Hacienda de Atrisco some twenty-four miles to the north, might have acquired his estancia through marriage. His wife was Catalina López Mederos, daughter of Juan López Mederos, who was in this area earlier.[109] Tomé II was alcalde mayor of Isleta jurisdiction in 1659 and Sandia jurisdiction in 1666 and fled with his family in 1680.[110]

Juan Ruiz de Cáceres, who came to New Mexico in 1600 and died in 1636 at his estancia in Isleta jurisdiction, was another very early settler in this area.[111] He is also known to have owned land in the Santa Fe River valley and the Española basin.[112] Another man with the same name who was a soldier-escort in 1652 might possibly have been his son, and a Juan Ruiz de Cáceres who returned with Governor Vargas to New Mexico, where he participated in the Granillo survey and acquired a property in the Española basin in the 1690s, might also have been related to Juan I, thus establishing this family's continuity in New Mexico in the 1600–1680 period.[113] Whether there was prerevolt continuity of landholding in Isleta jurisdiction remains unknown.

Juan García Holgado was a resident of Isleta jurisdiction in 1638. In 1667 when he was alcalde mayor of Socorro jurisdiction in the Southern Rio Grande region, he was mentioned as a resident of the Rio Abajo but his home was possibly still in the Isleta district, where he might have been a landowner.[114] Earlier, in 1650, he was alcalde mayor of Alameda in Sandia jurisdiction. Juan's father, Álvaro, came to New Mexico in 1600 and in 1625 was living in Santa Fe; however, it is possible that in the 1620s or 1630s he acquired land in the Isleta district, where he was connected to the López de Gracia family, and that his son Juan inherited this land.[115] Juan's brother Francisco García was residing in Isleta jurisdiction in 1665 and might have been living there with Juan or on a separate property of his own.[116] Francisco was born in San Gabriel in 1615 and was living in Santa Fe with his family in 1632; sometime later he lived in the vicinity of Tajique and Cuarac (Quarai), possibly as a soldier, before moving to the Isleta district where he was a weaver.[117] Diego García Holgado, possibly a grandson of Álvaro, represented family continuity up to the revolt, when he answered the 1681 muster with his family, but it is not known where he had been living.[118]

In addition, there is Juan Fresqui (Fresco), who, with two other Flemish miners, first came to New Mexico in 1617 looking for mines and in 1625 returned to Santa Fe with mining and smelting equipment that was then destroyed by local residents.[119] Fresqui stayed in New Mexico, but where he lived was not mentioned. He might have remained in the Santa Fe area and worked mines in the Cerrillos Hills or San Pedro Mountains, but at some point he might have moved to the Rio Abajo, where his son Juan Fresqui II declared himself to be a vecino in 1661, most likely in the jurisdiction of Isleta where he was alcalde mayor by 1667.[120] Juan I was most probably dead by that time, but earlier he might have been involved in initiating mining activity in the area. Although no one with the Fresqui name is listed on the 1680 or 1681 musters, Pedro Fresqui, who was born in the Rio Abajo circa 1679, was living in Socorro del Paso in 1712, as were his parents Francisco Fresqui and María Ortiz, both natives of New Mexico.[121] The uniqueness of this name in the colony argues that Francisco and Pedro were most likely descendants of old Juan Fresqui the miner.

A habitation site occupied by Spaniards in the latter part of the seventeenth century is Comanche Springs (LA 14904). The site covers about fifteen acres and contains three structures built near two perennial springs. It is located about eleven miles east of the Rio Grande and five to six miles west of the Manzano Mountains, where Comanche Canyon (see map 8, p. 212) provides access to the settlements east of the mountains. Features of the three structures that were discovered, cobble footings that supported thick adobe brick walls, large room size, and linear arrangement of rooms, are characteristic of Spanish colonial buildings. The largest of the three buildings contained six rooms and the other two had two rooms each. Artifacts found at the site made of iron, copper, and silver, along with sherds of Mexican majolica and Chinese porcelain and bones of domesticated animals, indicate that the site was established by Spanish people. Although Spaniards in New Mexico also used Puebloan-made pottery, the presence of local ceramics in addition to stone tools and the remains of wild birds indicate that native people also lived at Comanche Springs at that time. Dating of the site rests largely with the ceramics found there. By far the largest amount of ceramic material (78 percent) found is of the traditional utilitarian type and of that, Salinas Redware, which was made by the Tiwa people in the pueblos east of the Manzanos from about 1630 to the 1670s, was dominant. The bulk of evidence, acquired using various dating methods on this and other materials at the site, indicates a period of settlement from about 1650 to 1680.[122] The abundance of Salinas Redware at the site indicates a strong link, via Comanche Canyon, to the Salinas pueblos, which suggests that the native people who lived at Comanche Springs might have been from those Tiwa pueblos. There might also have been a connection with the Spanish landholdings to the west along the Rio Grande. The presence of cattle, sheep, and goat bones at the site may mean that ranching took place there and that it was established as an outpost of one of the Rio Grande estancias to take advantage of the extensive grasslands and the water provided by the springs. This water might also have irrigated some crops, although evidence of this kind of agriculture activity is lacking.[123] The nearest known estancia in this period belonged to Tomé Domínguez de Mendoza II, and perhaps he might have developed this site (Comanche Springs was included in the Tome community land grant of 1739).

What makes the Comanche Springs site notable is evidence of metal production, the main evidence being the slag and other metallurgical debris found there. In a room in the largest of the three buildings was a raised charcoal-covered adobe platform that could be interpreted to be a metallurgical hearth. The bloomery slag indicates that it was iron that was produced—a scarce but much-needed metal. The ore presumably came from mines in the Manzano Mountains, but neither historic nor modern information about mines in these mountains is sufficient to identify just where the source of the ore was located. Knowledge of simple metal production such as that carried out at Comanche Springs might have been present among the Spanish population in New Mexico. The only known miner who might have lived in this area was Juan Fresqui. He was probably dead by midcentury, but his possible prior influence and the presence of his son might have contributed to the beginning of metal production at Comanche Springs. Although metal working has been thought to have been the purpose of this settlement, the small amount of slag and related debris recovered at the site has led some investigators to suggest that such activity was only carried on occasionally or seasonally—possibly as an adjunct to ranching and farming.[124]

A site to the east of Comanche Springs, the Metzler site (LA 103997), located at a small spring near the approach to Comanche Canyon and perhaps contemporaneous with the Comanche Springs site, has been identified as a "fortified hacienda of Spanish date," but no further description is reported.[125] It might have served, among other things, as a refuge for Spaniards and Puebloans fleeing the Apache attacks on their settlements east of the Manzanos that intensified during the 1660s and 1670s.

CHAPTER SEVENTEEN

The Estancia Basin

✣ EAST OF THE MANZANO MOUNTAINS THAT FORM THE EASTERN boundary of the Middle Rio Grande region lies the vast Estancia basin, an old Pleistocene lake bed with no external drainage that at its lowest point, some seventeen to twenty-three miles east of the mountains, encompasses a series of salt flats (see map 2, p. 206). Seventeenth-century Puebloan settlement in the basin was confined to its western and southern margins. Five villages occupied by Tiwa people, often referred to as the "Salinas" pueblos, were established along the eastern foothills of the Manzanos: Chilili (LA 874), LA 371, LA 372, Tajique (LA 381), and Quarai/Quarac (LA 95). Pueblos occupied by Tompiro people were Abó (LA 97) and Tenabó (LA 200), in the Abó Pass area at the southern end of the Manzanos. Farther east along the southern rim of the basin, there were four more Tompiro pueblos: Las Humanas (LA 120), Pueblo Pardo (LA 83), Pueblo Colorado (LA 476), and Pueblo Blanco (LA 51) (see map 1, p. 205). After a major demographic collapse in the late 1630s, only Chilili, Tajique, Quarai, and Abó on the west side and Las Humanas and Pueblo Blanco (also known as Tabirá) on the south survived, but in the 1670s they, too, were abandoned (see map 1, p. 205).[1]

What little information is available about seventeenth-century Spanish settlement in the Estancia basin suggests that it centered on the area of the Salinas pueblos, particularly in the vicinity of Tajique Pueblo. Three of the known Estancia basin settlers were descended from original colonists, but it cannot be established if their forbearers acquired land in the basin earlier in the century. Hernán Martín Serrano II, heir of encomendero and 1598 colonist Hernán I, was reported living in the Salinas district after about 1664 with his second wife and their children.² Juan Martín Serrano, Hernán's son by his first wife Isabel de Monuera, had a house in the vicinity of Quarai Pueblo in 1667–68.³ The family was possibly living on land acquired by Hernán I, but when he might have received such a grant is unknown. During the 1670s the family likely left the region when Apache attacks forced abandonment of the Salinas pueblos, and they possibly moved to the Galisteo basin, where in 1675 Hernán II testified that he was sixty-eight years old and a vecino of Santa Fe.⁴ In 1680 he fled the colony with his extended family.⁵

Bartolomé de Ledesma, possible son of Francisco de Ledesma, who came to New Mexico in 1598, was reported to be residing in the Spanish settlements near the Salinas pueblos before he died in 1662.⁶ He might have acquired his property through marriage to María Martín Monuera, daughter of Hernán Martín Serrano II, who was also the executor of Bartolomé's estate.⁷ Bartolomé and his wife were also residents of Santa Fe, where he was appointed *procurador del cabildo* by Governor Peñalosa.⁸

Alférez Alonso Martín Barba II was living in Chilili in 1660 at the same time that his father Alonso I, likely an original colonist (1597 muster), was living in the La Cañada district, leaving unanswered the question of when this family acquired property in the Estancia basin.⁹ Toward the end of the decade, Alonso II was charged with concubinage and exiled by Pedro de Leyva, the alcalde mayor.¹⁰ Alonso was dead by 1669, and his younger brother Esteban Barba was killed at Santo Domingo during the revolt, leaving only another younger brother, Domingo, and various other family members to pass the 1680–81 musters.¹¹

Pedro de Leyva, who came to New Mexico in 1637 was appointed alcalde mayor of the Salinas jurisdiction by Governor Juan Manso de Contreras in the late 1650s, the earliest known such official for this jurisdiction.¹² He was residing on his estancia in the Tajique district when he was replaced by Nicolás de Aguilar, who was appointed to the position by Governor López de Mendizábal.¹³ Pedro continued to live in the area, being cited as a resident and vecino of the Salinas jurisdiction in the 1660s.¹⁴ In 1664 he was appointed lieutenant governor of the Salinas jurisdiction by the succeeding governor, Juan Durán de Miranda.¹⁵ Although alcaldes mayores were forbidden to own land in the jurisdictions they were administrating, there is the suggestion that in the remote Salinas jurisdiction, land rights were included with the office.¹⁶ By the time of the revolt, Pedro and his family were living in the Galisteo basin, probably having acquired land there in the 1670s, when the Salinas pueblos were being abandoned—if not earlier, before his official appointments in the Salinas jurisdiction. In 1680 Pedro's sons, Nicolás and Juan, along with their families, including their sister and mother, were killed at their hacienda in the vicinity of Galisteo Pueblo while Pedro and another son were away on a mission to El Paso to escort to Santa Fe the supply train that was coming from Mexico City.[17]

José Nieto, a native of Santa Fe, had a house in 1661 between Tajique and Quarai, 1 league (2.6 miles) from Tajique, possibly at the site of the present village of Torreon, which is at the eastern end of the main route across the Manzano Mountains.[18] He was still living there in 1665, and in 1668 he was alcalde mayor, having been appointed in 1662, following the banishment of Nicolás de Aguilar.[19] However, in 1680 he and most of his family were killed at their estancia near Galisteo Pueblo.[20] It seems likely that the Nieto family, as well the Leyvas and possibly Hernán Martín Serrano II, had moved to the Galisteo basin as drought, epidemic disease, and Apachean attacks during the 1660s and 1670s caused the pueblos in the Estancia basin to be abandoned.

Only four other Spaniards were mentioned as living in the Estancia basin in the seventeenth century, and they, too, were located in the Salinas jurisdiction. There is no information about when Nicolás de Aguilar came to New Mexico (apparently having previously committed a murder in the Parral district of northern New Spain), but during 1659–61, when he was the henchman of Governor López de Mendizábal, he was named alcalde mayor of the Salinas jurisdiction and moved to the Tajique area from his estancia near Chilili Pueblo.[21] In the early 1660s he was cited as living with his family near Tajique Pueblo, where he had an estancia, but his nefarious activities as alcalde mayor led him to be recalled to New Spain. He was found guilty and banished from New Mexico for ten years.[22]

Diego González de Apodaca came to New Mexico in 1642 and in 1661 was living in the Salinas district with his family. That same year his wife, Sebastiana López de Gracia, was described as "estanciera que vive una legua del Pueblo de Quarac," a somewhat more precise location.[23] Diego was involved in the murder of Governor Luis de Rosas in 1642 but not executed, and two years later he and his family were staying with his wife's brother Andrés López de Gracia at the Estancia de Pajarito near Isleta Pueblo on the Rio Grande.[24] Just when they moved to the Salinas jurisdiction is unknown, but they might have been one of the earliest families to take up land there. Like other families in the district, they were probably forced to leave in the

1670s, but to where is another question—possibly to the Pajarito estancia. Their son José and family were among the refugees in El Paso in 1681.[25]

Antonio de Ávalos, born in New Mexico in 1630, was superintendent of the Salinas salt mines in 1660 and was most probably living in Tajique with his family. His wife's mother, Isabel Baca—at this time a widow—cooked for the priest at Tajique Pueblo.[26] Antonio and his family passed muster in 1680, but where they went when they were forced to leave Tajique in the 1670s remains unknown. As superintendent of the salt mines, he must have also spent time at the camps where the workers from the pueblos lived during their assigned terms of work.

Sebastián Montaño, who was reported to be ill in Las Salinas in 1669, might have been a settler in that jurisdiction, but by 1680 he had a house at La Cañada. Nothing certain is known about his antecedents.[27]

Habitation sites for these settlers have not been found, but a small L-shaped masonry structure (LA 383) located near present Manzano village might have been the residence of one of them or of some as yet unidentified settler. Although LA 383 had been identified by earlier archaeologists as a pueblo, its size and shape and the Glaze-F ceramics at the site suggest that it might have been a Spanish residence that was occupied during the latter part of the seventeenth century, when there were other Spanish estancias still in the area.[28]

No Spanish settlers are known to have resided in the even more remote and arid Jumanos district in the southern Estancia basin. Diego González Bernal, who was the alcalde mayor of Las Humanas jurisdiction in 1663, was probably only a temporary resident; he was also alcalde mayor of San Marcos and Galisteo pueblos in that decade.[29] Nor were encomenderos likely settlers in this district. A number of Spaniards were noted as encomenderos or escuderos of the principal pueblo, Las Humanas (Alonso Rodríguez Cisneros, Juan Domínguez de Mendoza, Juan González Bernal, Toribio de la Huerta, and Miguel de Hinojos).[30] But these men (except Rodríguez Cisneros) had landholdings elsewhere and were unlikely to have established residence in such a remote area. Two other Estancia basin encomenderos probably did not reside in the area either. Francisco Gómez was encomendero of half of Abó Pueblo, which gave him authority in an area tributary to his Estancia de las Barrancas on the Rio Grande above its confluence with Abó Arroyo.[31] Francisco de Anaya Almazán held half of the encomienda of Cuarac (Quarai), but he also had encomiendas in other regions.[32] His son-in-law was Alonso Rodríguez Cisneros, who seems to have been encomendero of one-third of Las Humanas Pueblo in the 1660s.[33] So far no seventeenth-century Spanish habitation sites have been discovered by archaeologists in this district.

The Estancia basin probably attracted few Spanish settlers in the seventeenth century, being a frontier open to Apachean attacks and lacking good sources of water except along the eastern margin of the Manzano Mountains, where the few known settlers clustered. The record of settlement, as elsewhere, remains incomplete but is probably indicative of what the actual pattern of settlement of that time was like.

CHAPTER EIGHTEEN

The Southern Rio Grande Region

✢ RETURNING TO THE RIO GRANDE FROM THE ESTANCIA BASIN through Abó Pass, one reaches the northern end of the Southern Rio Grande region, which begins a short distance above the confluence of that river with Abó Arroyo. The district includes the southern part of the Albuquerque-Belen basin, the Socorro basin, and continues south to Senecú Pueblo—in all a distance of some sixty miles (see map 2, p. 206). Extensive wetlands exist in the area below where the Rio Puerco joins the Rio Grande from the west and at Bosque del Apache National Wildlife Refuge some thirty-six miles to the south. Between these areas of wetlands are large open areas suitable for agriculture, while the springs that occur throughout the canyon lands along the margins of the flood plain of the Rio Grande provide for more limited settlement.[1] The area from about the Rio Puerco-Rio Grande confluence south to Senecú Pueblo was the homeland of the Piro people, who occupied fourteen pueblos at the beginning of the seventeenth century. Their number was reduced to four by about 1640, leaving only Sevilleta (LA 774), Alamillo (no LA number), Socorro (LA 791), and, in the far south, Senecú (no LA number).[2]

In the northern part of the Southern Rio Grande region, in the Sevilleta jurisdiction, were properties of four known Spanish settlers. One was the Estancia de San Nicolás de las Barrancas, which belonged to the Gómez family.[3] It was located on the east bank of the Rio Grande about ten leagues (twenty-six miles) south of Isleta Pueblo, five leagues (thirteen miles) south of the Tomé Domínguez de Mendoza II property, and some fifteen miles

155

north of Sevilleta Pueblo.[4] This site was probably chosen for its location in the vicinity of where the route from the Estancia basin through Abó Pass reached the Rio Grande and the Camino Real (see map 2, p. 206). The Sevilleta area was a strategic location; it was here that products such as piñon nuts and salt from the basin's salt pans were brought by native laborers for transshipment and that the wagon trains made final preparation for the journey south to Parral, Zacatecas, Durango, and Mexico City.[5] The estancia was inherited by Francisco Gómez Robledo, eldest son of 1604 colonist Francisco Gómez, upon the latter's death in 1656 or 1657, and it was where Francisco II's brother Andrés was living in 1663.[6] Their father might well have acquired this estancia as early as the 1620s. Francisco II managed the family's many additional properties in the Middle Rio Grande, Española, and Far North regions as well.[7] He also inherited his father's numerous encomiendas, including half of Abó Pueblo obtained in exchange for half of Sandia Pueblo, thus giving the family access to a labor force that could be used to haul salt and other goods from the Estancia basin, probably commuting tribute goods to labor as they did with their Tesuque encomienda—an illegal practice.[8] In 1680 he and his family, along with numerous other members of this clan, fled the revolt.[9]

Owners of other Spanish properties in this area also brought goods from the Estancia basin. Besides the Gómez Robledo family, members of the Romero family—to whom many other landholders in the region were related by marriage—were important landholders. Felipe Romero de Pedraza's estancia, San Antonio de Sevilleta, was located near Sevilleta Pueblo. It was 8 or more leagues (more than 21 miles) from Abó Pueblo, about 3 leagues (7.8 miles) south of the Gómez estancia of Las Barrancas and some 7 leagues (18 miles) north of Alamillo Pueblo, all on the east side of the Rio Grande.[10] Felipe was a grandson of Bartolomé Romero I, who came to New Mexico in 1598.[11] Some other members of the Romero family also seem to have settled early in the Southern Rio Grande region. Felipe's uncle Bartolomé II and his wife were living in the Senecú Pueblo area as early as 1628, and possibly the patriarch himself settled here even earlier.[12] Felipe married the daughter of Diego de Guadalajara, another landowner in the area.[13] His home, along with the home of his neighbor Vicente de Cisneros, was attacked by Apaches in 1668.[14] In 1680 Felipe and his family joined other settler families in the flight to El Paso. His father-in-law's family, however, had left the colony the previous decade.

Vicente de Cisneros was possibly the son of Diego de Cisneros, who was mentioned as being in New Mexico in 1632. Little else is known about

Vicente except that he and a brother named Bartolomé were captains in the military guard in the Zuni jurisdiction in 1662 and that Bartolomé's son Antonio accompanied Governor Otermín in a failed attempt to take back the pueblos in 1681–82.[15]

Diego de Guadalajara, who came to New Mexico in 1628 with the new governor, was still in Santa Fe in 1636, serving as a member of its cabildo and in 1640 as its *alguacil mayor*.[16] In 1643 he accompanied the wagon train to Mexico City, and perhaps because of his involvement in the caravan trade and his position as encomendero of Sevilleta Pueblo, he acquired land in that district that was described in 1660 as a flourishing estancia.[17] This property, neighboring that of Felipe Romero's Estancia de San Antonio, was located on the Rio Grande 1 league (2.6 miles) north of Sevilleta Pueblo and 6 leagues (16 miles) north of Alamillo Pueblo.[18] In the late 1650s Governor Juan Manso de Contreras congregated the people of Sevilleta Pueblo with those of Alamillo Pueblo at the request of the clergy, who accused Diego of denying the Sevilletans access to religious services and of "enslaving" them by making them haul salt from the Estancia basin. But after three years, the new governor, Bernardo López de Mendizábal, restored the Sevilletans to their pueblo.[19] Despite his powerful position, Diego apparently did not remain in New Mexico after his wife's death but returned to New Spain, where by 1679 he was serving as alcalde mayor in the Valle de Toluca.[20] Diego's son Francisco had previously moved to New Spain, and no one with the Guadalajara name appears on the 1680 or 1681 musters.

Farther south, between the pueblos of Sevilleta and Alamillo, was the Estancia Acomilla that belonged to Gerónimo Márquez, who came to New Mexico with Governor Oñate.[21] The estancia was located on the west side of the Rio Grande at the southwest base of San Acacia Butte in the area called "Vueltas de Acomilla," where, at that time, the great Alamillo meander ran some three hundred meters to the west of the site.[22] The estancia is believed to have occupied the site of LA 286, a Hispanic site that had a prior late-Piro pueblo component.[23] In 1631 Gerónimo, then seventy-one, was living at the estancia, possibly with his eldest son Francisco, who was married to a woman from Socorro Pueblo.[24] Francisco was forty-three at the time and likely died well before the revolt; his only surviving brother in 1631 was Diego, who held Los Cerrillos estancia in the Galisteo basin, but he was beheaded in 1643 in connection with the murder of Governor Luis de Rosas. Although neither Gerónimo nor his sons were alive in 1680, a number of Márquez men of the next generation were on Governor Otermín's muster list.

Two brothers, Francisco and Alonso Pérez Granillo, had estancias south of Alamillo Pueblo. They were the sons of Francisco Pérez Granillo I, who was in New Mexico by 1617 as clerk of the colonial government.²⁵ The sons were both in charge of the wagon trains to and from Mexico City in 1661 and 1664 but might well have been involved in this business earlier and established their estancias in the Southern Rio Grande region for that reason.²⁶ Either might have been the Granillo who was alcalde mayor of Senecú in 1663.²⁷ Alonso's property was 2 leagues (5.2 miles) below Alamillo Pueblo, where he was cited as living in 1631.²⁸ His brother Francisco II might have been residing in the area at that time, too, although the location of his estancia, 2 leagues (5.2 miles) south of Socorro Pueblo, is not mentioned in available records until 1660–62.²⁹ Francisco II, who was married to Sebastiana Romero de Salazar, had five sons who answered the Otermín musters, one of whom, Luis, returned and was the leader of the team that conducted the survey of Spanish properties in the La Cañada district.³⁰ Francisco's property might have been one of the four abandoned estancias that Governor Otermín encountered in the 6 leagues (15.6 miles) between Socorro Pueblo and the ruins of San Pascual Pueblo in 1681, but, unfortunately, he did not mention who their owners were (see map 1, p. 205).³¹ Alonso left New Mexico before the revolt of 1680, at which time he was alcalde mayor of the jurisdiction of Janos in Sonora.³²

Another property in the Socorro area, also perhaps one of Governor Otermín's four abandoned estancias, belonged to Sebastián Rodríguez de Salazar and his wife, Luisa Díaz de Betanzos. He had come to New Mexico in 1619, and in 1626 they were living in Santa Fe.³³ When they acquired their property in the Socorro jurisdiction is unknown, but in 1662 Luisa, a widow aged eighty, declared that she was a vecina of the pueblo of Socorro.³⁴ She also mentioned that her daughter Isabel de Salazar was the wife of Agustín Romero I and that their daughter Sebastiana as well as Agustín's brother Bartolomé II and his nephew Felipe Romero de Pedraza were all landowners in the Southern Rio Grande region.³⁵

"The hacienda they call that of Luis López" was mentioned by Governor Otermín in January 1682 as he and his men returned to El Paso, having failed to restore Spanish rule to the pueblos.³⁶ It was located about eight miles south of Socorro Pueblo, or halfway between Socorro and the Qualacú pueblo ruin on the east side of the Rio Grande, and was perhaps another of Governor Otermín's four abandoned estancias (see map 1, p. 205).³⁷ Little else is known about Luis López except that in 1665–67 he was alcalde mayor of the Piro pueblos.[38] He was also mentioned as a vecino of the Senecú jurisdiction for the years 1659–68.[39]

At the extreme southern end of the Southern Rio Grande region were the properties of Bartolomé Romero II and José Telles Jirón. Bartolomé II, son of the family founder who came to New Mexico with Governor Oñate, was born in 1602 in the Spaniards' first capital, San Gabriel.[40] In 1628 he was described as living in the jurisdiction of Senecú with his wife, María del Moral Granillo, a member of the Granillo clan that lived to the north in the vicinity of Socorro Pueblo. In 1632 María was taking treatment at the mission in Senecú Pueblo for a spell that had been cast on her.[41] Although it is not clear where in Senecú jurisdiction they lived, from his wife's condition it might be surmised it was near Senecú Pueblo. Whether their estancia continued to be held by the family is uncertain. Their son, Bartolomé III, was an alcalde of Santa Fe in 1661 and a landowner in the Far North region.[42] Whether Bartolomé II and his wife stayed on in the Senecú area that was increasingly subject to the Apache raids in the 1670s that led to the temporary abandonment of Senecú Pueblo is unknown, but, if they did, they probably sought refuge at Socorro Pueblo along with their neighbors.[43] None of the 1680 Romero refugees can be directly linked to this family.

José Telles Jirón came to New Mexico in 1649 as a soldier accompanying Governor Ugarte y la Concha and after serving him in the casas reales remained in the colony, where he married Catalina Romero, niece of his Senecú neighbor Bartolomé Romero II and sister of Felipe Romero de Pedraza, landowner in the Sevilleta jurisdiction.[44] It was possibly through these connections that he acquired the estancia on which he raised livestock—principally sheep. Just where in the jurisdiction of Senecú their property was located was not stated, but possibly they established themselves in the vicinity of Senecú Pueblo, that being the only pueblo in this vast area, in order to be close to a source of labor. As late as 1667 José described himself as an estanciero and vecino of Senecú jurisdiction.[45] Earlier he had been awarded the encomiendas of San Felipe and Cochiti pueblos by Governor Juan Manso de Contreras, but they were revoked by the succeeding governor, Bernardo López de Mendizábal, who granted him the encomienda of Taos Pueblo, part of which had belonged to Francisco Gómez Robledo until he was arrested by the Inquisition.[46] José also owned land in the Agua Fria section of the Santa Fe River valley, and it is not known if he held both properties contemporaneously. In 1668, after Felipe Romero and Vicente Cisneros were attacked by Apaches, Governor Fernando de Villanueva ordered the Telles Jirón family to move to Socorro Pueblo, where they possibly continued to live as Apache attacks intensified into the 1670s.[47] It is possible that the family returned from their refuge in Socorro when there was an attempt to resettle Senecú Pueblo in 1677, but the revolt in 1680 ultimately made it impossible for them even to remain in New Mexico.[48]

Additional settlers with interests in the Southern Rio Grande region but who are not mentioned in the available records as landowners or residents are two encomenderos and one alcalde mayor. Juan García Holgado, alcalde mayor of Socorro in 1667, was a landowner in the Middle Rio Grande region but might have also have had land in the Southern Rio Grande region.[49] Felis de Carvajal was encomendero of part of Senecú in 1661, and Juan Alonso Mondragón held this pueblo in 1660.[50] Carvajal owned the Estancia de San Nicolás in the Middle Rio Grande region, but any landholdings of Mondragón are as yet unknown; either or both might have acquired land in the Southern Rio Grande region.

Conclusion

✣ A NEW LANDSCAPE WAS CREATED IN NEW MEXICO WITH THE SPANISH conquest and occupation. The five-hundred-strong expedition led by Juan de Oñate that reached Pueblo country in 1598 brought with it different concepts of governance and resource use, as well as new technologies that greatly transformed the human and natural landscapes. The Spaniards brought with them an emphasis on the individual that stood in contrast to the communalistic approach to land and labor that characterized Pueblo society. Because the Spaniards came to New Mexico to acquire wealth and prestige for themselves and their families, their negative perception of the province's resources led to a major defection a few years after the colony's initiation, resulting in the loss of almost two-thirds of the men and a majority of the families that had come from New Spain. Such a reduced number of settlers led the Crown to consider abandoning the colony, but the desire to continue the work of converting the Pueblo population to Christianity prevailed, and the remaining soldier-colonists and the civil authorities were meant to provide support for this effort. The Franciscan missionaries added a new element to the Pueblo landscape as they built, using Pueblo labor, impressive church-convents in the larger pueblos. The Spanish settlers initially resided in a pueblo converted for their use, which they named San Gabriel. Continuing problems led to the resignation of Governor Oñate in 1607 and the conversion of the colony from proprietary to Crown status. A new capital, the villa of Santa Fe, was formally established in 1610, although some colonists apparently had settled at the site a few years earlier. It remained the only official settlement until the Spaniards were forced to abandon the colony, at least for a time, in the face of a revolt by the Pueblo peoples some seven decades later in 1680. At that time the Spanish settler population (not counting servants and others) numbered some fourteen hundred, of whom about two hundred were men who could bear arms, a number larger than the approximately two hundred who remained after the defection of 1601, of whom about seventy were soldier-settlers. In 1680 the Puebloan population of about thirteen thousand greatly outnumbered the Spaniards, although it was much reduced from some fifty thousand in 1598.

In the absence of significant mineral wealth, the sixty to seventy soldier-colonists who remained after the defection in 1601 looked to the land to provide for them and to the Puebloan population to work that land. It was the scattered rural landholdings of the colonists, rather than towns or villages, that typified the Spanish settlement landscape, and it was these haciendas and estancias that had the greatest impact on the landscape of New Mexico. They tended to be located in the vicinity of pueblos, where the source of labor resided and from which those fortunate enough to have been awarded encomienda grants could more readily collect the tribute goods to which they were entitled. The wheat and various European fruits and vegetables the Spaniards brought with them generally required irrigation in dry New Mexico as did the maize and other crops of the Pueblo peoples. Hence there was a certain competition for irrigable land, most of which had already been taken up by the Puebloans. Although Crown laws were meant to prevent the exploitation of native land and labor, they did not always hold sway on this remote frontier, and the area devoted to Spanish crops expanded with the aid of native labor, more robust irrigation technology, and the introduction of the plow. But the introduction of grazing livestock to the vast virgin grasslands of New Mexico had an even greater impact on the landscape. Cattle, sheep, and goats provided meat, tallow, and hides, while the wool from sheep provided the raw material for textile workshops (using Pueblo labor) that gradually displaced the cotton that was originally raised by the Puebloans. Horses brought by the Spaniards provided a means of transportation, and their oxen pulled the plows and the carts they introduced.

Although the number of Spaniards in New Mexico remained small, they expanded their activities throughout the former Pueblo domain centered on the Rio Grande—from Taos Pueblo in the north some 215 miles south to near present San Marcial and east to Pecos and the Salinas pueblos of the Estancia basin. The earliest expansion of settlement away from San Gabriel seems to have taken place even before the provincial capital was officially moved to Santa Fe in 1610. The nearby Santa Cruz River valley, at the time bereft of occupied pueblos but not far from some eight Tewa pueblos that could provide workers, attracted early settlers, as did the Santa Fe River valley some twenty-three miles farther south, where permanent Pueblo villages had been abandoned there for over a century. A new pueblo, La Cienega, was created in the Santa Fe River valley, probably by the Spanish authorities, who congregated residents from other pueblos at a site that was more convenient to the villa and the landholders in the valley. Few Spanish landholdings were established to the north, where there were only two pueblos, Taos and Picurís, and where the growing season was much shorter. It was not until 1626–27 that permanent mission-convents were established at these pueblos. The presence of a mission was often the precursor to settlement of an area by colonists, even though the clergy tried to keep settlers at a distance from the lands of the pueblos, which they considered their domain.

South of Santa Fe, in the vicinity of the Cerrillos Hills, mining prospects attracted early settlement. But it was southward along the Rio Grande, where there were more pueblos and a more congenial climate, that greater numbers of Spaniards looked to acquire land. An estancia some five miles from Sandia Pueblo had been established by 1614, the mission at Sandia having been founded in 1610 or soon thereafter. In the 1620s there was an estancia north of Isleta Pueblo, where a mission had been established in 1612 or 1613. In 1626 one family is known to have had a hacienda in the vicinity of San Felipe Pueblo, where a convent was built in 1621. Even in the vicinity of the southernmost pueblo, Senecú, a settler family was living in 1628. On the eastern frontier, where exposure to Apachean attacks was greatest, no information about settlement before the 1650s and 1660s is available, although there might have been some before this time. Mission-convents were established earlier at Pecos, the Salinas pueblos, and Las Humanas, although the mission at Las Humanas that was established in 1629 was soon abandoned and not reestablished until 1659–60.

The absence of land grant records makes it difficult to get a better idea of how early settlement spread out from its beginnings in San Gabriel and Santa Fe and to know how many properties were involved. The available information can provide only an approximation of the settlement pattern, but it does indicate that it was widespread and also thinly spread except in a few areas of concentration: the Santa Cruz River valley and adjacent areas, the Santa Fe River valley, and the Bernalillo-Atrisco areas of the Middle Rio

Grande region. Dispersion of Spanish settlement increased significantly after the devastating epidemic of the late 1630s and early 1640s, when large numbers of pueblos were abandoned, especially in the Middle and Southern Rio Grande regions. Political upheaval related to the murder of Governor Luis de Rosas in 1642 led some settlers to seek new land in these areas. The Spaniards' most tenuous hold on the land was in the Estancia basin, where drought, epidemics, and Apachean raiding in the 1660s and 1670s forced abandonment of the Salinas pueblos and, along with them, the estancias of the Spanish settlers.

The Spaniards not only changed the physical landscape through their farming and ranching operations but also changed the human landscape to one characterized by a dominant and a subordinate population. But the lines between these categories became blurred when Spanish men took Puebloan or other native wives and thus established ties with some Puebloan families. Mexican Indians and other groups of mixed racial heritage (including African) who came in 1598 or with later supply trains added to the diversity of New Mexican society in which race and social status were very much entwined. Early on, a distinct class formed among those soldier-colonists who claimed Spanish heritage, held higher military rank, and were officials of the Santa Fe cabildo. These men, the most prominent among whom were the encomenderos, were able to amass the largest landholdings by receiving land grants and forming family alliances in which a bride's dowry of land often played a role. In some areas, such groups came to be dominant. Over time, in the absence of immigration of Spanish women from New Spain, intermarriage with Puebloan or mixed-race women changed the racial heritage of this class, but its elite status remained intact. The term "Spanish" took on a social rather than a biological connotation. Some members of this class were able to carry on commercial trading activities via the triennial supply train from Mexico City, but the majority were land poor and shared, in varying degrees, a marginal economic existence with the remaining nonnative population of the colony. The establishment of landholdings scattered over a far-flung area by a small number of Spanish colonists left them vulnerable to attacks by Apacheans and uprisings by the subject Puebloans. Nevertheless, they were able to prevail for eight decades until an unprecedented alliance among the northern pueblos forced them to retreat. Despite their expulsion from 1680 to 1692, the persistence of the Spaniards on this difficult, impoverished, and isolated frontier during the seventeenth century set the stage for an ongoing Hispanic presence in New Mexico to this day.

Appendix Tables

Appendix Table A. Palmer Drought Severity Index Values for New Mexico,* 1598–1680

YEAR	CHUP.	S. FE	CHAM.	TAOS	YEAR	CHUP.	S. FE	CHAM.	TAOS
1598	-4.238	-1.408	-.541	-3.043	1623	-1.776	1.799	.061	.790
1599	-.431	.434	2.566	.129	1624	-1.541	-1.365	-1.985	-2.586
1600	-4.031	-.932	-.743	-2.913	1625	-4.301	-1.772	.070	-2.639
1601	-2.737	-2.388	-.259	-1.637	1626	-.482	.035	-.735	-.606
1602	-1.880	.577	1.295	.044	1627	1.674	.221	1.800	.340
1603	2.025	1.760	2.314	.403	1628	-.758	-1.742	-3.202	-2.329
1604	2.163	.698	1.345	-1.193	1629	2.525	2.336	1.897	.466
1605	2.433	.785	.116	.544	1630	1.663	,811	-.831	1.216
1606	-.051	-.624	.739	-.919	1631	-.218	.087	-.819	-1.109
1607	-1.983	.512	.672	-.807	1632	-1.886	.711	-1.871	-1.334
1608	2.663	-.619	.356	-.497	1633	-1.512	.551	.651	-1.513
1609	1.277	.481	-.208	-.040	1634	.823	1.812	.248	-1.531
1610	3.900	2.492	3.425	2.137	1635	1.507	2.401	1.425	2.731
1611	3.261	1.985	2.183	.758	1636	1.306	1.197	-2.166	-.332
1613	1.024	.993	-.600	1.163	1637	-2.041	2.237	.453	-.279
1614	.927	.065	-.250	-.560	1638	-4.094	-1.599	-.903	-1.809
1615	-3.220	1,002	-.528	-1.538	1639	2.675	1.847	.166	1.455
1616	-2.915	-1.703	1.375	-2.456	1640	1.674	1.409	-.482	2.995
1617	.127	.889	.347	1.718	1641	-2.576	-1.543	-1.059	-1.433
1618	1.490	2.280	1.063	.364	1642	-1.483	-.082	-1.598	-.515
1619	.127	-.446	.209	-1.183	1643	.495	.542	-1.160	-.441
1620	.627	1.686	-1.025	1.205	1644	-1.109	-.550	-.154	.681
1621	-.166	2.701	3.749	1.367	1645	-3.248	-1.543	-.756	-1.700
1622	.650	.026	1.223	-1.591	1646	3.658	1.270	1.467	2.492

Appendix Table A. continued

YEAR	CHUP.	S. FE	CHAM.	TAOS	YEAR	CHUP.	S. FE	CHAM.	TAOS
1647	3.549	.113	-.726	1.124	1665	.035	.464	-.840	.927
1648	-.879	-1.421	-3.092	-1.774	1666	-2.558	-1.738	-.608	-2.343
1649	1.352	1.058	1.295	.973	1667	-2.144	-1.404	.082	-2.164
1650	-.678	-.632	-.095	-2.498	1668	-1.978	-.927	-.027	-.715
1651	3.871	1.379	1.905	3.551	1669	-2.311	-.776	-.474	-.916
1652	.616	.806	1.324	.523	1670	.058	-.802	-1.968	-1.760
1653	-1.057	-.407	-.145	-1.193	1671	-.563	.178	-1.185	-1.440
1654	-3.358	-.940	-.621	-2.646	1672	.794	-.034	-.680	1.075
1655	3.313	.841	1.505	3.804	1673	.852	.611	-.031	-.378
1656	-.321	-.329	-.023	.857	1674	.225	1.101	-.575	-.223
1657	-2.185	-.398	-2.221	-1.278	1675	-1.144	-.052	.482	-1.039
1658	-2.737	-.563	-1.930	-.835	1676	-3.662	-1.278	-1.105	-1.728
1659	-1.713	-1.153	2.251	-.828	1677	-.132	1.140	.802	.741
1660	2.146	.897	-1.488	1.560	1678	-.540	-.533	.133	-.525
1661	1.657	1.426	-.781	-.325	1679	-1.880	1.110	-.499	-.202
1662	1.007	2.406	1.501	2.527	1680	2.755	2.579	.861	1.212
1663	-.770	-.078	.920	.653					

Source: Laboratory of Tree-Ring Research, Southwest Paleoclimate Project.

*Palmer Drought Severity Index values, which integrate precipitation and temperature, are for June of each year for the four areas: Chupadera Mesa, Santa Fe, Chama Valley, and Taos (northern Rio Grande). Values of less than 1.00 indicate increasing dryness.

Appendix Table B. Precipitation,* Albuquerque, New Mexico, 1602–80

YEAR	WINTER	SPRING	SUMMER	FALL	ANNUAL TOTAL
1602	0.76	2.69	3.06	2.11	8.62
1603	0.88	2.46	3.22	2.00	8.56
1604	0.83	2.68	2.72	2.22	8.45
1605	0.63	2.93	2.74	1.89	8.18
1606	0.76	1.73	2.92	2.35	7.75
1607	0.87	1.85	2.97	2.72	8.40
1608	1.26	1.44	2.76	2.44	7.91
1609	1.18	1.32	3.15	2.68	8.35
1610	1.14	2.49	3.18	2.22	9.02
1611	1.30	0.86	3.04	3.13	8.32
1612	0.65	1.06	2.50	2.72	6.91
1613	0.61	0.79	2.21	2.80	6.40
1614	1.03	2.05	2.92	2.45	8.43
1615	1.07	3.30	2.30	2.60	9.26
1616	1.05	3.52	2.63	2.58	9.78
1617	1.60	3.02	2.60	2.74	9.97
1618	1.36	3.83	2.82	2.62	10.64
1619	1.00	2.46	3.30	2.56	9.32
1620	1.66	3.80	2.88	2.48	10.80
1621	1.09	3.34	2.89	2.04	9.37
1622	0.80	1.77	2.94	1.89	7.40
1623	0.02	1.75	2.82	1.53	6.13
1624	0.00	1.99	2.63	1.36	5.97
1625	0.16	1.66	3.17	1.58	6.56
1626	0.00	2.35	3.24	1.99	7.59
1627	0.74	2.86	3.15	1.71	8.45
1628	0.36	1.81	3.79	2.06	8.02
1629	0.63	2.97	3.39	1.98	8.97
1630	0.51	2.41	3.64	1.60	8.16
1631	0.40	2.06	3.71	2.41	8.59
1632	0.00	2.42	3.18	2.73	8.35
1633	0.79	2.21	3.22	1.93	8.16

Appendix Table B. continued

YEAR	WINTER	SPRING	SUMMER	FALL	ANNUAL TOTAL
1634	0.68	3.76	3.54	1.99	9.97
1635	0.59	3.08	3.19	2.17	9.02
1636	0.23	2.07	3.41	2.17	7.89
1637	0.26	2.46	3.51	1.66	7.89
1638	0.53	2.54	3.56	2.16	8.78
1639	0.57	3.40	3.52	2.39	9.89
1640	1.00	3.28	3.41	2.12	9.81
1641	0.58	2.43	3.05	2.51	8.59
1642	0.38	2.80	3.13	1.82	8.13
1643	0.73	3.50	3.57	2.00	9.81
1644	0.53	3.46	3.38	1.97	9.35
1645	0.66	2.34	3.47	2.46	8.94
1646	1.02	3.56	3.16	2.51	10.24
1647	0.93	2.38	2.65	2.09	8.05
1648	0.66	1.28	2.81	2.86	7.62
1649	1.05	3.57	2.95	2.48	10.05
1650	1.17	2.31	3.04	2.66	9.18
1651	1.72	2.68	3.38	2.81	10.59
1652	1.04	1.30	2.95	2.69	7.99
1653	0.68	1.69	2.46	2.46	7.29
1654	0.77	-.90	3.35	2.35	6.48
1655	1.16	3.28	3.01	1.87	9.32
1656	0.98	3.04	3.29	1.25	8.56
1657	0.49	3.09	3.18	1.70	8.45
1658	0.60	3.05	3.21	1.76	8.62
1659	0.86	2.59	3.34	2.08	8.86
1660	1.38	3.01	3.39	1.91	9.67
1661	0.97	3.40	3.27	2.00	9.64
1662	0.73	2.07	3.75	2.32	8.86
1663	0.84	2.54	3.13	2.16	8.67
1664	0.14	2.37	2.85	2.58	7.94
1665	0.99	1.97	3.05	1.66	7.67

Appendix Table B. continued

YEAR	WINTER	SPRING	SUMMER	FALL	ANNUAL TOTAL
1666	0.68	1.42	3.21	1.72	7.02
1667	0.46	0.75	2.66	1.86	5.73
1668	0.20	-.09	2.57	1.78	4.54
1669	0.65	1.44	2.89	1.48	6.48
1670	0.71	0.64	3.06	1.72	6.13
1671	0.74	2.74	2.93	1.93	8.35
1672	0.78	0.29	3.32	1.94	6.32
1673	1.14	2.90	2.76	1.72	8.54
1674	1.18	3.12	3.22	2.54	10.05
1675	1.02	1.04	3.01	1.89	6.97
1676	0.46	1.28	3.01	1.91	6.67
1677	0.94	3.00	3.28	1.87	9.08
1678	0.84	2.45	2.98	2.11	8.37
1679	0.89	2.30	3.05	2.12	8.37
1680	1.16	3.32	3.01	2.05	9.99
av.	0.82	2.33	3.08	2.39	8.37

Source: Fritts, *Reconstructing Large-scale Climatic Patterns.* Data are from the computer file related to this volume made available through the courtesy of Louis A. Scuderi, University of New Mexico.

*Inches.

Appendix Table C. Precipitation,* Southern Rio Grande Basin,** New Mexico, 1600–1680

YEAR	PRECIP	YEAR	PRECIP	YEAR	PRECIP
1600	8.35	1627	12.36	1654	7.86
1601	5.94	1628	8.96	1655	11.00
1602	9.36	1629	14.34	1656	8.48
1603	11.52	1630	10.47	1657	6.87
1604	10.33	1631	7.10	1658	9.36
1605	8.42	1632	6.38	1659	8.87
1606	9.55	1633	9.48	1660	9.64
1607	12.36	1634	11.30	1661	11.99
1608	10.94	1635	10.22	1662	10.86
1609	9.42	1636	10.02	1663	10.02
1610	11.39	1637	12.16	1664	8.39
1611	11.33	1638	9.31	1665	11.64
1612	13.23	1639	11.61	1666	8.08
1613	8.36	1640	12.32	1667	5.34
1614	6.77	1641	11.28	1668	4.10
1615	8.65	1642	8.85	1669	7.69
1616	9.38	1643	8.35	1670	5.86
1617	7.65	1644	10.65	1671	8.84
1618	11.53	1645	10.52	1672	7.69
1619	10.28	1646	10.06	1673	6.03
1620	10.49	1647	10.94	1674	8.96
1621	12.43	1648	6.08	1675	9.73
1622	10.37	1649	9.47	1676	9.35
1623	8.71	1650	10.19	1677	11.95
1624	4.87	1651	12.53	1678	10.72
1625	7.78	1652	9.62	1679	10.30
1626	7.65	1653	8.81	1680	12.10
				av.	9.34

Source: Grissino-Mayer, Baisan, and Swetnam, *A 1,373 Year Reconstruction.*

*Inches.
**Data sites are in the Magdalena, San Mateo, and Organ Mountains of New Mexico.

Appendix Table D. Temperature,* Santa Fe, New Mexico, 1602–80

YEAR	WINTER	SPRING	SUMMER	FALL	ANNUAL TOTAL
1602	34.06	50.95	68.51	50.52	49.55
1603	32.80	51.55	67.95	50.52	49.33
1604	34.28	51.62	68.58	50.28	49.78
1605	31.86	51.85	67.72	50.36	49.12
1606	32.32	53.53	68.14	50.59	49.93
1607	30.69	52.70	67.98	50.78	49.26
1608	33.65	52.67	67.81	50.59	49.91
1609	32.66	51.72	66.82	50.76	49.23
1610	34.79	51.03	67.22	51.53	49.80
1611	35.52	52.23	67.94	50.63	50.27
1612	31.71	51.27	67.94	51.00	49.10
1613	33.14	52.34	69.55	51.24	50.12
1614	30.93	52.83	67.88	51.96	49.64
1615	35.81	50.07	69.55	51.85	50.20
1616	33.14	50.21	68.34	52.12	49.44
1617	37.58	50.22	69.18	51.98	50.67
1618	33.04	49.71	68.81	51.39	49.13
1619	34.47	49.72	68.98	51.55	49.57
1620	33.82	50.91	68.24	51.42	49.65
1621	34.86	49.45	68.55	51.55	49.52
1622	31.86	51.56	68.15	50.92	49.25
1623	33.60	51.75	69.11	51.02	49.93
1624	33.31	52.02	68.54	51.03	49.86
1625	33.77	51.46	69.10	50.84	49.82
1626	32.46	51.08	68.98	50.99	49.39
1627	33.33	52.23	69.14	51.05	50.04
1628	34.26	51.67	68.31	50.68	49.83
1629	33.72	50.80	69.67	50.03	49.48
1630	32.61	52.81	69.15	50.36	49.88
1631	35.20	52.75	68.75	49.98	50.35
1632	35.11	52.39	68.27	51.16	50.41
1633	34.77	52.98	68.25	50.81	50.43

Appendix Table D. *continued*

YEAR	WINTER	SPRING	SUMMER	FALL	ANNUAL TOTAL
1634	31.64	51.62	67.74	50.43	49.01
1635	33.33	51.08	68.97	51.16	49.64
1636	34.06	52.42	69.37	49.87	50.02
1637	31.06	52.67	69.34	50.31	49.46
1638	32.83	53.57	68.10	49.93	49.89
1639	32.20	50.77	67.78	50.22	48.83
1640	32.56	51.27	67.88	49.85	49.01
1641	34.94	51.56	68.00	50.09	49.78
1642	32.95	51.46	67.98	51.02	49.48
1643	32.78	50.89	67.65	50.44	49.05
1644	35.08	49.81	68.64	50.38	49.41
1645	32.78	52.40	68.52	50.39	49.68
1646	31.47	50.79	68.51	50.46	48.83
1647	32.70	52.58	68.25	50.19	49.62
1648	31.03	53.83	68.80	50.25	49.73
1649	31.90	51.15	68.37	50.79	49.12
1650	32.80	53.51	68.12	50.71	50.07
1651	30.45	51.97	69.63	50.76	49.23
1652	33.43	54.17	69.94	50.70	50.74
1653	31.59	52.77	69.90	50.83	49.83
1654	30.47	55.67	69.14	49.99	50.20
1655	29.12	51.40	69.07	50.59	48.56
1556	31.15	52.83	68.41	50.46	49.41
1657	32.68	51.82	69.17	49.80	49.42
1658	33.04	2.78	68.64	49.46	49.65
1659	32.68	52.93	68.27	50.31	49.77
1660	32.97	53.31	67.44	50.23	49.82
1661	33.07	52.43	68.92	50.01	49.73
1662	32.24	52.60	67.95	49.10	49.18
1663	34.21	52.80	68.58	50.55	50.22
1664	32.10	53.50	69.55	49.62	49.86
1665	30.33	53.89	68.14	49.74	49.33

Appendix Table D. continued

YEAR	WINTER	SPRING	SUMMER	FALL	ANNUAL TOTAL
1666	32.34	53.53	67.91	49.40	49.60
1667	30.59	52.64	69.12	49.58	49.12
1668	32.41	55.41	68.32	50.22	50.52
1669	30.33	52.61	67.82	49.83	48.89
1670	31.95	54.30	69.11	49.85	49.91
1671	31.54	52.74	68.14	49.83	49.28
1672	43.26	53.22	67.79	50.11	50.12
1673	33.99	51.26	69.40	50.35	49.57
1674	32.00	52.37	68.18	50.36	49.41
1675	34.89	52.32	68.12	50.28	50.09
1676	32.75	52.03	68.91	50.06	49.54
1677	28.70	52.20	67.79	49.83	48.32
1678	31.81	51.12	68.72	50.17	48.99
1679	32.78	53.66	68.34	50.17	50.02
1680	30.69	51.20	68.57	49.80	48.61
av.	32.80	52.11	68.48	50.51	49.61

Source: Fritts, *Reconstructing Large-scale Climatic Patterns*. Data are from the computer file related to this volume made available through the courtesy of Louis A. Scuderi, University of New Mexico.

*Reconstructed values are in degrees Fahrenheit.

Appendix Table E. Known New Mexico Encomenderos, 1610–80

NAME	PUEBLO	DATE REPORTED
Albizu, Antonio de	Ácoma: twenty houses Alameda Picurís: part San Cristóbal	1659–61
Albizu, Tomás de	Zuni	1632
Anaya Almazán, Francisco I	Cuarac (Quarai): half?	1662
Anaya Almazán, Cristóbal	La Ciénega	
Anaya Almazán, Francisco II	Picurís: half	
*Archuleta, Asencio de	Cochiti	1611–14
*Archuleta, Gregoria de	Jemez, San Juan: half	1661–63
*Carvajal, Felis de	Senecú: thirty houses	1661
*Carvajal, Gerónimo de	Awatobi: half	1661
*Cruz, Juan de la ("el Catalán")	n.a.	1628
Cruz, Pedro de la	Cuquina (Kwakina)	n.a.
Domínguez de Mendoza, Francisco	Zia: half Cochiti: half	1665
Domínguez de Mendoza, Juan	Humanas: one-third	1664
		1669
	Jemez: part	n.a.
	Isleta	1678

SOURCE AND COMMENT
Kessell, *Kiva*, 186; Esquibel, private communication, citing Tierras, t. 3268, ff. 54v–56r, AGN.
Chávez, *Origins*, 2. He was the father of Antonio de Albizu.
Chávez, *Origins*, 3–4. He died July 18, 1662; his heir was his son Cristóbal. Cristóbal was imprisoned by the Inquisition at the time and unable to inherit. His younger son, Francisco, was made escudero of the family encomienda pueblos. Hackett, *Historical Documents*, 3:247–48, 249; Scholes, *Troublous Times*, 35–36, 132; Anderson, "Encomienda," 368.
Scholes, "Church and State," pt. 1, 48; Esquibel, private communication, citing Inquisition, t. 316, exp. 2, f. 171, AGN. He was dead by 1626.
This encomienda was transferred from Diego Romero to Gregoria. Esquibel, "Romero Family," 18, citing Real Audiencia, Concurso de Peñalosa, vol. 2, exp. 495, leg. 1, no. 7, 81 ff., AGN. She gave her half of the encomienda to Andrés Peralta as part of her daughter Isabel's dowry. Esquibel, private communication, citing Tierras, t. 3268, f. 295, AGN; Chávez, *Origins*, 6, 86, 103. She was the widow of Diego de Santa Cruz.
Esquibel, private communication, citing Tierras, t. 3268, ff. 133v–135r, AGN; Chávez, *Origins*, 15.
Chávez, *Origins*, 15. He was the son of Juan Vitoria Carvajal and the brother of Felis.
Snow, "Note," 356; Esquibel, "Vecino Estancia," 2, citing Inquisition, t. 304, exp. 27, f. 186, AGN.
Snow, "Note," 355. He was the son of Diego de la Cruz. Chávez, *Origins*, 103.
Both of these encomiendas were granted by Governor Fernando de Villanueva, superseding escudero Cristóbal Durán y Chávez, the encomiendas having previously belonged to Diego Romero. Esquibel, "Romero Family," 19, citing Inquisition, t. 583, exp. 3, ff. 99–99v, AGN.
Brother of Francisco Domínguez de Mendoza. He was named escudero for Francisco Gómez Robledo. Scholes, *Troublous Times*, 133, 214–15.
He was granted the part taken from Juan González Bas. Kessell and Hendricks, *By Force of Arms*, 480n29; Esquibel, private communication, citing MS. 19258, ff. 55–57, BN.
He was granted the part originally held by the López Ocanto family. Esquibel, personal communication, citing Tierras, t. 3268, f. 109v–110r, AGN.
This encomienda was granted upon the death of encomendero Francisco de Valencia. Esquibel, personal communication, citing MS. 19258, ff. 137–38, BN.

Appendix Table E. continued

NAME	PUEBLO	DATE REPORTED
*Durán y Chávez, Pedro I	San Felipe	n.a.
*Durán y Chávez, Fernando I	San Felipe	ca. 1638
*Durán y Chávez, Cristóbal	Zia: half Cochiti	1664
	Cuyamunge	n.a.
*Escarramad, Juan	n.a.	n.a.
Gómez de Luna, Juan	San Lázaro	1618–25
*Gómez, Francisco	Ácoma: half Abó Sandía Pecos Shongopavi: half Taos: half Tesuque	ca. 1620s
Gómez, Elena	Aguatobi: half?	ca. 1664
González, Sebastián I	Humanas: half	n.a.
González Bernal, Juan	Humanas: one-third	n.a.
González Bas, Juan	Humanas: one-third	1668–69
*Griego, Juan II	n.a.	1662
Guadalajara, Diego de	Sevilleta	ca. 1659
*Herrera, Juan de I	Jemez	n.a.
	Santa Clara	n.a.
*Hinojos, Hernando de	Humanas	n.a.
*Hinojos, Miguel de	Humanas	1661

SOURCE AND COMMENT
Scholes, "Church and State," pt. 2, 149–50; Anderson, "Encomienda," 366, 375–76n46; Chávez, *Origins*, 21. He was dead by 1637.
He inherited the encomienda from his father, Pedro I. Anderson, "Encomienda," 366, 375–76n46; Chávez, *Origins*, 19–20.
He was named escudero of Zia and Cochiti for Diego Romero. Scholes, *Troublous Times*, 133, 214–15; Hackett, *Historical Documents*, 3:251–52; Chávez, *Origins*, 20. He was the son of Fernando I.
He was the escudero who superseded Pedro de Montoya for Diego Romero. Scholes, *Troublous Times*, 133.
Anderson, "Encomienda," 366; Chávez, *Origins*, 29. He probably left New Mexico after 1617.
Scholes, "Church and State," pt. 2, 148, 149–50.
Twenty houses were held by Antonio de Albizu. Kessell, *Kiva*, 186.
Kessell, *Kiva*, 186.
He exchanged Sandía for half of Abó. Kessell, *Kiva*, 186.
Twenty-four houses were held by Pedro Lucero de Godoy. Kessell, *Kiva*, 186.
Kessell, *Kiva*, 186.
Kessell, *Kiva*, 186; Hackett, *Historical Documents*, 3:221.
Kessell, *Kiva*, 186; Hackett, *Historical Documents*, 3:223.
Hackett, *Historical Documents*, 3:243–44, 260, 267; Chávez, *Origins*, 58. She was the wife of Hernán López Sambrano. She was dead by 1665.
Snow, "Note," 355.
Snow, "Note," 355. He was the son of Sebastián. Chávez, *Origins*, 40.
He inherited the encomienda from his father, Juan, but then lost it for failing to meet military obligations, at which point it was granted to Juan Domínguez de Mendoza. Esquibel, private communication, citing MS. 19258, ff. 55–57, BN.
Esquibel, "Vecino Estancias," 2, citing Inquisition, trial of Mendizábal, leg. 1, no. 9, f. 21, AGN.
Hackett, *Historical Documents*, 3:189, 206, 259; Scholes, *Troublous Times*, 29; Chávez, *Origins*, 42.
Chávez, *Origins*, 45.
Chávez, *Origins*, 45.
Chávez, *Origins*, 48.
He was the temporary escudero for Alonso Rodríguez Cisneros's encomienda; Toribio de la Huerta was appointed escudero after him, and then the encomienda was returned to Rodríguez Cisneros. Scholes, *Troublous Times*, 40. He was the son of Hernando. Chávez, *Origins*, 48.

Appendix Table E. continued

NAME	PUEBLO	DATE REPORTED
Huerta, Toribio de la	Humanas	n.a.
Hurtado, Andrés I	Santa Ana	1661
*López del Ocanto, Juan	Jemez	n.a.
	Nambé	n.a.
López del Castillo, Diego	n.a.	1662
López Palomino, Francisco	n.a.	1656
Lucero de Godoy, Juan	Aguatobi: half	1661
Lucero de Godoy, Pedro	Pecos: twenty-four houses	1662
*Madrid, Lorenzo de	Pecos	pre-1680
*Márquez, Cristóbal	Cieneguilla (La Ciénega)	late 1650s
*Martín Serrano, Hernán I	n.a.	1664
*Martínez de Montoya, Juan	Jemez, Santiago de	1606
Mondragón, Juan Alonso	Senecú	ca. 1660
*Montoya, Diego de I	San Pedro (Paako?)	n.a.
*Montoya, Pedro de	Cuyamunge	1664
Peralta, Andrés de	Jemez, San Juan: half	1661-63
Rodríguez Cisneros, Alonso	Humanas: one-third	n.a.
Romero, Bartolomé III	Picurís	1659-61

SOURCE AND COMMENT
He was the temporary escudero for Alonso Rodríguez Cisneros encomienda. Scholes, *Troublous Times*, 40.
Chávez, *Origins*, 49.
Both pueblos were inherited by his son Domingo. Chávez, *Origins*, 57.
Esquibel, private communication, citing Real Audiencia, Concurso de Peñalosa, no. 4, vol.1, exp. 605, leg. 1, f. 96r, AGN.
His encomiendas were confiscated by Governor Mansos. Esquibel, private communication, citing Real Audiencia, Concurso de Peñalosa, vol. 3, leg. 1, no. 1, f. 196v, AGN.
This encomienda was confiscated from Elena Gómez by Governor Manso and granted to Juan Lucero de Godoy but then taken from him by Governor López de Mendizábal, who appointed Francisco Romero de Pedraza escudero. Esquibel, private communication, citing Tierras, t. 3268, ff. 136, 138, AGN, and Real Audiencia, Concurso de Peñalosa, no. 4, vol. 1, exp. 605, leg. 1, no. 1, f. 196v, AGN.
Kessell, *Kiva*, 186.
Kessell and Hendricks, *By Force of Arms*, 319n5.
Snow, "Note," 356. This encomienda was taken from Francisco de Anaya Almazán and granted to Cristóbal by Governor Manso but restored to the former by Governor López de Mendizábal. Esquibel, private communication, citing Tierras, t. 3268, f. 47, AGN.
Hackett, *Historical Documents*, 3:248–49; Chávez, *Origins*, 72.
Scholes, "Juan Martínez de Montoya," 340; Anderson, "Encomienda," 360.
Hackett, *Historical Documents*, 3:58.
He was dead by 1661. His encomienda was inherited by son Bartolomé II. Chávez, *Origins*, 77.
He was named escudero for Diego Romero by Governor Peñalosa, but apparently this was a fraudulent move by the governor. Scholes, *Troublous Times*, 132–33; Hackett, *Historical Documents*, 3:249. He was the son of Diego I. Chávez, *Origins*, 77.
This encomienda was a dowry from Gregoria Archuleta when he married her daughter Isabel. Esquibel, private communication, citing Tierras, t. 3268, f. 295, AGN; Chávez, *Origins*, 6, 86, 103.
This encomienda was confiscated by Governor Manso and restored by Governor López de Mendizábal. Scholes, *Troublous Times*, 35, 40; Anderson, "Encomienda," 368.
Esquibel, private communication, citing Tierras, t. 3268, ff. 50–51, AGN, and Real Audiencia, Concurso de Peñalosa, no. 4, vol. 1, exp. 605, leg. 1, f. 164, AGN.

Appendix Table E. continued

NAME	PUEBLO	DATE REPORTED
Romero, Diego Pérez	Cochiti: half?	1662
	Cuyamunge	1662
	Jemez, San Juan: half	1661–63
	Zia: half	1662
Romero de Pedraza, Francisco	Aguatobi	1659–61
Salas, Antonio de	Pojoaque	1639
	Jemez: part	1659–61
*Tapia, Juan Fernández de	Taos: one-fourth	ca. 1625
Telles Jirón, José	Cochiti: half?	ca. 1661
	San Felipe	ca. 1661
Trujillo, Diego de	Picurís: part	1659–61
Valencia, Francisco de	Isleta	1670s
Vera Perdomo, Diego de	n.a.	n.a.
Xavier, Francisco	n.a	1662

Appendix table E is modified from Snow, "Note," 354.

*Descendant of original colonist who came to New Mexico in 1598 or 1600. Francisco Gomez came in 1604 and Francisco de Madrid in 1603.

SOURCE AND COMMENT
Esquibel, "Vecino Estancias," 18, citing Real Audiencia, Concurso de Peñalosa, vol. 2, exp. 495, leg. 1, no. 7, 81ff, AGN.
Esquibel, "Vecino Estancias," 18, citing Real Audiencia, Concurso de Peñalosa, vol. 2, exp. 495, leg. 1, no. 7, 81ff, AGN.
See Gregoria Archuleta above.
Esquibel, "Vecino Estancias," 18, citing Real Audiencia, Concurso de Peñalosa, vol. 2, exp. 495, leg. 1, no. 7, 81ff, AGN; Scholes, *Troublous Times*, 147n3.
Esquibel, private communication, citing Tierras, t. 3268, ff. 136, 138, AGN, and Real Audiencia, Concurso de Peñalosa, no. 4, vol. 1, exp. 605, leg. 1, no. 1, f. 196v, AGN. He was appointed escudero after Governor López de Mendizábal confiscated Aguatobi from Juan Lucero de Godoy.
Scholes, *Troublous Times*, 42; Chávez, *Origins*, 100.
Esquibel, private communication, citing Tierras, t. 3268, f. 150, AGN.
Hodge, Hammond, and Ray, *Revised Memorial*, 110; Snow, "Note," 355; Chávez, *Origins*, 105.
Chávez, *Origins*, 106.
Chávez, *Origins*, 106.
Esquibel, private communication, citing Tierras, t. 3268, f. 94r, 185r, AGN, and Real Audiencia, Concurso de Peñalosa, vol. 1, f. 235/382, AGN. This encomienda was confiscated by Governor López de Mendizábal.
Esquibel, private communication, citing MS. 19258, ff. 137–38, BN. He died in 1678, at which point his encomienda was granted to Juan Domínguez de Mendoza.
Chávez, *Origins*, 112. He left New Mexico in 1626.
Esquibel, private communication, citing Real Audiencia, Concurso de Peñalosa, no. 4, vol. 1, exp. 605, leg. 1, no. 9, f. 33r, AGN.

Appendix Table F. Known New Mexico Alcaldes Mayores, 1610–80

NAME	JURISDICTION	DATE REPORTED
Aguilar, Nicolás de	Salinas	1660
Anaya Almazán, Francisco II	Tanos	1664
*Carvajal, Gerónimo	Tanos	1661, 1665
Domínguez de Mendoza, Tomé II	Isleta	1659
	Sandia	1666
*Durán y Chávez, Fernando I	n.a.	1643
Fontes, Cristóbal	Cochiti	1663
Fresqui, Juan II	Isleta	pre-1667
*García Holgado, Juan	Alameda	ca. 1650
	Socorro	1667
García, Alonso	Sandia	pre-1661, 1670
González Bernal, Diego	Tanos	ca. 1659–61
	Humanas	1663
Heras, Marcos de las	Taos	1667
*Hinojos, Miguel	Cochiti	1661
	Jemez	1663
Leyva, Pedro de	Salinas	1669
	Senecú	1670
López, Luis	Piros	1665–67
López de Gracia, Andrés	n.a.	1643
	El Paso	1661
López Sambrano, Andrés	Keres	1663
*Luján, Francisco	Cochiti	1643
*Luján, Juan II	n.a.	1643
	La Cañada	1660–61
	Taos	1661

SOURCE AND COMMENT
Hackett, *Historical Documents*, 3:145, 159, 169, 174; Scholes, *Troublous Times*, 6–7, 40–41, 48, 54; Chávez, *Origins*, 1.
Hackett, *Historical Documents*, 3:253; Chávez, *Origins*, 2–3. He was part of an encomendero family.
Hackett, *Historical Documents*, 3:249, 254; Chávez, *Origins*, 14–16. He was part of an of encomendero family.
Scholes, *Troublous Times*, 27, 40. He was succeeded by his brother Juan.
Scholes, *Troublous Times*, 247.
Scholes, "Church and State," pt. 5, 86.
Chávez, *Origins*, 30; Snow, "Evolution," 219.
Chávez, *Origins*, 30.
Chávez, *Origins*, 32.
Esquibel, "Beyond Origins," vol. 8.
Scholes, *Troublous Times*, 6. Hackett, *Historical Documents*, 3:277.
Scholes, *Troublous Times*, 72, 74; Hackett, *Historical Documents*, 3:170; Chávez, *Origins*, 40.
Hackett, *Historical Documents*, 3:169; Chávez, *Origins*, 40. He was part of an encomendero family.
Chávez, *Origins*, 44. Hackett and Shelby, *Revolt* 1:xxvn10 (his name was misinterpreted as Dehezas).
Hackett, *Historical Documents*, 3:182; Scholes, *Troublous Times*, 140. He was part of an encomendero family.
Chávez, *Origins*, 48.
Hackett, *Historical Documents*, 3:163; Chávez, *Origins*, 53.
Sánchez, *Rio Abajo*, 103.
Scholes, *Troublous Times*, 7; Chávez, *Origins*, 58; Hendricks and Mandell, "Juan Manso," 350.
Scholes, "Church and State," pt. 5, 86.
Chávez, *Origins*, 55–56.
Hackett, *Historical Documents*, 3:244; Scholes, *Troublous Times*, 218. He was part of an encomendero family.
Brother of Juan Luján II. Snow, "Evolution," 219. He was assistant alcalde mayor.
Scholes, "Church and State," pt. 5, 86.
Hackett, *Historical Documents*, 3:152.
Hackett, *Historical Documents*, 3:265; Scholes, *Troublous Times*, 69, 73; Chávez, *Origins*, 63.

Appendix Table F. continued

NAME	JURISDICTION	DATE REPORTED
*Martín Serrano, Luis I	Tewa	pre-1663
Nieto, Joseph	Salinas	1668
Peralta, Andrés de	Santo Domingo	pre-1680
Pérez Granillo, Francisco II or Alonso	Piros (Senecú)	1663
Pérez Granillo, Luis	Jemez	pre-1680
	Keres	pre-1680
Pérez Granillo, Diego	n.a.	1643
Quintana, Luis de	La Cañada	pre-1680
Ramírez de Salazar, Juan	n.a.	1643
Romero, Pedro	Nambé	1660s
Romero de Pedraza, Francisco	Santo Domingo	1664
Serna, Diego de la	n.a.	1643
*Valencia, Francisco de	Isleta	1669
*Varela de Losada, Juan	Cochiti	1662

Appendix table F is modified from Lycette, "Archaeological Implications," 538.

*Descendant of original colonist who came to New Mexico in 1598 or 1600.

SOURCE AND COMMENT
Chávez, *Origins*, 72; Hendricks and Mandell, "Juan Manso," 345; Esquibel, "Analysis," 6, citing Tierras, t. 3268, ff. 143–44, AGN. He was part of an encomendero family.
Hackett, *Historical Documents*, 3:276; Scholes, *Troublous Times*, 7; Chávez, *Origins*, 80–81.
Hackett, *Historical Documents*, 3:330. He was killed in 1680.
Hackett, *Historical Documents*, 3:206.
Son of Francisco Pérez Granillo II. Chávez, *Origins*, 88; Preucel, *Archaeologies*, 47.
Chávez, *Origins*, 88; Preucel, *Archaeologies*, 47.
Nephew of Francisco Pérez Granillo II. Scholes, "Church and State," pt. 5, 86.
Hackett, *Historical Documents*, 3:330.
Scholes, "Church and State," pt. 5, 86.
Hackett, *Historical Documents*, 3:259.
Chávez, *Origins*, 98. He was assistant alcalde mayor.
Scholes, "Church and State," pt. 5, 86.
Hackett, *Historical Documents*, 3:276; Chávez, *Origins*, 109. He was part of an encomendero family.
Hackett, *Historical Documents*, 3:238, 261; Scholes, *Troublous Times*, 140.

Appendix Table G. Spanish Men in New Mexico before 1601

	NUMBER
Frías Salazar muster of January 8, 1598 (including Juan de Oñate and son)*	133
Gordejuela-Sotelo muster of August 26–28, 1600**	81
Men not on the 1598 or 1600 musters according to Villagrá (see below)	13
Men not on the 1598 or 1600 musters according to Hammond and Rey (see below)	21
Total	248
Loss of Spanish men in New Mexico before the 1601 desertion (see below)	31
Total	217

NAME	MUSTER	SOURCE
MEN NOT ON THE 1598 OR 1600 MUSTERS ACCORDING TO VILLAGRÁ		
Carvajal, Estevan de	—	Villagrá, *History*, 223, 226
Castillo, Alonso or Diego del	February 17, 1597	Villagrá, *History*, 224
Díaz, Juan	—	Villagrá, *History*, 224, 226
García Holgado, Juan	—	Villagrá, *History*, 179, 183
Guerra, Juan	January 4, 1598	Villagrá, *History*, 156, 161
Hernández, Gerónimo	—	Villagrá, *History*, 226
Hernández, Pedro	—	Villagrá, *History*, 224
López, Juan	February 17, 1597	Villagrá, *History*, 236, 248
Lucas, Alonso	—	Villagrá, *History*, 102, 104, 225
Márquez, Francisco	—	Villagrá, *History*, 224
Nieves, Francisco de las	—	Villagrá, *History*, 172
S(Z)umaya, Jorge de	February 17, 1597, January 1, 1598	Villagrá, *History*, 236, 239
Vega, Jorge de la	—	Villagrá, *History*, 156, 162, 236
MEN NOT ON THE 1598 OR 1600 MUSTERS ACCORDING TO HAMMOND AND REY		
Bañuelos, Dionisio de	—	Hammond and Rey, *Don Juan*, 846, 1120–21
Castañeda, Juan de	—	Hammond and Rey, *Don Juan*, 705, 787

Appendix Table G. continued

Coronda, Joseph de	—	Hammond and Rey, *Don Juan*, 609
Correa, Rodrigo	February 10, 1597	Hammond and Rey, *Don Juan*, 163, 701–2
Cortés, Juan	February 17, 1597	Hammond and Rey, *Don Juan*, 156, 451
González, Juan	—	Hammond and Rey, *Don Juan*, 324, 1117
González, Juan, Alférez	February 17, 1597	Hammond and Rey, *Don Juan*, 153, 1082
Lucero de Godoy, Pedro	February 17, 1597	Hammond and Rey, *Don Juan*, 160, 701–2
Mallea, Juan de	January 4, 1598	Hammond and Rey, *Don Juan*, 759
Martín Barba, Alonso	February 10, 1597	Hammond and Rey, *Don Juan*, 164, 701–2
Medina, Juan de	January 4, 1598	Hammond and Rey, *Don Juan*, 283, 701–2
Paz, Simón de la	—	Hammond and Rey, *Don Juan*, 759
Pereira, Marcos	February 24, 1597	Hammond and Rey, *Don Juan*, 166, 325, 426
Portugués, Manuel	—	Hammond and Rey, *Don Juan*, 324, 1117
Riveros (Biveros), Martín de	—	Hammond and Rey, *Don Juan*, 325, 440, 618
Ruiz de Cabrera, Juan	February 10, 1597	Hammond and Rey, *Don Juan*, 162, 833
Salas, Juan de	February 17, 1597	Hammond and Rey, *Don Juan*, 156, 701–2
Torres (la Torre), Juan de	February 17, 1597	Hammond and Rey, *Don Juan*, 157, 1102
Valle, Pedro Alonso	—	Hammond and Rey, *Don Juan*, 707
Vitoria, Juan de (not Carvajal)	February 17, 1597, December 6, 1597	Hammond and Rey, *Don Juan*, 160, 275
Ynojosa, Juan de	—	Hammond and Rey, *Don Juan*, 762

Appendix Table G. continued

LOSS OF SPANISH MEN IN NEW MEXICO BEFORE THE 1601 DESERTION		
DIED OF NATURAL CAUSES	MUSTER	SOURCE
Robledo, Pedro I	January 8, 1598	Hammond and Rey, *Don Juan*, 316
Pérez de Donís, Juan	January 8, 1598	Villagrá, *History*, 207
SENT TO MEXICO CITY BY OÑATE		
Landín (Blandín), Diego	January 8, 1598	Hammond and Rey, *Don Juan*, 312, 1110; Villagrá, *History*, 109
EXECUTED BY ORDER OF OÑATE		
Aguilar Ynojosa, Pablo de	January 8, 1598	Hammond and Rey, *Don Juan*, 612, 1111, 1120, 1130
Sosa Albornoz, Alonso de	January 8, 1598	Hammond and Rey, *Don Juan*, 612, 1111, 1114, 1120
DESERTED AND KILLED		
González, Juan	—	Hammond and Rey, *Don Juan*, 324, 1116–17
Portugués, Manuel	—	Hammond and Rey, *Don Juan*, 324, 1117
Castañeda, Juan de	—	Hammond and Rey, *Don Juan*, 704–5
Santillán, Bernabé de	1600	Hammond and Rey, *Don Juan*, 704–5, 791
DESERTED		
Rodríguez Moreno, Juan	1598	Hammond and Rey, *Don Juan*, 324, 1116
Rodríguez (Sánchez?), Matías	—	Hammond and Rey, *Don Juan*, 324, 1116
KILLED AT ÁCOMA, DECEMBER 1598		
Araujo, Luis de	1598	Hammond and Rey, *Don Juan*, 325
Camacho, Juan	1598	Hammond and Rey, *Don Juan*, 325
Escalante, Felipe de	1598	Hammond and Rey, *Don Juan*, 325, 426
Núñez de Chávez, Diego	1598	Hammond and Rey, *Don Juan*, 325, 426

Appendix Table G. continued

Pereira, Marcos	1597	Hammond and Rey, *Don Juan*, 325, 426; Villagrá, *History*, 193
Ramírez, Martín	1598	Hammond and Rey, *Don Juan*, 325
Rivera, Pedro de	1598	Hammond and Rey, *Don Juan*, 325
Riveros (Biveros), Martín de	—	Hammond and Rey, *Don Juan*, 325, 440, 618; Villagrá, *History*, 193
Robledo, Pedro II	1598	Hammond and Rey, *Don Juan*, 325
Rodríguez (de Hinojos), Sebastián	1598	Hammond and Rey, *Don Juan*, 325
Salado de Rivadeneira, Lorenzo	1598	Hammond and Rey, *Don Juan*, 451; Villagrá, *History*, 220, 225, 244
Segura, Hernando de (Juan de?)	1598	Hammond and Rey, *Don Juan*, 325
Zaldívar, Juan de	1598	Hammond and Rey, *Don Juan*, 325

FAILED TO RETURN TO NEW MEXICO WITH REINFORCEMENTS THAT ARRIVED IN 1600

Farfán de los Godos, Marcos	1598	Hammond and Rey, *Don Juan*, 24, 488
Piñeiro, Juan, Alférez	1598	Hammond and Rey, *Don Juan*, 24, 488
Villagrá, Gaspar Pérez de	1598	Hammond and Rey, *Don Juan*, 24, 488, 576, 577

VALVERDE WITNESSES IN MEXICO CITY, JULY 1601

Brondate, Joseph	1598	Hammond and Rey, *Don Juan*, 624–25
Espinosa, Marcelo de	1598	Hammond and Rey, *Don Juan*, 632–33
Herrera Horta, Ginés de	1600	Hammond and Rey, *Don Juan*, 616–17, 643–44, 1134
Ortega, Juan de	1600	Hammond and Rey, *Don Juan*, 658

*Hammond and Rey, *Don Juan*, 289–300.
**Ibid., 548–65, 572, 587–89, 837.

Appendix Table H. Spanish Men Who Brought Families to New Mexico before 1601

MUSTER OF JANUARY 8, 1598, AT THE MINES OF TODOS SANTOS*

César, Gregorio, Captain: wife, three sons, one daughter
García, Francisco, soldier: wife and small daughter
García, Lázaro: wife and children (February 17, 1597, muster)
Gasco de Velasco, Luis, Treasurer: wife
Gómez de Montesinos, Alonso, Captain: wife and family
Griego, Juan, soldier: wife and family
Hernández Cordero, Francisco, soldier and carpenter: wife and father-in-law
Hernández Guillén, Francisco: wife, one married daughter and son-in-law, granddaughter, and one single daughter
Hernández, Gonzalo, Caudillo: wife, children and family
Márquez, Gerónimo, Captain: married and taking whole household including five sons and a daughter
Martín Serrano, Hernán, Sargento: wife and family
Morán, Juan: wife and children
Pérez de Bustillo, Juan, Alférez: wife, seven daughters, and two adult sons
Pereira, Marcos, Alférez: wife, sons, daughters, and household
Robledo, Pedro I, Alférez: wife and five children, including four adult sons
Romero, Bartolomé, Alférez: wife, family, and household
Sánchez, Alonso, Contador: wife, two married daughters, three unmarried daughters, and two adult sons
Sánchez de Monroy, Pedro: wife, children, and family
Sosa Albornoz, Alonso de, Captain and Alférez: wife, one daughter, two adult sons
Sosa Peñalosa, Francisco de, Captain and Alférez: wife, one daughter, two adult sons
Vitoria Carvajal, Juan de, Alférez: children and family, two adult sons
Zubía, Diego de, Captain and purveyor general: family

Number of families: 22

Appendix Table H. continued

MUSTER OF AUGUST 28, 1600, IN THE VALLEY OF SAN BARTOLOMÉ*

Baca, Cristóbal, Captain: wife, one minor son, three daughters

Conde de Herrera, Antonio, Captain and Sargento Mayor: wife, adult son, minor son and daughter, three sisters-in law, and one brother-in-law

Figueroa, Gregorio del, Alférez: wife

Hernández de Benhumea, Gonzalo: wife, two adult sons and one daughter

López Villasaña, Juan: wife, two daughters, and one adult son

Montoya, Bartolomé, del: wife, three boys and two girls

Rua, Gerónimo Moreno de la: wife

Ruiz Fernández, Juan: wife

Number of families: 8

ADDITIONAL SPANISH MEN WITH WIVES IN NEW MEXICO BEFORE 1601**

Archuleta, Asencio de

Gutiérrez Bocanegra, Juan

Lucas, Alonso

Monzón, Baltasar de, soldier

Núñez de Chávez, Diego, Alférez

Quesada, Alonso de, Captain

San Martín, Pedro de

Sánchez, Francisco, Caudillo

Number of families: 8

*Hammond and Rey, *Don Juan*.
**Villagrá, *History*.

Appendix Table I. Colonists Who Signed the October 2, 1601, Loyalty Petition

NAME	MUSTER	EARLIEST KNOWN POST-1601 DATE
Angulo, Pedro de	1600	—
Archuleta, Asensio de	1598	1603
Barba, Alonso (Martín)	1597	1604
Cháves, Alonso de	?	—
Correa, Rodrigo	1597	—
Días/Díez de Castro, Diego	1600	—
Fernández, Juan	1597	1604
García (Holgado), Álvaro	1600	1609
Gómez Montesinos, Alonso	1598	1602
Hernández, Gonzalo	1598	1602
López Olguín, Juan	1600	1604
Lucero de Godoy, Pedro	1597	1609
Luxán, Juan	1600	1604
Márquez, Gerónimo	1598	1609
Martín Gómez, Hernán	1598	1604
Martín Serrano, Hernán	1598	1604
Medina, Juan de	1598	1604
Monzón, Baltasar de	1598	—
Pérez de Bustillo, Juan (father)	1598	1613
Pérez de Bustillo, Simón (son)	1598	1613
Romero, Bartolomé	1598	1602
Salas, Juan de (son of Gonzalo Hernández)	1597	—
Vaca (Baca), Cristóbal	1600	1603
Varela (Jaramillo), Alonso	1598	1604
Vega, Alonso de la	1600	—
Total	25	

Sources: Hammond and Rey, *Don Juan*; Esquibel, "Soldados-Vecinos," citing Colección Antigua, t. 316, f. 139 ff., AH (for 1604 dates).

Appendix Table J. Additional Colonists Who Remained in New Mexico after 1601

COLONIST	MUSTER	EARLIEST KNOWN POST-1601 DATE
Cadimo, Francisco	1598	1631 (daughter?)
Cruz, Juan de la (changed to Juan Durán)	1598	1628
Cruz, Juan de la ("el Catalán")	1598	1613
Escarramad, Juan de	1598	1617
García, Marcos	1598	1608
Griego, Juan	1598	1631
Herrera, Juan de	1600	1642
Hinojos, Hernando de	1598	1613
Jorge, Juan	1600	1655 (son)
Ledesma, Francisco de	1598	1662 (son ?)
López del Ocanto, Juan	1598	1642 (son ?)
Morán, Juan	1598	1663 (son ?)
Robledo, Diego (son of Pedro I)	1598	1607
Ruiz Cáceres, Juan	1600	1631
Santa Cruz, Diego de*	1598	1617
Torres, Juan de	1597	1608
Varela, Pedro	1598	1613
Vásquez, Francisco	1598	1608
Vitoria, Juan de (not Carvajal)	1597	1614
Vitoria Carvajal, Juan de	1598	1614
Ximénez (Hurtado?), Juan	1598	1665 (son)

Source: Chávez, *Origins*.

*Son of Juan Pérez de Bustillo.

Durán y Chávez, Pedro I	—	1613
Francisco, Manuel	1598	1609
González, Juan	1597	1609
Gutiérrez Bocanegra, Juan/Antonio	1598	1602
Rascón, Francisco	1600	1604
Sánchez Monroy, Pedro	1598	1602
Velarde Colodro, Juan	1598	1604
Vido, Francisco	1598	1604
Ynojosa, Juan de	—	1602

Source: Hammond and Rey, *Don Juan*.

Appendix Table J. continued

COLONIST	MUSTER	EARLIEST KNOWN POST-1601 DATE
Fernández de Tapia, Juan	1600	1604
García, Lázaro	1597	1604
Gil, Juan	1600	1604
González (Lobón), Domingo	1600	1608
Hernández de Benhumea, Gonzalo	1600	1604
López de Áviles, Cristóbal	1598	1604
López Mederos, Juan	1600	1604
Mallea, Juan de	—	1612
Martínez de Montoya, Juan	1600	1604
Medel, Juan	1598	1604
Montoya, Bartolomé de I	1600	1604
Núñez Ynojosa, Alonso	1598	1612
Robledo, Francisco (son of Pedro I)	1598	1621
Rodríguez, Pedro	1600	1604
Rodríguez Bellido, Juan	1600	1604
Valencia, Blas	1600	1604

Source: Esquibel, "Soldados-Vecinos," citing Colección Antigua, t. 316, f. 139 ff., AH.

Ayardi, Diego de	1598	1603
Suárez de Figueroa (Montaño), Isidro	1598	1603
Zapata, Rodrigo	1598	1603

Source: Scholes, unpublished notes.

Appendix Table K. Known Spanish Families in New Mexico in the Early Post-1601 Years

NAME	MUSTER	EARLIEST KNOWN POST-1601 DATE
MEN WHO BROUGHT FAMILIES FROM NEW SPAIN (17)		
Archuleta, Asensio de	1598	1603
García, Lázaro	1597	1604
Gómez Montesinos, Alonso	1598	1602
Griego, Juan	1598	1631
Gutiérrez Bocanegra, Juan	1598	1602
Hernández, Gonzalo	1598	1602
López Paredes, Francisco*	—	1660 (grandson)
Márquez, Gerónimo	1598	1609
Martín Serrano, Hernán	1598	1604
Montoya, Bartolomé de I	1600	1604
Morán, Juan	1598	1663 (son?)
Pérez de Bustillo, Juan	1598	1613
Robledo, Diego (son of Pedro I)	1598	1607
Romero, Bartolomé	1598	1602
Sánchez de Monroy, Pedro	1598	1602
Vaca (Baca), Cristóbal	1600	1603
Vitoria Carbajal, Juan de	1598	1614
MEN WHO FOUNDED FAMILIES IN NEW MEXICO (17)		
Cadimo, Francisco	1598	1631 (daughter?)
Cruz, Juan de la (Durán)	1598	1628
Cruz, Juan de la ("el Catalán")	1598	1613
Durán y Chávez, Pedro I	—	1613
Escarramad, Juan de	1598	1617
García (Holgado), Álvaro	1600	1609
Herrera, Juan de	1600	1642
Hinojos, Hernando de	1598	1613
Ledesma, Francisco de	1598	1662 (son?)
López del Ocanto, Juan	1598	1642 (son?)
Luxán, Juan	1600	1604
Martín Barba, Alonso	1597	1604
Ruiz Cáceres, Juan	1600	1631

Appendix Table K. continued

NAME	MUSTER	EARLIEST KNOWN POST-1601 DATE
MEN WHO FOUNDED FAMILIES IN NEW MEXICO (17)		
Santa Cruz, Diego de (son of Juan Pérez de Bustillo)	1598	1617
Varela Jaramillo, Alonso	1598	1604
Varela de Losada, Pedro	1598	1613
Ximénez (Hurtado?), Juan	1598	1665 (son)

Sources: Hammond and Rey, *Don Juan*; Chávez, *Origins*; Esquibel, "Soldado-Vecinos," citing Colección Antigua, t. 316, f. 139ff., AH.

*Esquibel, personal communication, citing Inquisition, t. 582, exp. 2, ff. 309v–310, AGN.

Appendix Table L. Known *Vecinos* of Santa Fe, 1610–32

NAME	COMMENT
Anaya Almazán, Francisco de	His wife was Juana López de Villafuerte, *india ladina*.
Archuleta, María de	She was the wife of Juan Márquez and the daughter of Asencio de Archuleta.
Baca, Antonio	His wife was Yumar Pérez de Bustillo. He was the son of Cristóbal Baca; he was executed in 1643.
Bellido, Diego Rodríguez	He was the son of Juan Rodríguez Bellido.
Bernal, María	She was the wife of Juan Gómez Barragán and the daughter of Juan Griego and Pascuala Bernal.
Bustillo, Ana de	She was the wife of Asencio de Archuleta and the daughter of Juan Pérez de Bustillo.
Bustillo, Beatris de	She was the wife of Hernando de Hinojos and the daughter of Juan Pérez de Bustillo.
Durán, Juan	His wife was Catalina Bernal. He had previously been known as Juan de la Cruz.
*Durán y Chávez, Pedro II	His wife was Elena Domínguez de Mendoza. He was the son of Pedro Durán y Chávez I.
Escarramad, Juan de	He was living in Santa Fe with his family (his wife is not named) in 1617.
Figueroa, Lucas de	He was a single soldier in New Mexico for six years, ca. 1620.
Fresqui (Fresco), Juan	His wife is unnamed. He was Flemish miner who came to New Mexico in 1617.
García Holgaldo, Álvaro	His wife was Juana de los Reyes, a *mulata*.
García, Diego	His wife is unnamed. He was the son of Álvaro.
*Gómez, Francisco	His wife was Ana Robledo.
Gómez de Luna, Juan	Hi wife was Juana Sánchez, a mulata.
González, Domingo	His wife was Magdelena de Carvajal. He was the brother of Sebastián.
González, Sebastián I	His wife was Isabel Bernal. He was the brother of Domingo.
*Griego, Juan	His wife was Pascuala Bernal.
Griego, Juan II	His wife was Juana de la Cruz, an *india ladina mexicana*.
Guadalajara, Diego de	His wife was Josefa de Zamora.

Appendix Table L. continued

NAME	COMMENT
Gutiérrez, Alonso	His wife was Ana Cadimo.
Herrera, Juan de	His wife was Leonor Hernández, a mulata.
*López Olguín, Juan I	His wife was Catalina de Villanueva.
López del Castillo, Matías	His wife was the daughter of Asencio Archuleta and Ana Pérez de Bustillo.
Lucero de Godoy, Pedro	His wife was Petronila de Zamora.
*Madrid, Francisco	His wife was María de la Vega Márquez.
Márquez, Pedro	His wife was Catalina Pérez de Bustillo, daughter of Simon Pérez de Bustillo.
*Martín Serrano, Hernán I	His wife was Juana Rodríguez.
Moraga, Diego de	His wife was Juana Bernal.
Ortiz, Ana	She was the wife of Cristóbal Baca.
Pacheco, Luis	He was a soldier in Santa Fe in 1632; he was killed by Taoseños in 1639.
Pérez, Gaspar	His wife was María Romero. He was an armorer.
Pérez Granillo, Francisco	His wife is unnamed.
Robledo, Luisa	She was the wife of Bartolomé Romero and the daughter of Pedro Robledo I and Catalina López.
*Rodríguez Bellido, Juan	His wife was Isabel (?). He was the father of Diego Bellido.
Romero, Bartolomé II	His wife was María Pérez Granillo.
Romero, Matías	His wife was Isabel de Pedraza.
Santa Cruz, Diego de	His wife was Gregoria de Archleta. He was possibly an adopted son of Juan Pérez de Bustillo.
*Varela, Alonso	His wife was Catalina Pérez de Bustillo, who was the daughter of Juan Pérez de Bustillo.
Vera, Diego de	His wife was María de Abendaño.
Vitoria Carvajal, Juan	His wife was Isabel Holguín.

Sources: Esquibel, "Founders"; Chávez, *Origins*.

*Known founders of Santa Fe.

Appendix Table M. Spanish Settlers Reported Killed in the 1680 Revolt

SPANISH MEN ONLY (13; 10 NONCONVICT)

Anaya Almazán, Francisco ("el Mozo")
Barba, Estevan, Alférez
Gamboa, Lucas
García de Noriega, Lázaro
Goitia, Joseph de (convict)
Gómez Robledo, Andrés, maese de campo
Griego, Bartolomé (youth)
Herrera, Cristóbal de (youth)
López, Felipe (convict)
López, Nicolás
Peralta, Andrés de, alcalde mayor
Ramos, Marcos (convict)
Vega, Francisco Blanco de la

SPANISH MEN AND THEIR FAMILIES* (8)

Anaya Almazán, Cristóbal de, Captain; his wife was Leonor de Mendoza
Carvajal, Agustin de, Captain; his wife was Damiana Domínguez de Mendoza
Guadarrama, Joseph de
Leyva, Juan de
Leyva, Nicolás de
Nieto, Joseph, Captain; his wife was Lucia López de Gracia
Torres, Sebastián de
Ximénez, Francisco, Captain

SPANISH MEN WHOSE WIVES AND FAMILIES WERE KILLED* (12)

Anaya Almazán, Francisco de II; his wife was Gerónima Pérez de Bustillo
Cuellar, Pedro de
Durán y Chávez, Fernándo, sargento mayor; his wife was Elena Ruiz Cáceres
Herrera Corrales, Sebastián de, sargento mayor; his wife was Juana de Aragón
Herrera, Domingo de; his wife was María Ramos
Leyva, Pedro I de; his wife was Catalina García Holgado
Lucero de Godoy, Antonio, Alférez
Lucero de Godoy, Diego
Lucero de Godoy, Pedro; his wife was Francisca Gómez Robledo

Appendix Table M. continued

SPANISH MEN WHOSE WIVES AND FAMILIES WERE KILLED* (12)

Romero, Pedro; his wife was Petronila de Salas
Varela (Losada), Francisco, Alférez
Xavier, Francisco; his wife was Graciana Griego

Sources: Hackett and Shelby, *Revolt*, vol. 1; Chávez, *Origins*.

*Names of wives are given where known.

Appendix Table N. Known Spanish Men Descended from Original New Mexico Colonists

1680–81 MUSTERS (54)	FAMILY FOUNDER*
Archuleta, Juan de Archuleta, Juan de	Archuleta, Asencio de
Baca, Cristóbal II Baca, Ignacio	Baca, Cristóbal I
Bernal, Francisco II	Griego, Juan
Carvajal, Ambrosio de Carvajal, Antonio de	Carvajal, Juan de Vitoria
Durán, Juan II Durán, Salvador	Durán, Juan (de la Cruz)
Durán y Chávez, Fernando II Durán y Chávez, José Durán y Chávez, Pedro II	Durán y Chávez, Pedro I
González Lobón, Domingo	González, Domingo
González (Bas), Sebastián II	González (Bernal), Sebastián
Griego, Agustín Griego, Blas Griego, Juan Griego, Juan	Griego, Juan
Hinojos, Hernando II	Hinojos, Hernando
Jorge, Antonio	Jorge, Juan
López del Ocanto, Domingo (?)**	López del Ocanto, Juan

Appendix Table N. continued

1680–81 MUSTERS (54)	FAMILY FOUNDER*
López Olguín, Juan II	López Holguín, Juan I
(López) Olguín, Cristóbal	
(López) Olguín, Salvador	
Luján, Agustín	Luxán, Juan
Luján, Antonio	
Luján, Domingo	
Luján, Matías	
Márquez, Antonio	Márquez, Geronímo
Márquez, Bernabé	
Márquez, Pedro I	
Márquez, Pedro II	
Martín Barba, Domingo	Martín Barba, Alonso I
Martín (Serrano), Apolinar	Martín Serrano, Hernán
Martín Serrano, Domingo	
Martín Serrano, Hernán II	
Martín Serrano, Luis II	
Martín Serrano, Luis (the younger)	
Montoya, Antonio de	Montoya, Bartolomé de I
Montoya, Bartolomé de II	
Montoya, Diego de II	
Montoya, Felipe de	
Montoya Francisco de	
Romero de Pedraza, Bartolomé	Romero, Bartolomé
Romero de Pedraza, Felipe	
Romero de Pedraza, Francisco	
Sánchez de Monroy (Nontoi), Sebastián (?)	Sánchez de Monrroy, Pedro

Appendix Table N. continued

1680–81 MUSTERS (54)	FAMILY FOUNDER*
Tapia, Cristóbal de (?)	Fernández (de Tapia), Juan
Valencia, Juan de Valencia, Manuel de	Valencia, Blas de
Varela de Losada, Alonso Varela de Losada, Diego Varela de Losada, Eugenio Varela de Losada, Francisco	Varela, Pedro

1681 MUSTERS (35)	FAMILY FOUNDER
Baca, José Baca, Manuel	Baca, Cristóbal
Barba, Juan (Martín)	Martín Barba, Alonso
Carvajal, Luis de Carvajal, Nicolás de	Carvajal, Juan de Vitoria
Durán, Luis	Durán, Juan (de la Cruz)
Durán y Chávez, Fernando, Sargento Mayor Durán y Chávez, Cristóbal II Durán y Chávez, Juan Durán y Chávez, Tomás	Durán y Chávez, Pedro I
García Holgado, Diego	García Holgado, Álvaro
González, Sebastián, Adjutant	González, Domingo
Herrera, Antonio de Herrera, Juan II de	Herrera, Juan de

Appendix Table N. continued

1681 MUSTERS (35)	FAMILY FOUNDER
Hinojos, Diego de	Hinojos, Hernando de
López Mederos, Pedro	López Medel, Juan
López Olguín, Juan (the younger)	López Holguín, Juan
Luján, Diego Luján, Miguel	Luxán, Juan
Márquez, Francisco Márquez, Diego	Márquez, Gerónimo
Martín Serrano, Antonio Martín Serrano, Cristóbal Martín Serrano, Pedro	Martín Serrano, Hernán
Montoya, Juan de	Montoya, Bartolomé de
Romero, Juan Romero, Salvador Romero, Sebastián	Romero, Bartolomé
Ruiz de Cáceres, Juan	Ruiz Cáceres, Juan
Varela Jaramillo, Cristóbal Varela Jaramillo, Pedro	Varela, Alonso
Varela de Losada, Pedro III Varela de Losada, Joseph Varela de Losada, Cristóbal	Varela, Pedro

Sources: Hackett and Shelby, *Revolt*, vols. 1 and 2; Chávez, *Origins*.

*Men who came with Governor Juan de Oñate in 1598 or with reinforcements in 1600.
**(?) indicates that the relation to family founder is uncertain.

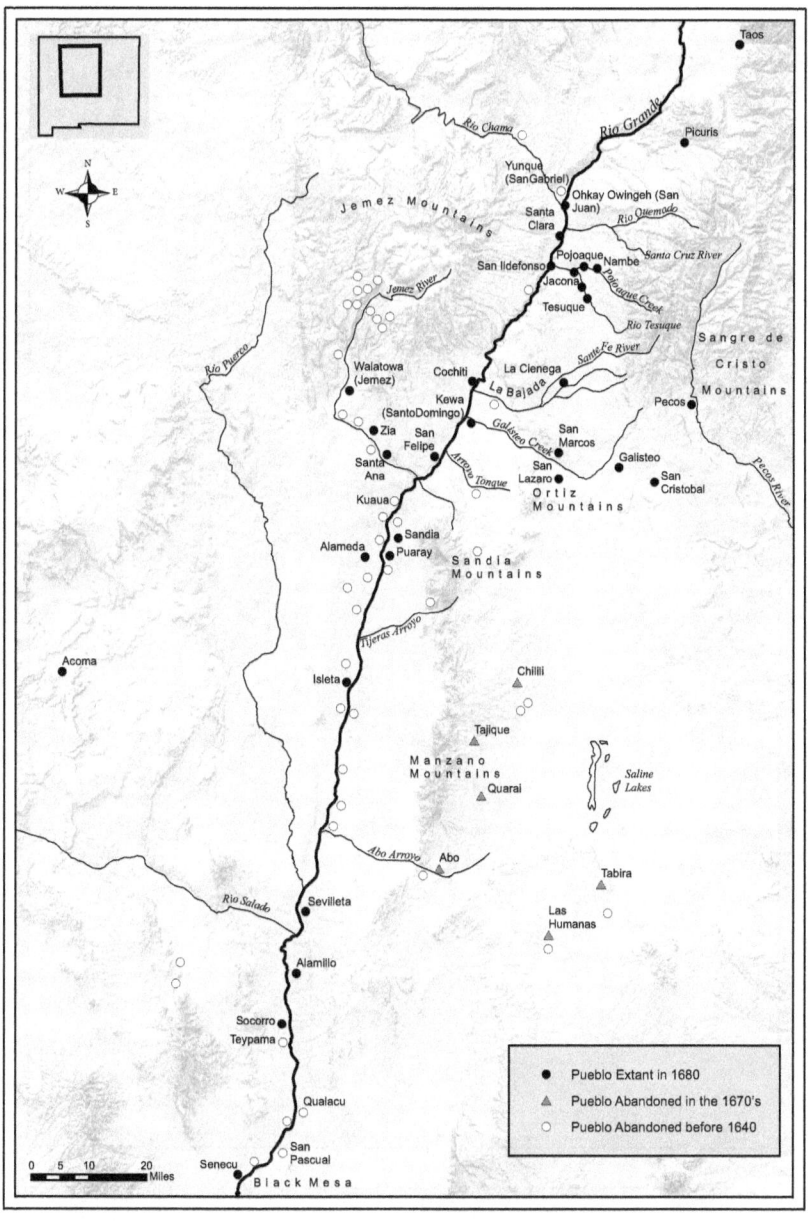

Map 1. Seventeenth-Century New Mexico Pueblos
Created by Natalie Heberling

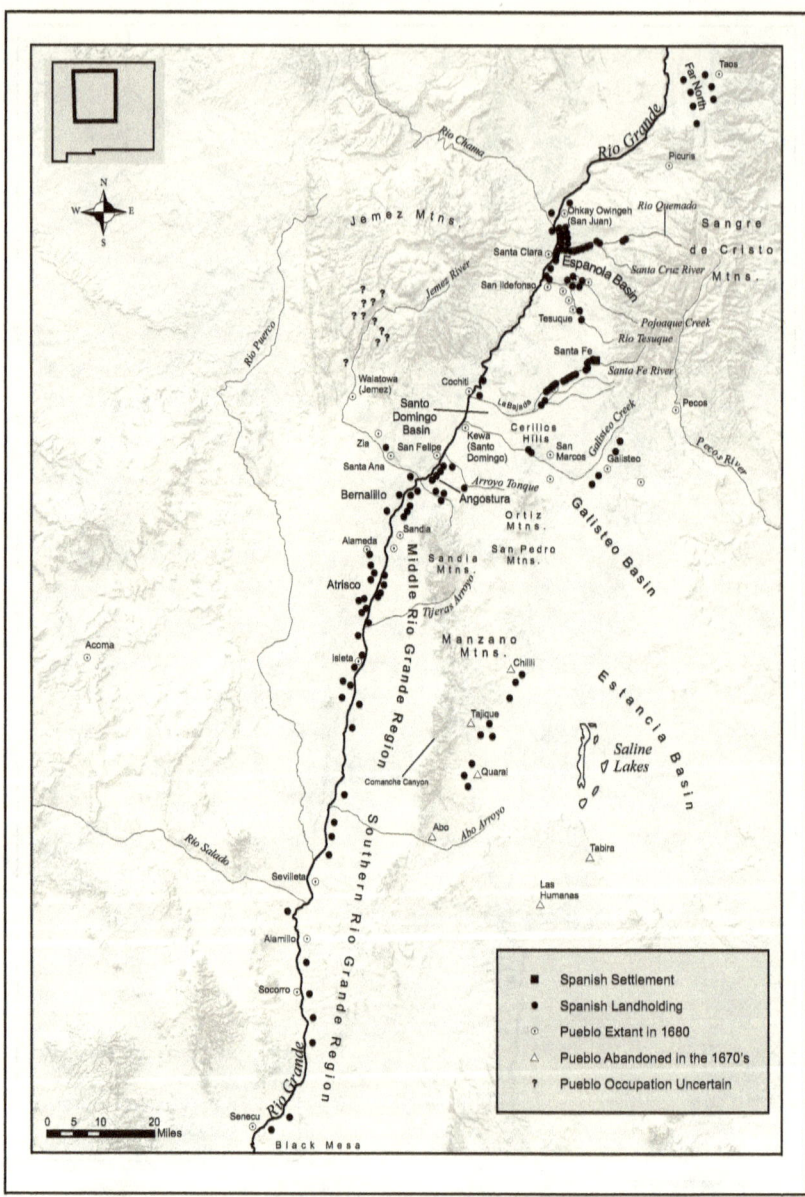

Map 2. Spanish Landholdings in New Mexico, 1610–80, an Approximation
Created by Natalie Heberling

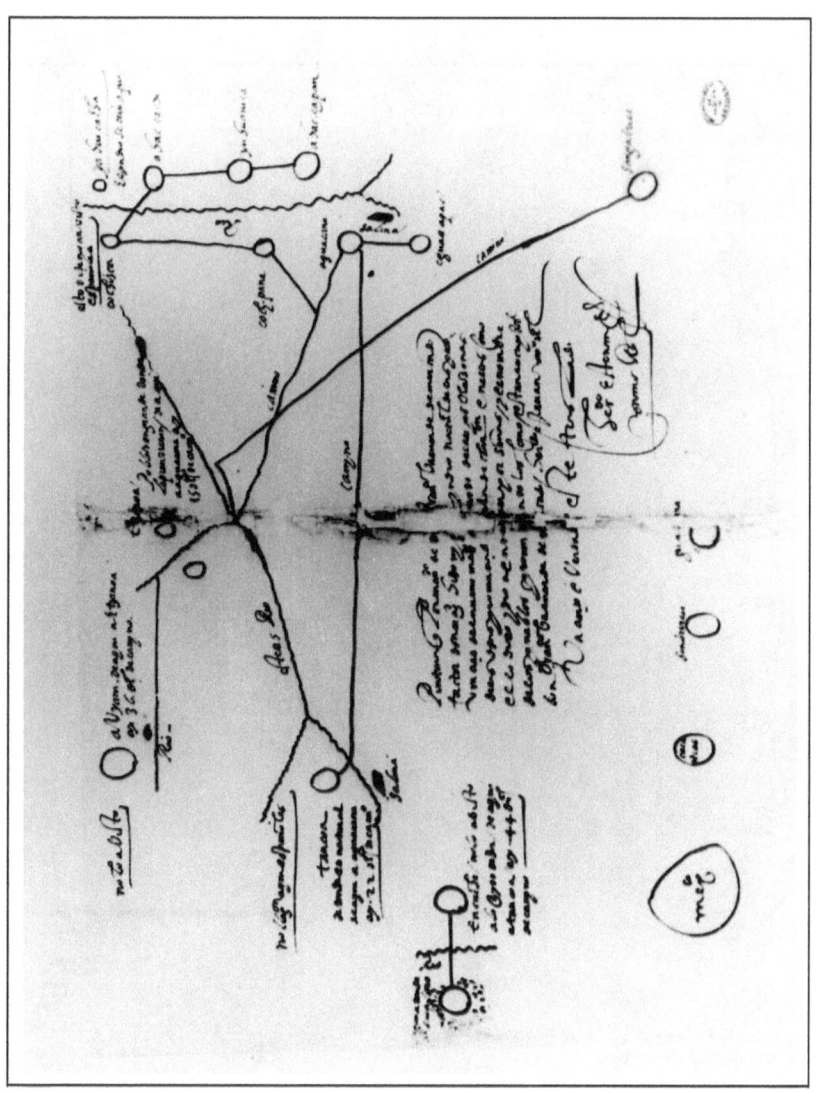

Map 3. Zaldívar's Route to the Eastern Plains from San Gabriel, 1599. Courtesy: Archivo General de Indias, Seville, Spain

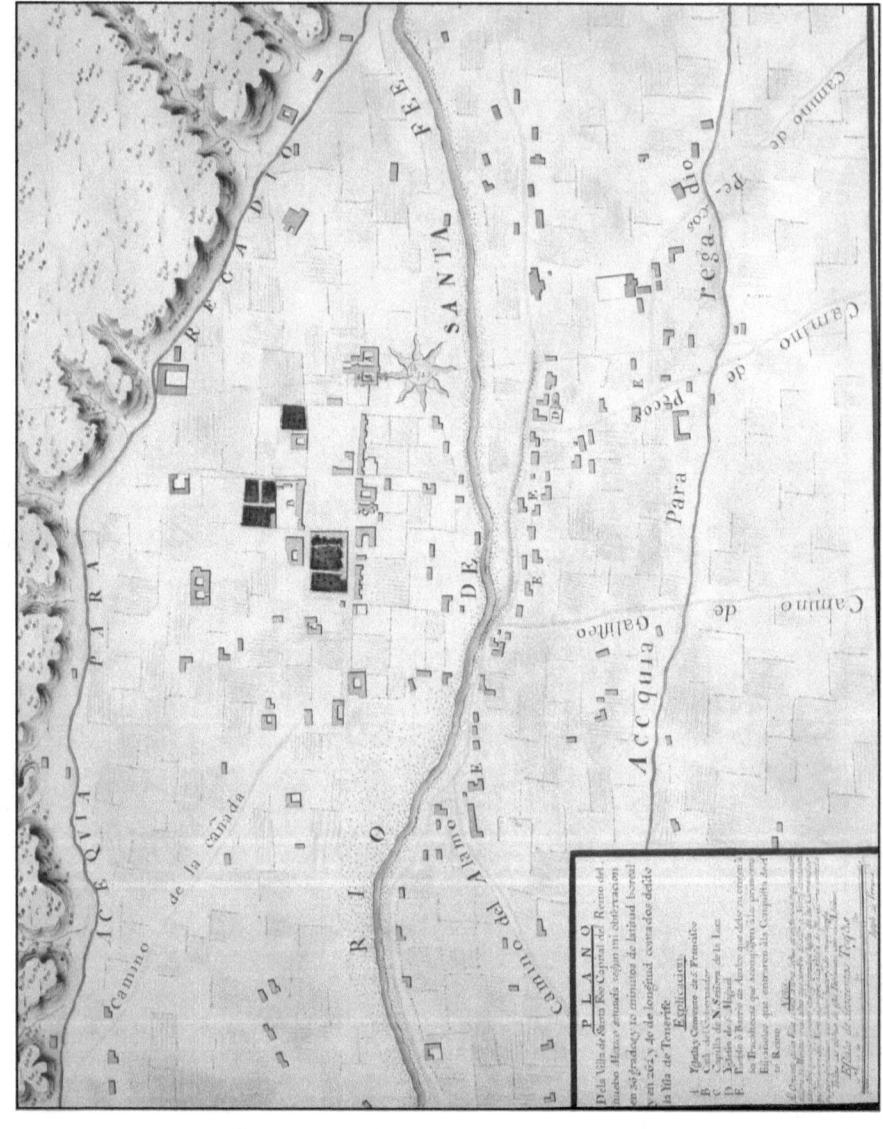

Map 4. Urrutia Map of Santa Fe, 1766

A. Church and convent of Saint Francis
B. Palace of the Governors
C. Chapel of Nuestra Señora de la Luz
D. Church of San Miguel
E. Pueblo or barrio of Analco

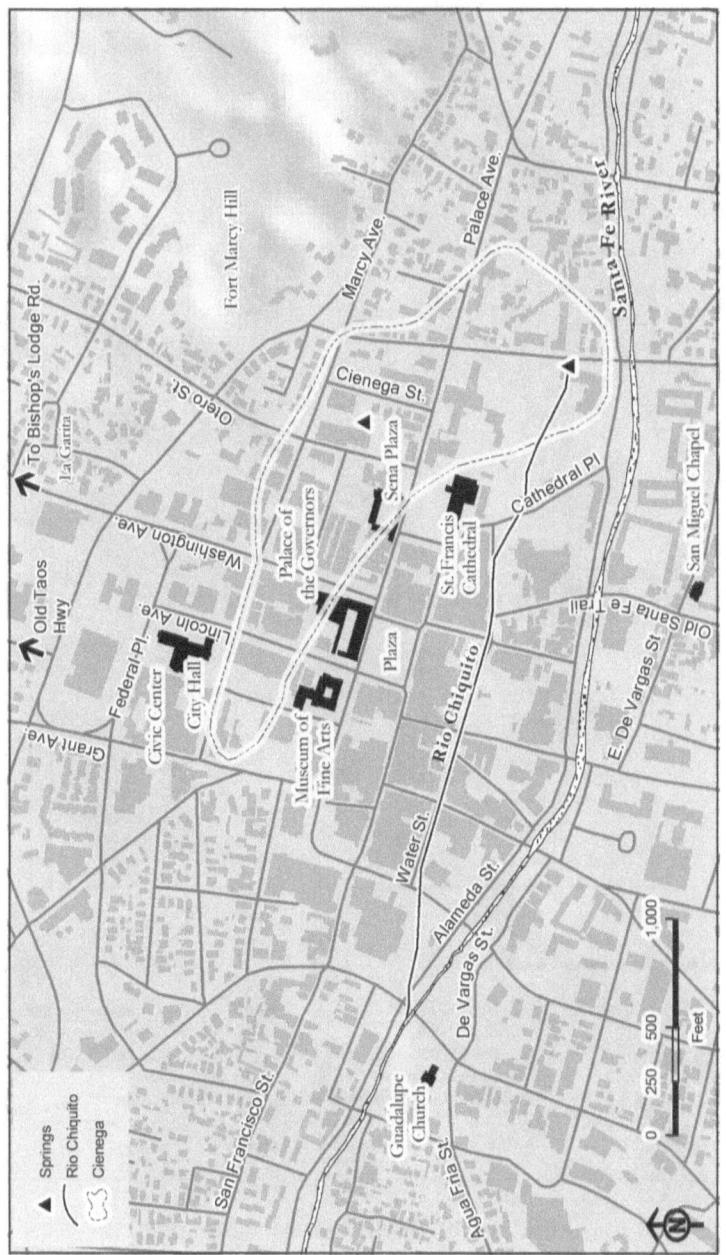

Map 5. Santa Fe Placenames and Seventeenth-Century Hydrologic Features.
Created by Andrew Ruiz; location of the cienega (Tigges, "Soil Tests"); location of the Rio Chiquito (Plewa, "Trickle")

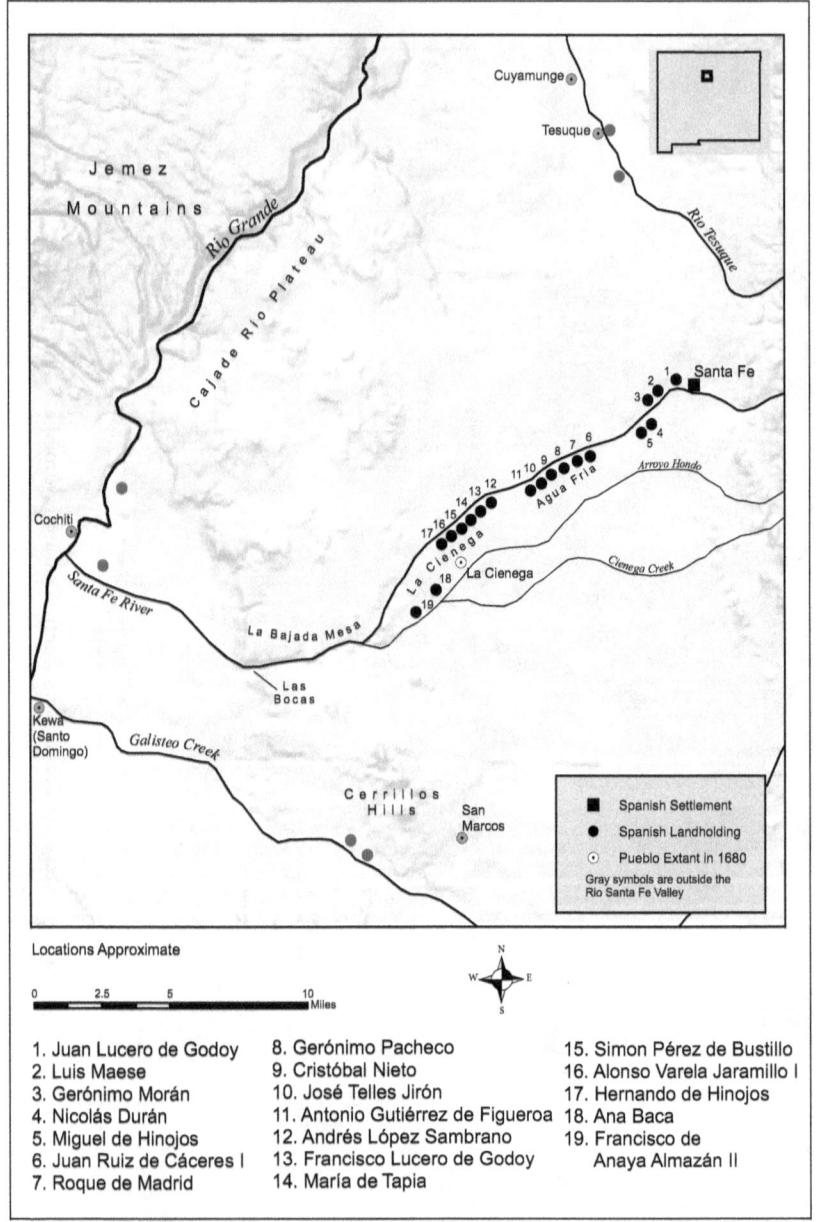

1. Juan Lucero de Godoy
2. Luis Maese
3. Gerónimo Morán
4. Nicolás Durán
5. Miguel de Hinojos
6. Juan Ruiz de Cáceres I
7. Roque de Madrid
8. Gerónimo Pacheco
9. Cristóbal Nieto
10. José Telles Jirón
11. Antonio Gutiérrez de Figueroa
12. Andrés López Sambrano
13. Francisco Lucero de Godoy
14. María de Tapia
15. Simon Pérez de Bustillo
16. Alonso Varela Jaramillo I
17. Hernando de Hinojos
18. Ana Baca
19. Francisco de Anaya Almazán II

Map 6. Known Seventeenth-Century Spanish Landholdings: Santa Fe River Valley
Created by Natalie Heberling

MAPS

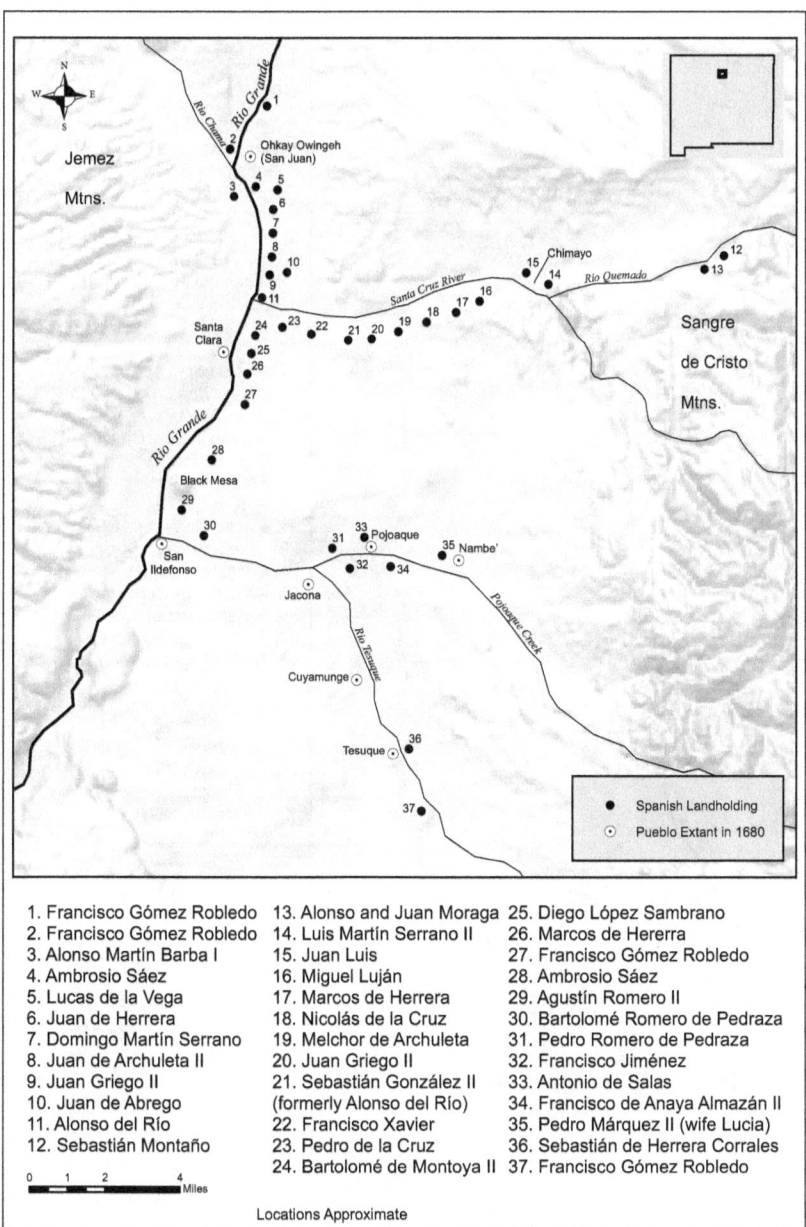

1. Francisco Gómez Robledo
2. Francisco Gómez Robledo
3. Alonso Martín Barba I
4. Ambrosio Sáez
5. Lucas de la Vega
6. Juan de Herrera
7. Domingo Martín Serrano
8. Juan de Archuleta II
9. Juan Griego II
10. Juan de Abrego
11. Alonso del Río
12. Sebastián Montaño
13. Alonso and Juan Moraga
14. Luis Martín Serrano II
15. Juan Luis
16. Miguel Luján
17. Marcos de Herrera
18. Nicolás de la Cruz
19. Melchor de Archuleta
20. Juan Griego II
21. Sebastián González II (formerly Alonso del Río)
22. Francisco Xavier
23. Pedro de la Cruz
24. Bartolomé de Montoya II
25. Diego López Sambrano
26. Marcos de Hererra
27. Francisco Gómez Robledo
28. Ambrosio Sáez
29. Agustín Romero II
30. Bartolomé Romero de Pedraza
31. Pedro Romero de Pedraza
32. Francisco Jiménez
33. Antonio de Salas
34. Francisco de Anaya Almazán II
35. Pedro Márquez II (wife Lucia)
36. Sebastián de Herrera Corrales
37. Francisco Gómez Robledo

Locations Approximate

Map 7. Known Spanish Landholdings: Española Basin, 1680
Created by Natalie Heberling

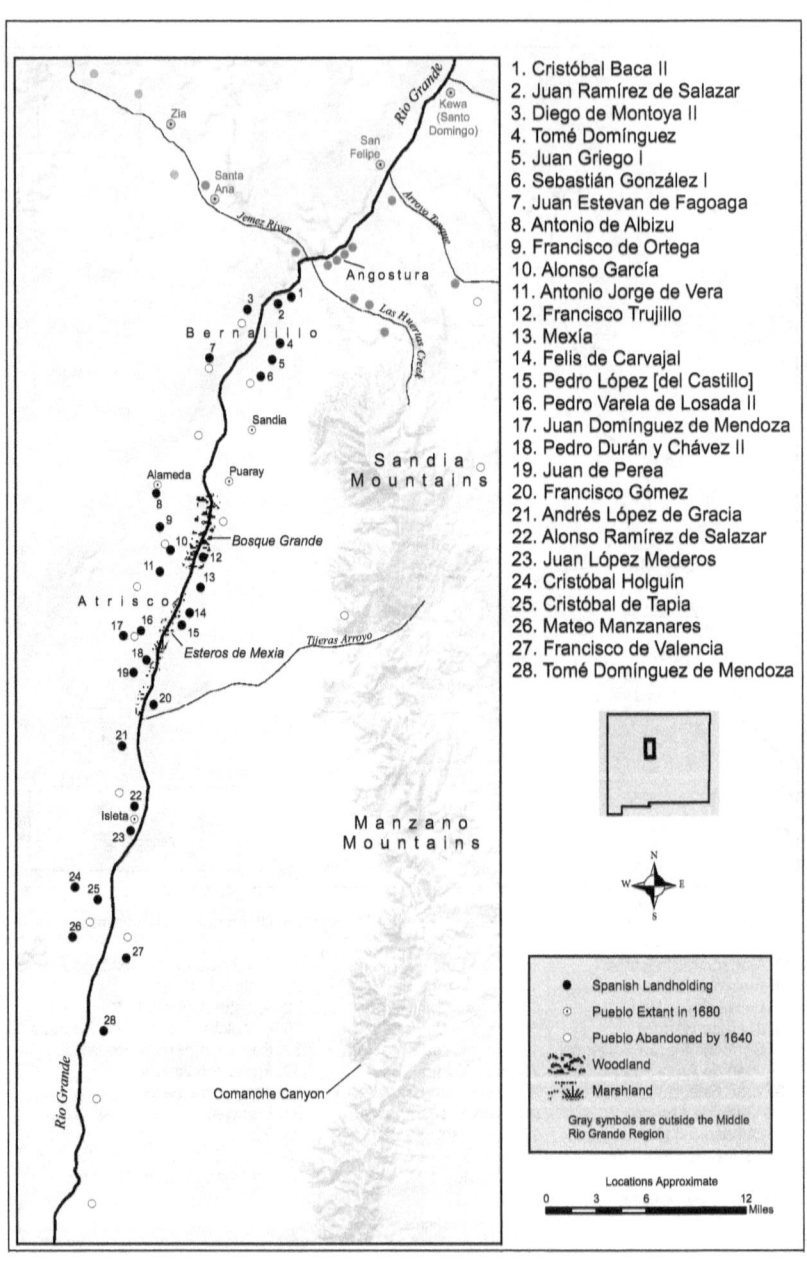

Map 8. Known Seventeenth-Century Spanish Landholdings: Middle Rio Grande Region.
Created by Natalie Heberling

Notes

PREFACE

1. So far copies of these land grants have not been located in archives in either Mexico or Spain or in private hands (some fleeing settlers might have been able to take their documents with them, but as yet none have been found).

CHAPTER ONE

1. Hammond and Rey, *Narratives*, 3, 5.
2. For documents on the Coronado expedition, especially the account of chronicler Pedro de Castañeda, see Flint and Flint, *Documents*, 378–496; Hammond and Rey, *Narratives*, 191–293; and Winship, *Coronado Expedition*, 470–546.
3. Hammond and Rey, *Rediscovery*, 7, 8, 12–14.
4. Hammond and Rey, *Rediscovery*, 19.
5. Ibid., 16–19, 27–28.
6. In 1590 Captain Gaspar Castaño de Sosa led an unauthorized group of colonists into New Mexico from Nuevo Leon in northern New Spain but was soon forced to withdraw (Schroeder and Matson, *Colony*, 175; Hammond and Rey, *Rediscovery*, 294–95).
7. Hammond and Rey, *Don Juan*, 1:6.
8. Ibid., 42–57.
9. Ibid., 58.
10. Hammond, *Don Juan*, 33–34.
11. Hammond and Rey, *Don Juan*, 1:8.
12. Ibid., 86–87, 89–90.
13. Ibid., 93.
14. Ibid., 169.
15. Ibid., 94–97.
16. Ibid., 194, 196, 197–98.
17. Hammond, *Don Juan*, 70–71; Hammond and Rey, *Don Juan*, 1:98–168.
18. Hammond and Rey, *Don Juan*, 1:197–98, 199–202.

19. Hammond, *Don Juan*, 88–89; Hammond and Rey, *Don Juan*, 1:202–308.
20. Hammond, *Don Juan*, 90.
21. Ibid., 90; Hammond and Rey, *Don Juan*, 1:311, 314; Simmons, *Last Conquistador*, 91–93.
22. Hammond and Rey, *Don Juan*, 1:314, 329–36.
23. Ibid., 315.
24. Ibid., 316–18.
25. Oñate claimed there were sixty men in his party (Hammond and Rey, *Don Juan*, 1:480), but Villagrá stated that there were thirty (*History*, 139–40).
26. Hammond and Rey, *Don Juan*, 1:319, 481.
27. Ibid., 319–20.
28. Ibid., 320, 320n21. For identification of Caypa as San Juan, see Sánchez, *Rio Abajo Frontier*, 47; Anderson, "Encomienda," 357; Hammond, *Don Juan*, 100.
29. Hammond and Rey, *Don Juan*, 1:320–23.
30. Barrett, *Conquest*, 45, table 10.
31. Flint and Flint, *Documents*, 412, 468; Hammond and Rey, *Narratives*, 244; Winship, *Coronado Expedition*, 445, 511. For the argument that Barrionuevo visited San Ildefonso and Santa Clara pueblos, not Yunque and Ohkay, see Schaafsma, *Apaches de Navajo*, 202.
32. Schroeder and Matson, *Colony*, 110–21; Hammond and Rey, *Don Juan*, 1:280–83. An unauthorized expedition led by Francisco de Leyba y Bonilla and Antonio Gutiérrez de Humaña visited among the Rio Grande pueblos during 1593, staying mainly at the Tewa pueblo of San Ildefonso, but nothing is known about their treatment of the local people (Hammond and Rey, *Don Juan*, 1:416–19).

CHAPTER TWO

1. Hammond and Rey, *Don Juan*, 2:656.
2. Flint and Flint, *Documents*, 407; Hammond and Rey, *Narratives*, 234; Winship, *Coronado Expedition*, 503; Hammond and Rey, *Don Juan*, 2:610.
3. Hammond and Rey, *Don Juan*, 2:645.
4. Ibid., 2:610, 626, 634, 645, 660.
5. Ayer, Hodge, and Lummis, *Memorial*, 38–39; Hodge, Hammond, and Rey, *Revised Memorial*, 37–38.
6. Fritts, *Reconstructing Large-Scale Climatic Patterns*, xix, 176, 190.
7. Hammond and Rey, *Don Juan*, 2:696–97.
8. Kessell, Hendricks, and Dodge, *Blood*, 2:645.
9. Kessell, Hendricks, and Dodge, *Blood*, 1:219–21; Twitchell, *Spanish Archives*, no. 818, 1:229.
10. Tuan et al., *Climate*, 79; Pratt and Snow, *North Central*, 13. According to the *1941 Yearbook of Agriculture*, the optimal frostless period for growing corn is over 140 days (U.S. Department of Agriculture, *Climate and Man*, 310).

11. Pratt and Snow, *North Central*, 13.
12. Domínguez, *Missions*, 98.
13. Crawford et al., *Middle Rio Grande Ecosystem*, 8.
14. Ibid., 8, 19, 28.
15. A settler in the El Paso area in 1773 confirms the fertilizing effect of silt deposition when he mentions "the benefit furnished by the water in bringing with it a thick mud which serves as manure for the land" (Hackett, *Historical Documents*, 3:507).
16. Kelley, *Albuquerque*, 13, 15; Scurlock, *From the Rio*, 186; Barrett, *Conquest*, 30, 125–26n59.
17. Kelley, *Albuquerque*, 15; Crawford et al., *Middle Rio Grande Ecosystem*, 20–21; Simmons, *Albuquerque*, 11.
18. Scurlock, *From the Rio*, 185; Simmons, *Albuquerque*, 40, 112.
19. Kelley, *Albuquerque*, 15; Simmons, *Albuquerque*, 40.
20. Kessell et al., *Disturbances*, 200, 201.
21. Crawford et al., *Middle Rio Grande Ecosystem*, 27, 28, 29.
22. Flint and Flint, *Documents*, 305, 307; Hammond and Rey, *Narratives*, 183; Winship, *Coronado Expedition*, 594.
23. Hammond and Rey, *Rediscovery*, 219.
24. Domínguez, *Missions*, 145n1; Scurlock, *From the Rio*, 185; Simmons, *Albuquerque*, 40.
25. Domínguez, *Missions*, 145n1.
26. Lafora, *Relación del viaje*, 96.
27. Lafora, *Relación del viaje*, 94, 104; Scurlock, *From the Rio*, 222.
28. Dick-Peddie, *New Mexico Vegetation*, 104–5; Scurlock, *From the Rio*, 201, 205.
29. Dick-Peddie, *New Mexico Vegetation*, 88–89; Scurlock, *From the Rio*, 206.
30. Dick-Peddie, *New Mexico Vegetation*, 51, 58, 66–67; Scurlock, *From the Rio*, 206–7.

CHAPTER THREE

1. The Zuni and Hopi pueblos, located farther west, are not included in this study because its focus is on the Rio Grande Pueblo region.
2. Hammond and Rey, *Don Juan*, 1:483; Barrett, *Conquest*, 12–13, 54–59, 65.
3. Ford, Schroeder, and Peckham, "Three Perspectives," 25, 28–29, 30–32, 34–36; Riley, *Rio del Norte*, 96–103.
4. Two other Piro pueblos, Magdalena (LA 284) and Bear Mountain (LA 285), were located to the west just north of the Magdalena Mountains.
5. Hammond and Rey, *Don Juan*, 1:318. Later, the name "Socorro" came to be applied to a pueblo about three miles north, Pilabó (LA 791), located in the present town of Socorro.
6. Ibid., 318–19.

7. Ibid., 319.
8. More information about the Puebloans' way of life is to be found in the reports of previous Spanish expeditions. See Flint and Flint, *Documents*; Hammond and Rey, *Narratives*; Winship, *Coronado Expedition*; and Hammond and Rey, *Rediscovery* for the Chamuscado-Rodríguez, Espejo, and Castaño de Sosa expeditions, as well as Schroeder and Matson, *Colony*, for the last.
9. Hammond and Rey, *Don Juan*, 2:625, 633, 644, 851.
10. Flint and Flint, *Documents*, 414, 470; Hammond and Rey, *Narratives*, 246; Winship, *Coronado Expedition*, 446–47; 512.
11. See Flint and Flint, *Documents*, 298, 301; Hammond and Rey, *Narratives*, 309; and Winship, *Coronado Expedition*, 567, 569, who cite the *Relación postrera de Cibola*. Hammond and Rey and Winship state that the pueblos downstream from Tiguex province are smaller, whereas Flint and Flint state that "upstream and downstream along the river all the pueblos are small." The Spanish transcriptions provided by Winship and Flint and Flint could allow for either interpretation. Hammond and Rey, *Rediscovery*, 130, 221–22, cite the expeditions of Chamuscado (1581–82) and Espejo (1583) respectively. They approached Tiguex province from the south along the Rio Grande rather from the Zuni pueblos to the west. The chroniclers of both expeditions stated that as they traveled north from Tiguex the pueblos were increasingly larger and better.
12. Hammond and Rey, *Rediscovery*, 82, 83, 129, 130, 134, 172, 173, 223; Villagrá, *History*, 140.
13. Flint and Flint, *Documents*, 417, 473; Hammond and Rey, *Narratives*, 252; Winship, *Coronado Expedition*, 450, 517; Hammond and Rey, *Rediscovery*, 85, 172, 278; Hammond and Rey, *Don Juan*, 1:483.
14. Flint and Flint, *Documents*, 418, 475; Hammond and Rey, *Narratives*, 255; Winship, *Coronado Expedition*, 452, 521; Hammond and Rey, *Don Juan*, 2:610; 627, 636, 645, 660; Webster, "Economics," 181.
15. Flint and Flint, *Documents*, 417, 473; Hammond and Rey, *Narratives*, 252; Winship, *Coronado Expedition*, 450, 517; Hammond and Rey, *Don Juan*, 2:626, 634, 645, 659, 850–51, 862; Hammond and Rey, *Rediscovery*, 172, 185, 192, 220, 278.
16. Webster, "Economics," 180.
17. Hammond and Rey, *Rediscovery*, 85; Hammond and Rey, *Don Juan*, 2:636.
18. Flint and Flint, *Documents*, 420, 476; Hammond and Rey, *Narratives*, 256; Winship, *Coronado Expedition*, 452, 522.
19. Hammond and Rey, *Rediscovery*, 182, 224, 282; Hammond and Rey, *Don Juan*, 2:610, 626; Schroeder and Matson, *Colony*, 118.
20. Hammond and Rey, *Don Juan*, 1:317–18, 2:693, 698.
21. Hammond and Rey, *Rediscovery*, 85, 278; Hammond and Rey, *Don Juan*, 2:660.
22. Hammond and Rey, *Rediscovery*, 82, 172.
23. Hammond and Rey, *Don Juan*, 2:626, 634, 652.
24. Webster, "Economics," 180–82.

25. Ibid., 187.
26. Scholes, "Civil Government," 84.

CHAPTER FOUR

1. Hackett, *Historical Documents*, 3:109–110; Anderson, "Encomienda," 353–54.
2. Hammond and Rey, *Don Juan*, 1:49, 508–9, 2:603–5; Hackett, *Historical Documents*, 3:120.
3. Hammond Rey, *Don Juan*, 1:50, 509–10, 2:605–6; Anderson, "Encomienda," 356.
4. Hackett, *Historical Documents*, 3:111.
5. Scholes, "Civil Government," 102n51.
6. Hackett, *Historical Documents*, 3:110, 120.
7. Scholes, *Troublous Times*, 131; Snow, "Note," 350–51.
8. Hodge, Hammond, and Ray, *Revised Memorial*, 170; Hackett, *Historical Documents*, 3:110, 120.
9. Hammond and Rey, *Don Juan*, 2:630.
10. Scholes, "Juan Martínez," 340.
11. Hammond and Rey, *Don Juan*, 2:1048, 1052, 1081; Scholes, "Juan Martínez," 337, 341.
12. Hammond and Rey, *Don Juan*, 2:1044.
13. Ibid., 653, 667.
14. Ibid., 630, 641.
15. Ibid., 630, 641, 654.
16. Scholes, "Church and State," pt. 1, 32–33.
17. Hackett, *Historical Documents*, 3:252; Scholes, "Civil Government," 79; Anderson, "Encomienda," 367, citing *Recopilación*, libro 1, tit. 10, ley 10.
18. Scholes, "Church and State," pt. 5, 91; Anderson, "Encomienda," 367.
19. The term "escudero" literally means "shield bearer," reflecting the requirement of the person so named to carry out the military obligation of the encomendero. An encomendero could be replaced when he was not able to carry out his duties in the event of ill health or death, he had no male heirs who had achieved their majority, or because he was incarcerated or had to travel out of the colony (José Antonio Esquibel, personal communication). "Escudero" is translated as "trustee" by Hackett (*Historical Documents*, 3:250), but this term does not cover the military obligation of the escudero, only his role in seeing to the collection of encomienda tribute. In this study, the term "escudero" is used because there is no equivalent word in English.
20. Hackett, *Historical Documents*, 3:250; Scholes, *Troublous Times*, 131; Anderson, "Encomienda," 368–69.
21. Hackett, *Historical Documents*, 3:247–49, 251; Anderson, "Encomienda," 369.
22. Scholes, *Troublous Times*, 41–42.
23. Scholes, "Church and State," pt. 5, 91; Forbes, *Apache*, 139.

24. Barrett, *Conquest*, 58
25. Snow, "Note," 353–54; Barrett, *Conquest*, 64.
26. Hackett, *Historical Documents*, 3:110.
27. Esquibel, "Political and Economic Influences," 10.
28. Hammond Rey, *Don Juan*, 1:49–50, 509; Hall, "Pueblo Grant," 72.
29. Hammond and Rey, *Don Juan*, 2:734; Scholes, *Juan Martínez*, 341; Ivey, "Uncertain Founding," 3–4.
30. Hammond and Rey, *Don Juan*, 2:1088.
31. *Recopilación*, libro 4, título 12, ley 9.
32. *Recopilación*, libro 6, título 3, ley 8
33. Kessell and Hendricks, *By Force of Arms*, 125n15.
34. *Recopilación*, libro 6, título 3, ley 20; Hall, "Pueblo Grant," 75.
35. Bloom, "Glimpse," 368–69; Scholes, "Civil Government," 106n55; Ivey, "Pueblo and Estancia," 225; Esquibel, "Political and Economic Influences," 6, citing México, 29, exp. 2, n. 45, ff. 4r–4v, AGI.
36. Hackett, *Historical Documents*, 3:131.
37. Scholes, *Troublous Times*, 42–43.
38. Esquibel, personal communication, citing Real Audiencia, Concurso de Peñalosa, t. 3, exp. 455, leg. 1, no. 22, 44 ff., AGN; Chávez, *Origins*, 4, 25.
39. Chávez, *Origins*, 41, 113.
40. Kessell, Hendricks, and Dodge, *Blood*, 1:613; Esquibel, personal communication, citing land records of New Mexico, series 1, roll 50, fr. 818 ff., Santa Cruz de la Cañada Private Land Claim Case, 194, SANM.
41. Chávez, *Origins*, 55–56.
42. Chávez, *Origins*, 90; Inquisition, t. 594, exp. 1, ff. 228–28v, AGN, cited in Esquibel, "Vecino Estancias," 7.
43. Hackett, *Historical Documents*, 3:175.
44. *Recopilación*, libro 6, título 3, leyes 9, 14 and libro 4, título 12, ley 14; Gibson, *Aztecs*, 283.
45. Gibson, *Aztecs*, 282.
46. *Recopilación*, libro 6, título1, ley 30.
47. Barrett, *Conquest*, 78–80.
48. Hackett, *Historical Documents*, 3:5.
49. Scholes, "Documents," 46–49, 52–56.
50. Ivey, "Greatest Misfortune," 78; Ivey, "Estancia," 80–82; Esquibel, personal communication, citing Real Audiencia, Concurso de Peñalosa, t. 1, f. 328r, AGN.
51. Scholes, "Documents," 46–50, 52–56; Ivey, "Pueblo and Estancia," 225; Ivey, "Greatest Misfortune," 78.
52. Bloom, "Ynstrucción," 184; Cháves, "Instructions," 183.
53. Hackett, *Historical Documents*, 3:119.
54. Hackett and Shelby, *Revolt*, 1:95.
55. Esquibel, "Political and Economic Influences," 10–12.

56. Hackett and Shelby, *Revolt*, 2:228.
57. Pratt and Snow, *North Central*, 55–57, 62; Snow, "Review," 189; Hackett, *Historical Documents*, 3. Hackett translates the term "estancia" as "farm."
58. Chevalier, *Land and Society*, 264.
59. Simmons, "Settlement Patterns," 10, 11.
60. Pratt and Snow, *North Central*, 54–55; Snow, "Review," 189.
61. Pratt and Snow, *North Central*, 57, 62.
62. Kessell, Hendricks, and Dodge, *Blood*, 1:613–14.
63. Hackett, *Historical Documents*, 3:119
64. *Recopilación*, libro 6, título 5, ley 24 and ley 25; Hammond and Rey, *Don Juan*, 1:511; Hackett, *Historical Documents*, 1:32n148, 32–35; Hackett, *Historical Documents*, 3:262n88.
65. Gibson, *Aztecs*, 62, 224; Hammond and Rey, *Don Juan*, 2:603.
66. Gibson, *Aztecs*, 224–26.
67. Ibid., 233–35.
68. Espinosa, *Crusaders*, 303.
69. Hackett and Shelby, *Revolt*, 1:206.
70. Hammond and Rey, *Don Juan*, 2:322–23.
71. Ibid., 68.
72. Ibid., 630, 641.
73. Scholes, "Church and State," pt. 1, 32.
74. Kessell, Hendricks, and Dodge, *Blood*, 2:1073.
75. Scholes, *Troublous Times*, 39–40.
76. Scholes, "Church and State," pt. 2, 151, 155; Bloom, "Glimpse," 366–67.
77. Scholes, *Troublous Times*, 25.
78. Bloom, "Glimpse," 366–67.
79. Scholes, *Troublous Times*, 48; Scholes, "Civil Government," 81; Bloom, "Glimpse," 367.
80. Hackett, *Historical Documents*, 3:206.
81. Scholes, "Church and State," pt. 2, 155.
82. *Recopilación*, libro 5, título 2, ley 47; Scholes, "Civil Government," 82.
83. Scholes, "Civil Government," 93; Scholes, *Troublous Times*, 39–40.
84. Kessell, *Kiva*, 186.
85. Kessell, *Kiva*, 186; Scholes, *Troublous Times*, 48.
86. Simmons, "Settlement Patterns," 11.
87. *Recopilación*, libro 5, título 2, ley 47.
88. Chávez, *Origins*, 1; Ivey, *In the Midst of Loneliness*, 25; Scholes, *Troublous Times*, 47–48.
89. Scholes, *Troublous Times*, 48–49.
90. Hackett, *Historical Documents*, 3:153.
91. Scholes, "Civil Government," 81; Scholes, "Church and State," pt. 4, 300.
92. Scholes, *Troublous Times*, 48.

93. Scholes, *Troublous Times*, 49.
94. Scholes, "Civil Government," 83.
95. Scholes "Civil Government," 83–85.
96. Barrett, *Conquest*, 55–58.
97. The total Puebloan population, which included the Zuni and Hopi pueblos, was estimated by Governor Oñate in 1599 to have been at least sixty thousand (Hammond and Rey, *Don Juan*, 1:483; Barrett, *Conquest*, 65).
98. Scholes, "Documents," 47–50; Scholes, "Juan Martínez," 245–46; Barrett, *Conquest*, 65; Hackett, *Historical Documents*, 3:119. The Spaniards living in the Zuni and Hopi districts were mainly Crown officials and clergy.
99. Barrett, *Conquest*, 64.
100. Barrett, ibid., 64.
101. Barrett, ibid., 58, 65.
102. Snow, "Note," 353.
103. Scholes, "Civil Government," 77.
104. Bloom, "Beginnings," 129–30.
105. Scholes, "Civil Government," 94–95; Bloom, "Ynstrucción," 180.
106. Scholes, "Civil Government," 91–92.
107. Scholes, "Civil Government," 92–93; Scholes, *Troublous Times*, 39–40; *Recopilación*, libro 6, título 1, ley 77.
108. Lycett, "Archaeological Implications," 536–37.
109. Hammond and Rey, *Don Juan*, 1:53.
110. Scholes, "Church and State," pt. 5, 86.
111. Scholes, "Civil Government," 91, 91n35; Lycett, "Archaeological Implications," 536–38; Sánchez, *Rio Abajo*, 73.
112. Scholes, "Civil Government," 91. In 1665 Governor Fernando de Villanueva considered the jurisdiction of Rio Abajo to encompass the area from La Cienega in the north to Senecú in the south, including the Keres and Jemez pueblos (MS #19258, photos 37–38, BN, cited in Esquibel, "Vecino Estancias," 1).
113. Real Audiencia, Concurso de Peñalosa, t. 3, leg. 1, no. 2, f. 6 ff, October 2, 1661, AGN, cited in Esquibel, "Vecino Estancias," 1.

CHAPTER FIVE

1. Scholes and Bloom, "Friar Personnel," pt. 1, 320–21.
2. Ibid., 326.
3. Ibid., 328, 332, 333.
4. Ibid., 332–335.
5. Scholes and Bloom, "Friar Personnel," pt. 2, 66.
6. Ibid., 64, 65, 73, 74.
7. Ibid., 67, 75.
8. Ibid., 67, 75–77.

9. Ibid., 81.
10. Ibid., 68.
11. Ibid., 78, 80.
12. Ibid., 68, 74, 75.
13. Ayer, Hodge, and Lummis, *Memorial*; Hodge, Hammond, and Rey, *Revised Memorial*.
14. Scholes and Bloom, "Friar Personnel," pt. 2, 81.
15. Scholes, "Documents," 45–56.
16. Gibson, *Aztecs*, 124; Scholes, "Civil Government," 107.
17. Scholes, "Civil Government," 107.
18. Hackett, *Historical Documents*, 3:71.
19. Ibid., 71, 72, 73. At this time the triennial supply service, although underwritten by the Crown, was administered by the Franciscan *procurador general* for New Mexico under the terms of a contract signed in 1631. This arrangement persisted until 1664, when control of the supply trains was contracted out by the Crown to a lay person (Scholes, "Supply Service," pt. 3, 93, 95, 96–113; pt. 3, 386, 392–94).
20. Ivey, "Pueblo and Estancia," 225.
21. Hackett, *Historical Documents*, 3:67–74; Esquibel, "Political and Economic Influences," 3–4.
22. See chapter 15 of this book and map 2.
23. Esquibel, "Political and Economic Influences," 4–5.
24. Hackett, *Historical Documents*, 3:113, 190–91.
25. Webster, "Economics," 183–84; Hackett, *Historical Documents*, 3:144.
26. Hackett, *Historical Documents*, 3:213; Webster, "Economics," 184.
27. Webster, "Economics," 184.

CHAPTER SIX

1. Flint and Flint, *Documents*, 262; Hammond and Rey, *Narratives*, 177; Winship, *Coronado Expedition*, 563.
2. Warren and Weber, "Indian and Spanish Mining," 7–9; Schroeder, "Cerrillos Mining Area," 13–14; Vaughn, "Taking the Measure," 278–79. The Santa Catalina mines mentioned in 1583 by the chronicler of the Espejo expedition were possibly the mines near San Marcos Pueblo, but another view holds that they were on the north end of the Sandia Mountains (Hammond and Rey, *Rediscovery*, 27, 205n124).
3. Hammond and Rey, *Don Juan*, 1:223, 225, 327–28, 396, 2:950; Simmons, *Last Conquistador*, 63.
4. Hammond and Rey, *Don Juan*, 1:321, 2:622, 653–54; Simmons, *Last Conquistador*, 150; Bakewell, *Silver Mining*, 147.
5. Hammond and Rey, *Don Juan*, 1:225, 2:787, 815, 821, 829, 948.
6. Ibid., 813, 820.

7. Ibid., 641–42.
8. Warren and Weber, "Indian and Spanish Mining," 9; Simmons, *Last Conquistador*, 150.
9. Hammond and Rey, *Don Juan*, 2:630, 641–42.
10. Ibid., 2:653, 667.
11. Esquibel, "Founders," 6–8; Esquibel, "Vecinos," n.p. Juan Martínez de Montoya came to New Mexico in 1600 with the reinforcements and played a prominent role, for which he sought recognition from Governor Juan de Oñate and his son Cristóbal, who succeeded him after the cabildo of San Gabriel rejected the viceroy's appointment of Martínez de Montoya to replace the former when he resigned in 1607 (Scholes, "Juan Martínez," 337–41; Hammond and Rey, *Don Juan*, 2:1040, 1044, 1048, 1052–52, 1081).
12. Esquibel, "Thirty-eight Adobe Houses," 113. The first mission church at Las Humanas Pueblo was established by Fray Alonso de Benavides in 1629 and named for San Isidro, but it did not last long and was reestablished in 1659–60 with the new name of San Buenaventura, possibly because this name had persisted as part of the name of the pueblo from the time of the Real (Scholes and Bloom, "Friar Personnel," pt. 2, 74).
13. Hammond and Rey, *Don Juan*, 2:914.
14. Zárate Salmerón, *Relaciones*, 56.
15. Ibid., 56–57; Chávez, *Origins*, 30; Esquibel, personal communication, citing, Inquisition, t. 356, exp 133m f, 266r, AGN.
16. Zárate Salmerón, *Relaciones*, 57.
17. Hackett, *Historical Documents*, 3:72.
18. Warren and Weber, "Indian and Spanish Mining," 8.
19. Kessell, Hendricks, and Dodge, *Blood*, 1:125.
20. See discussion in chapter 16.
21. Hackett, *Historical Documents*, 3:71–72, 73.
22. Bakewell, *Silver Mining*, 181.
23. Esquibel, personal communication, citing Real Audiencia, Concurso de Peñalosa, t. 1, f. 29v, testimony of Sargento Mayor Diego del Castillo, August 16, 1662, Villa de Santa Fe, AGN.
24. Hammond and Rey, *Rediscovery*, 106–7, 131–32, 137, 143, 216.
25. Flint, "La Salina," 40; Kraemer, "Salt Trade," 22–23; Northrop, *Minerals*, 276; Talmage and Wootton, *Non-Metallic Mineral Resources*, 144.
26. *Recopilación*, libro 8, título. 23, ley 13; Flint, "La Salina," 42.
27. Kraemer, "New Mexico's Ancient Salt, 24; Ewald, *Mexican Salt Industry*, 21.
28. Scholes, "Civil Government," 81.
29. Scholes, *Troublous Times*, 29; Kraemer, "Salt Trade," 26.
30. West, *Mining Community*, 36–37; Flint, "La Salina," 42; Kraemer, "Salt Trade," Bakewell, *Silver Mining*, 140, 147–48.
31. West, *Mining Community*, 37; Ewald, *Mexican Salt Industry*, 12–13.
32. Scholes, *Troublous Times*, 44–45; Flint, "La Salina," 42.

33. Kraemer, "New Mexico's Ancient Salt," 27; Chávez, Origins, 8.
34. Talmage and Wootton, *Non-Metallic Mineral Resources*, 147.
35. West, *Mining Community*, 38; Bakewell, *Silver Mining*, 148; Ewald, *The Mexican Salt*, 12–13; Parsons, *Last Salt Makers*, 152.
36. Flint, "La Salina," 42.

CHAPTER SEVEN

1. Hammond and Rey, *Don Juan*, 1:289–300; Gerhard, *Northern Frontier*, map, 217.
2. Hammond and Rey, *Don Juan*, 1:390.
3. Ibid., 1:150–68, 229–86. The three men on the 1600 muster were Diego Díaz de Castro, Juan Fernández, and Francisco Rascón.
4. Ibid., 1:379, 391.
5. Ibid., 1:548–65, 572, 578–79, 2:837. There were eighty-six names on the muster, including two latecomers and an advance party of seven, but five of these officers had come from New Mexico and returned as escorts of the newcomers: Bernabé de las Casas, Gerónimo Márquez, Isidro Suárez de Figueroa, Juan de Victoria Carbajal, and Caudillo Robledo. The total does not include three officers from New Mexico who did not return: Captains Gaspar Pérez de Villagrá, Juan Piñeiro, and Marcos Farfán de los Godos.
6. Ibid., 609. Zárate Salmerón, who was in New Mexico from 1621 to 1626, gave a figure of four hundred men (Zárate Salmerón, *Relaciones*, 54), and Benavides, who was in New Mexico between 1626 and 1629, gave one of seven hundred men (Hodge, Hammond, and Rey, *Revised Memorial*, 57).
7. Hammond and Rey, *Don Juan*, 2:628, 638.
8. Ibid., 2:651, 665.
9. Ibid., 2:770.
10. Ibid., 2:837.
11. Hammond, *Don Juan*, 138.
12. Hammond and Rey, *Don Juan*, 1:28, 481.
13. Ibid., 557–8; Villagrá, *History of New Mexico*, 224–25.
14. Hammond and Rey, *Don Juan*, 2:628, 638, 651. Zárate Salmerón stated that 135 of Oñate's 400 colonists had brought families (*Relaciones*, 54), and Benavides said that about half of Oñate's army of 700 had brought their wives and children (Hodge, Hammond, and Rey, *Revised Memorial*, 57, 68)—both obvious exaggerations.
15. Hammond and Rey, *Don Juan*, 2:687. However, by the fall of 1601 Bernabé had come to favor the abandonment of New Mexico (ibid., 2:686–77, 707). In October 1602 he left with his wife for Saltillo, where her father had a ranch (Esquibel, "Beyond Origins of New Mexico Families," vol. 7).
16. Hammond and Rey, *Don Juan*, 2:758.
17. Ibid., 2:672, 698; Hammond, *Don Juan*, 152. The Quivira report is dated December 14, 1601, and Vicente de Zaldívar's name is on it; therefore, the

expedition to hunt down the deserters did not leave New Mexico until after this date, or some twenty days after their return to San Gabriel (Hammond and Rey, *Don Juan*, 2:758–59, 849).

18. Hammond and Rey, *Don Juan*, 2:701–2, 702–39.
19. Ibid., 2:665.
20. Ibid., 2:703, passim 707–36.
21. Ibid., 2:746.
22. Ibid., 2:773. Zárate Salmerón said he took eighty soldiers (*Relaciones*, 58).
23. Hammond and Rey, *Don Juan*, 2:836.
24. Ibid., 2:837, 850, 862.
25. Scholes, unpublished notes; Scholes, "Royal Treasury Records," 139.
26. Scholes, unpublished notes.
27. Hammond and Rey, *Don Juan*, 2:770–71.
28. Ibid., 1013, 1030, 1076. Esquibel states that about 121 soldiers, many with wives and children, remained after the desertion ("New Light," 176).
29. Hammond and Rey, *Don Juan*, 2:933–34.
30. Ibid., 2:1052–53.
31. Ibid., 2:691, 683, 685, 710.
32. Ibid., 2:686, 688, 707, 1112.
33. Ibid., 2:690–91.
34. Ibid., 2:1013, 1030. Zárate Salmerón cited thirty soldiers, mostly raw recruits (*Relaciones*, 64, 76).
35. Chávez, *Origins*, 65–66, 35–36. Descendants of Francisco Gómez added the name of his wife, Ana Robledo. Members of these two families answered the roll call at Salineta in 1680.
36. Hammond and Rey, *Don Juan*, 2:1076–77.
37. Ibid., 2:1096.
38. Chávez, *Origins*, 65.
39. Scholes, "Royal Treasury Records," 142, 146.
40. Scholes, "Juan Martínez," 337–41.
41. Hammond and Rey, *Don Juan*, 2:1040, 1044, 1048, 1051–2, 1081.
42. Bloom, "Ynstrucción," 178; Cháves, "Instructions," 179.
43. Hammond and Rey, *Don Juan*, 2:1082.
44. Ibid., 2:1114–21.
45. Scholes, "Church and State," pt. 1, 56–57.
46. Hackett and Shelby, *Revolt*, 1:148, 152; Chávez, *Origins*, 69–70.

CHAPTER EIGHT

1. Hammond and Rey, *Don Juan*, 2:1140.
2. Hackett, *Historical Documents*, 3:47.
3. Scholes, "Civil Government," 102, 102n51.

4. Tierras, t. 3268, f. 60v ff., AGN, cited in Esquibel, "Beyond Origins of New Mexico Families," vols. 1 and 9.
5. Ayer, Hodges, and Lummis, *Memorial*, 22–23; Hodge, Hammond, and Rey, *Revised Memorial*, 68.
6. Hackett, *Historical Documents*, 3:108.
7. Ibid., 119.
8. Ibid., 69.
9. Esquibel, personal communication.
10. Hackett, *Historical Documents*, 3:108; Barrett, *Conquest*, 78.
11. Esquibel, "Palace Echoes," 5–6. The nine widows and their deceased husbands were: Ana Robledo (Francisco Gómez), Elena Gómez (Hernán López Sambrano), Gregoria de Archuleta (Diego de Santa Cruz), Antonia González (Estevan López), Francisca Martín (Domingo González), María Ortiz de Vera (Diego de Montoya), Juana Moedana, Catalina Bernal (Juan Durán), and Isabel de Pedraza (Matías Romero) (Esquibel, "Founders," pt. 2:n.p.).
12. Hackett, *Historical Documents*, 3:119; Scholes, *Troublous Times*, 6.
13. Hackett, *Historical Documents*, 299.
14. Ibid., 287–89, 317–22, 323–24.
15. Kessell, Hendricks, and Dodge, *To the Royal Crown*, 509.
16. Scholes, *Troublous Times*, 6.
17. Hackett and Shelby, *Revolt*, 1:136–53, 157–59.
18. Ibid., 90.
19. Ibid., 159–317; Lycette, "Archaeological Implications," 528.
20. Hackett and Shelby, *Revolt*, 1:178. Scholes holds that the total nonaboriginal population in New Mexico never exceeded twenty-five hundred, including servants ("Civil Government," 96, 96n44). According to Hackett, New Mexico had a population of between twenty-five hundred and three thousand in 1680, including servants but excluding indigenous tribes (*Historical Documents*, 3:19, 327–28n133). Hackett and Shelby state that there were approximately twenty-eight hundred Spanish inhabitants in New Mexico in 1680 (*Revolt*, 1:xx).
21. Hackett and Shelby, *Revolt*, 1:153, 161.
22. Ibid., 136–59.
23. Ibid., 130–32.
24. Governor Otermín reported that on the muster there were 155 men capable of bearing arms, but this figure includes 14 who were specifically designated Mexican, Mexican Indian, mestizo, or mulatto (Hackett and Shelby, *Revolt*, 1:157–59, 161). There were twenty-three family members declared by convict Francisco de la Muerte, but he was probably mistaken, and so they are not included in this count (Hackett and Shelby, *Revolt*, 149).
25. Scholes, "Civil Government," 96n44.
26. A party of thirty Spaniards led by Pedro de Leyva was in El Paso to meet the supply train from Mexico City when the revolt broke out, but they joined

Governor Otermín south of Las Nutrias and their names appear on the 1680 muster (Hackett and Shelby, *Revolt*, 1:lxxiv, 78, 104).
27. Figures are adjusted here to exclude populations at Zuni and Hopi (Moqui) Pueblos (Barrett, *Conquest*, 65, table 13).
28. Hackett and Shelby, *Revolt*, li, lix, lxix.
29. The cabildo reported that among those killed in the revolt were seventy-three Spanish men of military age, but this number might have included many very young teen-aged males (Hackett and Shelby, *Revolt*, 1:178).
30. Hackett, *Historical Documents*, 3:299.
31. The great majority have been identified by Chávez in *Origins*. Others have been tracked down by Esquibel, who has continued the work of identifying New Mexico's earliest settlers. Other names have been gleaned from Hackett, *Historical Documents*, vol. 3, and Hackett and Shelby, *Revolt*.
32. Scholes, "Civil Government," 97; Hackett and Shelby, *Revolt*, 2:94–134.

CHAPTER NINE

1. Ellis, "Long Lost 'City,'" 11, 15; ARMS site files for San Juan (Ohkay Owingeh [LA 874]) and Yunque Yunque (Yunque Owingeh [LA 59]).
2. Ellis, "Long Lost 'City,'" 14, 16; Ortiz, "San Juan Pueblo," 280–81.
3. Hammond and Rey, *Don Juan*, 1:320–23, 1:322–23.
4. Ibid., 1:318; Ellis, "Long Lost 'City,'" 17, 18.
5. Hammond and Rey, *Don Juan*, 1:323.
6. Ayer, Hodge, and Lummis, *Memorial*, 234n30, citing Fray Agustín de Vetancurt, *Teatro mexicano*, 318.
7. Ellis, "Long Lost 'City,'" 10.
8. Ibid., 21–22; Ellis, *San Gabriel*, 653.
9. Hammond and Rey, *Don Juan*, 1:397.
10. Ibid., 1:17, 2:609n3; Simmons, *Last Conquistador*, 148; Simmons, "Spaniards of San Gabriel," 39; Schroeder and Matson, *Colony*, 129.
11. Ellis, "Long Lost 'City,'" 17, 18; Ellis, *San Gabriel*, 11.
12. Ortiz, "San Juan Pueblo," 280; Ortiz, *Tewa World*, 61.
13. Villagrá, *History*, 147. Florence Ellis is mistaken in stating that Oñate used the term "San Juan de los Caballeros" ("Long Lost 'City,'" 18). Hammond and Rey only mention it in their introduction and in a footnote (*Don Juan*, 17, 609n3). For alternate interpretations of the name, see Hammond, *Don Juan*, 100n383; and Simmons, *Last Conquistador*, 117.
14. Hammond and Rey, *Don Juan*, 1:398, 404; see also Hammond and Rey, *Don Juan*, 1:350, 416, 427, for other instances in which San Juan or San Juan Bautista was used in early 1599.
15. Sánchez, *Rio Abajo*, 46.
16. Hammond and Rey, *Don Juan*, 2:837.

17. An exception is found in the 1602 testimony of Juan de León; he stated that San Juan was the first town established (Hammond and Rey, *Don Juan*, 2:851).
18. Ibid., 609; Jenkins, "Oñate's Administration," 63.
19. Hammond and Rey, *Don Juan*, 2:639.
20. Ibid., 643–44.
21. Ellis, "Long Lost 'City,'" 22–35; Ellis, *San Gabriel*, 47–64.
22. Hammond and Rey, *Don Juan*, 2:652, 666.
23. Ellis, *San Gabriel*, 26–27; Ellis and Dodge, "Window," 177, 180.
24. Ellis, "Long Lost 'City,'" 19; Hammond and Rey, *Don Juan*, 2:610, 656.
25. Ellis, "Long Lost 'City,'" 20, 21; Ellis, *San Gabriel*, 26.
26. Hammond and Rey, *Don Juan*, 2:629, 639.
27. Ellis, "Long Lost 'City,'" 17, 33–34; Ellis and Dodge, "Window," 182.
28. Hammond and Rey, *Don Juan*, 2:629, 652, 666.
29. Ibid., 2:652, 666.
30. Ibid., 1:481.
31. Ibid., 2:609–10, 675.
32. Ibid., 2:674, 675, 679–80, 684, 686, 687, 688, 692–93, 696.
33. Ibid., 2:619, 628–29, 638–39, 707–8, 710, 714–15, 718–19, 722, 726.
34. Ibid., 2:628–29, 638–39, 651–52, 654, 665–66.
35. Ibid., 1:584, 2:619, 654.
36. Ibid., 2:654, 661.
37. Ibid., 2:1096.
38. *Recopilación*, libro 6, título 3, leyes 21–22.
39. Rey, "Cristóbal de Oñate," 198; Scholes, "Juan Martínez," 340.
40. Simmons, "Spaniards of San Gabriel," 44.
41. Hammond and Rey, *Don Juan*, 2:1076–77.
42. Hackett, *Historical Documents*, 3:254.
43. Hammond and Rey, *Don Juan*, 2:599.
44. Ibid., 2:1096.
45. Ibid., 2:1140.

CHAPTER TEN

1. For ordinance 110 of the royal ordinances relating to the founding of new towns promulgated by Phillip II on July 13, 1573, and part of the Laws of the Indies, see Zelia Nuttall, "Royal Ordinances," 743–53, 749–50; Crouch, Garr, and Mundigo, *Spanish City Planning*, 13; Scholes, "Civil Government," 93; and Elliott, *Archeology*, 21.
2. Scheick, "Land and Water," 13.
3. Peckham, "Anasazi," 279; Elliott, *Archeology*, 21; Levine, "Down Under," 10–11; Scheick, "Land and Water," 16.
4. Kelley, *Contemporary Ecology*, 15–16; Moke, "Santa Fe," 21, 118–19.

5. Kelley, *Contemporary Ecology*, 24. Although the Santa Fe River is considered a perennial stream, there are stretches below the city where the flow is subsurface during dry years (Scurlock, *From the Rio*, 188–89; Moke, "Santa Fe," 23).
6. Kelley, *Contemporary Ecology*, 30, 33, 36, 39. Santa Fe rainfall and temperature data are for 1850–1970 and 1874–1960 respectively.
7. Rose, Dean, and Robinson, *Past Climate*, 105, fig. 34, pt. 2.
8. Kessell, Hendricks, and Dodge, *To the Royal Crown*, 509.
9. Adams, *Bishop Tamarón's Visitation*, 47.
10. Bloom, "When Was Santa Fe Founded?" 192–94; Ivey, "Uncertain Founding," 1–5.
11. Scholes, "Juan Martínez," 341; Bloom, "Ynstrucción," 178; Cháves, "Instructions," 179.
12. Bandelier, *Final Report*, 1:124n1 ("La villa de Santa-Fé . . . descubrióla el año de 1605 el Adelantado D. Juan de Oñate"); Ivey, "Viceroy's Order," 97, 97n2. Fray Alonso Posadas's complete statement was: "The villa of Santa Fe, center of New Mexico, is at 37 degrees in a straight line south, having the sea on the west, at a distance of 200 leagues. It was discovered in the year 1605 by the Adelantado Juan de Oñate" (Lansing Bloom, cited in Twitchell, "Notes, Reviews, Communications," 336). Governor Oñate led an expedition to the Gulf of California from October 27, 1604, to April 25, 1605, during which he discovered this "sea" (Zárate Salmerón, *Relaciones*, 64, 76; Hammond and Rey, *Don Juan*, 2:1013). For further discussion of the 1605 date, see Hammond, *Don Juan*, 180n693; Twitchell, *Leading Facts*, 333n336; and Ayer, Hodge, and Lummis, *Memorial*, 234.
13. Fray Alonso de Benavides claimed that Santa Fe was founded by Governor Oñate: "This city was founded by the *adelantado*, Don Juan de Oñate, when he entered with seven hundred married Spaniards, but the majority returned to Mexico" (Hodge, Hammond, and Rey, *Revised Memorial*, 68). This statement refers to the capital that Oñate founded when he arrived in New Mexico in 1598; Benavides glosses over the earlier capital, San Gabriel, from which the 1601 desertion took place, by calling it Santa Fe. His statement, therefore, does not indicate when Santa Fe itself was founded except that it was sometime before 1610, when Oñate left New Mexico.
14. Bloom, "Ynstrucción," 178–86; Cháves, "Instructions," 179–87; Hodge, Hammond, and Rey, *Revised Memorial*, 273–74n86.
15. Scholes, "Juan Martínez," 337n1, 338n2, 341; Ivey, "Uncertain Founding," 3–4.
16. Juan Martínez de Montoya Collection, AC, Box 1, f. 18ff., cited by Esquibel, "On the Founding," 6.
17. Ivey, "Viceroy's Order," 101; Scholes, "Juan Martínez," 339.
18. Inquisition, t. 586, f. 49, AGN, cited in Esquibel," On the Founding," 7; Chávez, *Origins*, 41.
19. Inquisition, t. 593, f. 288, AGN, cited in Esquibel "On the Founding," 7; Chávez, *Origins*, 72.
20. Esquibel, "On the Founding," 2–3, 8; Hammond and Rey, *Don Juan*, 2:1053.
21. Esquibel, "Founders," 13–14.

22. Ibid.
23. Peralta was appointed governor of New Mexico by the viceroy on March 5, 1609, and his instructions were issued March 30, 1609 (Hammond and Rey, *Don Juan*, 2:1082, 1087–91; Bloom, "Ynstrucción," 186; Cháves, "Instructions," 187).
24. Hammond and Rey, *Don Juan*, 2:1042–43, 1052–53, 1081.
25. Ivey, "Viceroy's Order," 102. Ivey suggests that Martínez de Montoya had been lobbying the viceroy to make Santa Fe the capital even before 1608.
26. Hackett, *Historical Documents*, 3:47.
27. It's possible landowners were able to escape the revolt with their land grant documents, but so far no documents have been recovered.
28. Wroth, "Barrio de Analco," 164, 170, 172.
29. Ivey, "Viceroy's Order," 105.
30. Bloom, "Ynstrucción," 180; Cháves, "Instructions," 181; Carrera Stampa, "Evolution," 19–20; Snow, "Review," 90–92.
31. Map 4 is the earliest extant map of Santa Fe. It is the work of Joseph de Urrutia, a draftsman attached to the Marqués de Rubí expedition that was charged with inspecting the presidios of the Provincias Internas of New Spain from 1766 to 1768 (Moorhead, *The Presidio*, 56–57n25, 148–49).
32. Adams, *Bishop Tamerón's Visitation*, 47; Domínguez, *Missions*, 10, 39–40.
33. Ivey, "Viceroy's Order," 103.
34. Ordinance 128 (Nuttall, "Royal Ordinances," 752; Crouch, Garr, and Mundigo, *Spanish City Planning*, 16).
35. Snow, "Brief History," 4.
36. Hordes, "History," 5–6.
37. Bloom, "Glimpse," 66–68; Scholes, "Civil Government," 81; Lycett, "Archaeological Implications," 537.
38. Levine, "Down Under," 12–13, 17, 23; Peckham and Snow, "Clues," 40; Scheick, "Land and Water," 13; Ellis, "La Garita," 12, 14, 18; Pratt and Snow, *North Central*, 166–67; Lentz, *Excavations*, 8.
39. Cross-Cultural Research Systems, *Santa Fe Historic Plaza Study II*, 15; Snow, "Hypothetical Configurations," 56–57.
40. Plewa, "Trickle," 264–66.
41. Tigges, "Soil Tests," 75–76, 84; Cross-Cultural Research Systems, *Santa Fe Historic Plaza Study II*, 87–88; Ellis, "La Garita," 6, 21n1; Twitchell, *Old Santa Fe*, 52.
42. Plewa, "Trickle," 276; Ellis, "Santa Fe's Seventeenth-Century Plaza," 186–88; Snow, *Santa Fe Acequia*, 10–11. The map is based on Tigges, "Soil Tests," 84; and Viklund, "Roads Old and New," 69–70—the 1846-47 Gilmer map.
43. Cross-Cultural Research Systems, *Santa Fe Historic Plaza Study II*, 14, 18.
44. Hackett and Shelby, *Historical Documents*, 1:101; Kessell and Hendricks, *By Force of Arms*, 393.
45. Snow, *Santa Fe Acequia*, 21n2; Snow, "Review," 28; Tigges, "Soil Tests," 84.
46. Lentz, *Excavations*, 26, 67, 69, 70.

47. Bloom, "Ynstrucción," 180; Cháves, "Instructions," 181. For ordinance 112, see Nuttall, "Royal Ordinances," 750; and Crouch, Garr, and Mundigo, *Spanish City Planning*, 13.
48. Snow, "Brief History," 15; Levine, "Down Under," 22; Cross-Cultural Research Systems, *Santa Fe Historic Plaza Study II*, 22; Post, "Archaeology, History, and Cartography," 174; Wiseman, "Early Spanish Colonial Occupations," 214.
49. Twitchell, *Old Santa Fe*, 56–57; Ellis, "Santa Fe's Seventeenth-Century Plaza," 185–86, 190–91; Hordes, "The History of the Santa Fe Plaza," 6–7; Snow, "Plazas," 40; Snow, "Hypothetical Configurations," 61–62; Levine, "Down Under," 22; Pratt and Snow, *North Central*, 161–62; Pratt, "Santa Fe Plaza," 37–40.
50. Nuttall, "Royal Ordinances," 750; Crouch, Garr, and Mundigo, *Spanish City Planning*, 13; Ellis, "Santa Fe's Seventeenth-Century Plaza," 186; Pratt and Snow, *North Central*, 161-2.
51. Snow, "Hypothetical Configurations," 61–62; Snow, "Review," 102; Cross-Cultural Research Systems, *Santa Fe Historic Plaza Study II*, 18–19, 24.
52. Snow, "Hypothetical Configurations," 63.
53. Hordes, "History," 6–7.
54. Hackett, *Historical Documents*, 3:47; Nuttall, "Royal Ordinances," 751; Crouch, Garr, and Mundigo, *Spanish City Planning*, 15.
55. Two mid-seventeenth-century foundations resting on earlier seventeenth-century debris were found in room 7, and two adobe brick floors with the lower floor laid in diagonal pattern were found in room 5 (Snow, "Brief History," 15, 19; Snow, "Living Artifact," 17; Seifert, *Archaeological Excavations*, 6–11; Post, "Archaeology, History, and Cartography," 173–74).
56. Post, "Archaeology, History, and Cartography," 174–75; Post, "Archaeology Behind the Palace of the Governors," 7–8.
57. Twitchell, *Old Santa Fe*, 55, 136; Arnold, "Palace," 131.
58. Schaafsma, "Window," 32; Snow, "Plazas," 44–45; Post, personal communication; Lentz, personal communication.
59. Tigges, "Soil Tests," 75–76, 84.
60. Snow, "Plazas," 40.
61. Cháves, "Instructions," 181; Bloom, "Ynstrucción," 180; Nuttall, "Royal Ordinances," 751; Crouch, Garr, and Mundigo, *Spanish City Planning*, 15.
62. Cordelia Snow, personal communication.
63. Hammond and Rey, *Don Juan*, 2:1046, 1059; Esquibel, "Founding," 4–6; Torrez, "The Presidio," 52.
64. Hackett, *Historical Documents*, 3:69.
65. Rey, "Cristóbal de Oñate," 198; Scholes, "Juan Martínez," 340.
66. Wroth, "Barrio de Analco," 171.
67. Ordinance 133 (Nuttall, "Royal Ordinances," 752; Crouch, Garr, and Mundigo, *Spanish City Planning*, 17).

68. Ordinance 128 (Nuttall, "Royal Ordinances," 752; Crouch, Garr, and Mundigo, *Spanish City Planning*, 16).
69. Moorhead, "Rebuilding," 123, 124, following Twitchell, *Old Santa Fe*, 55. Twitchell places *cuarteles* north and west of the palace. Moorhead states that a presidio of sorts, namely, a military quadrangle, was in existence from the founding of the city in about 1610 until the Pueblo Revolt of 1680 and that it was part of the compound that included the Palace of the Governors. Neither Moorhead nor Twitchell cite documentary or archeological evidence.
70. Ordinance 124 (Nuttall, "Royal Ordinances," 751; Crouch, Garr, and Mundigo, *Spanish City Planning*, 15).
71. Hackett and Shelby, *Revolt*, 1:100.
72. Chávez, "Santa Fe Church," 86; Snow, "Plazas," 41.
73. Scholes, "Church and State," pt. 1, 38, 40; Snow, "Window," 148; Sánchez, "Peralta-Ordóñez Affair," 30. *Analco* means "on the other side" in Nahuatl, referring to the location of this satellite settlement on the south side of the Santa Fe River; the villa, by contrast, was located on the north side.
74. Snow, "Window," 148; Sánchez, "Peralta-Ordóñez Affair," 31.
75. Bloom, "Glimpse," 370.
76. Snow, "Plazuela," 81, 88.
77. Bloom, "Glimpse," 369–70.
78. Bloom, "Glimpse," 369–70.
79. Kessell, Hendricks, and Dodge, *To the Royal Crown*, 110–11.
80. Hammond and Rey, *Don Juan*, 2:1140; Hackett, *Historical Documents*, 3:47.
81. Ayer, Hodge, and Lummis, *Memorial*, 22–23; Hodge, Hammond, and Rey, *Revised Memorial*, 68.
82. Snow, "Plazuela," 88; Kessell, *Kiva*, 123, 123n34, citing Civil, leg. 77, exp. 14, AGN; Kubler, *Religious Architecture*, 100.
83. Hodge, Hammond, and Rey, *Revised Memorial*, 2–3.
84. Hodge, Hammond, and Rey, *Revised Memorial*, 129.
85. Snow, "Window," 150.
86. Ayer, Hodge, and Lummis, *Memorial*, 23; Hodge, Hammond, and Rey, *Revised Memorial*, 68.
87. Scholes, "Church and State," pt. 4, 333n56.
88. Ayer, Hodge, and Lummis, *Memorial*, 23; Hodge, Hammond, and Rey, *Revised Memorial*, 68.
89. Hodge, Hammond, and Rey, *Revised Memorial*, 109–24; Ivey, "Viceroy's Order," 21.
90. Hodge, Hammond, and Rey, *Revised Memorial*, 68.
91. Chávez, "Santa Fe Church," 89–90, 90n4, citing Inquisition, t. 372, ff. 3–14, AGN; Scholes, "Church and State," pt. 4, 333n56; Kubler, *Religious Architecture*, 100; Hackett, *Historical Documents*, 3:54.
92. Chávez, "How Old Is San Miguel?" 143, 145.
93. Kessell, Hendricks, and Dodge, *To the Royal Crown*, 477.

94. Archeological work at San Miguel yields evidence of a structure that was destroyed in 1640, rebuilt in 1650, and partly destroyed again when rebels burned it during the 1680 revolt, after which it was rebuilt again in 1710 (Stubbs and Ellis, *Archaeological Investigations*, 2–3; Ivey, "San Miguel Archaeology," n.p.; Hackett and Shelby, *Revolt*, 2:171).
95. Chávez, "Santa Fe Church," 86, 93; Hackett and Shelby, *Revolt*, 1:100, 101.
96. Ordinance 121 (Nuttall, "Royal Ordinances," 751; Crouch, Garr, and Mundigo, *Spanish City Planning*, 15).
97. Chávez, "How Old is San Miguel?" 145.
98. Kubler, *Religious Architecture*, 79n2, citing Patronato, t. 247, exp. 7, AGI. Fray Angélico holds that the chapel was closed but that the infirmary was torn down on the orders of Governor Rosas ("How Old is San Miguel?" 146), whereas Scholes claims that Governor Rosas, after closing the Hermita de San Miguel, had the bells and vigas removed before razing the remains ("Church and State," pt. 4, 319, 323, 333n56). Archeological work reported in 1955 indicates that the chapel was destroyed in 1640 and rebuilt in 1650 (Stubbs and Ellis, *Archaeological Investigations*, 3; see also Ivey, "San Miguel Archaeology," n.p.).
99. Ordinance 121 (Nuttall, "Royal Ordinances," 751; Crouch, Garr, and Mundigo, *Spanish City Planning*, 15; Scholes, "Civil Government," 101; Snow, "Hypothetical Configurations," 65, 68).
100. Cross-Cultural Research Systems, *Santa Fe Historic Plaza Study II*, 24, 106.
101. Real Audiencia, Concurso de Peñalosa, t. 1, leg. 1, n. 2, f. 4, AGN, cited in Esquibel, "Palace Echoes," 6; Real Audiencia, Concurso de Peñalosa, t. 1, leg. 1, no. 6, ff. 33–34v, AGN, cited in Esquibel, "Palace Echoes," 11.
102. Esquibel, "Palace Echoes," 11–24.
103. Esquibel, "Palace Echoes," 11–24. See Gavin, "La Sala de Estrada," 51, for a plan of the reconstructed palace. Recent excavation at the site of the current community stage on the plaza in front of the portal of the Palace of the Governors yielded evidence of seventeenth-century use and a radiocarbon date of 1660 plus or minus sixty years (Lentz, *Excavations*, 33).
104. Substantial seventeenth-century cobble foundations embedded in adobe mortar discovered during excavation indicate walls strong enough to support a second story (Post, "Archaeology Behind the Palace," 8; Post, "Archaeology, History and Cartography," 174–75; Cordelia Snow, personal communication). A second floor was also noted in a 1716 report on the condition of the Palace of the Governors that stated that above there was one room and an apartment with a room that served as a chapel and that below the walls were collapsing ("Solamente Una sala alta Y un aposento Con un Salon q[u]e Sirve de Capilla ... y Vajos estan come ba d[ic]ho Cayendose " [Ivey, "Reconnaissance," n.p.]). However, it should be noted that the palace was subject to considerable modification during its twelve-year occupation by Puebloans, and further changes were made after the reconquest (Kessell et al., *A Settling of Accounts*, 209).

105. Gavin, "La Sala de Estrada," 48–55.
106. The description of the palace at the time of Governor López de Mendizábal is based on Esquibel, "Palace Echoes," 11–24.
107. Post, personal communication.
108. Bloom, "Glimpse," 369.
109. Hackett and Shelby, *Revolt*, 1:74.
110. Scholes, "First Decade," 204n15.
111. Scholes, "First Decade," 204–5n15; Snow, "La Plazuela," 89. Another gunpowder tower that seems to have been on the west side of the palace at the northwest corner of the plaza was mentioned in the 1715 survey of Santa Fe ("Writ," 240; Snow, "Presentation," 11).
112. Hackett and Shelby, *Revolt*, 1:101; Snow, "Plazas," 45–46; Lentz, *Excavations*, 69.
113. Hackett and Shelby, *Revolt of the Pueblo*, 1:207–8.
114. Ibid., 101.
115. Kessell and Hendricks, *By Force of Arms*, 388–94; Kessell, Hendricks, and Dodge, *To the Royal Crown*, 469, 471, 495, 525, 528, 530–33; Kessell et al., *A Settling of Accounts*, 209.
116. Hackett and Shelby, *Revolt*, 1:101; Kessell and Hendricks, *By Force of Arms*, 393.
117. Nuttall, "Royal Ordinances," 750; Crouch, Garr, and Mundigo, *Spanish City Planning*, 14.
118. Snow, "Hypothetical Configurations," 64–66; Snow, "Presentation," 13–15; "Writ," 236. Members of the survey group were Lorenzo Madrid, Roque Madrid, and Miguel Morán, assisted by master of carpentry Diego de Velasco and master of masonry Juan Lorenzo de Medina.
119. Snow, "Hypothetical Configurations," 65.
120. Ibid., 66.
121. Snow, "Presentation," 11, 15; "Writ," 240, 247.
122. Ellis, "Santa Fe's Seventeenth-Century Plaza," 189–90.
123. Snow, "Hypothetical Configurations," 64.
124. Pratt, "Santa Fe Plaza," 50; Crouch, Garr, and Mundigo, *Spanish City Planning*, 2–3; Stanislawski, "Early Spanish Town Planning," 94.
125. Domínguez, *Missions*, 40.
126. Esquibel, personal communication, citing lands records of New Mexico, series 1, no. 422, SANM; Twitchell, *Spanish Archives*, 1:129–31; Twitchell, *Spanish Archives*, 2:85–88; ARMS files for LA 1051 and LA 4450 locality 33; David Snow, personal communication.
127. Snow, "Presentation," 11, 15; "Writ," 240, 247.
128. Cordelia Snow, personal communication.
129. Marshall, *Cultural Properties Assessment*, 30; ARMS file for LA 54785, Camino de los Carros.
130. Hordes, "History," 10; Ellis, "Santa Fe's Seventeenth-Century Plaza," 189.
131. Snow, "Plazas," 41, 46; Snow, "Hypothetical Configurations," 65.

132. Real Audiencia, Concurso de Peñalosa, t. 1, leg. 1, no. 6, f. 33–34v, AGN, cited in Esquibel, "Palace Echoes," 11.
133. Esquibel, personal communication, citing land records of New Mexico, series 1, no. 929, SANM. The father of Antonia was Juan González Bernal (Chávez, *Origins*, 189).
134. Esquibel, personal communication, citing Real Audiencia, Concurso de Peñalosa, t. 1, leg. 4, f. 33, AGN.
135. Esquibel, personal communication, citing land records of New Mexico, series 1, no. 929, SANM; Snow, "Hypothetical Configurations," 64.
136. Esquibel, personal communication, citing land records of New Mexico, series 1, nos. 294 and 929, SANM.
137. Esquibel, personal communication, citing land records of New Mexico, series 1, no. 929, SANM; Ellis, "La Garita," 6.
138. Esquibel, personal communication, citing land records of New Mexico, series 1, no. 491, SANM; Chávez, *Origins*, 92.
139. Esquibel, personal communication, citing land records of New Mexico, series 1, no. 491, SANM; Snow, "Hypothetical Configurations," 64.
140. Chávez, *Origins*, 27–28, 170.
141. Hackett and Shelby, *Revolt*, 1:100–101, 103.
142. Chávez, *Origins*, 113.
143. Esquibel, personal communication, citing land records of New Mexico, series 1, nos. 2 and 411, SANM.
144. Esquibel, personal communication, citing land records of New Mexico, series 1, no. 411, SANM; Chávez, *Origins*, 9–10.
145. Hordes, "History," 6, 12.
146. Chávez, *Origins*, 2, 10.
147. Ibid., 65–66, 216; Kessell and Hendricks, *By Force of Arms*, 319n5. Lorenzo was not the son of Francisco II but rather his younger stepbrother and son of Francisco I (Esquibel, personal communication, citing Inquisition, t. 596, f. 156r–156v, testimony of doña Teresa de Aguilera y Roche, 1663, Mexico City, AGN).
148. Esquibel, personal communication, citing land records of New Mexico, series 1, no. 2, SANM.
149. Esquibel, personal communication, citing Tierras, t. 3268, f. 295, AGN.
150. Chávez, *Origins*, 6, 87, 102–3.
151. Ibid., 10, 87–88; Hordes "History," 6.
152. Chávez, *Origins*, 27–28.
153. Ibid., 25, 63–64, 212; Esquibel, personal communication, citing DM 1707, June 9, no. 3, Santa Fe, AASF.
154. Chávez, *Origins*, 27, 64, 212.
155. "Writ," 240, 247; Snow, "Presentation," 11, 15; Snow, "Hypothetical Configurations," 66.
156. Chávez, *Origins*, 62, 212.

157. ARMS files for LA 1051 and LA 4450 locality 33; David Snow, personal communication; Esquibel, personal communication, citing land records of New Mexico, series 1, no. 422, SANM; Twitchell, *Spanish Archives*, 2:86.
158. Esquibel, personal communication, citing Inquisition, t. 587, exp. 1, f. 312r, 1660, AGN.
159. Chávez, *Origins*, 38–39.
160. Kessell, Hendricks, and Dodge, *To the Royal Crown*, 509.
161. Chávez, *Origins*, 72.
162. Real Audiencia, Concurso de Peñalosa, t. 3, exp. 455, leg. 1, no. 1, f. 74, AGN, cited in Esquibel, "Vecinos," n.p.
163. Tierras, t. 3268, f. 247, AGN, cited in Esquibel, "Palace Echoes," 11; Chávez, *Origins*, 36.
164. Chávez, *Origins*, 87.
165. Ibid., 51; Real Audiencia, Concurso de Peñalosa, t. 1, leg. 1, no. 10, f. 51, 57v, AGN, cited in Esquibel, "Vecinos," n.p.
166. Inquisition, t. 587, exp. 1, ff. 154, 386–88, AGN, cited in Chávez, *Origins*, 79; Inquisition, t. 372, exp. 16, f. 9v, f. 15, AGN, cited in Esquibel, "Analysis," 11.
167. Tierras, t. 3268, f.42, AGN, cited in Esquibel, "Vecinos," n.p.
168. Chávez, *Origins*, 79–80; Hackett and Shelby, *Revolt*, 1:148.
169. Hackett, *Historical Documents*, 3:72; Snow, "Hypothetical Configurations," 66.
170. Tierras, t. 3268, ff. 208–208v, AGN, cited in Esquibel, "Palace Echoes," 16, 26–27.
171. Hackett and Shelby, *Revolt*, 1:157–59; Provincias Internas, t. 37, f. 112, AGN, cited in Esquibel, "Palace Echoes," 12.
172. Esquibel, personal communication, citing Inquisition, t. 356, exp. 133, f. 308r, testimony of Lucas de Figueroa, January 26, 1626, Villa de Santa Fe, AGN.
173. Inquisition, t. 372, exp. 16, f. 8, AGN, cited in Esquibel, "Founders," 17.
174. Barrett, *Conquest*, 116.
175. Kessell, Hendricks, and Dodge, *To the Royal Crown*, 509.</notetxt>

CHAPTER ELEVEN

1. Kessell, Hendricks, and Dodge, *To the Royal Crown*, 509.
2. Domínguez, *Missions*, 40–41; Adams, *Bishop Tamarón's Visitation*, 47.
3. Bandelier, *Final Report*, 2:88.
4. Esquibel, personal communication, citing land records of New Mexico, series 1, nos. 422 and 423, SANM; Twitchell, *Spanish Archives*, 1:129–131; Twitchell, *Spanish Archives*, 2:85–88.
5. Twitchell, *Spanish Archives*, 2:87; Kessell, Hendricks, and Dodge, *To the Royal Crown*, 495. "La Cuma" is located between Del Norte Lane, Rosario Blvd., and Rio Grande Avenue in Santa Fe (report by David Snow and Jerry Porter in ARMS file for LA 4450 locality 20).

6. Juan Lucero de Godoy stated that the road to Tesuque in use in 1693 ran closer to the villa de Santa Fe than the one that defined the eastern boundary of his property in 1680 (Twitchell, *Spanish Archives*, 2:88).
7. Chávez, *Origins*, 59–60.
8. Esquibel, personal communication, citing Real Audiencia, land records of New Mexico, series 1, no. 478, SANM; Chávez, *Origins*, 68.
9. Esquibel, personal communication, citing land records of New Mexico, series 1, no. 478, SANM, and Real Audiencia, Concurso de Peñalosa, t. 3, leg. 1, ff. 8 and 116v, AGN; Chávez, *Origins*, 79.
10. Real Audiencia, Concurso de Peñalosa, t. 3, leg. 1, no. 1, ff. 73, 73v, 79v, 80, 80v, AGN, and Inquisition, t. 586, exp. 1, f. 78v., AGN, cited in Esquibel, "Beyond Origins of New Mexico Families," vol. 10.
11. Esquibel, personal communication, citing Inquisition, t. 372, exp. 16, ff. 7v–8r, AGN; Chávez, *Origins*, 27.
12. Chávez, *Origins*, 27–28.
13. Twitchell, *Spanish Archives*, 1:488; Chávez, *Origins*, 48.
14. Hackett, *Historical Documents*, 3:182.
15. Chávez, *Origins*, 48; Scholes, *Troublous Times*, 40.
16. Chávez, *Origins*, 48–49.
17. Kessell and Hendricks, *By Force of Arms*, 387; Kessell, Hendricks, and Dodge, *To the Royal Crown*, 467–68.
18. ARMS file for LA 2, Schoolhouse/Agua Fria, 1275–1425; Payne, "Valley of Faith," 29, 31, 62; Cordelia Snow, personal communication.
19. Chávez, *Origins*, 65–66, 99; Esquibel, personal communication, citing land records of New Mexico, series 1, nos. 486, 487, 488. The only person with this surname known to have survived the revolt was Juan Ruiz de Cáceres, who lived in the Española basin where the family also had property and was a Tewa interpreter.
20. Chávez, *Origins*, 216.
21. Esquibel, personal communication, land records of New Mexico, series 1, nos. 486, 487, 488, SANM.
22. Chávez, *Origins*, 83–84.
23. Esquibel, personal communication, citing land records of New Mexico, series 1, no. 4, SANM.
24. Chávez, *Origins*, 80–81, 242; Kessell and Hendricks, *By Force of Arms*, 488n73.
25. Kessell and Hendricks, *By Force of Arms*, 444, 525; Chávez, *Origins*, 81.
26. Esquibel, personal communication, citing land records of New Mexico, series 1, no. 4, SANM.
27. Kessell and Hendricks, *By Force of Arms*, 140; Chávez, *Origins*, 106.
28. Chávez, *Origins*, 106.
29. Esquibel, personal communication, citing land records of New Mexico, series 1, no. 4, SANM; Chávez, *Origins*, 44.

30. Esquibel, personal communication, citing miscellaneous documents, series 2, 1704, roll 21, fols. 264–71 and 272–75, SANM; Chávez, *Origins*, 60.
31. Ibid.
32. Esquibel, personal communication, citing land records of New Mexico, series 1, no. 747, SANM.
33. Chávez, *Origins*, 44, 105.
34. Sankawi Black on Cream, Tewa Polychrome, and Tewa Polished Red (ARMS file for LA 69996).
35. G—p Kotyiti, Tewa Polychrome, Tewa Red, and Kapo Black, which might indicate a late seveneenth-century reoccupation (ARMS file for LA 146).
36. Boyd, Application for Registration, 16/6; (ARMS file for LA 16773); Payne, "Valley of Faith," 62.
37. Pratt and Snow, *North Central*, 176; Payne, "Valley of Faith," 62; Boyd, Application for Registration, 16/3; (ARMS file for LA 16768).
38. Boyd, Application for Registration, 16/2; (ARMS file for LA 16767); Payne, "Valley of Faith," 62; Pratt and Snow, *North Central*, 176.
39. ARMS file for LA 16; Mera, *Population Changes*, 29. Glaze F ceramics are usually dated between 1650 and 1700, but an earlier beginning date of 1575 has been proposed (Snow, "'Por alli no ay losa,'" 353).
40. ARMS file for LA 44; Mera, *Population Changes*, 29.
41. Cordelia Snow, personal communication.
42. Espinosa, *Pueblo Indian Revolt*, 261, 262.
43. Tewa Polychrome (including a soup plate rim), Tsia Polychrome, Polished Red, Polished Black, and European ware (ARMS file for LA 163).
44. Esquibel, personal communication, citing Inquisition, t. 361, f. 158r, AGN; Chávez, *Origins*, 87.
45. Chávez, *Origins*, 87; Esquibel, personal communication, citing Inquisition, t. 372, exp. 16, f. 6, AGN.
46. Chávez, *Origins*, 110; Inquisition, t. 304, exp. 27, f. 187, AGN, cited in Esquibel, "Vecino Estancias," 4.
47. Chávez, *Origins*, 110.
48. Ibid., 4. Gerónima used her mother's surname.
49. Ibid., 48–49.
50. Ibid., 54; Pratt and Snow, *North Central*, 167; Payne, "Valley of Faith," 72.
51. Chávez, *Origins*, 10, 54; Tierras, t. 3268, ff. 63v–64, AGN, cited in Esquibel, "Vecino Estancias," 3–4.
52. Chávez, *Origins*, 51.
53. Kessell, Hendricks, and Dodge, *To the Royal Crown*, 111, 465; Payne, "Valley of Faith," 44.
54. Chávez, *Origins*, 4, 48; Esquibel, personal communication, citing land records of New Mexico, series 1, no. 497, SANM.

55. Chávez, *Origins*, 3–4; ARMS file for LA 16 (see Boyd, Application for Registration).
56. Esquibel, personal communication, citing land records of New Mexico, series 1, no. 497, SANM; Tierras, t. 3268, f. 22v, October 29, 1661, AGN, cited in Esquibel, "Vecino Estancias," 4; Scholes, *Troublous Times*, 132.
57. Espinosa, *Pueblo Indian Revolt*, 113.
58. Chávez, *Origins*, 4–5.
59. Snow, "'Por alli no ay losa,'" 353.
60. Pratt and Snow, *North Central*, 176; Snow, "Review," 192; ARMS file for LA 20000.
61. David Snow, personal communication.
62. LA 164: G—p Kotyiti, Tewa Polychrome (and soup plate rim), Tewa Red (and soup plate rim), and Kapo Black, which indicates a possible late seventeenth-century reoccupation. LA 165: Rio Grande Polychrome, Tewa Polychrome, Tsia Polychrome, Polished Red, Polished Black, and European ware (ARMS files for LA 164 and LA 165).
63. Cordelia Snow, personal communication.
64. The name "La Cienega" also applies to the pueblo site LA 3 located on a mesa between the confluence of the Santa Fe River and Cienega Creek, but it was a prehistoric pueblo (ca. 1175–1300) (ARMS file for LA 3).
65. Hackett, *Historical Documents*, 3:249, 261; Esquibel, personal communication, citing land records of New Mexico, series 1, no. 497, SANM; Scholes, "Documents," 48, 53; Vetancurt, *Teatro mexicano*, 3:324.
66. Hackett and Shelby, *Revolt*, 1:3, 11, 13.

CHAPTER TWELVE

1. Hammond and Rey, *Don Juan*, 2:733–34.
2. Esquibel, "Analysis," 12.
3. Esquibel, "Analysis," 1–24; land records of New Mexico, series 1, roll 50, fols. 1143 ff., case no. 194, private land claims series, Santa Cruz de la Cañada land grant records, SANM, cited in Esquibel, "Analysis," 9–15; Kessell, Hendricks, and Dodge, *Blood*, 1:604–16, based on Historia 39, AGN; Kessell, Hendricks, and Dodge, *Blood*, 2:1074–75; Twitchell, *Spanish Archives*, 1:247–51, based on land records of New Mexico, series 1, no. 882, SANM.
4. Chávez, *Origins*, 41; Kessell, Hendricks, and Dodge, *Blood*, 1:613; Twitchell, *Spanish Archives*, 1:249–50.
5. Inquisition, leg. 1, no. 9, ff 33–334v, trial of López de Mendizábal, AGN, cited in Esquibel, "Vecino Estancias," 2.
6. Chávez, *Origins*, 35–36.
7. Land records of New Mexico, series 1, no. 829, SANM, cited in Esquibel, "Analysis," 8; Land records of New Mexico, series 1, no. 819, SANM, cited in Esquibel, "Analysis," 19.

8. Chávez, *Origins*, 71; Hackett, *Historical Documents*, 3:154; Kessell, Hendricks, and Dodge, *To the Royal Crown*, 62, 94n102.
9. Chávez, *Origins*, 71.
10. Land records of New Mexico, series 1, no. 823, SANM, cited in Esquibel, "Analysis," 15.
11. Chávez, *Origins*, 45–46; land records of New Mexico, series 1, no. 311, SANM, cited in Esquibel, "Analysis," 17.
12. Land records of New Mexico, series 1, no. 823, SANM, cited in Esquibel, "Analysis," 16.
13. Chávez, *Origins*, 100; Kessell, Hendricks, and Dodge, *To the Royal Crown*, 431.
14. Esquibel, "Parientes," 45; Chávez, *Origins*, 71–73.
15. Land records of New Mexico, series 1, no. 311, SANM, cited in Esquibel, "Analysis," 17.
16. Chávez, *Origins*, 6.
17. Ibid., 6–7.
18. Land records of New Mexico, series 1, no. 311, SANM, cited in Esquibel, "Analysis," 17.
19. Ibid., Chávez, *Origins*, 12.
20. Chávez, *Origins*, 41.
21. Land records of New Mexico, series 1, no. 311, SANM, cited in Esquibel, "Analysis," 17.
22. Land records of New Mexico, series 1, no. 293, SANM, cited in Esquibel, "Analysis," 18.
23. Chávez, *Origins*, 92.
24. Kessell, Hendricks, and Dodge, *Blood*, 1:613; Kessell, Hendricks, and Dodge, *To the Royal Crown*, 50, 86n58; land records of New Mexico, series 1, no. 400, SANM, cited in Esquibel, "Analysis," 13–14.
25. Land records of New Mexico, series 1, roll 50, fol. 950, case no. 194, private land claims series, Santa Cruz de la Cañada land grant records, SANM, and land records of New Mexico, series 1, no. 882, SANM, cited in Esquibel, "Analysis," 10–11; Kessell, Hendricks, and Dodge, *Blood*, 1:606, 616.
26. Inquisition, t. 372, exp. 16, f. 15, AGN, and Inquisition, t. 372, exp. 16, f. 9v, AGN, cited in Esquibel, "Analysis," 11; Chávez, *Origins*, 79.
27. Land records of New Mexico, series 1, no. 491, SANM, cited in Esquibel, "Analysis," 11.
28. Land records of New Mexico, series 1, no. 491, SANM, and land records of New Mexico, series 1, no. 818, SANM, cited in Esquibel, "Analysis," 10–11.
29. Land records of New Mexico, series 1, no. 882, SANM, cited in Esquibel, "Analysis," 11; Kessell, Hendricks, and Dodge, *Blood*, 2:1074; Chávez, *Origins*, 76; Hackett, *Historical Documents*, 3:273.
30. Chávez, *Origins*, 76.
31. Kessell, Hendricks, and Dodge, *Blood*, 1:606, 612–13; Esquibel, "Analysis," 11.

32. Hackett, *Historical Documents*, 3:185.
33. Tierras, t. 3268, ff. 143–44, AGN, cited in Esquibel, "Analysis," 6; Chávez, *Origins*, 72–73.
34. Chávez, *Origins*, 72–73; Kessell et al., *A Settling of Accounts*, 185–86.
35. Chávez, *Origins*, 72, 222.
36. Chávez, *Origins*, 72; Inquisition, t. 593, f. 288 and t. 304, f. 184, AGN, cited in Esquibel, "Beyond Origins of New Mexico Families," vol. 2.
37. Kessell, Hendricks, and Dodge, *Blood*, 1:606, 612–13; Esquibel, "Analysis," 9–10.
38. Esquibel, "Analysis," 10; Chávez, *Origins*, 62, 367.
39. Chávez, *Origins*, 63, 99.
40. Esquibel, "Beyond Origins of New Mexico Families," vol. 2.
41. Hackett and Shelby, *Revolt*, 1:140; Chávez, *Origins*, 62, 367.
42. Kessell, Hendricks, and Dodge, *Blood*, 1:606, 610, 614.
43. Chávez, *Origins*, 99.
44. Kessell, Hendricks, and Dodge, *Blood*, 1:613. According to the Granillo survey, it was the Rio del Norte (Rio Grande) that they crossed, but this is probably mistaken because the party had not gone far enough to reach that river (Esquibel, "Analysis," 4, 12).
45. Chávez, *Origins*, 63; Kessell et al., *A Settling of Accounts*, 186; Esquibel, "Analysis," 6.
46. Land records of New Mexico, series 1, roll 50, fol. 818 ff., case no. 194, private land claims series, Santa Cruz de la Cañada land grant records, SANM, cited in Esquibel, "Analysis," 12. Conflicting statements about whether or not San Cristóbal people occupied a pueblo called Tsawari (LA 36), located in the area in question, were reported by ethnolinguist John Harrington in 1916 (*Ethnography*, 254–55; ARMS site file for LA 36). The Tano people of San Lázaro also transferred their pueblo to the Santa Cruz River valley and located it on the north side of the river, where the villa of Santa Cruz was established in 1695 (Kessell, Hendricks, and Dodge, *Blood*, 1:621; Esquibel, "Analysis," 2).
47. Scholes, *Troublous Times*, 69; Hackett, *Historical Documents*, 3:265; Chávez, *Origins*, 63.
48. That Matías could have been the son of Juan Luis Luján is based on birth dates worked out by Esquibel, who states that the relationship is purely a matter of supposition (personal communication).
49. Chávez, *Origins*, 64, 213, 369; Kessell and Hendricks, *By Force of Arms*, 413, 487n57.
50. Kessell, Hendricks, and Dodge, *Blood*, 1:613.
51. Ibid., 614.
52. Chávez, *Origins*, 45–46.
53. Ibid., 46.
54. Land records of New Mexico, series 1, no. 882, SANM, cited in Esquibel, "Analysis," 13.

55. Kessell, Hendricks, and Dodge, *Blood*, 1:613; Chávez, *Origins*, 6.
56. Chávez, *Origins*, 6.
57. Kessell, Hendricks, and Dodge, *Blood*, 1:613.
58. Chávez, *Origins*, 41.
59. Inquisition, t. 304, exp. 27, f. 186, and t. 372, exp. 16, f. 18v, AGN, cited in Esquibel, "Vecino Estancias," 2; Esquibel, "People," 159; Chávez, *Origins*, 41.
60. Inquisition, trial of López de Mendizábal, leg. 1, no. 9, f. 21, AGN, cited in Esquibel, "Vecino Estancias," 2.
61. Inquisition, t. 304, exp. 27, f. 189, AGN, cited in Esquibel, "Analysis," 13.
62. Chávez, *Origins*, 42.
63. Kessell, Hendricks, and Dodge, *Blood*, 1:613.
64. Land records of New Mexico, series 1, no. 400, SANM, cited in Esquibel, "Analysis," 13–14.
65. Chávez, *Origins*, 39, 40.
66. Ibid., 39.
67. Kessell, Hendricks, and Dodge, *Blood*, 1:613; Twitchell, *Spanish Archives*, 1:250; Chávez, *Origins*, 92.
68. Kessell, Hendricks, and Dodge, *To the Royal Crown*, 50, 86n58; land records of New Mexico, series 1, no. 400, SANM, cited in Esquibel, "Analysis," 14.
69. Chávez, *Origins*, 92.
70. Ibid., 99.
71. Kessell, Hendricks, and Dodge, *Blood*, 1:613.
72. In 1697 Governor Rodríguez Cubero granted a tract of land to Pedro de Ávila located "in La Cañada called San Cristóbal which was where Indians settled—when the Kingdom was lost—and which formerly belonged to Francisco Xavier" (land records of New Mexico, series 1, roll 50, fol. 888, private land claims series, Santa Cruz de la Cañada land grant records, SANM, cited in Esquibel, "Analysis," 6, 14).
73. Chávez, *Origins*, 113.
74. Ibid., 41, 113; Esquibel, "Analysis," 14.
75. Chávez, *Origins*, 113.
76. Kessell, Hendricks, and Dodge, *Blood*, 1:613; Chávez, *Origins*, 23–24; Inquisition, t. 304, f. 186, AGN, cited in Esquibel, "Vecino Estancias," 2; Esquibel, "Analysis," 14.
77. Chávez, *Origins*, 24.
78. Land records of New Mexico, series 1, roll 50, fol. 888, 1143 ff., case no. 194, private land claims series, Santa Cruz de la Cañada land grant records, SANM, cited in Esquibel, "Vecino Estancias," 3; Kessell, Hendricks, and Dodge, *Blood*, 1:614; Twitchell, *Spanish Archives*, 1:250.
79. Esquibel, personal communication, citing Inquisition, t. 467, exp. 78, f. 352r, AGN.
80. Chávez, *Origins*, 77–78.
81. Kessell, Hendricks, and Dodge, *Blood*, 1:614.
82. Chávez, *Origins*, 58.

83. Kessell, Hendricks, and Dodge, *Blood*, 1:614.
84. Land records of New Mexico, series 1, roll 50, fol. 888, 1143 ff., case no. 194, private land claims series, Santa Cruz de la Cañada land grant records, SANM, cited in Esquibel, "Vecino Estancias," 3; Kessell, Hendricks, and Dodge, *Blood*, 1:614; Twitchell, *Spanish Archives*, 1:250–51.
85. Kessell, Hendricks, and Dodge, *Blood*, 1:614.
86. Inquisition, trial of López de Mendizábal, leg. 1, no. 9, f. 28, AGN, cited in Esquibel and Martínez, "Additional Vecinos," 23; Chavez, *Origins*, 100.
87. Kessell, Hendricks, and Dodge, *Blood*, 1:614.
88. Inquisition, t. 586, exp. 1, ff. 70v–72v, AGN, cited in Esquibel, "Romero Family," pt. 1, 10; Esquibel, "Analysis," 15; Chávez, *Origins*, 95, 97.
89. Chávez, *Origins*, 97–98; Inquisition, t. 586, exp. 1, ff. 70v–72v, AGN, cited in Esquibel, "Romero Family," pt. 1, 10.
90. Chávez, *Origins*, 95, 97.
91. Ibid., 97, 100.
92. Land records of New Mexico, series 1, no. 545, SANM, cited in Esquibel, "Analysis," 21–22.
93. Hackett, *Historical Documents*, 3:150; Chávez, *Origins*, 97–98.
94. Hackett and Shelby, *Revolt*, 1:10, 96; Chávez, *Origins*, 97, 100.
95. Hackett, *Historical Documents*, 3:329; Hackett and Shelby, *Revolt*, 1:10, 96; Chávez, *Origins*, 50.
96. Chávez, *Origins*, 50.
97. Ibid., 50.
98. Scholes, *Troublous Times*, 42–43; Chávez, *Origins*, 100.
99. Chávez, *Origins*, 100.
100. Ibid., 100–101; Hackett and Shelby, *Revolt*, 1:76–77.
101. DM, 1692, no. 6, Real de San Lorenzo, El Paso, AASF, cited in Esquibel, "Analysis," 21.
102. Chávez, *Origins*, 69–70.
103. Kessell, Hendricks, and Dodge, *Blood*, 1:393.
104. Chávez, *Origins*, 47; Hackett, *Historical Documents*, 3:205.
105. Chávez, *Origins*, 47.
106. Kessell, Hendricks, and Dodge, *Blood*, 1:610; Twitchell, *Spanish Archives*, 1:247.
107. Chávez, *Origins*, 35; Kessell, *Kiva*, 186; Hackett, *Historical Documents*, 3:223.
108. Chávez, *Origins*, 87–88; Esquibel, personal communication.
109. Chávez, *Origins*, 69, 88.
110. Ibid., 40, 189.
111. Ibid., 107.
112. Ibid., 107.
113. Ibid., 89; Hackett, *Historical Documents*, 3:330; Hackett and Shelby, *Revolt*, 1:8–9, 139.
114. Inquisition, t. 593, exp. 1, ff. 291–92, AGN, cited in Esquibel, "Analysis," 22.

115. Chávez, *Origins*, 57.
116. Ibid., 87; Scholes, "Royal Treasury Records," 143; Real Audiencia, Concurso de Peñalosa, t. 2, exp. 495, leg. 1, no. 7, 81 ff., AGN, cited in Esquibel, "Romero Family," pt. 1, 18–19.
117. Six Tewa Polychrome soup plates are listed in an August 17, 1981, report in the ARMS file for LA 37549.
118. National Register of Historic Places Nomination Forms in ARMS file for LA 37549; Chávez, *Origins*, 223.
119. Chávez, *Origins*, 71–72, 222.
120. ARMS site file for LA 4994.
121. Land records of New Mexico, series 1, roll 50, fol. 888, case no. 194, private land claims series, Santa Cruz de la Cañada land grant records, SANM, cited in Esquibel, "Analysis," 6, 14.

CHAPTER THIRTEEN

1. Hackett, *Historical Documents*, 3:265.
2. Chávez, *Origins*, 63; Scholes, *Troublous Times*, 69, 73.
3. Inquisition, trial of López de Mendizábal, leg. 1, no. 9, ff. 33–34v, AGN, cited in Esquibel, "Vecino Estancias," 2.
4. Hackett, *Historical Documents*, 3:221; Kessell, *Kiva*, 186; Chávez, *Origins*, 36.
5. Esquibel, personal communication.
6. Esquibel, personal communication, citing Tierras, t. 3268, leg. 1, no. 6, ff. 42r–42v, AGN.
7. Chávez, *Origins*, 59, 60.
8. Esquibel, personal communication, citing land records of New Mexico, series 1, no. 503, SANM.
9. Domínguez, *Missions*, 111; Scurlock, *From the Rio*, 225.
10. Chávez, *Origins*, 46.
11. Ibid., 46.
12. Ibid., 21–22.
13. Esquibel, personal communication, citing land records of New Mexico, series 1, nos. 750 and 830, SANM.
14. Esquibel, personal communication, citing land records of New Mexico, series 1, no. 545, SANM.
15. Ibid.
16. Esquibel, personal communication, citing Tierras, t. 3268, ff. 50–51, AGN; and Real Audiencia, Concurso de Peñalosa, t. 1, exp. 605, leg. 1, f. 164, AGN; Chávez, *Origins*, 95.
17. Chávez, *Origins*, 97.
18. Ibid., 74.

19. Ibid., 74; Kessell, Hendricks, and Dodge, *To the Royal Crown*, 194; Jenkins, "Oñate's Administration," 90.
20. Jeffrey Boyer, personal communication.
21. Snow, "Note," 355; Chávez, *Origins*, 105; Hodge, Hammond, and Rey, *Revised Memorial*, 110.
22. Chávez, *Origins*, 93. Pedro Robledo was a member of the Oñate expedition, who died in New Mexico while en route to the colonists' destination at Ohkay Owingeh (San Juan Pueblo) (Chávez, *Origins*, 93).
23. Chávez, *Origins*, 3–4; Hackett, *Historical Documents*, 3:247–48.
24. Chávez, *Origins*, 44. Hackett and Shelby, *Revolt*, 1:xxvn10, gives the name Marcos de Dehezas as alcalde mayor of Taos at the time of the revolt, but such a person is otherwise not mentioned, and it is possible this name is a misreading of the text (Esquibel, personal communication).

CHAPTER FOURTEEN

1. San Marcos Pueblo is also considered a Keres pueblo and most likely had a mixed population. Barrett, *Conquest*, 40.
2. Hackett, *Historical Documents*, 3:153.
3. Esquibel, personal communication, citing Inquisition, t. 586, exp. 1, f. 6r, AGN; Chávez, *Origins*, 69, 70; Espinosa, *Pueblo Indian Revolt*, 261.
4. Chávez, *Origins*, 69–70; Hackett and Shelby, *Revolt*, 1:lviii, xc, 11, 20, 22, 57, 71, 97.
5. Hackett, *Historical Documents*, 3:249, 254; Chávez, *Origins*, 15; Hendricks and Mandell, "Juan Manso," 343; Inquisition, t. 587, f. 296, AGN, cited in Esquibel, "Vecino Estancias," 4.
6. Chávez, *Origins*, 15, 69.
7. Ibid., 14–15.
8. Ibid., 15–16.
9. Ibid., 28.
10. Esquibel, personal communication, citing Inquisition, t. 587, exp. 1, f. 457, AGN.
11. Chávez, *Origins*, 28–29.
12. Hackett and Shelby, *Revolt*, 1:97.
13. Chávez, *Origins*, 32–33.
14. Provincias internas, t. 34:1, AGN, cited in Esquibel, "Beyond Origins of New Mexico Families," vol. 2.
15. Inquisition, t. 608, exp. 6, f. 427 and t. 356, f. 260, AGN, cited in Esquibel, "Beyond Origins of New Mexico Families," vol. 8.
16. Chávez, *Origins*, 33, 80.
17. Hackett and Shelby, *Revolt*, 2:163; Hackett, *Historical Documents*, 3:161; Chávez, *Origins*, 53.
18. Hackett and Shelby, *Revolt*, 1:xl–xli, 11, 25; Hackett and Shelby, *Revolt*, 2:163.
19. Hackett and Shelby, *Revolt*, 1:24, 25.

20. Chávez, *Origins*, 80; Kessell, *Kiva*, 233, 235, 236.
21. Hackett and Shelby, *Revolt*, 1:24, 25; Chávez, *Origins*, 80–81—two of Nieto's sons, Francisco and Cristóbal, were away and escaped the massacre.
22. Esquibel, personal communication, citing Tierras, t. 3268, ff. 54v–56r, AGN; Chávez, *Origins*, 2.
23. Scholes, "Church and State," pt. 2, 148, 149–50.
24. Esquibel, personal communication, citing Inquisition, t. 356, exp. 133, f. 300, AGN; Chávez, *Origins*, 65.
25. Esquibel, personal communication, citing Inquisition, t. 372, exp. 16, f. 14v, AGN; Chávez, *Origins*, 65.
26. Chávez, *Origins*, 65.
27. Hackett, *Historical Documents*, 3:138; Scholes, *Troublous Times*, 72, 74; Chávez, *Origins*, 40.
28. Hackett, *Historical Documents*, 3: 253; Chávez, *Origins*, 4.
29. Real Audiencia, Concurso de Peñalosa, t. 2, exp. 495, leg. 1, no. 7, 81 ff., AGN, cited in Esquibel, "Romero Family," pt. 1, 18.
30. Inquisition, t. 586, pt. 2, exp. 1, f. 100v, AGN, cited in Esquibel, "Romero Family," pt. 1, 10; Kessell, *Kiva*, 186.
31. Weber, *Taos Trappers*, 18.

CHAPTER FIFTEEN

1. Chávez, *Origins*, 63; Snow, "Evolution," 219.
2. Chávez, *Origins*, 30.
3. Snow, "Evolution," 219; Twitchell, *Spanish Archives*, 1:230, no. 822; Esquibel, personal communication, citing land records of New Mexico, series 1, no. 822, SANM.
4. Snow, "Evolution," 219; Chávez, *Origins*, 30, 110–11; Hackett, *Historical Documents*, 3:238, 261.
5. Pratt and Snow, *North Central*, 167; Snow, "Evolution," 219.
6. Snow, "Evolution," 218; ARMS site file for LA 34.
7. Snow, "Evolution," 218; ARMS site file for LA 591.
8. Esquibel, personal communication, citing land records of New Mexico, series 1, no. 319, SANM.
9. Snow, "Evolution," 218; Snow, "Review," 192.
10. Snow, "Evolution," 218; Snow, "Review," 192.
11. Pratt and Snow, *North Central*, 169; Snow, "Review," 192.
12. Snow, "Evolution," 219.
13. Ibid., 220.
14. ARMS file for Signal Site, LA 9142; Pratt and Snow, *North Central*, 176.
15. Michael P. Marshall, personal communication.
16. Chávez, *Origins*, 9, 19; Esquibel and Durán y Cháves, "Durán y Cháves," 184–85.
17. Chávez, *Origins*, 19.

18. Scholes, "Church and State," pt. 2, 149–50; Anderson, "Encomienda," 366, 375–76n46; Chávez, *Origins*, 20.
19. Chávez, *Origins*, 20–21.
20. Provincias internas, t. 34:1, AGN, cited in Esquibel, "Beyond Origins of New Mexico Families," vol. 2.
21. Scurlock, *From the Rio*, 225.
22. Twitchell, *The Spanish Archives*, 1:141–41, no. 462.
23. Hackett and Shelby, *Revolt*, 1:xlvi, 22.
24. Chávez, *Origins*, 24.
25. Ibid., 20.
26. Hackett and Shelby, *Revolt*, 1:143; Chávez, *Origins*, 24.
27. Esquibel, personal communication, citing Inquisition, t. 593, exp. 1, ff. 331r–335r, AGN; Chávez, *Origins*, 15, 25. Álvaro de Paredes was killed by lightning in 1662 at the age of twenty-two (Chávez, *Origins*, 85).
28. Chávez, *Origins*, 24, 26.
29. Hackett and Shelby, *Revolt*, 1:23; Chávez, *Origins*, 15, 25.
30. Esquibel, personal communication, citing Inquisition, t. 582, exp. 2, ff. 324r and 345r, AGN, and Real Audiencia, Concurso de Peñalosa, vol. 3, exp. 455, leg. 1, no. 22, 44 folios, embargo of property of Captain Cristóbal de Anaya Almazán, May 25, 1662, Estancia de San Antonio, AGN. Use of the outbuilding was mentioned by Fray José de Paredes, brother of Álvaro de Paredes, who was son-in-law of landowner Tomé Domínguez (Esquibel, personal communication, citing Inquisition, t. 582, exp. 2, f. 42, April 23, 1662, Pueblo del Socorro, AGN).
31. Esquibel, personal communication, citing Real Audiencia, Concurso de Peñalosa, t. 3, exp. 455, leg. 1, no. 22, 44 ff., AGN; Chávez, *Origins*, 24.
32. Esquibel, personal communication, citing Inquisition, t. 666, exp. 10, f. 532, AGN.
33. Hackett and Shelby, *Revolt*, 1:23; Chávez, *Origins*, 4.
34. Inquisition, trial of López de Mendizábal, roll 1, leg. 1, no. 9, f. 28, AGN, cited in Esquibel and Martínez, "Additional Vecinos," 23; Chávez, *Origins*, 3, 94, 100.
35. Kessell, Hendricks, and Dodge, *To the Royal Crown*, 431, 449, 461.
36. Chávez, *Origins*, 49; AGN, Tierras, t. 3268, f. 60v ff., cited in Esquibel, "Beyond Origins of New Mexico Families," vols. 1 and 9.
37. Chávez, *Origins*, 49.
38. Ibid., 49–50.
39. Scurlock, *From the Rio*, 191–92, 223.
40. Bayer, *Santa Ana*, 76–77.
41. Kessell, Hendricks, and Dodge, *To the Royal Crown*, 113.
42. Scurlock, *From the Rio*, 192.
43. Chávez, *Origins*, 107–8; Inquisition, t. 304, exp. 27, ff. 181–82, AGN; and Inquisition, t. 593, exp. 1, f. 159, AGN, cited in Esquibel, "Vecinos Estancias," 5–6.
44. Chavez, *Origins*, 108.

45. National Register of Historic Places, Nomination Form, June 1982, LA 25674, item 7, page 1. Ceramic types: Tewa Polychrome, Ogapoge Polychrome, Kapo Black, Glazes D–F, and Majolica ware (Schaafsma, "Archaeological Reconnaissance").
46. Chávez, *Origins*, 107–8; Esquibel, personal communication, citing Tierras, t. 3268, f. 94r, 185r, AGN, and Real Audiencia, Concurso de Peñalosa, t. 1, f. 235/382, AGN.
47. Chávez, *Origins*, 80.
48. Ibid., 80; Hackett and Shelby, *Revolt*, 2:266.
49. Hackett and Shelby, *Revolt*, 2:250.
50. National Register of Historic Places Inventory Nomination Form, June 1982, LA 25674, item 7, pages 50 and 52. Postrevolt documentation supplied by historian Stanley M. Hordes that refers to the prerevolt period indicates that "Naranjo owned the 'Rancho de las Guertas'" and that a reference to "a watering hole known as that of Naranjo" could have meant the spring at the LA 50329 site (Marshall, "Rio Medio Report No. 166 in ARMS file for LA 25674").
51. Marshall, "Rio Medio Report in ARMS file for LA 44534." Ceramics found at the site were mainly late Glaze F plus minor amounts of Kapo Gray, Tewa Polychrome, and Puname.
52. Ibid.
53. Hackett, *Historical Documents*, 3:238; Chávez, *Origins*, 106.
54. Chávez, *Origins*, 87; Scholes, "Royal Treasury Records," 143.
55. Chávez, *Origins*, 106; Inquisition, t. 608, exp. 6, f. 425v, AGN, cited in Esquibel, "Vecinos Estancias," 9.
56. Chávez, *Origins*, 110–11.
57. Hackett, *Historical Documents*, 3:182, 243–44; Scholes, *Troublous Times*, 218; Chávez, *Origins*, 98.
58. Hackett, *Historical Documents*, 3:330; Chávez, *Origins*, 86.</notetxt>

CHAPTER SIXTEEN

1. Esquibel, personal communication, citing Real Audiencia, Concurso de Peñalosa, t. 2, exp. 495, leg. 1, no. 2, f. 192r, AGN.
2. Snow, "Santiago to Guache," 172; Hackett and Shelby, *Revolt*, 1:30, 39; Esquibel, "People," 159.
3. Snow, "Santiago to Guache," 172–75, 177; Scurlock, *From the Rio*, 186. As the channel of the Rio Grande shifted its course westward after about 1710, settlers in the area of Angostura and upper Bernalillo were forced to move to higher ground east of the river (Snow, "Santiago to Guache," 175).
4. Snow, "Santiago to Guache," 168.
5. Chávez, *Origins*, 9–10.
6. Bandelier, *Final Report*, 2:221n2; Pratt and Snow, *North Central*, 38; Snow, "Santiago to Guache," 167.
7. Bandelier, *Final Report*, 2:221n2; Chávez, *Origins*, 90.

8. Bandelier, *Final Report*, 2:221n2.
9. Snow, "Santiago to Guache," 164, 173; Chávez, *Origins*, 78; Bandelier, *Final Report*, 2:221n2.
10. Chávez, *Origins*, 77–78.
11. Snow, "Santiago to Guache," 163, 178; Pratt and Snow, *North Central*, 169; ARMS files for LA 50230, LA 187, and LA 4955.
12. Marshall, "Rio Medio Report for LA 50247"; see ARMS file for LA 50247.
13. Inquisition, t. 582, exp. 1, ff. 42, 323, AGN, cited in Esquibel, "Vecino Estancias," 5; Chávez, *Origins*, 24–25.
14. Esquibel, "The People of the Camino Real," 159; Chávez, *Origins*, 41.
15. Chávez, *Origins*, 41; Inquisition, t. 304, exp. 27, f. 186, AGN, cited in Esquibel, "Vecino Estancias," 2; Inquisition, t. 586, exp. 1, f. 49, AGN; and Inquisition, t. 583, exp. 3, f. 297, AGN, cited in Esquibel, "Founders," 13.
16. Chávez, *Origins*, 41.
17. Ibid., 12.
18. Twitchell, *Spanish Archives*, 1:101, no. 316; Chávez, *Origins*, 189.
19. Chávez, *Origins*, 40.
20. Ibid., 40, 189; Gerald González, personal communication.
21. Barrett, *Conquest*, 56.
22. Hackett, *Historical Documents*, 3:229, 232; Snow, "Santiago to Guache," 164, 167; Inquisition, t. 593, ff. 313–320 and t. 582, exp. 2, f. 38, AGN, cited in Esquibel, "Vecino Estancias," 4. Esquibel's source (t. 593) gives the distance from Santa Fe, and Hackett (*Historical Documents*, 3:229) gives the distance from Santo Domingo. Neither distance would put it at the site of LA 326.
23. Barrett, *Conquest*, 125n59; Kelley, *Albuquerque*, 15. The Valley of Atrisco was named for the Valley of Atlixco in Mexico, Atlixco being derived from the Nahuatl word meaning "on the water," an appropriate name given the large area of marshland along the river (Domínguez, *Missions*, 154n12; Hackett, "Location," 384).
24. Hackett and Shelby, *Revolt*, 2:227–28, 258, 380.
25. Bandelier, *Final Report*, 2:221n1.
26. Barrett, *Conquest*, 56, 78; Pratt and Snow, *North Central*, 62.
27. Esquibel, personal communication, citing Tierras, t. 3268, ff. 54v–56r, AGN. Albizu also held the pueblos of San Cristóbal, Ácoma, and Picurís (part).
28. Chávez, *Origins*, 2–3.
29. Hackett and Shelby, *Revolt*, 1:27, 64; Scholes, *Troublous Times*, 7; Hackett, *Historical Documents*, 3:231, 277; Chávez, *Origins*, 33–34.
30. Real Audiencia, Concurso de Peñalosa, t. 3, leg. 1, no. 1, f. 26v or 29v, AGN, cited in Esquibel, "Vecino Estancias," 6.
31. Hackett, *Historical Documents*, 3:271, 276; Chávez, *Origins*, 82; Hackett and Shelby, *Revolt*, 2:341; Tierras, t. 3268, pt.1, leg. 2, no. 32, f. 204, AGN, cited in Esquibel, "Vecino Estancias," 6.
32. Chávez, *Origins*, 82–83.

33. Ibid., 51.
34. Ibid., 41–42.
35. Hackett and Shelby, *Revolt*, 1:26–27; Kessell and Hendricks, *By Force of Arms*, 481n32; Chávez, *Origins*, 77, 108.
36. Hackett and Shelby, *Revolt*, 1:26; Marshall, *Cultural Properties Assessment*, 28.
37. Chávez, *Origins*, 108–9.
38. Espinosa, *First Expedition*, 182, 186; Kessell and Hendricks, *By Force of Arms*, 377, 481n31, 523–24, 531–32.
39. Hammond and Rey, *Don Juan*, 1:536, 552.
40. Espinosa, *First Expedition*, 68; Kessell and Hendricks, *By Force of Arms*, 377.
41. Hackett and Shelby, *Revolt*, 1:26–27; Domínguez, *Missions*, 145n1; Kessell and Hendricks, *By Force of Arms*, 481n32; Bandelier, *Final Report*, 2:221n1; Simmons, *Albuquerque*, 10, 40, 112; Scurlock, *From the Rio*, 185.
42. Chávez, *Origins*, 15.
43. Hackett and Shelby, *Revolt*, 1:clxxx–clxxxi; Hackett and Shelby, *Revolt*, 2:285.
44. Esquibel, personal communication, citing Inquisition., t. 593, exp. 1, f. 324–25, AGN, and land records of New Mexico, series 1, no. 1136, SANM.
45. Chávez, *Origins*, 16.
46. Twitchell, *Spanish Archives*, 1:333, no. 1136.
47. Chávez, *Origins*, 55.
48. Scurlock, *From the Rio*, 226
49. Chávez, *Origins*, 110.
50. Hackett, *Historical Documents*, 3:265.
51. Chávez, *Origins*, 111.
52. Ibid., 111.
53. Hackett, *Historical Documents*, 3:279.
54. Chávez, *Origins*, 25–26.
55. Hackett and Shelby, *Revolt*, 2:227, 257–58, 380; Kessell and Hendricks, *By Force of Arms*, 376; Bandelier, *Final Report*, 2:221n1.
56. Chávez, *Origins*, 19–21, 25; Esquibel and Durán y Cháves, "Durán y Cháves," 184–85.
57. Esquibel, personal communication, citing Real Audiencia, Concurso de Peñalosa, t. 1, leg. 1, no. 2, ff. 6r–6v, AGN; Scholes, *Troublous Times*, 133, 214–15.
58. Chávez, *Origins*, 21; Hackett, *Historical Documents*, 3:231; Scholes, *Troublous Times*, 203.
59. Chávez, *Origins*, 19–20.
60. Chávez, *Origins*, 20.
61. Scholes, *Troublous Times*, 133, 214–15; Hackett, *Historical Documents*, 3:251–52; Chávez, *Origins*, 20.
62. Land records of New Mexico, series 1, roll 37, fols. 727–28, U.S. surveyor general records, Court of Private Land Claims, Atrisco land grant, SANM, cited in Esquibel, "Beyond Origins of New Mexico Families," vol. 2.
63. Esquibel, "Beyond Origins of New Mexico Families," vol. 2.

64. Kessell, Hendricks, and Dodge, *To the Royal Crown*, 79n26; Chávez, *Origins*, 86–87.
65. Hackett and Shelby, *Revolt*, 1:xciv, 26–27; Hackett, "Retreat," pt. 1, 160; Bandelier, *Final Report*, 2:221n1.
66. Chávez, *Origins*, 35–36; Kessell, *Kiva*, 186; Hackett, *Historical Documents*, 3:221, 223, 249, 260; Anderson, "Encomienda," 368; Hodge, Hammond, and Rey, *Revised Memorial*, 110.
67. Chávez, *Origins*, 35–36.
68. Ibid., 94; Inquisition, t. 356, exp. 133, f. 268v, AGN, cited in Esquibel, "Founders," 13.
69. Inquisition, t. 372, exp. 16, f. 9, AGN, cited in Esquibel, "Vecino Estancias," 7.
70. Inquisition, t. 593, exp. 1, f. 335–37, AGN, cited in Esquibel, "Beyond Origins of New Mexico Families," vol. 5.
71. Chávez, *Origins*, 65.
72. Scholes, "Civil Government," 94n39.
73. Chávez, *Origins*, 17, 102.
74. Hackett, *Historical Documents*, 3:265.
75. Greenleaf, "Atrisco," 5; Domínguez, *Missions*, 154n12.
76. Hackett and Shelby, *Revolt*, 2:379–80.
77. Chávez, *Origins*, 56.
78. Barrett, *Conquest*, 56, 78.
79. Chavez, *Origins*, 55–56; Inquisition., t. 594, exp.1, f. 228v, AGN, cited in Esquibel, "Vecino Estancias," 7.
80. Chávez, *Origins*, 55–56; Hackett, *Historical Documents*, 3:251.
81. Inquisition, 594, exp. 1, f. 228v, AGN, cited in Esquibel, "Vecino Estancias," 7; Chávez, *Origins*, 90.
82. Hackett, *Historical Documents*, 3:75.
83. Chávez, *Origins*, 90.
84. Ibid., 56, 103.
85. Esquibel, personal communication, citing Inquisition, t. 610, exp. 7, f. 69v, AGN.
86. Chávez, *Origins*, 103.
87. Ibid., 90; Hackett and Shelby, *Revolt*, 1:38, 2:154–55.
88. Chávez, *Origins*, 57.
89. Ibid., 57.
90. Ibid., 57.
91. Esquibel, personal communication, citing Inquisition, t. 593, f. 60v, AGN.
92. Chávez, *Origins*, 81.
93. Ibid., 81.
94. Ibid., 82.
95. Chávez, *Origins*, 106; Esquibel personal communication, citing land records of New Mexico, series 1, no. 315, SANM.
96. Chávez, *Origins*, 105; Hammond and Rey, *Don Juan*, 1:155, 578, 2:702.

97. Chávez, *Origins*, 93.
98. Ibid., 106; Hackett and Shelby, *Revolt*, 1:142, 2:49.
99. Bandelier, *Final Report*, 1:141-42, no. 462.
100. Ibid.
101. Chávez, *Origins*, 14, 155-56, 219.
102. Hackett, *Historical Documents*, 3:177; Kessell and Hendricks, *By Force of Arms*, 376.
103. Hackett and Shelby, *Revolt*, 1:xcvi, 27.
104. Chávez, *Origins*, 109; Barrett, *Conquest*, 56; National Register of Historic Places Nomination Form in ARMS file for LA 953.
105. Chávez, *Origins*, 56, 109.
106. Ibid., 109; Hackett, *Historical Documents*, 3:276.
107. Chávez, *Origins*, 109.
108. Ibid., 24-25.
109. Ibid., 25, 57.
110. Ibid., 25.
111. Esquibel, "Beyond Origins of New Mexico Families," vol. 2; Chávez, *Origins*, 99.
112. Esquibel, personal communication, land records of New Mexico, series 1, nos. 486, 487, 488, SANM.
113. Chávez, *Origins*, 99.
114. Ibid., 32-33; Inquisition, t. 608, exp. 6, f. 427, and t. 356, f. 260, AGN, cited in Esquibel, "Beyond Origins of New Mexico Families," vol. 8.
115. Chávez, *Origins*, 32.
116. Ibid., 33.
117. Ibid., 33; Hackett, *Historical Documents*, 3:254.
118. Chávez, *Origins*, 33.
119. Ibid., 30; Zárate Salmerón, *Relaciones*, 56-57.
120. Esquibel, personal communication, citing Real Audiencia, Concurso de Peñalosa, t. 4, exp. 605, f. 62r, AGN; Chávez, *Origins*, 30
121. Esquibel, personal communication, citing DM 1712, August 31, no. 7, El Paso del Norte, AASF, and DM 1719, February 1, no. 4, El Paso del Norte, AASF.
122. Ramenofsky and Vaughn, "Comanche Springs," 31. Other sources for this discussion of the Comanche Springs site are Vaughn, "Taking the Measure," 186, 195; National Register of Historic Places Nomination Form in ARMS file for LA 14904; Hibben, Benjamin, and Adler, "Comanche Springs," 44-45, 55-57; and Pratt and Snow, *North Central*, 182-85.
123. National Register of Historic Places Nomination Form in ARMS file for LA 14904; Julyan, *Place Names*, 356.
124. Ramenofsky and Vaughn, "Comanche Springs," 19-20; Vaughan, "Taking the Measure," 195.
125. Hibben, Benjamin, and Adler, "Comanche Springs," 41, 42, 43; ARMS file for LA 103997, Metzler site.

CHAPTER SEVENTEEN

1. Barrett, *Conquest*, 55, 62, 63.
2. Chávez, *Origins*, 72.
3. Esquibel, personal communication, citing Inquisition, t. 666, exp. 10, ff. 375, 380, AGN.
4. Inquisition, t. 593, exp. 1, f. 288, and t. 304, f. 184, AGN, cited in Esquibel, "Beyond Origins of New Mexico Families," vol. 8. His mother was a Tano woman. Esquibel, personal communication.
5. Chávez, *Origins*, 72.
6. Ibid., 52.
7. Esquibel, personal communication, citing Inquisition, t. 593, exp. 1, ff. 292–94, and t. 586, f. 52, AGN.
8. Esquibel, personal communication, citing Inquisition, t. 596, exp, 1, f. 153r and 157r, AGN.
9. Hackett, *Historical Documents*, 3:151; Chávez, *Origins*, 71.
10. Chávez, *Origins*, 53, 71.
11. Ibid., 71.
12. Hackett and Shelby, *Revolt*, 2:163; Ivey, *In the Midst of Loneliness*, 24.
13. Hackett, *Historical Documents*, 3:161; Ivey, *In the Midst of Loneliness*, 24.
14. Esquibel, personal communication, citing Inquisition, t. 507, exp. 1 y 2, f. 303v, and t. 596, exp. 1, f. 26r, AGN.
15. Chávez, *Origins*, 53.
16. Ivey, *In the Midst of Loneliness*, 24–25.
17. Hackett and Shelby, *Revolt*, 1:25, 97, 2:163; Chávez, *Origins*, 53.
18. Hackett, *Historical Documents*, 3:224; Chávez, *Origins*, 80; Ivey, *In the Midst of Loneliness*, 25; Esquibel, personal communication, citing Inquisition, t. 593, f. 97, AGN.
19. Hackett, *Historical Documents*, 3:254, 273, 276; Ivey, *In the Midst of Loneliness*, 25.
20. Hackett and Shelby, *Revolt*, 1:25, 97; Chávez, *Origins*, 81.
21. Chávez, *Origins*, 1; Ivey, *In the Midst of Loneliness*, 25.
22. Chávez, *Origins*, 1; Hackett, *Historical Documents*, 3:136, 140, 160; Scholes, *Troublous Times*, 40–41, 178–79; Ivey, *In the Midst of Loneliness*, 25; Real Audiencia, Concurso de Peñalosa, t. 1, leg. 1, no. 10, f. 87, AGN, cited in Esquibel, "Vecino Estancias," 9.
23. Inquisition, t. 593, exp. 1, ff. 80–82, AGN, cited in Esquibel, "Vecino Estancias," 9; Chávez, *Origins*, 5, 55, 56.
24. Chávez, *Origins*, 5.
25. Ibid.
26. Ibid., 8, 99.
27. Hackett, *Historical Documents*, 3:273; Chávez, *Origins*, 76.

28. Mera, *Population Changes*, 23; ARMS file for LA 383 (Glaze F ceramics were G—p Kotyiti, G—p San Marcos, and Kapo Black, which date to 1650-1700/50 [Cordelia Snow, personal communication]).
29. Hackett, *Historical Documents*, 3:169; Chávez, *Origins*, 40.
30. Scholes, *Troublous Times*, 35, 40, 133, 214-15; Anderson, "Encomienda," 368; Kessell and Hendricks, *By Force of Arms*, 480n29; Snow, "Note," 354-56; Chávez, *Origins*, 48.
31. Kessell, *Kiva*, 186.
32. Scholes, *Troublous Times*, 132; Hackett, *Historical Documents*, 3:247-48; Chávez, *Origins*, 3-4.
33. Scholes, *Troublous Times*, 35, 40; Anderson, "Encomienda," 368.</notetxt>

CHAPTER EIGHTEEN

1. Marshall and Walt, *Rio Abajo*, 1-4.
2. Barrett, *Conquest*, 55. The other pueblos were Abó Confluence (LA 50241), Pueblo de Arena (LA 31717), El Barro (LA 283), Pueblito Point (LA 31751), Teypama (LA 282), Plaza Montoya (LA 31744), Qualacú (LA 757), Nuestra Señora (LA 19266), San Pascual (LA 487), and Tiffany (LA 244). Alamillo and Senecú pueblos have not been given LA numbers because their precise sites have not been discovered.
3. Inquisition, trial of López de Mendizábal, leg. 1, no. 9, ff. 33-33v, AGN, cited in Esquibel, "Vecino Estancias," 8.
4. Kessell and Hendricks, *By Force of Arms*, 375; Hackett and Shelby, *Revolt*, 2: 213; Marshall and Walt, *Rio Abajo*, 257.
5. Esquibel, "Romero Family," pt. 2, 13.
6. Chávez, *Origins*, 35-37.
7. Inquisition, trial of López de Mendizábal, Santa Fe, May 4, 1662, leg. 1, no. 6, ff. 4-4v, AGN, cited in Esquibel, "Vecino Estancias," 8.
8. Kessell, *Kiva*, 186.
9. Chávez, *Origins*, 36-37.
10. Ibid., 98; Tierras, t. 3268, pt. 1, leg. 2, no. 32, f. 212, Santa Fe, October 1661, AGN, cited in Esquibel, "Vecino Estancias," 8; Kessell and Hendricks, *By Force of Arms*, 375, 479-80n25.
11. Chávez, *Origins*, 95, 97.
12. Esquibel, "Romero Family," pt. 1, 12.
13. Chávez, *Origins*, 43, 97; Inquisition, t. 610, exp. 7, f. 63, AGN and Inquisition, t. 608, exp. 6, f. 419, AGN, cited in Esquibel, "Vecino Estancias," 8.
14. Leg. 1, doc. 29, BNM, cited in Esquibel, "Romero Family," pt. 2, 15, 18.
15. Chávez, *Origins*, 104; Sisneros, *Sisneros*, 5-7, 9.
16. Esquibel, personal communication, citing Patronato 244, R. 7, B. 14, f. 21v, AGI; Chávez, *Origins*, 42-43.
17. Hackett, *Historical Documents*, 3:189, 206; Chávez, *Origins*, 42-43.

18. Hackett, *Historical Documents*, 3:148, 189.
19. Ibid., 3:148, 188–89, 206; Esquibel, "Romero Family," pt. 2, 12–13.
20. Inquisition, 629, exp. 2, ff. 115v and 130, AGN, cited in Esquibel "Romero Family," pt. 2, 13–14.
21. Chávez, *Origins*, 69.
22. Marshall and Walt, *Rio Abajo*, 199, 256; Hackett and Shelby, *Revolt*, 2:363.
23. Marshall and Walt, *Rio Abajo*, 199–201, 256, 344.
24. Chávez, *Origins*, 69.
25. Ibid., 88.
26. Ibid., 88.
27. Hackett, *Historical Documents*, 3:206.
28. Chávez, *Origins*, 88; Hackett, *Historical Documents*, 3:148.
29. Sánchez, *Rio Abajo*, 93; Esquibel, personal communication, citing Inquisition, t. 593, exp. 1, ff. 320–21, AGN.
30. Chávez, *Origins*, 88–89.
31. Hackett and Shelby, *Revolt*, 2:204–5.
32. Ibid., 1:185; Chávez, *Origins*, 88.
33. Chávez, *Origins*, 95.
34. Esquibel, personal communication, citing Inquisition, t. 593, exp. 1, f. 327 ff., AGN.
35. Esquibel, "Romero Family," pt. 1, 10, 11.
36. Hackett and Shelby, *Revolt*, 2:364.
37. Chávez, *Origins*, 58; Marshall and Walt, *Rio Abajo*; Hackett, *Historical Documents*, 3:282.
38. Chávez, *Origins*, 58; Marshall and Walt, *Rio Abajo*, 277.
39. Esquibel, personal communication, citing Inquisition, t. 608, exp. 6, f. 417, AGN.
40. Chávez, *Origins*, 95, 97; Inquisition, t. 586, pt. 1, ff. 70v–72v, AGN, cited in Esquibel, "Romero Family," pt. 1, 10.
41. Chavez, *Origins*, 97; Inquisition, t. 586, pt. 1, ff. 70v–72v, AGN, cited in Esquibel, "Romero Family," pt. 1, 10.
42. Chávez, *Origins*, 97; Esquibel, personal communication, citing land records of New Mexico, series 1, no. 545, SANM.
43. Hackett, *Historical Documents*, 3:292, 297.
44. Kessell and Hendricks, *By Force of Arms*, 140; Chávez, *Origins*, 106.
45. Inquisition, t. 608, exp. 6, f. 425v, AGN, cited in Esquibel, "Vecino Estancias," 9; Chávez, *Origins*, 106.
46. Real Audiencia, Concurso de Peñalosa, vol. 1, exp. 605, leg. 1, no. 9, ff. 17–18, and leg. 1, no. 1, f. 164, AGN, cited in Esquibel, "Romero Family," pt. 2, 17–18.
47. Leg. 1, doc. 29, BNM, cited in Esquibel, "Romero Family," pt. 2, 18.
48. Hackett, *Historical Documents*, 3:292; Marshall and Walt, *Rio Abajo*, 252.
49. Inquisition, t. 608, exp. 6, f. 427, and t. 356, f. 260, AGN, cited in Esquibel, "Beyond Origins of New Mexico Families," vol. 8.
50. Chávez, *Origins*, 15, 75; Hackett, *Historical Documents*, 3:158.

Works Cited

Adams, Eleanor B., ed. *Bishop Tamarón's Visitation of New Mexico, 1760*. Albuquerque: Historical Society of New Mexico, 1954.
Anderson, H. Allen. "The Encomienda in New Mexico, 1598–1680." *New Mexico Historical Review* 60, no. 4 (1985): 353–77.
Arnold, Carrie Forman. "The Palace of the Governors." In *Santa Fe: History of an Ancient City*, edited by David Grant Noble, 128–49. Santa Fe, NM: School of American Research Press, 1989.
Ayer, Mrs. Edward E., trans., Frederick Webb Hodge, and Charles Fletcher Lummis, annot. *The Memorial of Fray Alonso de Benavides, 1630*. Albuquerque, NM: Horn and Wallace, 1965.
Bakewell, P. J. *Silver Mining and Society in Colonial Mexico, Zacatecas 1546–1700*. Cambridge: Cambridge University Press, 1971.
Bandelier, Adolph, F. A. *Final Report of Investigations among the Indians of the Southwestern United States Carried on Mainly in the Years from 1880 to 1885*. 2 vols. Cambridge, MA: John Wilson and Son, 1890, 1892.
Barrett, Elinore. *Conquest and Catastrophe: Changing Rio Grande Pueblo Settlement Patterns in the Sixteenth and Seventeenth Centuries*. Albuquerque: University of New Mexico Press, 2002.
Bayer, Laura, with Floyd Montoya and the Pueblo of Santa Ana. *Santa Ana: The People, the Pueblo, and the History of Tamaya*. Albuquerque: University of New Mexico Press, 1994.
Bloom, Lansing B. "Beginnings of Representative Government in New Mexico." *New Mexico Historical Review* 21, no. 2 (1946): 127–34.
———. "A Glimpse of New Mexico in 1620." *New Mexico Historical Review* 3, no. 4 (1928): 357–80.
———, transcr. "Ynstrucción a Peralta por Vi-Rey." *New Mexico Historical Review* 4, no. 2 (1929): 178–86.
———. "When Was Santa Fe Founded?" *New Mexico Historical Review* 4, no. 2 (1929): 188–94.
Boyd, Elizabeth. Application for Registration, State Register of Cultural Properties, Santa Fe River sites. File 200, New Mexico Historic Preservation Division. Santa Fe: New Mexico Office of Cultural Affairs, 1970.

Carrera Stampa, Manuel. "The Evolution of Weights and Measures in New Spain." *Hispanic American Historical Review* 29, no. 1 (1949): 2–24.

Cháves, Ireneo L., trans. "Instructions to Peralta by Vice-Roy." *New Mexico Historical Review* 4, no. 2 (1929): 179–87.

Chávez, Angélico. "How Old is San Miguel?" *El Palacio* 60, no. 4 (1953): 141–50.

———. *Origins of New Mexico Families in the Spanish Colonial Period: A Genealogy of the Spanish Colonial Period.* Santa Fe: Historical Society of New Mexico, 1992.

———. "Santa Fe Church and Convent Sites in the Seventeenth and Eighteenth Centuries." *New Mexico Historical Review* 24, no. 2 (1949): 85–93.

Chevalier, François. *Land and Society in Colonial Mexico: The Great Hacienda.* Edited by Lesley Byrd Simpson. Translated by Alvin Eustis. Berkeley: University of California Press, 1963.

Crawford, Clifford S., Anne C. Cully, Rob Leutheuser, Mark S. Sifuentes, Larry H. White, and James P. Wilber. *Middle Rio Grande Ecosystem: Bosque Biological Management Plan.* Albuquerque, NM: U.S. Fish and Wildlife Service, 1993.

Cross-Cultural Research Systems (David H. Snow). *Santa Fe Historic Plaza Study II: Plaza Excavation Final Report for the City of Santa Fe.* Santa Fe, NM, 1992.

Crouch, Dora P., Daniel J. Garr, and Alex I. Mundigo. *Spanish City Planning in North America.* Cambridge, MA: MIT Press, 1982.

Dick-Peddie, William A. *New Mexico Vegetation: Past, Present, and Future.* Albuquerque: University of New Mexico Press, 1993.

Domínguez, Fray Francisco Atanasio. *The Missions of New Mexico, 1776: A Description by Fray Francisco Atanasio Domínguez with Other Contemporary Documents.* Edited by Eleanor B. Adams. Albuquerque: University of New Mexico Press, 1956.

Elliott, Michael L. *The Archeology of Santa Fe: A Background Report.* Santa Fe, NM: City of Santa Fe Planning Department, 1988.

Ellis, Bruce T. "La Garita, Santa Fe's Little Spanish Fort." *El Palacio* 84, no. 2 (1978): 2–22.

———. "Santa Fe's Seventeenth-Century Plaza, Parish Church, and Convent Reconsidered." In *Collected Papers in Honor of Marjorie Ferguson Lambert,* edited by Albert H. Schroeder, 183–98. Albuquerque: Archaeological Society of New Mexico Press, 1976.

Ellis, Florence Hawley. "Isleta Pueblo." In *Handbook of North American Indians: Southwest,* vol. 9, edited by Alfonso Ortiz, 351–65. Washington, DC: Smithsonian Institution, 1979.

———. "The Long Lost 'City' of San Gabriel del Yungue, Second Oldest European Settlement in the United States." In *When Cultures Meet: Remembering San Gabriel del Yunge Oweenge,* 10–38. Santa Fe, NM: Sunstone Press, 1987.

———. *San Gabriel del Yunge as Seen by an Archaeologist.* Santa Fe, NM: Sunstone Press, 1989.

Ellis, Florence Hawley, and Andrea Ellis Dodge. "A Window on San Gabriel del Yunque." In *Current Research on the Late Prehistory and Early History of New Mexico,* edited by Bradley J. Vierra and Clara Gualtieri, 175–83. Albuquerque: New Mexico Archaeological Council, 1992.

Espinosa, J. Manuel. *Crusaders of the Rio Grande: The Story of Don Diego de Vargas and the Reconquest and Refounding of New Mexico.* Chicago, IL: Institute of Jesuit History, 1942.

———, ed. and trans. *First Expedition of Vargas into New Mexico, 1692.* Albuquerque: University of New Mexico Press, 1940.

———, ed. and trans. *The Pueblo Indian Revolt of 1696 and the Franciscan Missions in New Mexico: Letters of the Missionaries and Related Documents.* Norman: University of Oklahoma Press, 1988.

Esquibel, José Antonio. "Analysis of the Granillo Inspection of Pre-1680 Property Owners in the Vicinity of La Cañada." Unpublished manuscript, August 2008.

———. "Beyond Origins of New Mexico Families." 9 vols. http.//pages.prodigy.net/bluemountain/beyondorigins.htm.

———. "Founders of the Villa of Santa Fe, 1610–1632." Unpublished manuscript, 2007.

———. "New Light on the Jewish-Converso Ancestry of Don Juan de Oñate: A Research Note." *Colonial Latin American Historical Review* 7, no. 2 (1998): 175–90.

———. "On the Founding of the Villa of Santa Fe: Research Notes." Unpublished manuscript, January 2007.

———. "Palace Echoes: References to the Casas Reales de Palacio by Residents of the Villa de Santa Fe, 1659–1663." Unpublished manuscript, 2005.

———. "Parientes: Founders of the Villa of Santa Fe #2, the Martín Serrano Family." *Herencia* 15 (Winter 2007): 42–45.

———. "The People of the Camino Real: A Genealogical Appendix." In *The Royal Road: El Camino Real from Mexico City to Santa Fe*, edited by Christine and Douglas Preston and José Antonio Esquibel, 145–76. Albuquerque: University of New Mexico Press, 1998.

———. "Political and Economic Influences in the Establishment of Estancias in Seventeenth-Century New Mexico." Unpublished manuscript, February 2008.

———. "The Romero Family of Seventeenth Century New Mexico." Pt. 1. *Herencia* 11 (Jan. 2003): 1–32.

———. "The Romero Family of Seventeenth Century New Mexico." Pt. 2. *Herencia* 11 (July 2003): 1–25.

———. "*Soldados-Vecinos* of New Mexico, 1598 to 1610: A Preliminary Compilation." Unpublished manuscript, n.d.

———. "Thirty-eight Adobe Houses: The Villa de Santa Fe in the Seventeenth Century, 1608–1610." In *All Trails Lead to Santa Fe: An Anthology Commemorating the 400th Anniversary of the Founding of Santa Fe, New Mexico in 1610*, 109–28. Santa Fe: Sunstone Press, 2010.

———. "Vecino Estancias of Seventeenth-Century New Mexico." Unpublished manuscript 2004.

———. "Vecinos and Residents of the Villa de Santa Fe 1659–1663." Unpublished manuscript, 2007.

Esquibel, José Antonio, and Patryka Durán y Cháves. "Pedro Durán y Cháves and Juana de Montoya." In *Aquí Se Comienza: A Genealogical History of La Villa de San Felipe de Albuquerque*, edited by Gloria M. Valencia y Valdez et al., 179–227. Albuquerque: New Mexico Genealogical Society, 2007.

Esquibel, José Antonio, and Robert D. Martínez. "Additional Vecinos of New Mexico." In "Vecinos, Mineros y Hacendados: The Sáez Family of Nueva Vizcaya and Nuevo Mexico, 1600–1750." Unpublished manuscript, n.d.

Ewald, Ursula. *The Mexican Salt Industry, 1560–1980: A Study in Change*. Stuttgart, Ger.: Gustav Fischer, 1985.

Flint, Richard. "La Salina of the Estancia Valley, New Mexico: Community Use and Private Ownership, 1830s to 1930s." *New Mexico Historical Review* 83, no. 1 (2008): 39–55.

Flint, Richard, and Shirley Cushing Flint. *Documents of the Coronado Expedition, 1539–1542*. Dallas, TX: Southern Methodist University Press, 2005.

Forbes, Jack D. *Apache, Navajo, and Spaniard*. Norman: University of Oklahoma Press, 1960.

Ford, Richard I., Albert H. Schroeder, and Stewart L. Peckham. "Three Perspectives on Pueblan Prehistory." In *New Perspectives on the Pueblos*, edited by Alfonso Ortiz, 19–39. Albuquerque: University of New Mexico Press, 1972.

Fritts, Harold C. *Reconstructing Large-scale Climatic Patterns from Tree-Ring Data: A Diagnostic Analysis*. Tucson: University of Arizona Press, 1991. The computer file related to this volume was made available through the courtesy of Louis A. Scuderi, University of New Mexico.

Gavin, Robin Farwell. "La Sala de Estrado: Woman's Place in the Palace." *El Palacio* 115, no. 4 (2010): 48–55.

Gerhard, Peter. *The Northern Frontier of New Spain*. Princeton, NJ: Princeton University Press, 1982.

Gibson, Charles. *The Aztecs under Spanish Rule: A History of the Indians of the Valley of Mexico, 1519–1810*. Stanford, CA: Stanford University Press, 1964.

Greenleaf, Richard E. "Atrisco and Las Ciruelas, 1772–1769." *New Mexico Historical Review* 42, no. 1 (1967): 5–25.

Grissino-Mayer, Henri D., Christopher H. Baisan, and Thomas W. Swetnam. *A 1,373 Year Reconstruction of Annual Precipitation for the Southern Rio Grande Basin, Final Report*. Fort Bliss, TX: Department of the Army, Directorate of Environment, Natural Resources Division, 1997.

Grissino-Mayer, Henri D., Christopher H. Baisan, Kiyomi A. Morino, and Thomas W. Swetnam. *Multi-Century Trends in Past Climate for the Middle Rio Grande Basin, AD 622–1992*. Albuquerque, NM: Rocky Mountain Research Station, U.S. Forest Service, U.S. Department of Agriculture, 2002.

Hackett, Charles Wilson, ed. *Historical Documents Relating to New Mexico, Nueva Vizcaya, and Approaches Thereto to 1773*. Vols. 1 and 3. Washington, DC: Carnegie Institution, 1923, 1937.

———. "The Location of the Tigua Pueblos of Alameda, Puaray, and Sandia in 1680-81." *Old Santa Fe Trail* 2, no. 4 (1915): 381-91.

———. "The Retreat of the Spaniards from New Mexico in 1680 and the Beginnings of El Paso." Pt. 1. *Southwestern Historical Quarterly* 16, no. 2 (1912): 137-68.

———. "The Retreat of the Spaniards from New Mexico in 1680 and the Beginnings of El Paso." Pt. 2. *Southwestern Historical Quarterly* 16, no. 3 (1913): 259-76.

Hackett, Charles Wilson, and Charmion C. Shelby, eds. and trans. *Revolt of the Pueblo Indians of New Mexico and Otermín's Attempted Reconquest, 1680-1682*. 2 vols. Albuquerque: University of New Mexico Press, 1942.

Hall, Emlen G. "The Pueblo Grant Labyrinth." In *Land, Water, and Culture: New Perspectives on Hispanic Land Grants*, edited by Charles L. Briggs and John R. Van Ness, 67-138. Albuquerque: University of New Mexico Press, 1987.

Hammond, George P. *Don Juan de Oñate and the Founding of New Mexico*. Santa Fe: Historical Society of New Mexico, 1927.

Hammond, George P., and Agapito Rey, eds. and trans. *Don Juan de Oñate: Colonizer of New Mexico, 1595-1628*. 2 vols. Albuquerque: University of New Mexico Press, 1953.

———, eds. and trans. *Narratives of the Coronado Expedition, 1540-1542*. Albuquerque: University of New Mexico Press, 1940.

———, eds. and trans. *The Rediscovery of New Mexico, 1580-1594*. Albuquerque: University of New Mexico Press, 1966.

Harrington, John Peabody. *The Ethnogeography of the Tewa Indians*. Washington, DC: Smithsonian Institution, 1916.

Hendricks, Rick, and Gerald J. Mandell. "Juan Manso, Frontier Entrepreneur." *New Mexico Historical Review* 75, no. 3 (2000): 339-67.

Hibben, Frank C., Ben Benjamin, and Mildred S. Adler. "The Spanish Period at Comanche Springs, New Mexico: A Silver Assaying Station of the Early Seventeenth Century." *The Artifact* 23, no. 3 (1985): 41-58.

Hodge, Frederick Webb, George P. Hammond, and Agapito Rey, eds. *Fray Alonso de Benavides' Revised Memorial of 1634*. Albuquerque: University of New Mexico Press, 1945.

Hordes, Stanley M. "The History of the Santa Fe Plaza, 1610-1720." In *Santa Fe Historic Plaza Study I, with translations from Spanish Colonial Documents*, edited by Linda Tigges, 3-36. Santa Fe, NM: City Planning Department, 1990.

Ivey, James E. "The Estancia, the New Mexican Hacienda." In *Canyon Gardens: The Ancient Pueblo Landscapes of the American Southwest*, edited by V. B. Price and Baker H. Morrow, 75-85. Albuquerque: University of New Mexico Press, 2006.

———. "The Greatest Misfortune of All: Famine in the Province of New Mexico, 1667-1672." *Journal of the Southwest* 36, no. 1 (1994): 76-100.

———. *In the Midst of Loneliness: The Architectural History of the Salinas Missions.* Santa Fe, NM: National Park Service, U.S. Department of the Interior, 1988.

———. "Pueblo and Estancia: The Spanish Presence in the Pueblo, A.D. 1620–1680." In *Current Research on the Late Prehistory and Early History of New Mexico*, edited by Bradley J. Vierra and Clara Gualtieri, 221–26. Albuquerque: New Mexico Archaeological Council, 1992.

———, transcr. and trans. "Reconnaissance of the Palacio, Santa Fe, 1716." Miscellaneous documents, series 2, 253, roll 5, frames 564–67, SANM.

———. "San Miguel Archaeology." Unpublished manuscript, n.d.

———. "An Uncertain Founding: Santa Fe." *Common-Place* 3, no. 4 (2003): 1–6.

———. "The Viceroy's Order Founding the Villa of Santa Fe: A Reconsideration." In *All Trails Lead to Santa Fe: An Anthology Commemorating the 400th Anniversary of the Founding of Santa Fe, New Mexico in 1610*, 97–107. Santa Fe, NM: Sunstone Press, 2010.

Jenkins, Myra Ellen. "Oñate's Administration and the Pueblo Indians." In *When Cultures Meet: Remembering San Gabriel del Yunge Oweenge*, 63–72. Santa Fe, NM: Sandstone Press, 1987.

———. "Taos Pueblo and its Neighbors." *New Mexico Historical Review* 16, no. 2 (1966): 85–114.

Juan Martínez de Mendoza Collection, 1785–1835. AC 143, box 1, 18 ff., Fray Angelico Chávez Library, Palace of the Governors, Santa Fe.

Julyan, Robert. *The Place Names of New Mexico.* Albuquerque: University of New Mexico Press, 1996.

Kelley, N. Edmund. *The Contemporary Ecology of Arroyo Hondo, New Mexico.* Santa Fe, NM: School of American Research Press, 1980.

Kelley, Vincent C. *Albuquerque: Its Mountains, Valley, Water, and Volcanoes.* Socorro: New Mexico Bureau of Mines and Mineral Resources, 1969.

Kessell, John L. *Kiva, Cross, and Crown: The Pecos Indians and New Mexico, 1540–1840.* Washington, DC: National Park Service, U.S. Department of the Interior, 1979.

Kessell, John L., and Rick Hendricks, eds. and trans. *By Force of Arms: The Journals of Don Diego de Vargas, 1691–1693.* Albuquerque: University of New Mexico Press, 1992.

Kessell, John L., Rick Hendricks, and Meredith Dodge, eds. and trans. *Blood on the Boulders: The Journals of Don Diego de Vargas, New Mexico, 1694–97.* 2 vols. Albuquerque: University of New Mexico Press, 1998.

———. *To the Royal Crown Restored: The Journals of Don Diego de Vargas, New Mexico, 1692–1694.* Albuquerque: University of New Mexico Press, 1995.

Kessell, John L., Rick Hendricks, Meredith Dodge, and Larry D. Miller, eds. and trans. *A Settling of Accounts: The Journals of Don Diego de Vargas, New Mexico, 1700–1704.* Albuquerque: University of New Mexico Press, 2002.

———. *That Disturbances Cease: The Journals of Don Diego de Vargas, New Mexico, 1697–1700.* Albuquerque: University of New Mexico Press, 2000.

Kraemer, Paul K. "New Mexico's Ancient Salt Trade." *El Palacio* 82, no. 1 (1976): 22–30.
Kubler, George. *The Religious Architecture of New Mexico in the Colonial Period and since the American Occupation*. Colorado Springs, CO: Taylor Museum, 1940.
Laboratory of Tree-Ring Research. Southwest Paleoclimate Project. University of Arizona, Tucson. Unpublished data.
Lafora, Nicolás de. *Relación del viaje que hizo a los presidios internas situados en la frontera de la América Septentrional*. México, DF: Editorial Pedro Robredo, 1939.
Lentz, Stephen C. *Excavations at LA 80,000: The Santa Fe Plaza Community Stage Location, Santa Fe, New Mexico*. Santa Fe: Museum of New Mexico, Office of Archaeological Studies, 2004.
Levine, Frances. "Down Under an Ancient City: An Archaeologist's View of Santa Fe." In *Santa Fe: History of an Ancient City*, edited by David Grant Noble, 9–26. Santa Fe, NM: School of American Research Press, 1989.
Lycett, Mark Thomas. "Archaeological Implications of European Contact: Demography, Settlement, and Land Use in the Middle Rio Grande Valley, New Mexico." PhD diss., University of New Mexico, 1995.
Marshall, Michael P. *A Cultural Properties Assessment for the El Camino Real de Tierra Adentro National Historic Trail System*. Albuquerque, NM: National Park Service, Spanish Colonial Research Center, 2005.
———. "Rio Medio Report for LA 50247." See ARMS file, LA.
———. "Rio Medio Report for LA 44534." See ARMS file, LA.
———. "Rio Medio Report for LA 25674." See ARMS file, LA.
Marshall, Michael P., and Henry J. Walt. *Rio Abajo: Prehistory and History of a Rio Grande Province*. Santa Fe: Historic Preservation Division, New Mexico Office of Cultural Affairs, 1984.
Mera, Harry P. *Population Changes in the Rio Grande Glaze Paint Area*. Santa Fe: Laboratory of Anthropology, Museum of New Mexico, 1940.
Moke, Irene A. "Santa Fe, New Mexico: A Study in Urban Geography." PhD diss., University of Nebraska, n.d. (ca. 1950).
Moorhead, Max L. *The Presidio: The Bastion of the Spanish Borderlands*. Norman: University of Oklahoma Press, 1975.
———. "Rebuilding the Presidio of Santa Fe, 1789–1791." *New Mexico Historical Review* 49, no. 2 (1974): 123–42.
National Register of Historic Places Inventory Nomination Form. Reports prepared for nomination to the National Register of Historic Places, National Park Service, U.S. Department of the Interior. On file at the Historic Preservation Division, New Mexico Office of Cultural Affairs, Santa Fe, New Mexico.
Northrop, Stuart A. *Minerals of New Mexico*. Albuquerque: University of New Mexico Press, 1959.
Nuttall, Zelia. "Royal Ordinances Concerning the Laying Out of New Towns." *Hispanic American Historical Review* 4, no. 4 (1921): 743–53.

Ortiz, Alfonso. *The Tewa World: Space, Time, Being, and Becoming in a Pueblo Society.* Chicago, IL: University of Chicago Press, 1969.

———. "San Juan Pueblo." In *Handbook of North American Indians: Southwest*, vol. 9, edited by Alonso Ortiz, 278–95. Washington, DC: Smithsonian Institution, 1979.

Parsons, Jeffrey R. *The Last Salt Makers of Nexquipayac, Mexico: An Archaeological Ethnography.* Ann Arbor: University of Michigan, Museum of Anthropology, 2001.

Payne, Melissa. "Valley of Faith: Historical Archaeology of the Upper Santa Fe River Basin." PhD diss., University of New Mexico, 1999.

Peckham, Stewart. "The Anasazi of the Northern Rio Grande Rift." In *Rio Grande Rift: Northern New Mexico*, 275–81. Socorro: New Mexico Geological Society, 1984.

Peckham, Stewart, and David H. Snow. "Clues to Santa Fe's Past: Excavating the Fine Arts Site." *El Palacio* 88, no. 2 (1982): 38–42.

Plewa, Tara Marie. "A Trickle Runs Through It: An Environmental History of the Santa Fe River, New Mexico." PhD diss., University of South Carolina, 2009.

Post, Stephen S. "Archaeology behind the Palace of the Governors: A New Look At History and Cartography." *El Palacio* 108, no. 3 (2003): 6–11.

———. "Archaeology, History and Cartography of Pre-Statehood New Mexico: A View from the Backyard of the Palace of the Governors." In *Inscriptions: Papers in Honor of Richard and Natalie Woodbury*, edited by Regge N. Wiseman, Thomas C. O'Laughlin, and Cordelia T. Snow, 171–86. Albuquerque: Archaeological Society of New Mexico, 2005.

Pratt, Boyd C. "The Santa Fe Plaza: An Analysis of Various Theories of Its Size and Configuration, a Look at Several Crucial Documents, and a Comparison with Other Spanish Colonial Towns." In *Santa Fe Historic Plaza Study I, with Translations from Spanish Colonial Documents*, edited by Linda Tigges, 37–53. Santa Fe, NM: City Planning Department, 1990.

Pratt, Boyd C., and David H. Snow. *The North Central Regional Overview: Strategies for the Comprehensive Survey of the Architectural and Historic Archaeological Resources of North Central New Mexico.* Santa Fe: New Mexico Historic Preservation Division, 1988.

Preucel, Robert W. *Archaeologies of the Pueblo Revolt.* Albuquerque: University of New Mexico Press, 2002.

Ramenofsky, Ann F., C. D. Vaughn, and Philip Geib. "Comanche Springs: A 17th-Century Hybrid Community in Rio Abajo, New Mexico." Unpublished manuscript, n.d.

Recopilación de leyes de los reynos de las Indias. 3 vols. Madrid, 1943.

Rey, Agapito. "Cristóbal de Oñate." *New Mexico Historical Review* 26, no. 3 (1951): 197–203.

Riley, Carroll L. *Rio del Norte: People of the Upper Rio Grande from Earliest Times to the Pueblo Revolt.* Salt Lake City: University of Utah Press, 1995.

Rose, Martin R., Jeffrey S. Dean, and William J. Robinson. *The Past Climate of Arroyo Hondo, New Mexico, Reconstructed from Tree Rings.* Santa Fe, NM: School of American Research Press, 1981.

Sánchez, Joseph P. "The Peralta-Ordóñez Affair and the Founding of Santa Fe." In *Santa Fe: History of an Ancient City*, edited by David Grant Noble, 28–31. Santa Fe, NM: School of American Research Press, 1989.

———. *The Rio Abajo Frontier, 1540–1692: A History of Early Colonial New Mexico*. Albuquerque, NM: Albuquerque Museum, 1996.

Schaafsma, Curtis F. *Apaches de Navajo: Seventeenth Century Navajos in the Chama Valley of New Mexico*. Salt Lake City: University of Utah Press, 2002.

———. "Archaeological Reconnaissance of the Proposed MAPCO Pipeline from Bloomfield to Hobbs, New Mexico, MAPCO 2." Ms., 1972. See ARMS file for LA 25674.

———. "A Window on Santa Fe's History." *El Palacio* 88, no. 3 (1982): 29–39.

Scheick, Cherie L. "When Land and Water Were a Plenty: A View of Santa Fe's Early History as a Master Plan." In *Archaeology in Your Backyard*, 1–16. Santa Fe, NM: City of Santa Fe, 1999.

Scholes, France V. "Church and State in New Mexico, 1610–1650." Pts. 1–4. *New Mexico Historical Review* 11, nos. 1, 2, 3, 4 (1936): 9–76, 145–78, 283–94, 297–349.

———. "Church and State in New Mexico, 1610–1650." Pt. 5. *New Mexico Historical Review* 12, no. 1 (1937): 78–106.

———. "Civil Government and Society in New Mexico in the Seventeenth Century." *New Mexico Historical Review* 10, no. 2 (1935): 71–111.

———. "Documents for the History of the New Mexican Missions in the Seventeenth Century." *New Mexico Historical Review* 4, no. 1 (1929): 45–58.

———. "The First Decade of the Inquisition in New Mexico." *New Mexico Historical Review* 10, no. 3 (1935): 195–241.

———. "Juan Martínez de Montoya, Settler and Conquistador of New Mexico." *New Mexico Historical Review* 19, no. 4 (1944): 337–42.

———. "Royal Treasury Records Relating to the Province of New Mexico 1596–1683." Pts. 1–2. *New Mexico Historical Review* 50, nos. 1, 2 (1975): 5–23, 139–64.

———. "Supply Service of the New Mexico Missions of the Seventeenth Century." Pts. 1–3. *New Mexico Historical Review* 5, nos. 1, 2, 4 (1930): 93–114, 186–209, 386–404.

———. *Troublous Times in New Mexico: 1659–1670*. Albuquerque: University of New Mexico Press, 1942.

———. Unpublished notes from Contaduría, leg. 704, box 1, folder 85, AGI. In ZL.

Scholes, France V., and Lansing B. Bloom. "Friar Personnel and Mission Chronology, 1598–1629." Pt. 1. *New Mexico Historical Review* 19, no. 4 (1944): 319–36.

———. "Friar Personnel and Mission Chronology, 1598–1629." Pt. 2. *New Mexico Historical Review* 20, no. 1 (1945): 58–82.

Schroeder, Albert H. "The Cerrillos Mining Area." In *Archaeology and History of Santa Fe County*, edited by Ray V. Ingersoll, 13–16. Socorro: New Mexico Geological Society, 1979.

Schroeder, Albert H., and Dan S. Matson. *A Colony on the Move: Gaspar Castaño de Sosa's Journal, 1590–1591*. Santa Fe, NM: School of American Research, 1965.

Scurlock, Dan. *From the Rio to the Sierra: An Environmental History of the Middle Rio Grande Basin.* Fort Collins, CO: Rocky Mountain Research Station, U.S. Forest Service, U.S. Department of Agriculture, 1998.

Seifert, Donna J. *Archaeological Excavations at the Palace of the Governors, Santa Fe, New Mexico: 1974 and 1975.* Santa Fe: Museum of New Mexico, 1979.

Simmons, Marc. *Albuquerque: A Narrative History.* Albuquerque: University of New Mexico Press, 1982.

———. *The Last Conquistador: Juan de Oñate and the Settling of the Far Southwest.* Norman: University of Oklahoma Press, 1991.

———. "Settlement Patterns and Village Plans in Colonial New Mexico." *Journal of the West* 8, no. 1 (1969): 7–21.

———. "The Spaniards of San Gabriel." In *When Cultures Meet: Remembering San Gabriel del Yunge Oweenge*, 39–61. Santa Fe, NM: Sunstone Press, 1987.

Sisneros, Francisco. "Sisneros: A New Mexico Family History." Unpublished manuscript, n.d.

Snow, Cordelia Thomas. "A Brief History of the Palace of the Governors and a Preliminary Report on the 1974 Excavation." *El Palacio* 80, no. 3 (1974): 1–22.

———. "The Evolution of a Frontier: An Historical Interpretation of Archaeological Sites." In *Archeological Investigations in Cochiti Reservoir, New Mexico*, edited by Jan V. Biella and Richard C. Chapman, 217–34. Albuquerque: Office of Contract Archeology, University of New Mexico, 1979.

———. "Hypothetical Configurations of the Early Santa Fe Plaza Based on the 1573 Ordinances or the Law of the Indies." In *Santa Fe Historic Plaza Study I, with Translations from Spanish Colonial Documents*, edited by Linda Tigges, 55–72. Santa Fe, NM: City Planning Department, 1990.

———. "A Living Artifact, the Palace of the Governors: Archaeological Excavations from 1884 to 1987, and a Review of the History of the Building from 1610 to 1846." Getty Grant Program, Architectural Conservation Grants, application prepared for the Museum of New Mexico Foundation, 1994.

———. "The Plazas of Santa Fe, New Mexico." *El Palacio* 94, no. 2 (1988): 40–51.

———. "A Window to the Past: The San Miguel and La Conquistadora Chapels and Their Builders, 1610–1776." In *All Trails Lead to Santa Fe: An Anthology Commemorating the 400th Anniversary of the Founding of Santa Fe, New Mexico in 1610*, 147–62. Santa Fe, NM: Sunstone Press, 2010.

Snow, David H. *Archaeological Excavation of the Las Majadas Site, LA 591, Cochiti Dam, New Mexico.* Santa Fe: Laboratory of Anthropology Notes 75, Museum of New Mexico, 1973.

———, comp. and arr. *New Mexico's First Colonists: The 1597–1600 Enlistments for New Mexico under Juan de Oñate, Adelante and Gobernador.* Albuquerque, NM: Hispanic Genealogical Research Center, 1998.

———. "A Note on Encomienda Economics in Seventeenth Century New Mexico." In *Hispanic Arts and Ethnohistory in the Southwest: New Papers Inspired by the Work of E. Boyd*, edited by Marta Weigle, 347–57. Santa Fe, NM: Ancient City Press, 1983.

———. "La Plazuela de San Francisco: A Possible Case of Colonial Superposition?" In *Seeds of Struggle, Harvest of Faith*, edited by Thomas J. Steele, Paul Thetts, and Barbe Awalt, 81–99. Albuquerque, NM: LPD Press, 1998.

———. "'Por alli no ay losa, ni se hace': Guilded Men and Glazed Pottery on the Southern Plains." In *The Coronado Expedition to Tierra Nueva: The 1540–1542 Route Across the Southwest*, edited by Richard Flint and Shirley Cushing Flint, 344–64. Niwot: University Press of Colorado, 1997.

———, transcr. and trans. "Presentation by the Illustrious Cabildo, July 24, 1715." Land records of New Mexico, series 1, no. 169, SANM. Unpublished manuscript, n.d.

———. "Review of Agrarian and Linear Land Measurement of Land from 17th Century Documents in Colonial New Mexico." In *Santa Fe Historic Plaza Study I, with Translations from Spanish Colonial Documents*, edited by Linda Tigges, 85–108. Santa Fe, NM: City Planning Department, 1990.

———. "A Review of Spanish Colonial Archaeology in Northern New Mexico." In *Current Research on the Late Prehistory and Early History of New Mexico*, edited by Bradley J. Vierra and Clara Gualtieri, 185–93. Albuquerque: New Mexico Archaeological Council, 1992.

———. "Rural Hispanic Community Organization in Northern New Mexico: An Historical Perspective." In *The Survival of Spanish American Villages*, edited by Paul Kutsche, 45–52. Colorado Springs: Colorado College, 1979.

———. *The Santa Fe Acequia Systems*. Santa Fe, NM: City Planning Department, 1988.

———. "Santiago to Guache: Notes for a Tale of Two (or more) Bernalillos." In *Collected Papers in Honor of Marjorie Ferguson Lambert*, edited by Albert H. Schroeder, 161–81. Albuquerque, NM: Albuquerque Archeological Society Press, 1976.

Stanislawski, Dan. "Early Spanish Town Planning in the New World." *Geographical Review* 37, no. 1 (1947): 94–105.

Stubbs, Stanley A., and Bruce T. Ellis. *Archaeological Investigations at the Chapel of San Miguel and the Site of La Castrense, Santa Fe, New Mexico*. Santa Fe, NM: School of American Research, 1955.

Talmage, S. B., and T. P. Wootton. *The Non-Metallic Mineral Resources of New Mexico and Their Economic Features (Exclusive of Fuels)*. Socorro: New Mexico Bureau of Mines and Mineral Resources, 1937.

Tigges, Linda. "Soil Tests, the *Cienega*, and Spanish Colonial Occupation in Downtown Santa Fe." In *Santa Fe Historic Plaza Study I with Translations from Spanish Colonial Documents*, edited by Linda Tigges, 75–84. Santa Fe, NM: City Planning Department, 1990.

Tórrez, Robert. "The Presidio of Santa Fe." *Tradición Revista* 11, no. 1 (2006): 52–59.

Tuan, Yi-Fu, Cyril E. Everard, Jerold G. Widdison, and Iven Bennett. *The Climate of New Mexico*. Rev. ed. Santa Fe: New Mexico State Planning Office, 1973.

Twitchell, Ralph Emerson. *The Leading Facts of New Mexican History*. 5 vols. Cedar Rapids, IA: Torch, 1911–12.

———. *Old Santa Fe: The Story of New Mexico's Ancient Capital*. Chicago, IL: Rio Grande Press, 1963.

———. "Notes, Reviews, Communications." *Old Santa Fe* 1, no. 3 (1914): 335–43.

———. *The Spanish Archives of New Mexico*. 2 vols. Cedar Rapids, IA: Torch, 1914.

U.S. Department of Agriculture. *Climate and Man: 1941 Yearbook of Agriculture*. Washington, DC: U.S. Department of Agriculture, 1941.

U.S. National Oceanic and Atmospheric Agency. National Climatic Data Center. www.srh.noaa.gov.

Vaughn, Charles David. "Taking the Measure of New Mexico's Colonial Miners, Mining, and Metallurgy." PhD diss., University of New Mexico, 2006.

Vetancurt, Agustín de. *Teatro mexicano: Descripción breve de los sucesos ejemplares, históricos, politicos, militares, y religiosos del nuevo mundo occidental de las Indias*. Mexico City: Ed. Porrúa, SA, 1971.

Viklund, Lonyta. "Roads Old and New to Santa Fe: Historic Maps and Trails." In *Archaeology in Your Backyard*, 67–82. Santa Fe, NM: City of Santa Fe, 1999.

Villagrá, Gaspar Pérez de Acalá. *History of New Mexico*. Translated by Gilberto Espinosa. Los Angeles, CA: Quivira Society, 1933.

Warren, A. Helene, and Robert W. Weber. "Indian and Spanish Mining in the Galisteo and Hagan Basins." In *Archaeology and History of Santa Fe County*, edited by Ray V. Ingersoll, 7–11. Socorro: New Mexico Geological Society, 1979.

Weber, David J. *The Taos Trappers: The Fur Trade in the Far Southwest, 1540–1846*. Norman: University of Oklahoma Press, 1971.

Webster, Laurie D. "The Economics of Pueblo Textile Production and Exchange in Colonial New Mexico." In *Beyond Cloth and Cordage: Archaeological Textile Research in the Americas*, edited by Penelope Ballard Drooker and Laurie D. Webster, 179–204. Salt Lake City: University of Utah Press, 2000.

West, Robert C. *The Mining Community in Northern New Spain: The Parral Mining District*. New York: AMS Press, 1980.

Wilson, Christopher M. "The Santa Fe, New Mexico Plaza: An Architectural and Cultural History, 1610–1921." MA thesis, University of New Mexico, 1981.

Winship, George P., ed. *The Coronado Expedition, 1540–1542*. Fourteenth Annual Report, U.S. Bureau of Ethnology, Pt. 1. Washington, DC: Smithsonian Institution, 1896.

Wiseman, Regge N. "Early Spanish Colonial Occupation of Santa Fe: Excavations at the La Fonda Parking Lot Site (LA 54000)." In *Current Research on the Late Prehistory and Early History of New Mexico*, edited by Bradley J. Vierra and Clara Gualtieri, 207–14. Albuquerque: New Mexico Archaeological Council, 1992.

"Writ Concerning Diego Arias de Quiros at La Ciénega." In *Santa Fe Historic Plaza Study I, with Translations from Spanish Colonial Documents*, edited by Linda Tigges, 235–53. Santa Fe, NM: City Planning Department, 1991.

Wroth, William. "Barrio de Analco: Its Roots in Mexico and Role in Early Colonial Santa Fe, 1610–1780." In *All Trails Lead to Santa Fe: An Anthology Commemorating the 400th Anniversary of the Founding of Santa Fe, New Mexico in 1610*, 163–78. Santa Fe, NM: Sunstone Press, 2010.

Zárate Salmerón, Jerónimo de. *Relaciones: An Account of Things Seen and Learned by Father Jerónimo de Zárate Salmerón from the Year 1538 to Year 1626*. Translated by Alicia Ronstadt Milich. Albuquerque, NM: Horn and Wallace, 1966.

Index

Page numbers in italic text indicate tables and maps.

Abrego, Juan de, 112, *211*
Additional Colonists Who Remained in New Mexico after 1601, *193–95*
agriculture: implements, 17, 74; Puebloans, 17–18; San Gabriel, 73–74. *See also* cattle; chile; cotton; livestock; maize; wheat
Aguilar, Nicolás de, 47, 151–52, *182*
Aguilar Ynojosa, Pablo de, *188*
Albizu, Antonio de, 96, 127, 138–39, *174*, *212*
Albizu, Juana de, 139
Albizu, Tomás de, 138–39, *174*
Albuquerque, 12, 135, 137–39; Average Annual Precipitation, Albuquerque, New Mexico, 1602–80 and 1950–95, *9*; founding, 144; Precipitation, Albuquerque, New Mexico, 1602–80, *167–69*
alcaldes mayores, 33–34, *182–86*
Anaya Almazán, Cristóbal de, 24, 124, 131, 132, *174*, *199*, 246n30
Anaya Almazán, Francisco de ("el Mozo"), *199*
Anaya Almazán, Francisco de, I, 105, 124, 132, 153, *174*, *197*
Anaya Almazán, Francisco de, II, 105, 106, 118, 124, 127, *174*, *182*, *210*, *211*
Angulo, Pedro de, *192*
animal husbandry, 17–18

Antón, Juan, 133
Apache, 24; raids, 32, 33, 34, 74, 112, 149, 151, 156, 159–60, 163, 164
Araujo, Luis de, *188*
archaeological sites (Hispanic), 104, 106, 121, 130, 131, 133, 134, 136, 137, 148, 149, 153, 157
Archuleta, Ana de, 96
Archuleta, Asencio de, 54, 96, 115, 120, *174*, *191*, *192*, *195*
Archuleta, Gregoria de, 96, *174*
Archuleta, Juan de, I, 96, 111, 115
Archuleta, Juan de, II, 111, 115, *211*
Archuleta, María de, *197*
Archuleta, Melchor de, 110, 115, *211*
Arvide, Juana de, I, 102
Ávalos, Antonio de, 47, 153
Average Annual Precipitation, Albuquerque, New Mexico, 1602–80 and 1950–95, *9*
Average Seasonal Temperatures, Santa Fe, New Mexico, 1602–80 and 1950–95, *10*
Ávila, Pedro de, 116, 241n72
Ayardi, Diego de, 54, *194*
Ayeta, Francisco de, 61, 64

Baca, Ana, 105, *210*
Baca, Antonio, 95, 96, 104, 105, *197*
Baca, Cristóbal, I, 54, 95, 96, 105, 131, 136, *191*, *192*, *195*
Baca, Cristóbal, II, 136, *201*, *212*

268

INDEX

Baca, Gregoria, 96
Baca, Ignacio, *201*
Baca, Isabel, 153
Baca, José, *203*
Baca, Juana, 96
Baca, Manuel, 136, *203*
Baeza, Martínez de, 28
Balón, Francisco ("Pancho"), 98
Bañuelos, Dionisio de, *186*
Barba, Alonso (Martín). *See* Martín, Barba
Barba, Estevan, 111, 151, *199*
Barba, Juan, *203*
Bellido, Diego Rodríguez, 143, *197*
Beltrán, Bernadino, 3
Benavides, Alonso de, 7, 20, 39, 60, 85–86, 222n12
Bernal, Francisco, 112, 137
Bernal, Francisco, II, 137, *201*
Bernal, Isabel, 94, 119, 137
Bernal, Maria, *197*
Bernal, Pascuala, 137
Bernalillo. *See* Middle Rio Grande region
Bohórquez, Isabel de, 131
Bosque Grande de doña Luisa. *See* Middle Rio Grande region
Bosque Grande de San Francisco Xavier. *See* Middle Rio Grande region
Brondate, Joseph, *189*
Bustillo, Ana de, *197*
Bustillo, Beatris de, *197*

Cabeza de Vaca, Álvar Núñez, 3
cabildo: members, 33; San Gabriel, 58, 78, 222n11; Santa Fe, 20, 40, 59–60, 84–85, 89, 151, 157, 164
Cadimo, Francisco, *193*, *195*
Camacho, Juan, *188*
Camino Real, 5, 27, 28, 140; linking New Spain, 132; means to, 141
La Cañada, 28, 35–36, 78, 137, 151, 158; colonists, 109–21; refugees, 118; settlers, 23; survey, 28, 158. *See also* Santa Cruz River valley
Candelaria, Blas de la, 146

Carvajal, Agustín de, 132, *199*
Carvajal, Ambrosio de, 126, *201*
Carvajal, Antonio de, 126, *201*
Carvajal, Estevan de, *186*
Carvajal, Felis de, 139, 140, 160, *174*, 212
Carvajal, Gerónimo de, 125–26, *174*, *182*
Carvajal, Juan de Vitoria, 97, 126, 140, 145, *190*, *193*, *195*
Carvajal, Luis de, *203*
Carvajal, Melchora de, 145
Carvajal, Nicolás de, 141, *203*
Casas, Bernabé de las, 53, 56
casas reales, 81–85, 88–92
Casaus, Roque de, 143
Castañeda, Juan de, *186*, *188*
Castaño de Sosa, Gaspar, 4, 6, 213n6
Castillo, Alonso, *186*
Castillo, Diego del, *186*
cattle, 7, 24, 40, 90, 104, 162
ceramics, 17; Española basin, 120–21; Estancia basin, 153; Middle Rio Grande, 148–49; Salinas Redware, 148–49; Santa Fe River valley, 103–4, 106; Santo Domingo basin, 131, 134
César, Gregorio, 56, *190*
Chamiso, Juan, 98
Chamuscado, Francisco Sánchez, 3, 46
Chávez, Alonso de, *192*
Chávez, Angélico, 55, 64–65
chile, 11, 74
Christianity, 3, 19, 56; Puebloans and, 98, 161
La Cienega Pueblo, 80, 104, 105, 106–7, 163, 238n64
Cisneros, Diego, 156
Cisneros, Vincente de, 156–57, 159–60
clans, 22, 117, 124, 146, 156, 159. *See also* families
climate: Average Annual Precipitation, Albuquerque, New Mexico, 1602–80 and 1950–95, 9; Average Seasonal Temperatures, Santa Fe, New Mexico 1602–80 and 1950–95, *10*; drought, 8–9, 33, 73, 164, *165–66*; New Mexico, 7–9, 9, *10*, *11*, *165–66*; New Spain, 8; Number of Frost-Free

Days, Selected Sites in New Mexico, 11; Palmer Drought Severity Index 1598–1680, 8–9, *165–66*; Precipitation, Albuquerque, New Mexico, 1602–80, *167–69*; Precipitation, Southern Rio Grande Basin, 1600–1680, *170*; Santa Fe, 76; Temperature, Santa Fe, New Mexico, 1602–80, *171*
Coalition Period, 75
cobble footings, 148
colonists: Additional Colonists Who Remained in New Mexico after 1601, *193–95*; La Cañada, 109–21; Known Spanish Men Descended from Original New Mexico Colonists, *201–4*; New Spain, 5; Oñate, 7–8, 10, 17, 51–52, 54, 57–58, 64, 73, 223n14; signing loyalty petition, *192*; Spanish Men in New Mexico before 1601, *186*. See also Spanish colonial institutions; specific colonists
Colonists Who Signed the October 2, 1601, Loyalty Petition, *192*
Comanche Springs, 45, 148–49
Conde de Herrera, Antonio, 56, *191*
copper, 44, 148
Coronado, Francisco Vazquez de, 6, 42
Coronado State Monument, 136
Coronda, Joseph de, *187*
Correa, Rodrigo, *187, 192*
Cortés, Juan, *187*
cotton, 17, 18, 31, 162
cottonwood groves, 12–13, 140
Cruz, Juan de la (Durán), 101, *195*
Cruz, Juan de la, I ("el Catalán"), 110, 115, 116, 120, *174, 193, 195*
Cruz, Nicolás de la, 115, *211*
Cruz, Pedro de la, 116, *174, 211*
Cubero Rodríguez, 116, 241n72
Cuéllar, Pedro de, 131–32, *199*

del Moral Granillo, María, 159
del Río, Alonso, 94, 112, 114, 116, 119, *211*
del Río, Diego, 112
del Río, Juan, 94
Descalso, Juan, 44

desertions, 53–56, 60, 73, 223n15
Días Díez de Castro, Diego, *192*
Díaz, Juan, *186*
Diaz de Betranzos, Luisa, 158
Domínguez, Francisco Atanasio, 79
Domínguez, Juana, 96
Domínguez, Tomé, 24–25, 132, 137, 212
Domínguez de Mendoza, Damiana, 132
Domínguez de Mendoza, Francisco, 132, 137, *174*
Domínguez de Mendoza, José, 96–97
Domínguez de Mendoza, Juan, 132, 138, 141, 142, 153, *174*, 212
Domínguez de Mendoza, Leonor, 132
Domínguez de Mendoza, Tomé, I, 96, 145, 147, 212
Domínguez de Mendoza, Tomé, II, 145, 146–47, 149, 155, *182*
Donís, Francisco, 56
drought, 8–9, 33, 73, 164, *165–66*
Durán, Ayudante Nicolás, 101
Durán, Diego, 95
Durán, Juan, 95–96, *197*
Durán, Juan, II, *201*
Durán, Luis, 96, *203*
Durán, Nicolás ("el Mozo"), 101–2, *210*
Durán, Nicolás, Adjutant, 101
Durán, Salvador, *201*
Durán de Miranda, Juan, 101
Durán y Chávez, Cristóbal, 120, 142, *176*
Durán y Chávez, Cristóbal, II, *203*
Durán y Chávez, Fernándo, I, 34, 142, *176, 182*
Durán y Chávez, Fernándo, II, 131, 142, *201*
Durán y Chávez, Fernando, Sargeant Major, 123
Durán y Chávez, Isabel, 142
Durán y Chávez, José, *201*
Durán y Chávez, Juan, *203*
Durán y Chávez, Pedro I, 77, 131, 142, *176, 193, 195*
Durán y Chávez, Pedro, II, 142, *197, 201*, 212
Durán y Chávez, Tomás, *203*

encomienda, 162; clans rising from, 22; first granting, 20; Known New Mexico Ecomenderos, 1610–80, *174–81*; number in New Mexico, 21; in Santa Fe, 59, 86, 133; as Spanish colonial institution, 19–22; tribute paid to, 19, 22, 28. *See also specific encomenderos*
Enríquez, Cristóbal, 126
epidemics, 33, 60, 164
Escalante, Felipe de, *188*
Escarramad, Juan de, *176, 193, 195, 197*
Escobar, Francisco de, 57
escuderos, 102, 120, 124, 153, 217n19; duties, 21
Española basin: agriculture, 114; archaeological site (Hispanic), 121, 243n17; attraction to, 108; ceramics, 120–21; families, 121; Granillo survey, 109–21; Known Spanish Landholdings: Española Basin, 1680, *211*; plains, 115; settlers, 109–21; Tano occupation, 109, 240n46. *See also* La Cañada
Espejo, Antonio de, 3, 12, 46
Espinosa, Marcelo de, *189*
Esquibel, Jose Antonio, 55
Estancia basin, 150–54, 162, 164; archaeological site (Hispanic), 153, 253n28
estancias, 25–26, 27–28, 40, 110, 162
Esteros de Mexíca. *See* Middle Rio Grande region
Eulate, Juan de, 85, 89

Fagoaga, Juan Estevan de, 137, *212*
families, 53, 55–56, 65, 223n14; alliances, 164; Española basin, 121; Far North region, 122; Known Spanish Families in New Mexico in the Early Post-1601 Years, *195–96*; land, 164; New Spain, 161; Oñate, 53, 55–56; Puebloans, 164; Spanish Men Who Brought Families to New Mexico before 1601, *190–91*
Farfán de los Godos, Marcos, *189*
Far North region, 122–25

Fernández, Juan, *192*
Fernández de Tapia, Juan, *194*
Figueroa, Gregorio de, *191*
Figueroa, Lucas de, *197*
Fonte, Cristóbal, 129–30, *182*
food: missions, 39, 41; as pay for labor, 30, 45; production, 73, 79; Puebloans, 17–18, 56, 73; San Gabriel, 73
Franciscans, 36, 130, 161, 221n19
Francisco, Manuel, *193*
Fresqui, Francisco, 148
Fresqui, Juan, II, 148, *182*
Fresqui, Maria Ortiz, 148
Fresqui (Fresco), Juan, 44, 148, 149, *197*
frieze, 41

Galisteo basin, 125–28
Gamboa, Lucas, *199*
García, Alonso, 62, 139, *182, 212*
García, Diego, *197*
García, Lázaro, *194, 195*
García, Marcos, *193*
García de Noriega, Lázaro, 139, 147, *199*
García (Holgado), Francisco, 74, 126, 147, *190*
García Holgado, Álvaro, 126, 127, 147, *192*, 195, *197*
García Holgado, Catalina, 126
García Holgado, Diego, 147–48, *203*
García Holgado, Juan, 147, 160, *182, 186*
Gasco de Velasco, Luis, 56, *190*
Gil, Juan, *194*
Goitia Joseph de, *199*
Gómez, Elena, *176*
Gómez, Francisco, 31, 46, 57, 77, 95, 97, 110, 119, 122, 142, 153, 156, *176, 197, 212*; death of, 156
Gómez, Juan, 127
Gómez de Luna, Juan, 127, *176, 197*
Gómez de Montesinos, Alonso, *190, 192, 195*
Gómez de Torres, Francisco, 120
Gómez Durán, Pedro, *193*
Gómez Robledo, Andrés, 153, *199*
Gómez Robledo, Francisca, 123

Gómez Robledo, Francisco, 31, 88, 94, 95, 97, 110, 117, 119, 122, 123, 128, 143, 146, 159, *211*; inheritance, 156
González, Domingo, 94, 97, 115, *194*, *197*
González, Juan, *188*, *193*
González, Maria, 112, 116
González, Sebastián, Adjutant, 109, 115–16, 203, 211
González, Sebastián, I, 94, 115–16, 119, 127, 137, *176*, *197*, *212*
González (Bernal/Bas), Sebastián, II, 119, *201*
González Bas, Antonia, 94
González Bas, Juan, 137, *176*
González Bernal, Diego, 127, 153, *182*
González Bernal, Juan, 153, *176*
González de Apodaca, Diego, 152
González Lobón, Domingo, *201*
González Lobón, Juan, 94, 97, 101
Gordejuela Ybarguen, Juan de, 51
governance, as Spanish colonial institution, 33–35
Granillo, Luis (Pérez), 109–21, 158
grasslands, 13, 23, 162
Griego, Agustín, *201*
Griego, Bartolomé, *199*
Griego, Blas, 115, *201*
Griego, Graciana, 25, 116
Griego, Juan, I, 77, 94, 95, 111, 115, 120, 137, 139, *190*, *193*, *195*, *212*
Griego, Juan, II, 25, 109, 110, 112, 115, 137, *176*, *211*
growing season, 10
Guadalajara Diego de, 30, 157, *176*, *197*
Guadarrama, Joseph de, *199*
Guerra, Juan, *186*
Guijosa, Francisco Antonio de, 123
Gulf of California, 52, 55, 57, 76–77, 228n12
Gutiérrez, Alonso, *198*
Gutiérrez, Maria, 103
Gutiérrez, Roque, 103
Gutiérrez Bocanegra, Juan, *191*, *193*, *195*
Gutiérrez de Figueroa, Antonio, 103, *210*

haciendas, 27–28, 110, 132, 162
Harrington, John, 240n46
Heberling, Natalie, *205*, *206*, *210*, *211*, *212*
Heras, Marcos de las, 124, *182*, 244n24
Heredia, Alonso Pacheco y, 21
Hermita de San Miguel, 36, 232n98
Hernández, Gerónimo, *186*
Hernández, Gonzalo, *192*, *195*
Hernández, Pedro, *186*
Hernández Cordero, Francisco, *190*
Hernández de Benhumea, Gonzalo, *191*, *194*
Hernández Gonzalo, Caudillo, *190*
Hernández Guillén, Francisco, *190*
Herrera, Antonio de, *203*
Herrera, Cristóbal de, *199*
Herrera, Domingo de, 114, 123
Herrera, Juan de, I, 110, 111, 114, 120, *176*, *193*, *195*, *198*, *211*
Herrera, Juan de, II, *203*
Herrera, Marcos de, 114, 116, 120, 123, *211*
Herrera, Matías de, 120
Herrera Corrales, Sebastián de, 119, 120, *199*, *211*
Herrera Horta, Ginés de, *189*
hidalgo, 19
Hinojos, Diego de, 102, *204*
Hinojos, Hernando de, 102, 104–5, *176*, *193*, *195*, *210*
Hinojos, Hernando de, II, 107, *201*
Hinojos, Miguel de, 102, 105, 134, 153, *176*, *182*, *210*
Holguín, Cristóbal (López), 145, *202*, *212*
Holguín, Isabel (López), 140, 145
Holguín, Salvador (López), 145, *202*
Huerta, Toribio de la, 45, 153, *178*
Hurtado, Andrés, I, 59, 133, *178*

Inquisition, 21, 109, 124, 159
iron, 40, 45, 148, 149
irrigation, 11, 13, 17, 23, 27, 28, 29, 73
Isleta jurisdiction, Middle Rio Grande region, 144–49

INDEX

Jiménez, Francisco, 118, *211*
Jorge, Antonio, *201*
Jorge, Juan, 139, *193*
Jorge, Manuel, 97–98
Jorge de Vera, Antonio, 105, 139, *212*
Jorge de Vera, Isabel, 95–96
Jurado, Joseph, 98
jurisdictions, Known New Mexico Alcaldes Mayores, 1610–80, *182–85*

Keresan pueblos, 15–16
Keres people, 14, 15, 16
kivas, 16
Known New Mexico Alcaldes Mayores, 1610–80, *182–85*
Known New Mexico Ecomenderos, 1610–80, *174–81*
Known Spanish Landholdings: Española Basin, 1680, *211*
Known Seventeenth-Century Spanish Landholdings: Middle Rio Grande Region, *212*
Known Seventeenth-Century Spanish Landholdings: Santa Fe River Valley, *210*
Known Spanish Families in New Mexico in the Early Post-1601 Years, *195–96*
Known Spanish Men Descended from Original New Mexico Colonists, *201–4*
Known Vecinos of Santa Fe, 1610–32, *197–98*

labor: children, 32; drafts, 28–29, 33; encomenderos and, 31; food and, 29, 30, 45; mining, 45; payment, 28, 29–30; Puebloans, 18, 28, 29, 30, 32, 40, 41, 80, 162; repartimiento system, 28, 29, 30, 80; size of labor force, 32–33; as Spanish colonial institutions, 28–33; tribute, 28, 80; women, 30
Lafora, Nicolás de, 12
land: buffer zones, 24; Crown regulation, 23–24, 25; family, 164; grants (*mercedes de tierras*), xiii, 22–23;

Known Spanish Landholdings: Española Basin, 1680, *211*; Known Seventeenth-Century Spanish Landholdings: Middle Rio Grande Region, *212*; Known Seventeenth-Century Spanish Landholdings: Santa Fe River Valley, *210*; to Puebloans, 23–24; pueblos, 27; as Spanish colonial institution, 22–28; Spanish Landholdings in New Mexico, 1610–80, *206*
Landin, Diego, *188*
languages, 14–15, *15*, 109, 113
lead, 42, 43–44
Ledesma, Bartolomé de, 151
Ledesma, Francisco de, 151, *193*, *195*
Leon, Pedro Ponce de, 4
Leyva, Juan de, 127, 152, *199*
Leyva, Nicolás de, 127, 152, *199*
Leyva, Pedro de, 126–27, 151–52, *182*, *199*
Little Ice Age, 7
livestock, 13, 24, 40, 90, 159, 162
López, Felipe, *199*
López, Juan, *186*
López, Luis, 158–59, *182*
López, Nicolás, *199*
López, Pedro, 141
López (del Castillo), Pedro, 141, *212*
López de Aragón, Francisco, 21, 105
López de Áviles, Cristóbal, *194*
López de Gracia, Andrés, 25, 34, 144, 146, 152, *182*, *212*
López de Gracia, Isabel, 145
López de Gracia, José, 153
López de Gracia, Maria, 145
López de Gracia, Sebastiana, 152
López del Castillo, Diego, 94, 141, *178*
López del Castillo, Isabel, 113
López del Castillo, Matías, 141, *198*
López del Ocanto, Domingo, 120, *201*
López del Ocanto, Juan, 120, *178*, *193*, *195*
López de Mendizábal, Bernardo, 21, 24, 30, 31, 47, 59, 60; as governor, 117, 133, 135, 139, 142, 151–52, 157, 159; Santa Fe palace renovation, 88–90, 98

López Holguín (Olguìn), Juan, I, 77, 145, 192, *198*
López Medel, Juan, 145, *204*
López Mederos, Catalina, 147
López Mederos, Juan, 145, 147, *194*, *212*
López Mederos, Pedro, 145, *204*
López Millán, Maria, 146
López Olguín, Juan, II, *202*, *204*
López Palomino, Francisco, *178*
López Paredes, Francisco, *195*
López Sambrano, Andrés, 103, 117, 134, *182*, *210*
López Sambrano, Diego, 116–17, *211*
López Villasaña, Juan, *191*
Lorenzo, Rodrigo, 44, 98
loyalty petition, 54, 57, 110, 118, *192*
Lucas, Alonso, *186*, *191*
Lucero de Godoy, Antonio, *199*
Lucero de Godoy, Diego, 122–23, *199*
Lucero de Godoy, Francisco, 103, *210*
Lucero de Godoy, Juan, 76, 94, 97, 101, *210*
Lucero de Godoy, Pedro, 101, 118, 122–23, *178*, *187*, *192*, *198*
Luis, Juan, 113, 114, *211*
Luján, Agustín, *202*
Luján, Antonio, *202*
Luján, Diego, *204*
Luján, Domingo, 96–97, *202*
Luján, Francisco, 129, 130, *182*
Luján, Juan, II, 114, 122, *182*
Luján, Juan Luis, 97, 113, 114
Luján, Matías, 109, 114, *202*
Luján, Miguel, 114, *204*, *211*
Luján, Pedro, 97
Luján (Luxán), Juan, I, 23, 34, 96, 108, 113, 114, 129, *192*, *195*
Luna, Diego de, 127, 143

Madrid, Francisco de, 44, 57, 77, 96, 102, *198*
Madrid, Francisco de, II, 11, 102
Madrid, Lorenzo de, 95–96, *178*
Madrid, Roque de, 44, 101, 102, *210*
Maese, Juan, 101
Maese, Luis, 101, *210*
maize, 10, 11, 14, 28; as tribute, 17, 20

Mallea, Juan de, *187*, *194*
Manso de Contreras, Juan, 151, 159
Manzanares, Mateo, 126, 131, 146, *212*
Márquez, Antonio, *202*
Márquez, Bernabé, 125, *202*
Márquez, Cristóbal, *178*
Márquez, Diego, 118–19, 125–26, 157, *204*
Márquez, Francisco, 157, *186*, *204*
Márquez, Gerónimo, 54, 58, 118, 119, 125, 157, *190*, *192*, *195*
Márquez, Pedro, I, 119, *198*, *202*
Márquez, Pedro, II, 118, *202*, *211*
Martín, Luis (a.k.a. Luis Martín Serrano II), 113
Martín (Serrano), Apolinar, *202*
Martín Barba, Alonso, I, 110, 151, *187*, *192*, *195*, *211*
Martín Barba, Alonso, II, 110–11, 151
Martín Barba, Diego, 111
Martín Barba, Domingo, 151, *202*
Martínez, Antonio, 123
Martínez de Baeza, Francisco, 26, 28, 60
Martínez de Montoya, Juan, 20, 43, 45, 46, 58, 77, 78, *178*, *194*; prominence, 222n11; Santa Fe plaza creation, 81–82, 84
Martín Gómez, Hernán, *192*
Martín Monuera, María, 151
Martín Serrano, Antonio, *204*
Martín Serrano, Cristóbal, *204*
Martín Serrano, Domingo, 111, *202*, *211*
Martín Serrano, Hernán, I, 77, 113, 120, 121, 151, *178*, *190*, *192*
Martín Serrano, Hernán, II, 97, 113, 150–51, 152, *202*
Martín Serrano, Juan, 151
Martín Serrano, Luis (the younger), *202*
Martín Serrano, Luis, I, 113, *184*
Martín Serrano, Luis, II, 111, 113, *202*, *211*
Martín Serrano, Pedro, 113, *204*
Martín Serrano, Sebastián, 121
Martín Serrano de Salazar, Pedro, 121
Medel, Juan. *See* López Medel, Juan
Medina, Juan de, *192*
Mejía, Antonio, 140
Mexía, 140, *212*

Middle Rio Grande region, 164;
archaeological sites (Hispanic), 136,
137, 148, 149, 248n22; Atrisco valley,
138, 139, 141, 248n23; Bernalillo, 135–
37; Bosque Grande de doña Luisa, 12,
140; Bosque Grande de San Francisco
Xavier, 12, 140; ceramics, 148–49;
Comanche Springs, 148–49; Esteros
de Mexía, 12, 140; Isleta jurisdiction,
144–49; Known Seventeenth-Century
Spanish Landholdings: Middle Rio
Grande Region, 212; overview, 135;
Sandia jurisdiction, 135–43; La Villa
de Cerralvo, 143–44
mining, 148, 163; administration, 45;
copper, 44; equipment, 42, 44; iron,
40, 45, 148, 149; labor, 45; landscape,
42–47; lead, 42, 43–44; New Spain, 32,
39, 42, 47; Real de San Buenaventura,
43, 45, 222n12; salt, 13, 18, 45–47, 153,
156; silver, 42–43; turquoise, 42
Miranda, Blas de, 124
missionaries, 3, 36, 53
missions, 222n12; church-convents,
39, 163; farming and ranching on,
40–41; food, 39; foundation, 38–39;
landscape of, 36–41; Puebloan labor
on, 40–41; Seventeenth-Century New
Mexico Missions, 37–38; supply train,
39, 40, 164, 221n19; support of, 39–40
Mondragón, Juan Alonso, 160, 178
Montaño, Isidro Xuáres, 112
Montaño, Sebastián, 112, 153, 211
Montoya, Antonio de, 202
Montoya, Bartolomé de, I, 116, 136, 191,
194, 195
Montoya, Bartolomé de, II, 116–17, 136,
202, 211
Montoya, Diego de, I, 139–40, 178
Montoya, Diego de, II, 136, 202, 212
Montoya, Felipe de, 202
Montoya, Francisco de, 202
Montoya, Juan de, 204
Montoya, Luisa de, 139
Montoya, Pedro de, 120, 178
Monuera, Isabel de, 151

Monzón, Baltasar de, 191, 192
Moqui (Hopi), 18
Moraga, Alonso de, 112, 211
Moraga, Ana de, 94
Moraga, Diego de, 94, 98, 112, 198
Moraga, Juan de, 94, 95, 98, 112, 211
Moral. *See* del Moral Granillo, María
Moran, Gerónimo, 101, 210
Morán, Juan, 101, 190, 193, 195
Morán, Matías, 98, 101
Morán, Miguel, 98
muster rolls, 51–53, 58, 62–64, 225n24;
passing, 102, 116, 120, 139, 141

Naranjo, Alonso, 134
Naranjo, Bartolomé, 133–34, 247n50
Naranjo, Francisco, 118, 133–34
Naranjo, Juan, 133–34
Navajo, 24, 74
New Mexico: Additional Colonists Who
Remained in New Mexico after 1680,
193–94; climate, 7–9, 9, 10, 11, 165–73;
as Crown colony, 23, 161; economy,
98–99; Known New Mexico Alcaldes
Mayores, 1610–80, 182–85; Known
New Mexico Ecomenderos, 1610–80,
174–81; Known Spanish Families
in New Mexico in the Early Post-
1601 Years, 195–96; Known Spanish
Men Descended from Original New
Mexico Colonists, 201–4; native
born, 65; population, 61–64, 225n20;
saltpans, 13, 18, 156; Seventeenth-
Century New Mexico, Pueblos, 205;
Seventeenth-Century New Mexico
Missions, 37–38; Spanish entry,
3–6; Spanish Landholdings in New
Mexico, 1610–80, 206; Spanish Men
in New Mexico before 1601, 186–89;
Spanish Men Who Brought Families
to New Mexico before 1601, 190–91
New Spain: authority, 23, 161; Camino
Real linking, 132, 140, 141, 156;
exports to, 39, 46, 47, 98; families, 53,
55, 190; imports from, 39, 40, 45
Nieto, Cristóbal, 102, 103, 210

Nieto, José (Joseph), 102, 126–27, 152, *184*, *199*
Nieves, Francisco de las, *186*
Niza, Marcos de, 3
Number of Frost-Free Days, Selected Sites in New Mexico, *11*
Number of New Mexico Pueblos by District and Language, *15*
Núñez de Chávez, Diego, *188*, *191*
Núñez Ynojosa, Alonso, *194*

Oñate, Cristóbal de, 20
Oñate, Juan de: captains of, 20, 23, 52, 56, 72, 223n5; colonists, 7–8, 10, 17, 52, 54, 55, 57–58, 64, 73, 223n14; contract to crown, 4, 22–23; desertions from, 53–56, 60, 73; districts created by, 34; expeditions, 3–6, 14, 51–52, 55, 57, 77, 161; families, 53, 55–56; governorship, 29, 36, 69; loyalty petition, 54, 57, *192*; mining, 42; and Quivira, 52–56; resignation, 56, 58, 78, 161; trial, 58
Ordóñez, Isidro, 85
Ortega, Francisco de, 139, 140, *212*
Ortega, Juan de, *189*
Ortega, Pablo de, 139
Ortega, Tiburcio de, 139
Ortiz, Ana, 96, *198*
Otermín, Antonio de, 26, 29, 61–65, 81, 84, 106, 138; as governor, 144, 157; on Santa Fe palace renovation, 89–90

Pacheco, Alonso, 112
Pacheco, Gerónimo, 102, 103, *210*
Pacheco, Juan, 102, 103
Pacheco, Luis, *198*
Pacheco, Petrona, 103
Pacheco de Heredia, Alonso, 21, 22, 34
Palmer Drought Severity Index (PDSI), 8–9, *165–66*
Paredes, Álvaro de, 132, 246n27
Paz, Simón de la, *187*
PDSI. *See* Palmer Drought Severity Index
Pecos jurisdiction, 128
Peinado, Alonso de, 86–87

Peñalosa, Diego de, 144
Peralta, Andrés de, 134, *178*, *184*, *199*
Peralta, Pedro de: establishing capital, 76–79; excommunication, 85; as governor, 21, 23, 26, 29, 36, 44, 58, 95, 229n23; imprisonment, 136; Santa Fe plaza layout, 81–83, 91–93
Perea, Esteban de, 30
Perea, Juan de, 142, *212*
Pereira, Marcos, *187*, *189*, *190*
Pérez, Gaspar, 97–98, 120, 134, *198*
Pérez de Bustillo, Ana, 96
Pérez de Bustillo, Beatriz, 104
Pérez de Bustillo, Catalina, 104, 110, 119
Pérez de Bustillo, Gerónima, 105
Pérez de Bustillo, Juan, 77, 96, 104, 105, *190*, *192*, *195*
Pérez de Bustillo, Simón, 104, 106, 119, *192*, *210*
Pérez de Bustillo, Yumar, 104
Pérez de Donís, Juan, 56, *188*
Pérez de Villagrá, Gaspar, 52, 53, 56, 71, 97
Pérez Granillo, Alonso, 158, *184*
Pérez Granillo, Diego, 34, *184*
Pérez Granillo, Francisco, I, 158, *198*
Pérez Granillo, Francisco, II, 158, *184*
Pérez Granillo, Luis, 158, *184*
Pérez Romero, Diego, 120, 128, 134
Piñeiro, Juan Alférez, *189*
piñon, 13, 98, 139; transporting, 30–31, 156
Piro people, 14, 15, 16, 18, 62
Pojoaque massacre, 118–19
population: changing racial composition, 60–62, 225n24; decline, 61; dominant and subordinate, 164; New Mexico, 61–64, 225n20; Puebloans, 14, 25, 32–33, 220n97; Santa Fe, 59, 60, 61, 85–86, 88. *See also* colonists
Portugués, Manuel, *187*, *188*
Posada, Alonso de, 60–61, 76
Prada, Juan de, 60
Precipitation, Albuquerque, New Mexico, 1602–80, *167–69*
Precipitation, Southern Rio Grande Basin, New Mexico, 1600–1680, *170–73*

Puebloans, 3, 8; agriculture, 17–18; animal husbandry, 17–18; ceramic ware, 17; Christianizing, 98, 161; clothing, 16–17; epidemics, 32, 60, 164; families, 164; food, 11, 18, 56, 73; labor, 18, 28, 29, 30, 32, 40–41, 80, 162; land to, 23–24; maize and, 17, 20; at missions, 40; piñon and, 13; population, 14, 25, 32–33, 220n97; revolt, 61–62; society, 161; tribute, 19, 22, 28; wool, 18, 162. *See also* Keresan, Tano, Tiwa, and Tewa peoples
pueblos, 3, 5, 216n11; land, 27; languages, 14–15, *15*; number, *15*; Santa Fe, 75, 80; Seventeenth-Century New Mexico Pueblos, *205*; structure, 16

Quesada, Alonso de, 56, *191*
Quintana, Luis de, 120, *184*

Ramírez, Martin, *189*
Ramírez de Salazar, Alonso, 145, *212*
Ramírez de Salazar, Francisco, 25, 145
Ramírez de Salazar, Juan, 34, 136, *184*, *212*
Ramos, Marcos, *199*
ranchos, 27; Santa Fe, 79
Rangel, Juan, 126
Rascón, Francisco, *193*
refugees, 62–63, 118
repartimiento system, 28, 29, 30, 80
Río, Alonso. *See* del Río, Alonso
Rio Abajo/Rio Arriba, 34, 62, 143, 220n12
Rio Chiquito, 81–82, 95–96
Rio Grande, 5, 162; cottonwood groves, 12–13; flooding, 11–12; freezing over, 7; shifting course, 135, 138, 247n3; source and flow, 11–12; yazoos, 12. *See also* Middle Rio Grande region; Southern Rio Grande region
Rivera, Pedro de, *189*
Riveros, Martin de, *187*
Robledo, Ana, 97, 110
Robledo, Diego, *193*, *195*
Robledo, Francisca, 124, 146
Robledo, Francisco, *194*
Robledo, Luisa, *198*

Robledo, Pedro, I, 124, *188*, *190*, 244n22
Robledo, Pedro, II, *189*
Rodríguez, Agustín, 3
Rodríguez, Matías, *188*
Rodríguez, Pedro, *194*
Rodríguez, Sebastián, *189*
Rodríguez Bellido, Juan, 77, 143, *194*, *198*
Rodríguez Cisneros Alonso, 102, 153–54, *178*
Rodríguez de Anaya, Ana, 132
Rodríguez de Salazar, Sebastián, 158
Rodríguez Moreno, Juan, *188*
Romero, Agustín, I, 158
Romero, Agustín, II, 117, *211*
Romero, Bartolomé, I, 117–18, 124, 156, *190*, *192*
Romero, Bartolomé, II, 156, 158, 159, *198*
Romero, Bartolomé, III, 123–24, 158, *178*
Romero, Catalina, 159
Romero, Diego Pérez, 134, *180*
Romero, Felipe, 157, 159–60
Romero, Juan, *204*
Romero, Matías, 117, *198*
Romero, Pedro, *184*, 200
Romero, Salvador, *204*
Romero, Sebastián, *204*
Romero de Pedraza, Bartolomé, 117–18, *202*, *211*
Romero de Pedraza, Felipe, 118, 156, 158, 159, *202*
Romero de Pedraza, Francisco, 134, *180*, *184*, *202*
Romero de Pedraza, Pedro, 117–18, *211*
Romero de Salazar, Sebastiana, 158
Rosas, Luis de, 21, 25, 34, 60, 157; murder of, 96, 105, 111, 115, 119, 125–26, 136, 152
Rua, Gerónimo Moreno de la, *191*
Ruiz, Andrew, 209
Ruiz de Cabrera, Juan, *187*
Ruiz de Cáceres, Elena, 114
Ruiz de Cáceres, Juan, I, 102, 113, 147, *193*, *195*, 210
Ruiz de Cáceres, Juan Sargeant, 109, 113–14, 116, 147
Ruiz Fernández, Juan, *191*

sackcloth, 41
Sáez, Ambrosio, 111, 117, 132, *211*
Salado de Rivadeneira, Lorenzo, *189*
Salas, Antonio de, 24, 118, *180*, *211*
Salas, Juan de, 118, *187*, *192*
Salas, Petronila de, 118
Salazar, Isabel de, 158
Salazar, Juan de Frías, 5, 51, *186*
Salinas Redware, 148–49
salt: demand, 47; grading of, 47; lakes, 46; mining, 45–47, 153; pans, 13, 18, 156; transporting, 30, 31, 46
Sánchez, Alonso, 56, *190*
Sánchez, Francisco, 3, *191*
Sánchez de Monroy, Pedro, *190*, *193*, *195*
Sandia jurisdiction, Middle Rio Grande region, 135–43
Sandoval y Manzanares, Ana de, 131, 146
San Gabriel, 163; agriculture, 74; background, 69–70; cabildo, 58, 78, 222n11; capital moved to Santa Fe, 75, 78; food in, 73; modification of Yunque Owingeh, 72; Navajo attacks, 74; San Juan renamed, 70–71; Spanish capital, 71–72; as villa, 74; withering of, 74; Zaldivar's Route to the Easter Plains from San Gabriel, *207*
San Juan, 70–71, 227n17
San Juan de los Caballeros, 71, 226n13
San Martín, Pedro de, *191*
Santa Cruz, Diego de, 96, 143, *193*, *196*, *198*
Santa Cruz River valley, 78, 108, 112, 121
Santa Fe, 161–62, 228n12; Average Seasonal Temperatures, Santa Fe, New Mexico, 1602–80 and 1950–95, *10*; Bario de Analco, 78, 85, 98, 231n73; blacksmiths/armorer, 97–98; businesses, 97–98; cabildo, 20, 40, 59–60, 84–85, 89, 151, 157, 164; capital moved from San Gabriel, 74, 75, 78; casas reales, 83–84, 87–92; church, 84–87; climate, *11*, 76, 165–66; Coalition Period, 75; defenses, 84, 89–91, 233n111; deterioration, 85–87; encomienda in, 59, 86, 133; establishment, 78–79; founders, 77–78; founding, 76–77, 228n12, 228n13; hospital, 87; Known Vecinos of Santa Fe, 1610–32, *197–98*; land, 95–97; location advantages, 75; naming, 77; natural setting, 75–76; Otermín in, 89–90; palace, 88–89, 98, 230n55, 231n69, 232n103, 232n104; Placenames and Seventeenth-Century Hydrologic Features, *209*; plaza, 81–83; population, 59, 60, 61, 85–86, 88; prehispanic sites, 75, 80, 97, 235n157; pueblos, 75; ranchos, 79; residences, 94–97; roads, 93–94, 236n6; San Miguel chapel, 86–87, 232n97, 232n98; settlement pattern, 79; streets, 91–93, 233n18; Temperature, Santa Fe, New Mexico, 1602–80, *171*; urban component, 80–81; urban renewal, 87–88; Urrutia map, 82, 83, 91, 93, *208*, 229n31; Vargas in, 91; vecinos, 61, 97, *197–98*; villa organization, 79; water resources, 76, 80–81, 91, 228n5
Santa Fe River valley, 100–107; Agua Fria section, 100, 102–3; archaeological sites (Hispanic), 103, 104, 106, 237n34, 237n35, 238n62; attraction to, 100; ceramics, 103–4, 237n34, 237n39, 237n43, 238n62; La Cienega Pueblo, 80, 104, 105, 106–7, 163, 238n64; La Cienega section, 100, 104–5; Known Seventeenth-Century Spanish Landholdings, *210*; springs, 100, 102
Santillán, Bernabé de, *188*
Santo Domingo basin, 129–34; archaeological sites (Hispanic), 130, 131, 133, 134, 247n45, 247n50, 247n51, 247n52
Sedillo, Pedro de, 145
Segura, Hernándo de, *189*
Serna, Cristóbal de la, 123, 124
Serna, Diego de la, 34, *184*
settlement pattern, 26–27
settlers killed, 226n29; Spanish Settlers Reported Killed in the 1680 Revolt, *199–200*

Seventeenth-Century New Mexico
  Missions, *37–38*
Seventeenth-Century New Mexico
  Pueblos, *205*
silver, 42–43, 148
slavery, 28, 30; indigenous slaves as
  servants, 31–32; outlawed, 28
Sosa Albornoz, Alonso de, *188*, *190*
Sosa Peñalosa, Francisco de, 56, *190*
Sotelo, Phelipe, 89
Sotelo Cisneros, Juan de, 51
Southern Rio Grande region, 155–60,
  164; Precipitation, Southern Rio
  Grande Basin, New Mexico, 1600–
  1680, *170*
Spanish colonial institutions:
  encomienda, 19–22, 59; governance,
  33–35; labor as, 28–33; land as, 22–28
Spanish Landholdings in New Mexico,
  1610–80, *206*
Spanish Men in New Mexico before
  1601, *186–89*
Spanish Men Who Brought Families to
  New Mexico before 1601, *190–91*
Spanish Settlers Reported Killed in the
  1680 Revolt, *199–200*
springs, 132, 133; Comanche Springs,
  148–49; Santa Fe River valley, 100,
  102; Santo Domingo basin, 131, 134
Suárez de Figueroa, Isidro, 54, *194*
Sumaya, Jorge de, *186*
supply train, 39, 40, 164, 221n19
surveys: La Cañada, 28, 158; Española
  basin, 109–21. *See also* muster rolls

Tamarón y Romeral, Pedro, 76, 79
Tano people, 14, 15, 16, 109, 126, 240n46
Tapia, Cristóbal de, 145–46, *203*, *212*
Tapia, Juan de, 124
Tapia, Juan Fernández de, 124, 145–46, *180*
Tapia, María de, 103, *210*
Telles Jirón, José, 103, 134, 159–60, *180*, *210*
Tewa people, 6, 16, 24, 39, 108, 214n32;
  language, 15, 113; pueblos, 69
textile workshops (*obrajes*), 18, 31, 41,
  97, 162

Tiwa people, 15, 148–49, 150
Tompiro people, 15, 150
Torija, Gabriel de, 106
Torres, Juan de, 120, *187*, *193*
Torres, Sebastián de, *199*
Towa people, 15–16
tree-ring analysis, 9, 76
Trujillo, Baltasar, 123
Trujillo, Diego de, 94, 133, 140, *180*
Trujillo, Francisco de, 139–40, *212*
Trujillo, Luisa Montoya de, 12, 139–40
turquoise mining, 42

Ugarte de la Concha, Hernando de, 159
Ulloa y Lemos, Lope de, 4–5
Urrutia map of Santa Fe, 1766, 82, 83, 91,
  93, *208*, 229n31

Vaca, Cristóbal. *See* Baca, Cristóbal
Vaca, Núñez Cabeza de. *See* Cabeza de
  Vaca, Álvar Núñez
Valencia, Blas de, 78, 146, *194*
Valencia, Francisco de, 146–47, *180*, *184*,
  212
Valencia, Juan de, *203*
Valencia, Manuel de, *203*
Valverde, Francisco de, 7, 10, 20, 21, 29, 43
Valverde y Mercado, Francisco, 52, 53,
  54, 55
Varela de Losada, Alférez Alonso, 141,
  203
Varela de Losada, Cristóbal, *204*
Varela de Losada, Diego, *203*
Varela de Losada, Eugenio, *203*
Varela de Losada, Francisco, *200*, *203*
Varela de Losada, Joseph, *204*
Varela de Losada, Juan, 134, 141, *184*
Varela de Losada, Pedro, I, 141, *193*, *196*
Varela de Losada, Pedro, II, 141, *144*, *212*
Varela de Losada, Pedro, III, *204*
Varela de Losada, Teresa, 139
Varela Jaramillo, Alonso, 77, 104, 106,
  119, *192*, *196*, *210*
Varela Jaramillo, Cristóbal, *204*
Varela Jaramillo, Pedro, 104, *204*

Vargas, Diego de, 10, 81, 85, 133; as governor, 44, 140, 141; reconquering New Mexico, 109; in Santa Fe, 91
Vásquez, Francisco, *193*
Vayo (Valle), Alonso, 56
vecinos, 61, 97; Known Vecinos of Santa Fe, 1610–32, *197–98*
Vega, Alonso de la, 139, *192*
Vega, Francisco Blanco de la, *199*
Vega, Jorge de la, 139, *186*
Vega, Lucas de la, 111, *211*
Velarde Colodro, Juan, *193*
Velasco, Francisco de, 57, 74
Velasco, Luis de, II, 4, 5, 71
Vera Perdomo, Diego de, *180*
Vido, Francisco, *193*
La Villa de Cerralvo, 143–44
Villagrá, Gaspar Pérez de, *189*
Villanueva, Fernando, 159–60
Vitoria, Juan de, *187, 193*
Vitoria Carvajal, Juan de. *See* Carvajal, Juan de Vitoria

wheat, 11, 28, 73, 74
women: labor (Puebloan), 30; New Spain, 164; Spanish immigrant, 53, 61, 164
wool, 18, 162

Xavier, Francisco, 25, 95, 109, 116, 121, *180, 200, 211*
Ximénez, Francisco, *199*
Ximénez, Juan, *193, 196*

yazoos, 12
Ynojosa, Juan de, *187, 193*

Zaldívar, Juan de, 56, *189*
Zaldívar, Vicente de, 42, 52, 54–55, 56, 71; Route to the Eastern Plains from San Gabriel, 1599, *207*
Zamora, Maria de, 116
Zapata, Rodrigo, 54, *194*
Zárate Salmerón, Gerónimo de, 44, 127
Zubía, Diego de, 56, *190*
Zuñiga y Acevedo, Gaspar de, 4